# The Price of Freedom

David Foulk

# The Price of Freedom

## Financing French Resistance in World War II

palgrave
macmillan

David Foulk
Oriel College
University of Oxford
Oxford, UK

ISBN 978-3-031-09065-3 ISBN 978-3-031-09066-0 (eBook)
https://doi.org/10.1007/978-3-031-09066-0



Cover illustration: Archive Holdings Inc.

This Palgrave Macmillan imprint is published by the registered company Springer Nature Switzerland AG
The registered company address is: Gewerbestrasse 11, 6330 Cham, Switzerland

*For my family.*

# Acknowledgements

This book would not have been possible without the love and support of Mathilde and my son Jude. My thanks to my mother and stepfather for their unfailing help, notably with the proofreading and social network analysis. My aunt, without whom I would not have been able to complete this work, also deserves hearty recognition.

My sincere thanks to my supervisor, Robert Gildea, for his attentive reading and support throughout the project. In France, Christophe Bouneau, Christophe Lastécouères, Philippe Chassaigne, Laurent Coste and Philippe Meyzie of Université Bordeaux Montaigne have provided invaluable support over the years. The late Daniel Cordier provided much detail on the experience of everyday life in occupied France, and I am very fortunate to have been able to discuss this with him in person.

I wish to thank Steven Kippax, Philippe Oulmont, François Pacquement and Natacha Postel-Vinay for having generously given their time and assistance in various stages of the research for this book. For my friends who work on military and economic history—Robin Adams, Panarat Anamwathana, Mathieu Bideaux, Norma Cohen, Terence Cudbird, Vaida Nikšaitė and Kenneth Mouré—my thanks for all of your support.

In spite of the political and epidemiological difficulties experienced during the research and writing of this text—Brexit, IGI 1300 and the administrative closure of archives—here is the finished work.

# About This Book

The financing of French resistance is one of the least studied aspects pertaining to France's complex role in the Second World War.

By understanding how, and by whom, French resistance forces were funded, both within and without France's metropolitan borders, a fundamental reappraisal of the existing historiography of French resistance becomes possible.

The book takes a transnational approach. By using digital humanities techniques, including social network analysis (S.N.A.) and geographic information systems (G.I.S.), alongside forensic accountancy of the Free French and Special Operations Executive (S.O.E.) accounts, the thesis seeks to 'follow the money' across the planet, from donor to end-recipient. Those receiving the funds included *Maquis* forces and British- and French-run networks in France.

This work argues that, without concerted efforts by the British and U.S. governments and the Free French, this financing would not have been possible and, due to a lack of funds, nascent resistance activity would have been monetarily hampered, if not extinguished entirely. However, the development of these funding lines was convoluted and rendered difficult due to the transportation of agents and funds behind enemy lines. They were heavily impacted by political machinations and operational security protocols but, through the efforts of financial administrators, including intermediaries from the Bank of England, resistance activity in France was successfully supported by external funding from 1941.

It has been established that many who participated in fundraising were not French nationals and money was transferred across the planet which eventually arrived in France through clandestine landings and airdrops.

Having made use of a range of primary and secondary sources from France, Britain, the United States and Australia, this work builds upon the very limited existing historiography. Its primary sources include a 2017 interview with the late Daniel Cordier, the wartime secretary of Jean Moulin.

# Contents

# About the Author

**David Foulk** is a Briton in South-West France, where he has lived since 2008, surrounded by many wonderful dogs. Having studied at Université Bordeaux Montaigne and Oriel College, University of Oxford, he is a historian of the convergence between war and the economy. He can be found on Twitter (@davidfoulk9).

# Abbreviations

| | |
|---|---|
| A.M.G.O.T. | Allied Military Government of Occupied Territories |
| B.B.C. | British Broadcasting Corporation |
| B.C.R.A. | *Bureau central de renseignement et d'action* (Central Bureau of Intelligence and Operations) |
| C.C.F.L. | *Caisse centrale de la France libre* (Central Fund of the Free France) |
| C.F.L.N. | *Comité français de Libération nationale* (French Committee of National Liberation) |
| C.F.T.C. | *Confédération française des travailleurs chrétiens* (French Confederation of Christian Workers) |
| C.G.T. | *Confédération générale du travail* (General Confederation of Labour) |
| C.N.R. | *Conseil National de Résistance* (National Council of the Resistance) |
| D.M.R. | *Délégué militaire regional* (Regional Military Delegates) |
| F.F.I. | *Forces françaises de l'Intérieur* (French Forces of the Interior) |
| F.T.P. | *Franc-Tireurs et Partisans* |
| G.I.S. | Geographic Information Systems |
| I.L.O. | International Labour Organization |
| M.U.R. | *Mouvements unis de la résistance* (United Movements of the Resistance) |
| N.C.O. | Non-Commissioned Officer |
| N.P.B. | National Provincial Bank |
| O.S.S. | Office of Strategic Services |
| S.H.A.E.F. | Supreme Headquarters Allied Expeditionary Force |
| S.N.A. | Social Network Analysis |
| S.O.E. | Special Operations Executive |

## Abbreviations: Archives

| | |
|---|---|
| AN | Archives nationales, Pierrefitte-sur-Seine |
| ANOM | Archives nationales d'outre-mer, Aix-en-Provence |
| BdF | Banque de France, Paris |
| BoE | Bank of England, London |
| CHAR | Churchill Archives, Churchill College, Cambridge |
| NARA | National Archives and Records Administration, College Park, Maryland |
| SAEF | Service des archives économiques et financières, Savigny-Le-Temple |
| TNA | The National Archives, Kew |

# List of Figures

# List of Tables

CHAPTER 1

# Introduction

I first heard of Daniel Cordier when I came across a video of *On n'est pas couché*, presented by Laurent Ruquier, in which Cordier was presented as being the secretary of Jean Moulin or "*l'expert ès-Jean Moulin*". He had been invited to talk about a biopic which covered the contents of his 2009 book '*Alias Caracalla*'. The following day, I found the telefilm and was introduced to the early wartime life of Daniel Cordier.

Daniel Bouyjou was born in Bordeaux, on 10th August 1920. The son of a relatively well-to-do bourgeois couple, his parents took the uncommon step of divorcing when Daniel was about five. Dany, as he was known, was put in the custody of his father and was sent to school at *École Saint-Elme* in Arcachon. However, he spent substantial amounts of time, during the school holidays, with his mother and her new husband, Charles Cordier, near Pau.

Having been a member of the *Camelots du Roi*, the youth-wing of *Action française* which was a royalist, anti-parliamentarian movement that followed the ideology of Charles Maurras, the film opened with Cordier and his friend distributing flyers exclaiming that "France will never be the Boche's slave" and that "Young people can do nothing other than support Pétain".

Having read the memoir, I attempted to get in touch with Mr. Cordier. I wrote a letter, explaining that I was working on the financing of French resistance. I waited, time passed, but I didn't receive a response.



D. Foulk, *The Price of Freedom*,
https://doi.org/10.1007/978-3-031-09066-0_1

A year later, on 2nd May 2017, I was watching CNews, the 24-hour news broadcaster. It was in the period between the two rounds of the French presidential election, and Jean-Pierre Elkabbach was interviewing Daniel Cordier. Elkabbach asked him about the forthcoming run-off between Emmanuel Macron and Marine Le Pen and notably about the recent praise by Le Pen and Nicolas Dupont-Aignan for Charles de Gaulle:

> Ah, it's shameful. That needs to be said…because there was nobody who rallied to General de Gaulle in '40.

When de Gaulle arrived back in England, after his brief stay in Bordeaux during the government's flight from Paris, in mid-June 1940, de Gaulle would later say that he did not even have the "shadow of a force, nor an organisation". Nonetheless, he did have limited support from among the upper echelons of the British political class. Alongside Jean Monnet, René Pleven and others, a text was drafted that proposed a Franco-British union, whereby the two empires would unite: citizenry, military and resources. It never came to pass, however, as the idea was rejected in Paul Reynaud's final cabinet meeting.

Upon hearing of Reynaud's resignation, Marshal Philippe Pétain's accession and the armistice, Cordier was disconsolate and wept bitterly on his bed. It quickly passed and he decided to try to do something, rather than nothing. Along with a group of his friends, Cordier organised a meeting of local youths who wanted to continue the fight alongside French troops in Africa. His stepfather, a veteran of the Great War, was in full agreement and arranged transport for Cordier and a group of his friends on a Belgian vessel. However, unbeknownst to the young men, the ship's course was altered from North Africa, and they headed to Falmouth, in Cornwall, instead.

My own journey to see Cordier was no less hurried. Having seen him on CNews, I resolved to write again but, this time, a couple of days after having sent the letter, I received a phone-call from an elderly man, whose voice I recognised from the television. Despite my cut-glass accent, he understood my French and invited us to Cannes. His words were something along the lines of "Don't leave it too long, I am 97-years-old after all". The following day, after an 11-hour journey, we arrived in the late afternoon Mediterranean sunshine.

Upon landing in England, Cordier was taken into a school in a suburb of London that was serving as a refugee welcome centre. Having heard about General de Gaulle and the Free French, Cordier and his friends went to London to join the *Bataillon de chasseurs*. A couple of days later, the recruits left their temporary home at the Olympia and headed to Delville Camp.

Cordier's modern home, in Cannes, had a commanding view over the famous La Croisette. It resembled the home of a true bookworm with piles of books in every corner of the room. He beamed when we came through the door and shepherded us towards the table.

After a year in his battalion, in August 1941, Cordier was accepted into the secret services of the Free French movement, the B.C.R.A. (*Bureau central de renseignement et d'action*). His training involved learning to decrypt and encrypt messages—as he explained:

> You take the poem, and you begin with the sixth or seventh letter, writing the letters vertically and, then, horizontally. There were two codes to do, one after the other. You begin by the corresponding numbers and letters that came from the poem.[1]

He was parachuted back into France in July 1942, to begin his mission with Georges Bidault (*Bip*). To the British, Cordier was known by the codename *Bip.W*, where the 'W' stood for 'wireless', which reflected his intended role as a radio operator. To his comrades in France, he adopted the name *Alain*. Once in Lyon, he was seconded to Jean Moulin and became the secretary for Mission REX. In all, Cordier and his team handled and distributed around 300 million francs, between July 1942 and July 1943.

> ...they did not have a penny.[2]

Cordier's words indicate much about the relationship between French resistance members and the money that governed much of their paramilitary actions and underground lives. Firstly, they show that members of the clandestine movements, with whom Cordier interacted daily, felt poor.

[1] Author's interview with Daniel Bouyjou-Cordier, Translated Transcription, 11 May 2017.

[2] *Idem.*

Secondly, it was a sentiment that was generalised. As the wartime secretary of Jean Moulin, de Gaulle's representative in occupied France, Cordier controlled the purse strings for dozens of groups who looked to Moulin for pecuniary support. This work intends to show that, while Cordier was undoubtedly correct, his view does need to be nuanced.

It will place French resistance activity within a wider international context, by bringing together both the Free French movement and metropolitan resistance and underlining their interdependence. In order to better understand their connectedness, it is also necessary to underscore the limited financial autonomy of metropolitan resistance groups and to evaluate their dependence upon, firstly, the Free French, or *l'autre résistance*, as Muracciole referred to them[3]; and, secondly, on foreign powers, including the British and, to a lesser extent, the American government, via the direct injection of money, Lend-Lease and, later, Reverse Lend-Lease. By questioning this financial aspect of resistance activity, this work attempts to ascertain exactly how French were French resistance efforts? It also demonstrates the importance of French colonial territories and the French overseas diaspora towards the funding of sustained resistance efforts inside France.

The first contribution of this work involves the investigation of the economic development of the Free French movement, which began prior to the fall of France, in June 1940. Over the course of two years, they evolved into a political and military entity that relied largely on British credit, but which began to implement economic policy in the territories of the French Empire that rallied to de Gaulle, notably through their growing control over colonial budgets and monetary provision, with some exceptions, particularly in the Levant. Following the breakdown of personal relations between de Gaulle and Churchill, as well as Roosevelt's ambivalence towards the Free French, which bordered on outright animosity, the movement's economic emancipation came through the transfer of power from London to Algiers over the course of 1943, before they returned to France in 1944.

The second advancement involves reconsidering the manner in which money was transported into France. While resistance activity was largely self-funded at the beginning of the war, this work offers a vision of the networks' financial activity and how it was supported by external sources.

[3] MURACCIOLE Jean-François, *Les Français Libres, L'autre résistance*, Paris, Éditions Tallandier, 2009, 424p.

It is possible to track the foreign transfers sent into France which originated from Britain, Switzerland and further afield. By so doing, it greatly revises the existing historiography by applying a quantitative analysis that stretches from a global scale to the local level, as opposed to one that is exclusively focussed on events inside metropolitan France or, alternatively, those outside of her borders. By using such a framework, the complexity of operating covert missions in wartime is underlined, from both a strategic and tactical point of view.

The grammar that has been employed herein indicates a conscious choice. In the post-war era, many works pertaining to French resistance added the definite article to the proper noun, making it 'the French Resistance'.[4] This semantically renders French resistance a unified and monolithic entity. 'Unified' and 'monolithic' because using the definite article adds a singular nature to whatever is being described. By choosing to reject this, in favour of the more ambivalent 'French resistance', this work underlines a plurality of activities and enterprises that made up clandestine action. Additionally, using a frame that brings together the 'within' and 'without' of France's metropolitan borders, the question highlights the incontrovertible links that tied people and organisations in other countries, who helped to fund and equip those who rallied to de Gaulle, with those operating covertly in occupied France.

To offer a comparison with the funding that was received by the internal French resistance over the course of the war with similar movements in Western Europe, it is difficult to offer an analogous example, as other occupied nations had significantly smaller populations. In 1940, the Netherlands had a population of 8.8 million; the Belgians numbered 8.34 million; and the Norwegians were 2.98 million.[5] France, on the other

[4] BINOT Jean-Marc, BOYER Bernard, *L'argent de la Résistance*, Paris, Larousse, 2010, 175p.; FOOT Michael, *Des anglais dans la Résistance, le S.O.E. en France*, Paris, Tallandier, 2014, 816p.; GILDEA Robert, *Fighters in the Shadows: A New History of the French Resistance*, London, Faber and Faber, 2015, 608p.; PIKETTY Guillaume, *Pierre Brossolette: Un héros de la Résistance*, Paris, Éditions Odile Jacob, 1998, 416p.; WIEVIORKA Oliver, *Histoire de la Résistance*, Paris, Perrin, 2013, 588p.

[5] Statista, Population of the Netherlands from 1800 to 2020, https://www.statista.com/statistics/1016675/total-population-netherlands-1816-2020/; Statista, Population of Belgium from 1800 to 2020, https://www.statista.com/statistics/1008201/total-population-belgium-1816-2020/; Statista, Population of Norway from 1769 to 2020, https://www.statista.com/statistics/1016777/total-population-norway-1769-2020/, Consulted, 12 April 2022.

hand, had a population of 40.3 million.[6] It could therefore be argued that the most relevant of comparisons were the Dutch and Belgian resistance movements. In the first quarter of 1943, 10,000 people were involved in Dutch resistance, translating to 0.1% of the population,[7] whereas the Belgian resistance were composed of around 5,000 individuals,[8] showing that 0.05% of the Belgian population resisted the German occupation.[9] However, Ducarme estimated that one of the largest Belgian resistance groups, the Belgian National Movement, had 30,511 members, of whom 15,212 were recognised armed resistance members.[10] Nevertheless, those involved in both countries' resistance activities were significantly fewer in number than those in France, whom Wieviorka estimated as numbering somewhere between 300,000 and 500,000,[11] meaning that underground activities involved 0.7% to 1.2% of the French population. Relative to their demographic size, the Norwegians were similarly engaged in the underground struggle, with 0.6% taking part in resistance activities in 1943.[12] According to the British Special Operations Executive (S.O.E.), those involved in Dutch resistance remained at a stable size, with estimates showing that 9,350 people belonged to the movement in 1945.[13]

As the Dutch state was born from revolt in the sixteenth and seventeenth centuries, some felt compelled to recreate the efforts of their Calvinist forebears, by attempting to oust the invader.[14] Between February 1942 and May 1943, early S.O.E. attempts to foment resistance

[6] Statista, Population of France from 1700 to 2020, https://www.statista.com/statistics/1016777/total-population-norway-1769-2020/ Consulted, 12 April 2022.

[7] ((10,000/9170000)*100%).

[8] WIEVIORKA Olivier, *Une Histoire de la Résistance en Europe Occidentale*, Paris, Perrin, 2017, 476p., p. 186.

[9] ((5000/8420000)*100%).

[10] DUCARME Bernard, '*Le Financement de la Résistance Armée en Belgique: 1940–1944*', Courrier hebdomadaire du CRISP, 1970/11 n° 476–477, pp. 1–62, p. 48.

[11] WIEVORKA Olivier, *Histoire de la Résistance*, Paris, Perrin, 2013, 574p., (Ebook), Chapter 15, Para. 58.

[12] ((20,000/3060000)*100%).

[13] ((9350/9410000)*100%) = 0.09%; TNA, CAB 101–301, S. Passont, *Resistance and S.A.S. Operations in North-West Europe 1944–1945*, p. 58.

[14] ROMIJN Peter, 'La Résistance néerlandaise: L'unité dans la diversité ou l'autolimitation maîtrisée' in AZÉMA Jean-Pierre (Ed.), *Jean Moulin face à l'Histoire*, Paris, Flammarion, 2000, 418p., pp. 269–288, p. 269.

activity in the Netherlands were thwarted, as 43 agents were killed, with only three surviving.[15] In the country, three principal movements existed: *Orde Dienst*, who were, politically, right-wing; *Landelijke Knokploegen* was a left-wing movement; and *Raad van Verzet*, the Dutch equivalent of the French National Resistance Council.[16] Unlike in France, a separate organisation helped to provide money for the resistance movement between May 1943 and the liberation of the country, which was known as the *Nationaal Steunfonds* ('National Support Fund').

Having begun as separate groups, towards the end of 1941, which acquired funding for the families of Dutch sailors and merchants, they began to work more closely together and took the name of *Zeemanspot*. As the war began to have a greater impact on the Dutch population, the *Landrottenfonds* ('Landlubbers Fund') was created in spring 1943, and their name was subsequently changed to *Nationaal Steunfonds*. Many of the fundraising methods were similar to those practised by French resistance movements, including the soliciting of donations. Additionally, the Dutch government provided guarantees honouring the loans that were taken out by the *Nationaal Steunfonds*. The financial operation was complex, with different departments being devoted to the collection of monies owed, researching target organisations for fundraising, distributing the payments and an accounting department which kept the ledgers.

Throughout the war, 80 million guilders were raised.[17] Using the rate of 8.8225 guilders to the pound from 1939,[18] 80 million guilders would equate to £9,067,724 ($42,480,400 at $0.531005). By the end of the war, in 1945, this same amount would have translated into £7,445,427 ($30,047,619).[19] In the first six months of 1944, S.O.E. also tried to infiltrate 50,000 guilders for the benefit of their Dutch section, but the

[15] TNA, CAB 101–301, *Resistance and S.A.S. Operations...*, p. 52.

[16] Idem, p. 53.

[17] 'Nationaal Steun Fonds', 2018 Jaar van Verzet, https://www.jaarvanverzet.nl/verzet sactie/nationaal-steun-fonds/ , Consulted, 2 April 2022.

[18] Federal Reserve Bank, New York, *Monthly Review of Credit and Business Conditions, Second Federal Reserve District, Monthly Review*, 1939, March 1.

[19] EDVINSSON Rodney, 'Historical Statistics', https://www.historicalstatistics.org/Currencyconverter.html, Consulted, 2 April 2022.

money was delayed in Paris, as the addresses due to receive the funds were blown.[20]

Arguably, Dutch resistance financing was more secure than that received by French resistance groups, as they relied on the guarantees of the Dutch government-in-exile. However, French resistance movements received more money than their Dutch counterparts. £23.8 million were sent by S.O.E.'s Section 'F' and 'RF', or those sections who ran clandestine paramilitary activities in the country, between February 1942 and September 1944, as opposed to the £7.5 million that was raised by the *Nationaal Steunfonds*.

The historian, Bernard Ducarme, explained that Belgian resistance forces raised 942.8 million Belgian francs (£7.66 million at 123 Belgian francs to the pound, in 1944).[21] Their justifiable spending amounted to 717.5 million Belgian francs (£5.83 million) and 225.3 million Belgian francs of unjustified spending (£1.83 million).[22] However, the systematic financing of Belgian resistance only began in 1943. To procure the banknotes, a representative of the Belgian government-in-exile was despatched to Lisbon to change pound sterling or dollars with Belgian or French francs. This would have directly impacted on those seeking to procure funds for French resistance activity as the supply of French francs, outside the country, was limited. At the beginning of 1943, the British government requested that the Belgians avoid exporting too much sterling to Portugal.[23] As an alternative form of funding, the Belgians bought diamonds in London, which were subsequently despatched and sold through the Belgian black market. However, this only happened four times, all of which occurred in 1943, and was not a particularly successful undertaking, as only 492,000 Belgian francs (£4,000) were raised.[24] Another method of financing was a surcharge on the production of resistance newspapers. The printers did not charge for their services, other than the cost of the paper, with the savings being passed on to regional groups of the movement *Le Front de l'Indépendence*. While

[20] TNA, HS7-121, S.O.E. History 86 - *History of F Section by Colonel Buckmaster*, Expenditure in Field, p. 3.

[21] DUCARME, *Le Financement de la Résistance Armée en Belgique*, 1970, p. 53.

[22] Idem, Annex 7.

[23] *Idem*, p. 20.

[24] Idem, p. 22.

their readers paid ten francs per paper, only five francs were billed to the regional groups, meaning that the Brabant section made a profit of 347,000 Belgian francs (£2,821).[25]

Nonetheless, the level of funding open to Belgian resistance forces was less than for their French counterparts. One of the best-remunerated intelligence networks in Belgium, Group Luc-Marc, received close to 400,000 Belgian francs (£3,252) in July 1943.[26] If this is converted into French francs, the equivalent was 574,390 French francs. However, the REX Mission, led by Jean Moulin, received 81 million French francs in the same month, or £458,598. These figures underline the relative size and scale of French resistance against its Western European counterparts, through their finances.

Much of the primary literature and secondary historiography concerning French resistance and the Free French movement was written by those who participated in the conflict, either militarily or administratively. Despite their vast memoirs, Charles de Gaulle and Winston Churchill spent little time discussing the financial measures that aimed to help the Free French establish themselves as an alternative to the Vichy government.[27] Understandably, their literary efforts were concerned with other issues pertaining to war strategy, diplomacy and their own personal relationship, as opposed to financial minutiae. However, Pierre Denis, as the head of the Free French Financial Service, and André Postel-Vinay, who served as the director of the *Caisse centrale de la France libre*, both

[25] Idem, p. 42.

[26] DEBRUYNE Emmanuel, REMY Adeline, 'Les réseaux belges et leurs finances 1940–1944' in VANDENBUSSCHE Robert (Ed.), *La Clandestinité en Belgique et en Zone Interdite (1940–1944)*, Lille, Publications de l'Institut de recherches historiques du Septentrion, 2009, 265p., pp. 113–158, Graphique 2.

[27] CHURCHILL Winston, *The Second World War Vol. 1 'The Gathering Storm'*, New York, Houghton Mifflin Company, 1948, p. 527; CHURCHILL Winston, *The Second World War Vol. 2 'Their Finest Hour'*, New York, Houghton Mifflin Company, 1976, 556p.; CHURCHILL Winston, *The Second World War Vol. 3 'The Grand Alliance'*, New York, Houghton Mifflin Company, 1977, 630p.; CHURCHILL Winston, *The Second World War Vol. 4 'The Hinge of Fate'*, New York, Houghton Mifflin Company, 1978, 744p.; CHURCHILL Winston, *The Second World War Vol. 5 'Closing the Ring'*, New York, Houghton Mifflin Company, 1951, 558p.; CHURCHILL Winston, *The Second World War Vol. 6 'Triumph and Tragedy'*, New York, Houghton Mifflin Company, 1981, 584p.; DE GAULLE Charles, *Mémoires de guerre*, Paris, Plon, 1989, 1518p.

wrote their own memoirs of the war.[28] Denis' account of the financing of the Free French offers an insider's view of the mechanisms that helped to fund the ongoing combat but, due to the time elapsed between his experiences and the time at which he wrote, he freely admitted to missing many details from both his memoirs and the article that he authored, specifically on the subject.[29] Likewise, Postel-Vinay provided a post-war interview in which he discussed his role in helping to move the *Caisse* from London to Algiers before relocating to Paris, after the city's liberation.[30] Moreover, Lionel Fraser, the Treasury liaison official with the governments-in-exile in Britain, wrote of his wartime experiences with members of the Free French.[31] In order to have the perspective of those belonging to the French diaspora, Jean Monnet and Jacques Soustelle, both of whom would go on to have distinguished post-war political careers and who would, at different moments, fall out with de Gaulle, offered their respective viewpoints on the Free French.[32] Guillaume Piketty's compilation of letters by members of the Free French movement has helped to elucidate the role of René Pleven in the creation and furtherance of Gaullist objectives during the conflict, as the secretary of Jean Monnet in the Anglo-French Coordinating Committee and, later, in his roles within the *Comité National Français* and *Comité français de la Libération nationale*.[33] Furthermore, the works of those who acted as intermediaries between the resistance groups in France and the Free French have formed an important part of the historiographical context. Maurice Buckmaster, the head of the Special Operations Executive Section 'F', and Colonel Passy, the *nom-de-guerre* of André Dewavrin, wrote their memoirs after

[28] DENIS Pierre, *Souvenirs de la France Libre*, Paris, Éditions Berger-Levrault, 1947, 242p.; POSTEL-VINAY André, *Un fou s'évade: Souvenirs de 1941–1942*, Paris, Éditions du Félin, 1997.

[29] DENIS Pierre, 'Les finances de la France Libre', *Revue de la Deuxième Guerre mondiale*, PUF, N° 1, November 1950, pp. 20–27.

[30] POSTEL-VINAY André, PACQUEMENT François (Ed.), *La passion du développement—32 ans de Caisse centrale: Mémoires d'André Postel-Vinay*, Paris, Agence Française du Développement, 2019, 314p.

[31] FRASER W. Lionel, *All to the Good*, Kingswood, Heinemann, 1963, 275p.

[32] MONNET Jean, Mémoires, Paris, Fayard, 1976, 642p.; SOUSTELLE Jacques, *Envers et contre tout: De Londres à Alger (1940–1942)*, Paris, Robert Laffont, 1947, 470p.

[33] PIKETTY Guillaume (Ed.), *Français en Résistance: Carnets de guerre, correspondances, journaux personnels, Paris*, Éditions Robert Laffont, 2009.

the conflict and offered insight into the decisional processes that helped to fund the clandestine war in France.[34] Daniel Cordier, the secretary of Jean Moulin—de Gaulle's representative in occupied France—has posthumously published the second volume of his memoirs.[35] These supplement the first volume that covered the years 1940 to 1943, in which he explained how he came to meet and work with Moulin in Lyon and Paris. Moulin's rival, Henri Frenay, was the head of the movement '*Combat*', and his post-war writings often called into question the political motivations of Moulin.[36] However, in his leadership role, his reflections on wartime life in France have enriched our understanding of clandestine life under occupation.

The only book whose subject is directly comparable to the present work was written by Jean-Marc Binot and Bernard Boyer, one a journalist and the other is the son of a head of the BRUTUS network.[37] Their work, which they, themselves, critiqued as "having been too hastily done", suffered from a relative absence of contextualisation and did not consult archives other than those found in France. Many details are subsequently glossed over, and their conclusions are skewed by the lack of consultation of primary and secondary evidence. The work avoids asking fundamental questions as to where the money actually originated, and this present work intends to correct these oversights.

Important works of secondary historiography that have helped to shape this present work have included Sébastien Albertelli's volume on the *Bureau Centrale de Renseignements et d'Action* (B.C.R.A.) which looked at the work of the B.C.R.A. and their links with S.O.E. Section 'RF'.[38] Michael Foot's volume on S.O.E. Section 'F' provided important information on the funding of the British-run missions in France which, as

[34] BUCKMASTER Maurice, *They Fought Alone*, London, Biteback Publishing, 1958 (Ed. 2014), p. 304; PASSY Colonel, *Mémoires du chef des services secrets de la France Libre*, Paris, Éditions Odile Jacob, 2000, 801p.

[35] CORDIER Daniel, *La victoire en pleurant: Alias Caracalla 1943–1946*, Paris, Éditions Gallimard, 2021, 310p.

[36] FRENAY Henri, *La nuit finira: Mémoires de Résistance 1940–1945*, Paris, Éditions Robert Laffont, 1973, 607p.

[37] BINOT Jean-Marc, BOYER Bernard, *L'argent de la Résistance*, Paris, Larousse, 2010, 175p.

[38] ALBERTELLI Sébastien, *Les services secrets du général De Gaulle, Le BCRA 1940–1944*, Paris, Perrin, 2009, 624p.

it turned out, were incorrectly copied from the source material.[39] Foot therefore underestimated the amount of money that was received by those networks which were controlled by Maurice Buckmaster. Another set of important works were written in response to Henri Frenay's attacks on Jean Moulin; Daniel Cordier decided to write a two-volume biography of his former boss which has been accepted as being the seminal work on Moulin's life and underground career.[40] Moreover, another member of the Free French movement, Jean-Louis Crémieux-Brilhac wrote a two-volume work on the movement which, although light on details regarding the financing, provided an important addition to the historiography on the external resistance.[41] More recently, Eric Jennings has called into question the London-centricity of the movement by demonstrating the reliance of de Gaulle's enterprise upon the labour, materials and manpower provided by the rallied French colonies.[42] Jennings' work, as well as Robert Gildea's reappraisal of the Frenchness within French resistance, has provided much towards the intellectual outline of this present work.[43] Nonetheless, Gildea's work avoids the thorny topic of financing. As will be seen, this aspect helps to bind many of the seemingly disparate sinews of resistance activity inside France to the external resistance abroad.

Methodologically, this study also takes inspiration from works far outside of the historical discipline. Through Mark Granovetter's article on the 'strength of weak ties', John Scott's book on Social Network Analysis (S.N.A.) and Andrews' work on networks in the Islamic community in Britain, it has been seen that there is much merit in applying S.N.A. to historical sources.[44] Claire Lemercier's work on historical

[39] FOOT Michael, *Des anglais dans la Résistance, le S.O.E. en France*, Paris, Tallandier, 2014, 816p.

[40] CORDIER Daniel, *Jean Moulin: La République des catacombes (Tome I)*, Paris, Éditions Gallimard, 1999, (Ed. 2011), 976p., CORDIER Daniel, *Jean Moulin: La République des catacombes (Tome II)*, Paris, Éditions Gallimard, 1999 (Ed. 2011), 898p.

[41] CRÉMIEUX-BRILHAC Jean-Louis, *La France Libre, Vol. 1: De l'appel du 18 juin à la libération*, Paris, Éditions Gallimard, 1998 (Ed. 2013), 816p.

[42] JENNINGS Eric, *Free French Africa in World War II: The African Resistance*, New York, Cambridge University Press, 2015, 300p.

[43] GILDEA Robert, *Fighters in the Shadows: A New History of the French Resistance*, London, Faber and Faber, 2015, 608p. (Ebook), Chapter 8, Para. 1.

[44] GRANOVETTER Mark, 'The Strength of Weak Ties', *American Journal of Sociology*, Vol. 78, N° 6 (May, 1973), University of Chicago Press, pp. 1360–1380; SCOTT John,

network analysis, as well as the German school which is led by academics including Marten Düring and Tom Brughmans, has helped to guide this work despite the relative youth of the application of network analysis to historical sources.[45] Furthermore, the peer-reviewed work of 'The Programming Historian' has helped to further the understanding of various aspects of digital humanities for historians including social network analysis and geographic information systems (G.I.S.).[46]

Three approaches have been adopted which have helped to illuminate the arcane world of war financing. The first is traditional financial and accounting analysis. As the Free French were non-specialists in the area, they opted either for pre-existing solutions that had been applied elsewhere within the French empire, such as taking the statutes for the newly created *Caisse centrale* directly from those in place within the Moroccan central bank, or for the simplest techniques, such as double-entry bookkeeping. This has meant that, while there are no documents that actively explain how and why the Free French movement chose to do things as they did, from a financial standpoint, the methods that they applied are relatively clear. The most difficult aspect has been attempting to ascertain their economic policies, as they were governing countries in very specific diplomatic and political contexts, including Syria and Lebanon, alongside territories that were mandated to France following the First World War, such as Cameroon, and long-standing French colonies who had rallied to de Gaulle, including French Equatorial Africa or New Caledonia. The economic policies that were to be applied in these areas were

*Social Network Analysis (3rd Edition)*, London, Sage, 2013, 201p.; ANDREWS Ahmed, 'The importance of individual networks: network analysis as a means of understanding the significance of social barriers in religious conversion' in GÖRMAN Ulf (ed.), *Towards a New Understanding of Conversion*, Lund, Skrifter Utgivna Av Teologiska Institutionen I Lund, 1999, pp. 38–48.

[45] LEMERCIER Claire, 'Analyse de réseaux et histoire', *Revue d'histoire moderne et contemporaine*, Belin, 2005/2 n° 52–2, pp. 88–122; KERSCHBAUMER Florian (Ed.), VON KEYSERLINGK-REHBEIN Linda (Ed.), STARK Martin (Ed.), DÜRING Marten (Ed.), *The Power of Networks: Prospects of Historical Network Research*, Abingdon-on-Thames, Routledge, 2020, 302p.

[46] LEMERCIER Claire, 'Analyse de réseaux et histoire', *Revue d'histoire moderne et contemporaine*, Belin, 2005/2 n° 52–2, pp. 88–122; DÜRING Marten, 'From Hermeneutics to Data to Networks: Data Extraction and Network Visualization of Historical Sources', *The Programming Historian* 4, 2015, https://doi.org/10.46430/phen0044 COLSON Justin, 'Geocoding Historical Data using QGIS', *The Programming Historian* 6, 2017, https://doi.org/10.46430/phen0066.

not homogenous, nor could they apply a single policy for all the territories that fell under their control. Furthermore, as they were not an independent sovereign nation, the Free French relied upon the assistance of allies in order to keep their economies running, which invariably led to difficulties with supplying their territories and which caused friction in decision-making, as will be seen in the chapter on the colonial contributions.

Secondly, in order to make sense of these alliances and their impact on Free French policymaking, social network analysis has been applied as a means to highlight the important decision-makers in the Allied camp; these also altered throughout the course of the war. While network analysis does not explain the full importance of the decisions taken, it has raised the profile of those who were making the decisions and has allowed for focus to be placed on characters who are not usually present within the traditional historiography of the Free French or British wartime administrations. Moreover, it has helped to show differences within the structure of the competing branches in S.O.E. in France, between Section 'F', the British-run networks, and Section 'RF', the conjoined British-B.C.R.A. networks. A combination of these two approaches has not been previously attempted, and it has resulted in the questioning of traditional historiographical *aprioris* that continue to be perpetuated to this day, as to which of the branches were better funded and assisted during the war.

The final methodological approach has been the use of G.I.S analysis which, much like S.N.A., has helped to cartographically highlight details that have been mined from both historiographical and archival sources in a manner that enables deeper conclusions to be drawn.

This work is based on a chronological, rather than thematic, foundation, which allows for the investigation of the early financial growth of the Free French movement; before analysing the role played by foreign territories and countries towards French resistance financing; and, ultimately, concludes with the work of the internal resistance in France and the liberation of the country. This enables for a discussion of events that are well known to Second World War historians, but from a completely different perspective—that of the money which helped to serve as the framework of resistance.

The second chapter, covering 1939, titled **Coordinating Chaos** discusses the Phoney War period, prior to the invasion of France, and shows the creation of the Anglo-French Coordinating Committee.

Headed by Jean Monnet, the distinguished financier and future architect of European integration, who was assisted by Pierre Denis and René Pleven, both of whom were highly-skilled administrators, the Franco-British team worked towards ensuring that both empires would be able to source their primary necessities without stockpiling, and thus depriving the other of vital resources. All strategic goods and services, including shipping, oil, arms and food, fell under the Coordinating Committee's remit.

The third chapter, **Administrative Alliances**, looks at 1940 and 1941 and shows the establishment of the Free French financial administration. It underlines how reliant de Gaulle's movement was upon those who appeared unannounced before him. Pierre Denis was an invaluable London-based asset. Upon joining, Denis was sent to the virtually non-existent Financial Service and got to work. The progressive rallying of territories to the movement meant that they needed to conceptualise and enact coherent colonial economic and monetary policy. The organisation of an administration was undertaken by the Free French Financial Service, with the support of the British civil service, notably from members of the Treasury and the Bank of England, through the assistance of Major John S. Lithiby. However, the war caused a tightened of the money supply to the Free French colonies. A need to centralise payments pressed the Free French into action, which led to the establishment of the '*Caisse Centrale de la France Libre*', under Denis' stewardship.

Similarly, covering 1940–1941, the fourth chapter, titled **For a Few Dollars More?**, contrasts the wary warmth of the British governmental approach towards the Free French movement and the U.S. administration, under Roosevelt, which was incredibly reticent to allow them even the vaguest semblance of diplomatic recognition. When Pleven was sent, in 1941, to help organise the nascent delegation, he chose Adrien Tixier, a former high-ranking administrator for the International Labour Organization, in Geneva, and a disabled veteran of the trenches, as their leader. Nonetheless, according to Raoul Aglion, the delegation's secretary, Tixier's support for de Gaulle wavered, depending to whom he was talking. The American delegation principally served as a conduit through which information could be gleaned from the U.S. administration, as well as aiding the French community in America. Under the constraints of the 'Trading with the Enemy' legislation, the Free French delegation in the United States were unable to act as fundraisers for the movement. Instead, following the extension of the Lend-Lease programme to newly christened 'Fighting' French forces in September 1942, the U.S. delegation primarily became a communicative link and bureaucratic hub, through which French citizens could get passport visas and stamps for territories under the movement's control.

The second part of the book begins with **Viva la Resistencia!** during the period 1941 and 1942. It asks the question that if the U.S. delegation was unable to secure financing, exactly who did? A table has been produced showing the total payments that were made by these groups during the years 1941 and 1942. In conjunction with the movement's account books, this shows the early financing for French resistance efforts. Furthermore, when this is compared to monies sent via S.O.E. 'F' Section (the British section of the Special Operations Executive that operated independently of the Free French), a detailed picture of French resistance income is drawn. In relative terms, the most important providers of funds were the Free French delegations in Mexico and Argentina. These were countries that had sizeable French communities and established expatriate newspapers that were already aimed at this market. The delegations' funds were sent via wire transfer, or as cheques, to the Free French Financial Service in London, where the money helped to service both General de Gaulle's named current account and the movement's account.

Chapter six, **Colonial Contributions to French Freedom**, covers the years 1943 and 1944. It shows that the colonial support for the Free French was important not insofar as it provided a tax base for the group to funnel to London, but more for the fact that their natural resources provided a contribution towards the wider war effort and allowed the Free French to gain economic leverage with their allies. The manner in which Roosevelt was able to bypass Congress and provide aid was through the 'loaning' of American-produced equipment, ordnance and the provision of foodstuffs; with the expectation that the goods would be returned but that, if they were destroyed or used, the recipient would be subsequently charged. The introduction of Reciprocal Lend-Lease, in 1942, allowed the Fighting French to provide essential goods to the war effort for their allies and improve their balance of payments, notably in New Caledonia, in return for military ordnance and foodstuffs. The largest difficulty was in transporting the goods from their country of origin to their recipients. This notably affected the West African groundnut, which was of paramount importance for the British Ministry of Food, in order to help maintain the provision of the oil ration for British citizens. Equally, rubber production was quadrupled, in the Free French African territories, in comparison with 1938 levels. The most profitable resources included diamonds and gold, but phosphates, from North Africa, cocoa and wood, from French Equatorial Africa, all proved valuable items that could be exchanged. However, the Gaullists were aware of the difficulties with feeding their colonial populations, explaining that North African populations were, as of 1944, living almost exclusively on cereals and that this would play into the hands of their detractors in France.

The third part of the book, beginning in with **Of Pay and Parachutes**, revisits 1942–1943 and shows the development of the internal French resistance movement and increasing independence of its external counterpart. Following his escape from France, Jean Moulin rallied to de Gaulle at the end of 1941. Moulin had already begun preparing the terrain, having already written a detailed report on the nascent resistance groups and contacted various French leaders, including Henri Frenay of 'Combat', before leaving France. After an accelerated period of parachute training, Moulin was tasked with returning to unoccupied France, carrying one-and-a-half million francs. Moulin's funds would be kept by Daniel Cordier, whom he immediately relieved of other duties upon Cordier's arrival in France, in July 1942, in order to run the mission's secretariat. Despite the difficulties of operating under constant threat of discovery, a significant amount of money was accumulated and disseminated between the different groups. These funds would be folded inside a newspaper and handed to the contact, who belonged to the recipient movement. Payments increased dramatically from 1942 into 1943. Over 200 million francs were paid to the internal resistance, via his network, over the course of a fifteen-month period. Moulin's London-issued money and influence ensured that the resistance retained its British and Gaullist links, at least temporarily.

1943 and 1944 were years of increasing activity in the macro- and micro-spheres for the Free French and the internal resistance movements. **Converting the Caisse** shows the important movements of funds between Britain and France. Between January 1942 and September 1944, S.O.E. Section 'F', those run purely by the British, received 422 million francs. Concurrently, their Gaullist-assisted counterparts, Section 'RF', which were run in conjunction with the B.C.R.A., received nearly 3.8 billion francs, shows the transfer of the *Caisse centrale de la France libre*, from London to Algiers, which marked a step towards the restoration of the French republic and the reclamation of monetary sovereignty.

Previously, the movement had been entirely reliant upon Whitehall to function, to print their replacement currency and to manage their accounts. American-supported intrigues to replace de Gaulle with General Giraud, a more amenable intermediary in Washington's eyes, resulted in bad blood developing. Furthermore, De Gaulle's difficult nature left him distanced and isolated from his allies. The most surprising thing about the decision to transfer monetary and economic power, from London to Algiers, seems to have demonstrated how little an impact that this had on the bonhomie and continued assistance that was evident among members of the administration in London and their French counterparts. However, moving the headquarters to Algiers had little concrete effect on the money being sent into France, nor did the London office of the *Caisse centrale* close entirely, choosing instead to downsize. The issue of an invasion currency to be used in France was as contentious as it was vitally important for both the troops invading the country and for the local population. The introduction of the American Military Government of Occupied Territories (A.M.G.O.T.) dollar seems to have been intended as both a diplomatic slight and a functional economic measure; for it greatly resembled a traditional dollar, in both colour and design, but it was to be used as a means of ensuring that troops were able to pay for their goods with some form of exchangeable currency and to lessen the potential risk of looting.

**Planes, Loans and Bank Robbery** demonstrate that, following D-Day, different methods of fund acquisition emerged in France, including a growing reliance on borrowing and bank robbery. Borrowing was undertaken with the help of local industrialists. The other method involved the robbing of branches of the *Banque de France*. These 'patriotic hold-ups' were often undertaken with the complicity of those who worked there. The largest of the hold-ups was the Neuvic train robbery, on 26th July 1944. The astronomical amounts stolen in this one raid, or 2.28 billion francs, amounted to the largest single requisition of funds, during the war, in France. In August 1944, members of the Parisian personnel of the *Banque de France* assisted with the city's liberation as best they could. A cartographical picture has been drawn showing that fateful week from the perspective of a resistance member on the *Banque*'s staff.

The book concludes that funding of French resistance actions relied upon an international network of expatriate donors, British central banking assistance and the tenacity of General de Gaulle's supporters, both outside and within France. Through the use of digital methodologies, the international relationships that existed between the different administrations involved show a juxtaposing picture of plenty, as well as penury, that developed over the course of the conflict. This opens the path for a history of those bureaucratic and administrative actors who challenging fascistic tyranny.

CHAPTER 2

# Coordinating Chaos

Resistance to the invasion of France began long before the fall of the country, with war being declared on Germany, by Édouard Daladier, on 3rd September 1939.[1] The beginning of the Phoney War, which lasted from September 1939 to May 1940, was a time of belated mobilisation and conversion of British and French industry, from being consumer-focussed to preparing for a total war footing[2] and of being capable of equipping vast military forces. This chapter argues that coordinated Anglo-French economic activity acted as a precursor for the later funding of external resistance activity, which aimed to attack the Axis powers and their allies. This manifested itself through the Anglo-French Coordinating Committee, which was led by Jean Monnet and administered by Pierre Denis and René Pleven, who were to become future Gaullist representatives. Their task was to ensure that the British and French economies would operate in concert and not confrontationally.

[1] RAGACHE Gilles, *Juin 1940*, Paris, Perrin, 2020, 334p., p. 23.

[2] A comprehensive study of consumer behaviour during World War II is found in BERGHOFF Hartmut (Ed.), LOGEMANN Jan (Ed.), RÖMER Felix (Ed.), *The Consumer on the Home Front*, Oxford, Oxford University Press, 2017, 371p.



D. Foulk, *The Price of Freedom*,
https://doi.org/10.1007/978-3-031-09066-0_2

> Total warfare required the concentration of all the resources that states could draw on.[3]

From an administrative perspective, the relatively short period of 21 years that had elapsed between the First World War and the Second World War served all the major powers well, but some more so than others, as Harrison's edited volume on the major economies at war has helped to show.[4] They were able to conserve much of the institutional experience held by those who had previously fought, by reintegrating veterans and reserves into the forces and the corridors of power. They had retained many of the economic and financial lessons that had previously been learned and reintegrated them back into the state apparatus.

Jean Monnet was one such source of invaluable technical expertise, having served during the Great War as part of General Mauclair's Civilian Supply Services, where he had been inculcated into the importance of tonnage on the outcome of a war.[5] However, between the two wars, the requirements for logistics management had greatly changed. The Second World War was fought on a far wider geographical scale than the First, which had largely been confined to European shores.

In London, the skills that Jean Monnet had learned as an apprentice cognac trader were beneficial for his later diplomatic efforts.[6] Language acquisition, negotiating acumen and an understanding of the differences between English-speaking peoples were imperative to his position as an economic intermediary dealing with national governments. Monnet's reports went directly to Reynaud, Daladier, Chamberlain and Churchill. He cultivated a wide range of political contacts and so he was able to remain on the peripheries of the Gaullist circle of influence and yet retain independence. Moreover, Monnet's professional training enabled him to keep General Charles de Gaulle's ear at important moments during the conflict.

[3] Idem, p. 5.

[4] HARRISON Mark (Ed.), *The Economics of World War II: Six Great Powers in International Comparison*, Cambridge, Cambridge University Press, 1998, 331p.

[5] MONNET Jean, *Mémoires*, Paris, Fayard, 1976, 642p., p. 59.

[6] MONNET, *Mémoires*, 1976, p. 46.

## Monnet's Meetings

At the beginning of the war, Jean Monnet was one of the few men known to de Gaulle who had extensive contacts in the United States. Having met President Roosevelt, in March 1938, to discuss aircraft contracts for the French Air Force,[7] he was crucially important to General de Gaulle during the earliest days of the conflict. Monnet helped him to navigate Westminster's corridors of power, while being guided, himself, by Sir Edward Bridges[8] and Sir Horace Wilson.[9] In October 1939, Monnet was appointed chairman of the Anglo-French Coordinating Committee. This was the central body that was comprised of several committees, each tasked with collective purchasing and the division of their allotted materials between the French and British governments.

As shown in Fig. 2.1, these committees represented consequential economic sectors and were staffed by French and British personnel.[10] This ensured that both nations' armed forces were able to be prepared, without depriving the other of access to supplies, such as wood or machinery.

The committees were announced in the '*Journal Officiel*' on 2nd November 1939.[11] Having been selected by Daladier and Chamberlain, Monnet was given significant authority and was answerable only to the very highest echelons of the U.K. and French governments. In his view,

[7] BRUNET Luc-André, 'Jean Monnet et l'organisation des économies alliées pour la guerre (1939–1940)' in BOSSUAT Gérard (Ed.), *Jean Monnet et l'économie*, Brussels, Euroclio, Peter Lang, 2018, 14p., p. 1.

[8] MONNET, *Mémoires*, 1976, p. 149—"On September 26$^{th}$ (1939), I was in London where Sir Edward Bridges, secretary of the English War Cabinet, opened all the doors for me".

[9] TNA, CAB 21 1269, Machinery for Coordination of Anglo-French Economic War Effort, *Memorandum regarding Arrangements for the Coordination of the Economic War Efforts of the U.K. and France*, 24 April 1941, p. 1.

[10] TNA, CAB 21 1269, Machinery..., *Letter to Sean Nunan, Secretary of the High Commissioner for Eire, from Stephen Holmes, Dominions Office*—"Permanent executive committees, composed of United Kingdom and French representatives, deal with various separate aspects of the main problem. Among these are economic warfare, air production and supply, shipping, food, munitions and raw materials and certain specific commodities such as coal and oil. The general functions of each Committee are to organise the activities of each country within the sphere indicated, in order to make the best use of resources of raw materials and of means of production, and to arrange joint import programmes so as to avoid competition in purchases abroad and to make the best use of shipping facilities".

[11] TNA, CAB 21 1269, Machinery..., *Extract from 'Journal Officiel'*, 23 November 1939.

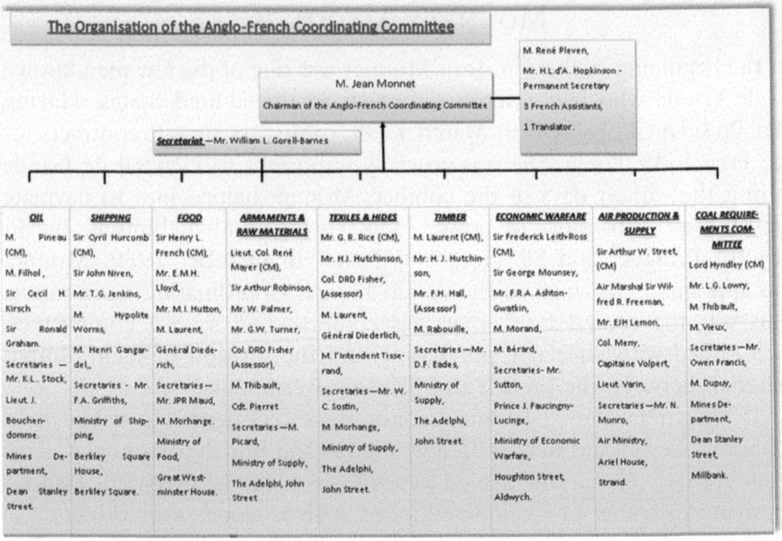


**Fig. 2.1** Organigram of the Anglo-French Coordinating Committee, 1939–1940 (TNA, CAB 21 1269)

without any obvious goals other than victory, it was difficult to engage the public in preparing for war.[12] At this point, the main preoccupation for the Anglo-French Coordinating Committee was the purchase of American planes. However, these constituted only thirty per cent of the sale enquiries that were being investigated in the United States.[13] The Timber Executive had insufficient French representation and there was a supposed lack of 'allied consciousness' on the British side. The other committees

[12] MONNET, *Mémoires*, 1976, pp. 16–17—"It was obvious that the coalition did not have a soul. We forgot to offer the people any clear war objectives. However, we can only achieve a common effort if we define common goals"; FOULK David, *Interview with Daniel Cordier*, 10 May 2017—This reflection was confirmed by Daniel Cordier, a schoolboy and soon-to-be member of the Free French forces, when he spoke of his astonishment seeing Britons continuing to holiday on the South coast, when he arrived at Falmouth, in June 1940.—"They were in bathing costumes, saying "Hello, hello!!!" and we were saying to ourselves, "But, we're at war…"".

[13] TNA, CAB 85 59, Anglo-French Purchasing Board in the USA—Coordination of British and French Purchases in the USA & Relations between the Board and the United States Administration, *Clipping from New York News*, 24 January 1940.

saw a limited level of success, but there was a reticence to share information on resources, and means of production, which severely hampered their collaborative effort.[14] This betrayed a lack of mutual confidence on the part of both governments. In a role that primarily revolved around "personal contacts with members and secretaries of Executive Committees",[15] such issues were serious ones to confront.

As Monnet said, on 6th December 1939, during the first meeting of the Anglo-French Coordinating Committee, "The Anglo-French Coordinating Committee was an experiment without precedent even in the last war, and only experience could show how it should work".[16] It was bilateral, highly centralised and oligarchic, being reliant on members of the military, peers and the private sector. When one considers that the entirety of two colonial empires' economies was being handled by only 67 people, the lives and livelihoods of 614.2 million people, across the planet, depended upon their decisions.[17] It was, therefore, a hugely influential body during its brief spell in existence.

René Pleven was one of Monnet's secretaries and European manager for Automatic Electric Telephone Company, an American telecommunications company, and had been living in the English capital for the previous eight years, with his wife and two daughters.[18] He left London on 14th December 1939 and arrived in New York, on 21st December, where he met the U.S. Treasury Secretary, Henry Morgenthau Jnr.[19]

[14] TNA, CAB 21 1269, Machinery..., *Memorandum regarding Arrangements for the Coordination of the Economic War Efforts of the U.K. and France*, 24 April 1941, p. 4.

[15] TNA, CAB 21 1269, Machinery..., *Memorandum regarding Arrangements for the Coordination of the Economic War Efforts of the U.K. and France*, 24 April 1941, p. 9.

[16] TNA, CAB 21 1269, Machinery..., *Record of the First Meeting of the Committee*, 6 December 1939.

[17] Table 1.1 'Population, Gross Domestic Product, Territory and Empires of the Allied and Axis Powers within Contemporary Frontiers, 1938', HARRISON Mark, 'The Economics of World War II: An Overview' in HARRISON Mark (Ed.), *The Economics of World War II: Six Great Powers in International Comparison*, Cambridge, Cambridge University Press, 1998, 331p.—(French Colonies + British Colonies + France + Britain)—(70.9 + 453.8 + 42 + 47.5 = 614.2).

[18] PLEVEN Françoise, 'À Quatre Mains' in PIKETTY Guillaume (Ed.), *Français en Résistance: Carnets de guerre, correspondances, journaux personnels*, Paris, Éditions Robert Laffont, 2009, pp. 925–927, p. 925.

[19] BOUGEARD Christian, *René Pleven: Un Français libre en politique*, Rennes, Presses universitaires de Rennes, 1994, 476p. (Ebook), Chap. 4, Para 9—"He was received on

This meeting resulted in an agreement being reached to deliver more than 8,000 aircraft, in October 1940, to Britain and France, costing a billion dollars. However, the price proved a stumbling block, in both in London and Paris.[20] During his visit, Pleven was also due to see Arthur Purvis, the chairman of the Anglo-French Purchasing Board in the United States, to update him as to the progress of the London committee.[21] The Purchasing Board acted as the buyer for the Anglo-French Coordinating Committee in the United States. He clearly left a positive impression upon Purvis, who, in a letter to Monnet, said: "Pleven's visit is an illustration of the value of personal contact which we believe should be instituted as continuing the practice".[22] The Purchasing Board was located at 15, Broad Street, in New York and held meetings on a weekly basis, as of January 1940.[23] Their aim was to organise the purchase of key goods and commodities from the United States. These included machine tools, as well as consumables, such as sugar, wheat, maize and dried fruits.[24] With levels of transportation at the rate of 40.5 million tons a year, British imports were insufficient for the country's needs, by about 6 million tons, while French imports, at the rate of 8 million tons a year, were 8 million tons in deficit.[25] The cooperation of neutral countries would be required to make up the shortfall, but it would come at a significant cost.

On 11th March 1940, the French Prime Minister, Édouard Daladier, wrote a letter to Jean Monnet, setting out the four French priorities for the Anglo-French Coordinating Committee: coal; aviation; arms;

December 21, 1939 by Secretary of State for the Treasury Morgenthau who was in favor of material aid if France managed to free up the financial means to pay for its orders".

[20] MONNET, *Mémoires*, 1976, pp. 156–157.

[21] TNA, CAB 85 59, Anglo-French Purchasing Board in the USA…, *Letter from Jean Monnet to Arthur Purvis*, 8 December 39.

[22] TNA, CAB 85 59, Anglo-French Purchasing Board in the USA…, *Annex II—Copy of Telegram N° 3 of the 29th December from Purvis to Monnet*, 29 December 1939.

[23] TNA, CAB 85 59, Anglo-French Purchasing Board in the USA…, *Letter from A. Purvis to J. Monnet*, 24 January 1940.

[24] TNA, CAB 85 59, Anglo-French Purchasing Board in the USA…, *Foodstuffs Purchased or Requisitioned from the USA—September 1939 to 20th January 1940*, 7 February 1940.

[25] TNA, CAB 85 40, *Anglo-French Permanent Executive Committee for Shipping: The Allied Import Position*, 30 April 1940, p. 4.

and food.[26] As a result of the decision regarding which goods were to be prioritised, on 19th March, the French Assembly heavily criticised Daladier.[27] However, by the end of the month, it was being reported that an agreement had been reached with the United States to supply both France and Britain with the aeroplanes that they required.[28]

Another import of great significance was toluol or toluene. This colourless solvent, a derivative of benzene, was produced by petroleum companies. It is also used in the production of trinitrotoluene (TNT). Buying toluol from the United States was not expected to become a frequent purchase for the British and French. It was merely being bought as a stopgap to help bridge the time-lag in their own production process; consequently, 9,326 tons were ordered from the Americans.[29] An additional 300 tons were ordered, on a month-by-month basis, with delivery beginning in May 1940. Nonetheless, Monnet's stipulated requirements meant that there was a shortfall of 12,134 tons for the year 1940. While this was only one product in the wider war effort, it demonstrates the broader difficulties experienced in the early Allied supply strategy. Converting industry from an export- and consumer-driven footing towards an economy devoting itself to preparing for war was a highly imprecise process. These problems were compounded by the "serious toluol shortage" that was being experienced, which forced prices even higher.[30] Over the course of four months, the price per gallon of

[26] TNA, CAB 85 40, Shipping Requirements for Period March–August 1940—Preparation of an Estimate of Total Imports, Showing Priorities, *Letter from Édouard Daladier to Jean Monnet*, 11 March 1940, p. 1.

[27] 'Biographie – Édouard Daladier', Assemblée nationale, http://www2.assemblee-nationale.fr/sycomore/bio/(num_dept)/2105, Consulted 17 August 2020—"On March 19th, before the House meeting in a secret committee, Edouard Daladier was the subject of violent attacks. 'The men who have not known how to avoid, nor to prepare for war, are not qualified to stop it, nor win it', declared Gaston Bergery".

[28] TNA, CAB 85 59, Anglo-French Purchasing Board in the USA..., *Unlimited Plane Sales to Allies Called Major Landmark of War*, Herald Tribune, 30 March 1940.

[29] TNA, CAB 85 67, Anglo-French Purchasing Board in the USA—Allied Purchases of Munitions in the U.S.A., *Telegram from A. Purvis to J. Monnet (N° 72)*, 27 March 1940.

[30] TNA, CAB 85 67, ...Allied Purchases of Munitions in the U.S.A., *Telegram from Purvis to Monnet (N° 61)*, 14 March 1940.

toluol rose from 45 to 50 cents,[31] representing an 11% increase. Explosives played a pivotal role in both sabotage activities and industrial mining efforts. The shipping trends were showing a decline in goods reaching the French, which pushed the Coordinating Committee to pressure the Shipping Committee to allocate more tonnage to the French.[32]

However, the events of 10th May 1940 would remain with Monnet, long after the war:

> I thought about it with even more anxiety that morning of May 10th as I looked up at the London sky, the fog had just receded. I learned that the sirens, at the same time, were blaring in Paris.[33]

Monnet's trade preoccupations remained largely the same—notably, to increase the number of aircraft available to the French and British. Arthur Purvis highlighted that transport planes, in the United States, were few in number.[34] To help alleviate this problem, and avoid breaching the Neutrality Act, it was suggested that planes could be flown to the U.S.-Canadian border and landed nearby. The aircraft could then be physically pushed across, before being flown to Botwood, Newfoundland, where an aircraft carrier would be waiting to transport them to Europe.[35] The Neutrality Act was first ratified on 31st August 1935[36] before being renewed in 1936, 1937 and, once again, in 1939. It acted as a legislative expression of American economic isolationism by imposing a general embargo on the arms trade with belligerent nations. However, under the 1939 version of the act, the total arms embargo was lifted in favour of purchases being made on the basis of cash-and-carry. Approved on 4th

[31] TNA, CAB 85 67, ...Allied Purchases of Munitions in the U.S.A., *Telegram from Purvis to Monnet (N° 89)*, 18 April 1940.

[32] TNA, CAB 85 40, Shipping Requirements..., *Shipping Capacity*, 30 April 1940, p. 4.

[33] MONNET, *Mémoires*, 1976, p. 15.

[34] TNA, CAB 85 71, Anglo-French Purchasing Board in the U.S.A—Effort to Expedite Supply of War Material to the Allies, *Telegram from A. Purvis to J. Monnet (N° 127)*, 15 May 1940.

[35] TNA, CAB 85 71, ...Effort to Expedite Supply of War Material, *Telegram from A. Purvis to J. Monnet (N° 125)*, 15 May 1940.

[36] 'The Neutrality Acts, 1930s', https://history.state.gov/milestones/1921-1936/neutrality-acts, Consulted 3 February 2017.

November of that year, the 1939 iteration attempted to preserve the neutral status of the United States by forbidding American citizens from partaking in commercial activity with states engaged in armed conflict.[37]

A few weeks later, the planes began crossing the U.S.-Canadian border in towns like Houlton, Maine.[38] Monnet's reasoning abilities were greatly needed at this point, as he sought to ensure that the delivery of American aircraft would not be delayed. To convince the Americans, he deftly argued that if the planes were delivered and the Allies succeeded in regaining the initiative, the debt to the U.S. would be speedily repaid. However, if the Allies succumbed, the United States would have already constructed a large proportion of an air force with which to fight.[39] Some of America's productive capacity had thus been encouraged by Britain and France, who had "at their own expense, created in the U.S.A., productive assets for the manufacture of engines, propellers, or accessories like starters, struts, etc.... at the expenditure of approximately $60,000,000".[40] Nevertheless, as Monnet recognised, in a letter to Sir Edward Bridges, "the U.S. Army and Navy stocks are small".[41]

The confusion sown by the Wehrmacht's rapid advance across Western Europe reached alarming levels in the corridors of power on both sides of the Atlantic. The British Supply Board, in Ottawa, was the British governmental body that organised the procuring of materials and goods in Canada. Its satellite, the British Purchasing Commission, in New York, was twinned with the French Purchasing Commission, under the name of the Anglo-French Purchasing Board, and was founded on 3rd June. Arthur Purvis, a naturalised Canadian who was originally from Scotland,

[37] 'Neutrality Act of 1939', *The American Journal of International Law*, Vol. 34, N° 1, Supplement: Official Documents (January 1940), pp. 47–74, p. 45.

[38] 'Plane Pulled Across Canadian Border in Houlton, 1940', Photograph (15.9 cm × 27.3 cm), Houlton, Aroosotook County, Maine, 2 June 1940, Maine Memory Network, https://www.mainememory.net/artifact/103726, Consulted 18 August 2020.

[39] TNA, CAB 85 71, ...Effort to Expedite Supply of War Material, *Note from J. Monnet to P. Reynaud*, 24 May 1940, p. 3.

[40] TNA, CAB 85 71, ...Effort to Expedite Supply of War Material, *Note from J. Monnet to P. Reynaud*, 24 May 1940, p. 1.

[41] TNA, CAB 85 71, ...Effort to Expedite Supply of War Material, *Letter from J. Monnet to Sir E. Bridges*, 30 May 1940.

was its chairman and served alongside French vice-chairman, Jean Bloch-Lainé.[42] As Purvis was already well known in the Americas, through his successful career in trading explosives, he was accorded a large remit to act on behalf of the British government.[43] With his ties to Roosevelt and Henry Morgenthau, the secretary of the United States Treasury, Purvis and Monnet were two of the most important war procurators at the outbreak of hostilities. However, by 11th June, Monnet proposed that the British Purchasing Commission, in New York, and the Supply Board, in Ottawa, should be separate organisations. However, Purvis was killed in an aeroplane accident, upon leaving Prestwick airport, on 14th August 1941. As Churchill later lamented: "Purvis was a grievous loss as he held so many British, American and Canadian threads in his hands…".[44] This administrative evolution was occurring at breakneck speed, in much a similar way as to how Morgenthau had described the efforts to pass an amendment permitting the provision of armaments.[45] Diplomatic language was heavily tinged by the events through which they were living.

On 13th June, alongside Sir Arthur Salter,[46] Monnet penned a five-page proposal for a union of the French and British Empires.[47] Salter had previously worked with Monnet during the First World War on a

[42] TNA, CAB 85 71, …Effort to Expedite Supply of War Material, *Note on the Functions of the Anglo-French Purchasing Board*, 3 June 1940.

[43] HALL H.D., 'Arthur Blaikie Purvis (1890–1941)', *Oxford Dictionary of National Biography*, 23 September 2004, p. 1, https://www.oxforddnb.com/view/10.1093/ref:odnb/9780198614128.001.0001/odnb-9780198614128-e-35635;jsessionid=1D3D45901F777C6671A5F7ACF7F27DFC, Consulted 24 May 2021.

[44] HALL, '*Purvis*', 2004, p. 2.

[45] TNA, CAB 85 71, …Effort to Expedite Supply of War Material, *Note by J. Monnet to W. Churchill and P. Reynaud*, 4 June 1940—"Mr. Morgenthau added that he wished me to inform both Prime Ministers, and also Ambassador Bullitt, that he and his colleagues were "breaking their necks" to get through with the greatest urgency, the amendment required to enable immediately delivery of armament material from US stock to the Allies".

[46] A colleague, in the Combined Allied Boards, between 1916 and 1918—MONNET, *Mémoires*, 1976, p. 16.

[47] MONNET, *Mémoires*, 1976, p. 18—"On 13$^{th}$ June, we put the finishing touches to a five-page document which examined the hypotheses which were presenting themselves: all of them led us to the conclusion that only the total union of France and England would safeguard the chances of final victory".

plan to coordinate maritime transport among the Allied powers.[48] Their plan was finalised the following day, having been completed by Pleven, Monnet, Salter and Desmond Morton.[49] Morton subsequently presented it to Churchill. It was shown to the British Cabinet, on 16th June, by a reticent Churchill, before being communicated to the French government, from where it was ultimately rejected. This was the final prime ministerial action for Paul Reynaud, before he stood down in favour of Marshal Philippe Pétain, the Victor of Verdun. By the morning of 17th June, de Gaulle met Churchill. He pushed the British prime minister for an appearance on the B.B.C. airwaves, to be allowed to issue his call-to-arms, with Monnet's full support behind him.[50] In order to manage the payments that would go on to support resistance activity, de Gaulle brought in some of Monnet's closest and most experienced collaborators to act on his financial behalf, like Pierre Denis and René Pleven.

## Pierre Denis: The Rebels' Chancellor

Pierre Denis arrived at Saint Stephen's House, in London, on 29th June 1940. General Charles de Gaulle, the leader of the Free French, needed a steady hand on the cashbox of his fledgling movement. Even basic administrative tasks, such as sending telegrams, posed funding difficulties. Within three years, the *Caisse centrale de la France libre* (C.C.F.L.) would become more akin to a central bank for the Free French-controlled colonial empire. This transformation occurred primarily because the mission of de Gaulle's movement changed from organising a military force to one of governing vast colonial territories, as well as managing their natural and human resources. Consequently, any payments made, and received, during the acquisition of armaments fell under the remit of the *Caisse centrale*, as well as those engendered by the sale of minerals, metals and other raw materials.

However, in order to reach this point, an intermediary step, between the creation of the movement and the establishment of the Caisse, was

[48] RICKETT Denis, 'Salter, (James) Arthur, Baron Salter', *Oxford Dictionary of National Biography*, 23 September 2004, p. 1, https://www.oxforddnb.com/view/10.1093/ref:odnb/9780198614128.001.0001/odnb-9780198614128-e-31651, Consulted 24 May 2021.

[49] MONNET, *Mémoires*, 1976, p. 21.

[50] BOUGEARD, *René Pleven*..., 1994, Chap. 4, Para. 41.

required. The C.C.F.L. built upon the foundations that had been laid out by Denis and his colleague, Henri Marais. In the days following the 'Call of 18th June 1940', the Free French Financial Service ran on a shoestring budget of fourteen shillings, with telegrams being sent with the small change that was found in Denis' and Marais' own back pockets.[51] The complexity of the task became clear as an increasing number of collaborators were needed in the day-to-day operations of the service.

The headquarters of the Financial Service were opened in St. Stephen's House, inside a small, triangular room on the third floor of the building, overlooking the Thames.[52] Marais' accounting methods were eccentric; for instance, he used probability calculations as a means of verifying his additions.[53] Marais did not survive the first winter and, on 7th November 1940,[54] he succumbed to a long illness. Nonetheless, his short service was recognised, and he was given honours by the Free French. His widow, Jeanne, continued to receive a pension of £10 per month from de Gaulle's personal account, until May 1942.[55] As pension payments are one of the hallmarks of a functioning social security regime, these payments could indicate the Free French movement's wish to 'shoulder the burden' of protecting their members.

Denis was one of the elders of the group. Having turned 57 a few days before his enrolment, his life experiences greatly added to the administrative competence of the movement. As the son of Ernest Denis, the eminent historian of Germany and Bohemia who had played a role in delimitating the newly founded Czech state in 1918, Pierre's own career began by teaching in Bar-le-Duc before becoming a researcher in Argentina, in 1912, at the Faculty of Philosophy at the University of

[51] OULMONT Philippe, '*Français libre et citoyen du monde: Pierre* Denis', 2 May 2015, http://www.memoresist.org/lecture/francais-libre-et-citoyen-du-monde-philippe-oulmont/, Consulted 4 December 2018.

[52] DENIS Pierre, *Souvenirs de la France Libre*, Paris, Éditions Berger-Levrault, 1947, 242p., p. 34.

[53] DENIS, *Souvenirs*, 1947, p. 35.

[54] Page of MARAIS Henri, http://www.francaislibres.net/liste/fiche.php?index=83276, Consulted 13 December 2018.

[55] Page of GEISMAR épouse MARAIS Jeanne, http://www.francaislibres.net/liste/fiche.php?index=83278, Consulted 13 December 2018; AN, 3 AG 1 302 Compte personnel du général de Gaulle, *Caisse journal novembre 1941–avril 1943*, p. 198.

Buenos Aires.[56] He had been asked to conduct a geographical study of the country as part of a project launched in 1910, the centenary year of Argentinian independence. Denis was chosen due to being a professor from France, in an effort to bring knowledge of Argentina to the wider world. In the balmy days of August 1914, he was mobilised in the initial wave of conscripts and fought as a *poilu* in the Infantry Regiment, achieving the rank of corporal, before being posted to the Macedonian front to become an intelligence officer in the Second Bureau of the Chief of General Staff of the Allied Armies in the Orient.[57] Following the Great War, he was subsequently appointed as an organiser in the League of Nations. As a member of the financial department, Denis served under the leadership of Jean Monnet.[58] Six years older than Monnet, Denis struck his boss as being a hard worker, as well as being:

> ...quick, conscientious...at ease in both analysis and synthesis, capable of seeing the bigger picture when addressing problems and with exceptional training combining the best of public and private experience.[59]

His professional experiences continued in the realm of high finance, by becoming the secretary of a Parisian bank, before being appointed as a monetary expert to the Venezuelan government. It is understandable, therefore, that René Cassin described him as being "our only financier with international experience".[60] Cassin became Denis' colleague in the French 'Empire Defence Council', which was the first political iteration of the Free French movement, in which de Gaulle's movement came to be treated as a quasi-government-in-exile by the British government. As head of the legal department, which was in much a similar position as the Financial Service, notably by lacking in experienced personnel, Cassin

[56] CASSIN René, *'Rauzan' (Pierre Denis)*, Fondation de la France Libre, 2011, http://www.france-libre.net/pierre-denis-rauzan/#2, Consulted 30 August 2017; OULMONT Philippe, *Pierre Denis: Free Frenchman and Citizen of the World*, Paris, Éditions Nouveau Monde, 2013 (Ebook) Chap. 4, Para. 62—"We know he finally left for Buenos Aires with his family on 17 April 1912".

[57] OULMONT, *Pierre Denis: Free Frenchman*..., 2013 (Ebook) Chap. 6, Para. 12.

[58] MONNET Jean, *Mémoires*, Paris, Librairie Arthème Fayard, 1976, 642p., p. 104.

[59] OULMONT, *Pierre Denis: Free Frenchman*..., 2013 (Ebook) Chap. 7, Para. 3.

[60] OULMONT Philippe, *Pierre Denis: Français libre et citoyen du monde*, Paris, Éditions Nouveau Monde, 2012, 480p., p. 270.

had spent a significant amount of time collaborating with Denis during the writing of the movement's economic statutes. It was this level of experience that led to Denis' immediate appointment as the head of the Free French Financial Service.

Denis was clearly a man who had travelled widely and had much experience in the professional, militarily and academic sectors. However, when offering his services to the Free French cause, he chose to do so in a manner that was contrary to the thinking of his colleagues and flew in the face of accepted French financial orthodoxy. The first example of this, cited by Oulmont,[61] is the manner in which Denis dealt with the liabilities of the Free French movement. As explained by Étienne Hirsch, the deputy director of Free French armaments, Denis simply paid funds into a bank account and stipulated that the debts were to be repaid within a five-day delay.[62] This allowed for the accumulation of discounts from suppliers. While this may hint at a gauche handling of public finances, Denis fully admitted to his own lack of formal experience. Moreover, the Free French movement were in a unique position among the other governments-in-exile as France still had a sitting government, in Vichy. The Free French were, therefore, obliged to adopt a bespoke method of managing their finances, as they had not been accorded official diplomatic recognition by many major powers, including the United States. Moreover, with the rapid evolutions in both the military and political context, an adaptable financial and monetary system was required in the Free French colonies. In de Gaulle's estimation, Denis was the man to implement such a project and his 'inexperience' appears to have been viewed as more of an asset than a hindrance.

While his manner of rectifying financial difficulties may have been unorthodox, Denis' methods should be seen within the context of an extremely confused situation. The political foundations of the movement had barely been established, despite Churchill's assurance to de Gaulle,

[61] OULMONT, *Pierre Denis*, 2012, p. 272.

[62] Étienne Hirsch was a civil engineer who was chosen as Deputy Director of Armaments in the Free French Forces. He was sent to Algiers in July 1943, where he worked with Jean Monnet on supplying the members of the resistance, before joining the invasion forces in Normandy following D-Day. See https://www.trumanlibrary.gov/library/oral-histories/hirsche, http://www.francaislibres.net/liste/fiche.php?index=110311, and http://clio.ish-lyon.cnrs.fr/patrons/AC000008015/AC000008015Doc1214.pdf, Consulted 15 January 2019.

on 28th June 1940.[63] The economic position was still subject to great upheaval. At this point, the only considerations that held Denis' and Marais' attention were the small personal loans that were requested by the personnel and their equipment costs. In the days following the 'Call of 18$^{th}$ June', a small group of soldiers, airmen and naval personnel rallied around General de Gaulle; these men would need monetary and material support, in order to pay their wages, feed, clothe and arm them. The soldier's pay book, in Fig. 2.2, belonged to Daniel Cordier. As can be seen, it is a British document that has been issued by de Gaulle's organisation, demonstrating the early Free French reliance upon their British hosts. These corps, who were restricted in number, formed the powerbase upon which the Free French based their political legitimacy.

Following the de facto recognition of General de Gaulle's movement by the British, the Bank of England opened a bank account for the movement which allowed for payments to be made by, and sent to, General de Gaulle. This enabled his services to draw and deposit money. The payments due to the British ministries for services or ordnance were remitted separately to each ministry, thus proving to be extremely cumbersome from a bureaucratic perspective. Pierre Denis created a vision for a financial and monetary system that would be suitable for the exceptional circumstances that surrounded the creation of the Free French movement—one that was freer, simpler and more adaptive. To help him, his ignorance of the arcane ways of the financial administrator allowed for a certain disregard for accepted rules.[64]

Beginning in July 1940, the costs incurred by French military personnel present in Great Britain were assured by the British Treasury, for the purposes of accounting. The eventual written agreement between Churchill and de Gaulle was signed on 7th August 1940, which created the need for a functioning accounts system.[65] These accounts were sent to the respective ministries who supplied the funds and placed the orders for other goods that were to be bought on behalf of the Free French.

[63] TNA, CAB/65/7/81, *Conclusions of a Meeting of the War Cabinet*, 28 June 1940, "His Majesty's Government recognise General de Gaulle as the Leader of all free Frenchmen, wherever they may be, who rally to him in support of the Allied cause".

[64] DENIS, *Souvenirs*..., 1947, p. 35—"But I had only a vague idea of these professional rules and, to violate them, my ignorance helped me more than my courage".

[65] Bank of England archives (BoE), OV45 129 Caisse centrale de la France libre, *Problèmes financiers et monétaires de la France Libre*, 15 July 1941, p. 1.

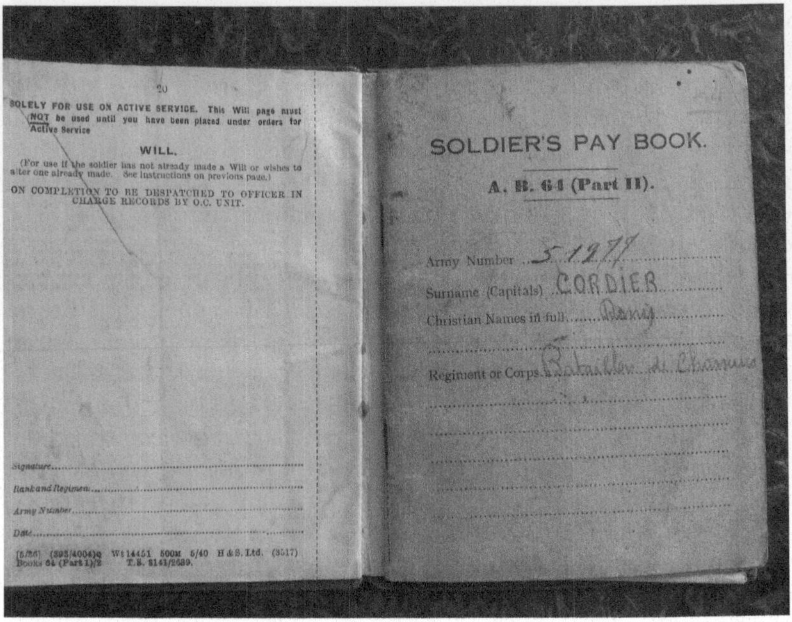


**Fig. 2.2** Daniel Cordier's Pay Book, 1940 (D. Cordier's collection, photograph by author)

Denis and de Gaulle both intended to limit any costs accumulated by the Free French Forces.[66] It was hoped that effective economic management and financial prudence would facilitate future diplomatic relations. The account opened at the Bank of England, in General de Gaulle's own name, would allow him to act as both a political chief and as a military leader. This account would be used as a 'holding account', meaning that the budget set out by the French National Committee would be sent to the respective British ministry, who would subsequently credit General de Gaulle's account, thus allowing for the payment of any outstanding bills. With credit and a bank account, the financial foundation of the Gaullist movement was laid.

[66] DE GAULLE, *Mémoires de guerre*, Paris, Plon, p. 89.

The primary task of the Free French Financial Service was to acquire, and account for, incoming money and to redistribute it among their creditors in the various British ministries. These payments covered all aspects of running a modern military force, which can be separated into two types of expenditure: firstly, living costs, which were comprised of food, clothing, training, health care and wages, and, secondly, military costs, including technology, ordnance and other capital expenditure, such as barracks. Using publicity and communication, including programmes broadcast by the B.B.C., such as '*Les Français parlent aux Français*', knowledge of the movement began to spread. With this steadily growing public recognition, unsolicited donations began to arrive at both Olympia[67] and Carlton Gardens.[68] These were two properties that had been lent to the movement by the British government. Concurrently, the Free French encouraged like-minded French expatriates and Francophiles to form their own 'delegations' in their adopted countries. The Free French delegations forwarded subscriptions and helped to finance projects, including the 'Spitfire Fund' which served as a means to equip the embryonic Free French Air Force with the newly designed fighter aircraft. However, to avoid squandering the generosity of their supporters, these funds needed to be managed.

According to Denis, the formalisation of economic interactions took place on 19th March 1941 with two agreements that were signed between the Free French and His Majesty's Treasury.[69] The importance of these accords is without question as they reflected the ongoing desire by both the British government and the Free French to attempt to resurrect the pre-war administrative cooperation. This is surprising as bilateral agreements are rarely signed between governments and private individuals. As has been seen, the Anglo-French Coordinating Committee used the economic heft of both Britain and France combined, in order to gain economies of scale and to avoid taxing already scarce resources too heavily. Under the agreements, the Free French were heavily dependent upon the British for both their money and the supplies that they needed. The continuity is clear, with both Denis and Pleven having been

[67] Idem, p. 82.

[68] Idem, p. 95.

[69] DENIS Pierre, 'Les finances de la France Libre', *Revue de la Deuxième Guerre mondiale*, PUF, N° 1, November 1950, pp. 20–27, p. 20.

involved in both ventures, but Monnet, a key figure in the Anglo-French Coordinating Committee, had decided that his talents were better suited elsewhere. This demonstrates that De Gaulle, with British support, was in the process of creating a powerbase to attempt to rival that of the Vichy government. Interallied collaboration and mutual assistance enabled the external resistance to embed itself within, and grow from, the colonies. Furthermore, this normalisation of political relations helped to seal the reputation of de Gaulle as being "leader of all free French people, wherever they may be".[70] However, a leader is predominantly judged by their ability to delegate. To manage the finances of the movement, de Gaulle's delegates implemented a makeshift method which ensured that the movement's debts would be repaid. From this perspective, the nascent Free French Financial Service was undoubtedly a collaborative success between the British and the Gaullists.

Denis tellingly remarked that "the question of money was secondary in our priorities, even my own",[71] when compared to the many difficult situations that the Free French were to face. However, this comment highlights Denis' modesty when considering the rapid development that was to come. In July 1940, it was little more than a two-man operation, but, less than a year later, they were discussing the planning of a public financial board, intended to manage colonial monetary questions and, by extension, the French external resistance. The following year would be marked by the creation of the *Caisse centrale de la France libre*. It reflected the evolution of the Free French movement, from a military fighting force to something more akin to a state-in-exile. Furthermore, the rallied colonies were to be supported in their effort to help supply the Allies and, by so doing, ensure that their economies remained solvent.

## The Peripatetic Plevens

René Pleven, Denis' colleague in the Anglo-French Coordinating Committee, was the recipient of many opportunities to demonstrate his myriad skills. As Raoul de Roussy de Sales, a French journalist in the United States, explained:

[70] TNA, CAB/66/39/41, *Relations with General de Gaulle*, 7 August 1943, p. 1.
[71] DENIS, *Souvenirs…*, 1947, p. 35.

> Pleven is a recruiter, and once his man has said yes, that is enough for him. He said to me, one day, apropos of something else, "Every man has a moment of weakness which does not last more than ten minutes. That is the moment to be seized". That is what he probably thought he was doing with me. It is perhaps what he did.[72]

However, being a 'recruiter' was certainly not Pleven's intended role within de Gaulle's fledgling movement. Having previously worked with Monnet and Denis, it was Pleven who wrote Monnet's resignation letter to Paul Reynaud on 1st July 1940.[73] Despite her initial misgivings at her husband's choice of wartime occupation, Annette Pleven served an important role in supporting René's activities, acting as a cheerleader for the movement and as an organiser of material aid that was destined for the Free French.

Pleven followed his friend, Denis, into the Free French movement on 8th July, with slightly more trepidation than was shown by his elderly colleague. This hesitancy was most likely due to Pleven's responsibilities as the head of a young family. Initially, his wife was disapproving of her husband's choice.[74] However, as René had ensured that she and the children, Françoise and Nicole, were safely expatriated to Canada, with the help of his contacts in the British government, there was little that she could do to change his mind. Whether this *fait accompli* was intentional is very much open to debate.

Beginning his career as a senior civil servant among the Free French on 13th July, Pleven was tasked with managing relations with the Foreign Office and the Colonial Office.[75] He was highly competent, having already proven himself by serving on the Anglo-French Coordinating Committee. However, even he was not expecting such a swift rise and assumed that this must have been due to the lack of professional politicians.[76] By the end of the month, Pleven was preparing to travel for the French African territories to try and bring them into the Free French

[72] DE ROUSSY DE SALES Raoul, *The Making of Yesterday*, New York, Reynal & Hitchcock, 1947, 310p., p. 226.

[73] PIKETTY Guillaume (Ed.), *Français en Résistance: Carnets de Guerre, Correspondances, Journaux Personnels*, Paris, Éditions Robert Laffont, 2009, 1169p., p. 934.

[74] Ibid., p. 939.

[75] Ibid., p. 937.

[76] Ibid., p. 941.

movement. It was recognised that the colonies' economies were highly reliant upon British cooperation and "good-will".[77] He intended that the Free French colonies should "not…be a burden on our allies" and "provide our allies with…the maximum war effort".[78] From his description of the journey, the wartime world of the 1940s appeared much larger—with a plane journey from London to Bathurst, in British Gambia, taking an entire day, for example. This was one of the recurring difficulties that the Free French movement faced from the outset, managing colonial territories that, by plane, were days away or weeks, when travelling by boat. Nonetheless, as Pleven explained, when discussing French Cameroon, "(they were) the only practical means of circulating around this country".[79]

As he was on secondment from his job for an American telecommunications firm, Pleven's thoughts often turned to the situation in the United States. Certain businesses felt compelled to look after their serving employees, as well as for their families. Annette was provided with living and educational stipend by her husband's employer, to the value of $14,437, with an additional $1,300 being paid on a monthly basis.[80] She had moved from Canada to New York and had begun to involve herself in the local expatriate community. Importantly, in addition to her assistance with acquiring medical equipment that could benefit the Free French movement, she collected information for her husband on the political sentiment being expressed among the French diaspora in the United States.[81] Concerning the request that Raoul de Roussy de Sales should join the American Free French committee, when René complained to Annette of his disappointment at having heard nothing back from his acquaintance, Annette took it upon herself to pay de Roussy a visit.[82] She had clearly conquered her initial reticence of de Gaulle's movement. While Roussy did not immediately acquiesce to her recruiting

[77] Ibid., p. 944.

[78] Archives nationales de la France d'Outre-mer (ANOM), 1AFF-POL 873, *Les réalisations coloniales de la France Combattante en Afrique Equatoriale Française*, Chap. 2, p. 10.

[79] Ibid., p. 953.

[80] Ibid., p. 963.

[81] Ibid., p. 961.

[82] DE ROUSSY DE SALES Raoul, *The Making of Yesterday*, 1947, p. 191.

advances, the Pleven brigading partnership worked and, by the end of 1941, de Roussy became one of the founding members of the Free French delegation in the United States.

In a foreshadowing of his future role, René became preoccupied by the problems that were hampering the American Free French delegation while he was on his mission to the Free French African territories. These seem to have been largely caused by two difficulties: firstly, the French diaspora organisation 'France Forever' was foundering in acrimony and, secondly, the American Neutrality Act of 1939 meant that no funds could be raised to finance foreign armed forces and militias. Pleven bemoaned that, while the other committees were sending £1,000 per month in subsidies, which will be seen in greater detail in Chapter 4, the New York committee had not sent a dime, despite requiring the Gaullist movement to pay for the expenses of Maurice Garreau-Dombasle, the leader at the time.[83]

It is clear from the journeys taken by these men, and woman, that those who were most intimately involved in the beginnings of the French external resistance were on the peripheries of the high politics of the day. De Gaulle, having been a junior minister in Reynaud's cabinet, was afforded a great deal of help by the British government. Monnet, despite not having wished to rally to the movement, had done his best to leave the Franco-British economic collaboration in a state fit to fight another global conflict. While circumstances did not allow the Anglo-French Coordinating Committee to progress much further than the drawing board, those whom he had hired were clearly of a calibre to offer significant help to de Gaulle in his self-proclaimed mission to keep the French empire's human capital and resources in the war. Having chosen to seize the opportunities that they were offered, Pleven and Denis would go on to become central figures in the Free French movement until the liberation of France and, in Pleven's case, far beyond. Moreover, the important role that Annette Pleven played in providing information, medical supplies and helping to recruit members, despite her initial hesitations, cannot be understated. She offered her husband a view of events happening on the other side of the Atlantic and prepared him for the difficult task that awaited him in 1941.

[83] PIKETTY, *Français en résistance...*, 2009, p. 970.

CHAPTER 3

# Administrative Alliances

Among the first preoccupations of de Gaulle's fledgling movement was ensuring their own financial stability. Having arrived in London with little more than the 100,000 francs in his possession (£566 2s 1d), which had been passed to him by Paul Reynaud, *Président* of the Council of Ministers, prior to de Gaulle's departure from Mérignac Airport, the movement quickly needed support.[1]

The Free French Financial Service was one of the central departments in the movement's civil administration. From July 1940, the service was headquartered at N° 4, Carlton Gardens, using a bank account opened in the name of General de Gaulle with the Bank of England.[2] By the end of August, the service began to keep a ledger, in an initial attempt at double-entry bookkeeping. Showing the movement's assets and liabilities, transactions began to be recorded from 29th August 1940, largely in an attempt to balance the payments that were to be made to Free French aviators.

[1] AGLAN Alya, *La France à l'envers: La guerre de Vichy 1940–1945*, Paris, Éditions Gallimard, 2020, 720p., p. 30.

[2] OULMONT, *Pierre Denis*, 2012, p. 270.



D. Foulk, *The Price of Freedom*,
https://doi.org/10.1007/978-3-031-09066-0_3

## Une Histoire D'argent

The *Caisse centrale* grew out of the Free French Financial Service. The agreement between Churchill and de Gaulle, on 7th August 1940, created the need for functioning accounts. Following the 'Call of $18^{th}$ June', a small group of soldiers, airmen and naval personnel rallied around de Gaulle. This armed corps, albeit restricted in number, formed the beginnings of a powerbase upon which the Free French movement could ground their political legitimacy. The task of the Financial Service was to acquire and account for the money, before redistributing it to their creditors in the various British ministries. These were payments that covered purchases concerning all aspects of leading a military.

Philippe Oulmont states that "in autumn 1940, the Free French authorities in Brazzaville decided to provisionally print new bills in the Belgian Congo, which were actually types of coupons known as "Larminat Bonds", and to put them into circulation in the rallied African colonies".[3] This sought to ensure that the pound sterling did not take precedence over the French franc in the rallied colonies. This demonstrates that one of de Gaulle's principal preoccupations was retaining the support of the newly rallied colonies, which, like Cameroon and parts of French Equatorial Africa, had been brought under the aegis of the Free French through the work of Pleven, Leclerc and Hettier de Boislambert in August 1940. The 'Empire Defence Council', to give the Free French their initial nomenclature, would try their best to live up to their name.

Beginning in July 1940, for Accounting purposes, the fees and charges incurred by French military personnel in Great Britain were underwritten by the British Treasury. These invoices were sent to the respective British ministries who issued the funds and placed orders for other goods bought on behalf of the Free French. Both Denis and de Gaulle intended to limit the costs accumulated by the movement.[4] It was hoped that effective financial management would facilitate diplomatic relations later in the war.

The movement's initial income was dominated by relatively small payments made by individuals from across the globe; from Rio de Janeiro, Montego Bay in Jamaica, Gillingham in Kent, Mexico and Afghanistan. However, some of the payments that were received by the Free French were missing from their ledgers, most notably from the '*Compte Général*

[3] Ibid., p. 275.

[4] DE GAULLE, *Mémoire*..., 1989, p. 89.

*de Gaulle*', which suggests that this was a form of secondary account that was intended for his personal expenses alone. The 'National Provincial Bank' (N.P.B.) account acted as a form of holding account. Invoices would be received by the respective British ministry, who would credit General de Gaulle's account, thus allowing for the payment of the outstanding bill. The reason that this was an innovative way of managing the Free French finances was that it bypassed the need for direct authorisation from their British hosts, thus underlining the close working relationship and level of monetary support available to the newly formed movement. However, this additional step risked causing great inefficiency, notably through time delays and bloated administration. While Denis' and Marais' initially conceived system, of paying expenditure with a week's delay, may have worked for a military organisation, impediments arose when additional levels of administration, notably concerning the management of colonial economies, were added to the burden.

The rallying of the territories of French Equatorial Africa, in August 1940, and New Caledonia, the following month, changed the nature of the Free French movement; from having been a military force, exclusively, to becoming a governmental administration. Discussions concerning monetary policy and finance were held over the course of March 1941. The principal result of the exchanging of letters, between Churchill and de Gaulle, was that a conversion rate was established between the pound sterling and the franc that was circulating in the rallied colonies.[5] This was fixed at 176.625 francs to the pound and no limits were set as to the amount that could be purchased by the Bank of England.[6] Through this agreement, a supply of foreign exchange was permitted to the Gaullists and this could be used to procure ordnance and the products necessary for supplying their territories. From the opening of credit in July 1940 to 1st April 1941, the British government provided £1,634,000 to the Free French movement, of which £1.15 million and £308,000 went, respectively, to French Equatorial Africa and Cameroon.[7]

The agreements provided a legitimate economic foundation upon which to support their growing colonial influence, largely due to the

[5] ANOM, 1 AFF-POL 879, Accords entre le Gouvernement de Sa Majesté Britannique et le Chef de la France Libre (Trésor et financier) 1941, *Letter from Winston Churchill to General de Gaulle, II – Texte d'accord financier*, 19 March 1941.

[6] BoE, OV45 129, *Problèmes financiers et monétaires de la France Libre*, p. 2.

[7] BoE, OV45 129, *Problèmes financiers et monétaires de la France Libre*, p. 3.

efforts of René Pleven, Claude Hettier de Boislambert and Philippe de Hautecloque, better known by his *nom-de-guerre* Leclerc. On 6th August, they flew from Poole to attempt to rally the African colonies to de Gaulle's movement.[8] For their audacious mission, the men were provided with £100 (17,662.50 F[9]). Denis later recounted the difficulties experienced with obtaining such a sum on short notice.[10] When it is considered that de Gaulle was issued the equivalent of £566 by Reynaud, prior to leaving Bordeaux on 17th June 1940, the sum issued to Pleven, Hettier de Boislambert and de Hautecloque represented about 17.6% of the Free French operating budget, *ceteris paribus*. Money was thus incredibly tight for the movement. Even at the time, Pleven's own monthly salary was viewed as being undervalued, as he accepted sixty pounds[11] (10,597.50 F). However, this remuneration should be put into perspective. According to Jennings, the official wage of road workers in Chad was around two francs per day and six francs for a porter.[12] These figures help to underline the difference in the cost of living between London and the soon-to-be Free French territories to which the men were travelling, specifically in French Equatorial Africa. More starkly, it shows the wage disparity between the hired colonial hands and the Free French personnel.

Donations were collected through the organisation of events, whose ticketing turnover would be donated, or through the sending of cheques directly to the Free French movement, as can be seen in Fig. 3.1. The two accounts, '*Compte Général de Gaulle*' and 'National Provincial Bank', grew rapidly during September and October, before increasing greatly in November. This was notably the case for the 'General de Gaulle' account, shown in blue. By December, donations became slightly more regular but on a declining trend, with the marked exception of March 1941, when very little money arrived in either account. Donations came from various sources; some were sent by individuals, others were sent by the Free French delegations; some were named, others were anonymous;

[8] BOUGEARD Christian, *René Pleven: Un Français libre en politique*, Rennes, Presses universitaires de Rennes, 1994, 476p. (Ebook), Chap. 5, Para. 33.

[9] £1:176.625 Francs, therefore £100 × 176.625 F = 17,662.50 F. For future foreign exchange calculations, the same operation will be undertaken.

[10] DENIS, *Souvenirs*..., 1947, p. 39.

[11] BOUGEARD, *René Pleven*..., Chap. 5, Para. 14.

[12] JENNINGS Eric, *Free French Africa*..., 2015, 300p., p. 231.

some religious, others secular. For instance, on 21st December 1940, a donation was received from the Israelite Community of Montévideo, for the value of £500, meaning that De Gaulle received support from both overtly Jewish and Christian organisations. These donations came from convents like Sacred Heart Convent at Hitchin, in Hertfordshire, or St. Paul de Chartres' Convent at Bloxwich. Recalling his schooldays at the convent school, the historian Robert Tombs remembered the mother superior:

> ...I was introduced to the Reverend Mother, who was French and spoke with a strong accent; being a child she seemed to me very old. She must have been old enough to remember when the Sisters of St. Paul of Chartres were forbidden to teach, dissolved and effectively expelled from France in the early 1900's. She remained a remote and awe-inspiring figure.[13]

Tombs was talking about *Sœur* Renée, Germaine Litter, who gave a total of £3 3s 0d to the Free French movement, over three separate occasions. As no accompanying correspondence has been recorded, Litter's motivation for sending money to de Gaulle is impossible to ascertain. Nonetheless, her small gifts contributed to funding French external resistance efforts.

As the summer of 1940 passed into autumn, in London, discussions began to help find ways of managing the economies of the newly rallied African and Pacific territories. Each posed their own difficulties, including problems linked to politically imposed characteristics, such as borders, and geographical considerations, such as the distances needing to be travelled when transporting goods and banknotes. However, it is important to understand more about the income and outgoings of the Free French before their methods for organising the colonial economies can be better explained.

[13] TOMBS Robert, 'St Paul's Convent Through the Eyes of a Pupil', Saint Peter's Catholic Church, Bloxwich, https://www.stpetersbloxwich.org.uk/history-of-st-pauls-convent.html, Consulted 20 September 2020.

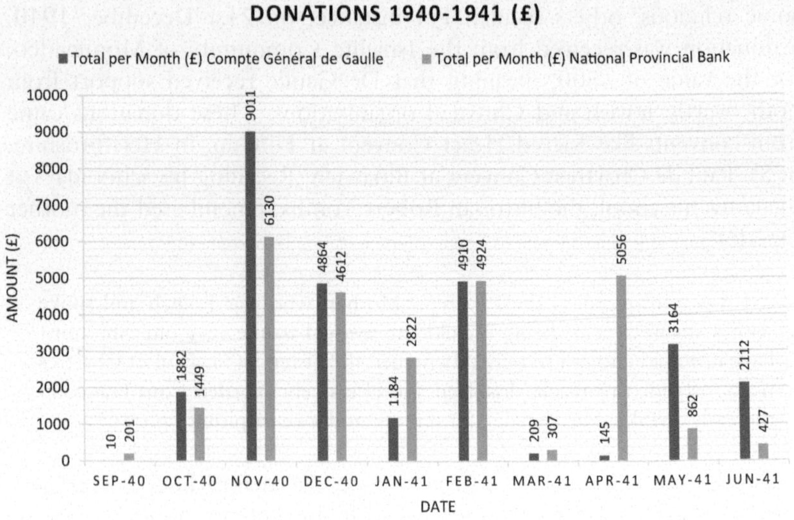


**Fig. 3.1** Donations to the General de Gaulle Account and the National Provincial Bank Account, 1940–1941 (AN, 3 AG 1 301)

## General Funds—De Gaulle's Private Accounts

> Although the Free French were, of course, without funds of their own, it was to General de Gaulle's credit that he declined to accept from (the British) Government a penny for his own personal expenses or for his entourage, these being provided from money donated for the purpose by Frenchmen from all over the world.[14]

Lionel Fraser's words, as the Treasury's representative to the governments-in-exile, indicate that de Gaulle did not receive a personal stipend from the British government. This section intends to investigate the General's personal finances in greater depth as the historical importance of his British bank account is abundantly clear; to have an idea as to what de Gaulle paid, and to whom, is as important as knowing about the missions and objectives that his movement pursued. Unfortunately, at the movement's beginning, from June until September 1940, due to

[14] FRASER W. Lionel, *All to the Good*, Kingswood, Heinemann, 1963, 275p., p. 134.

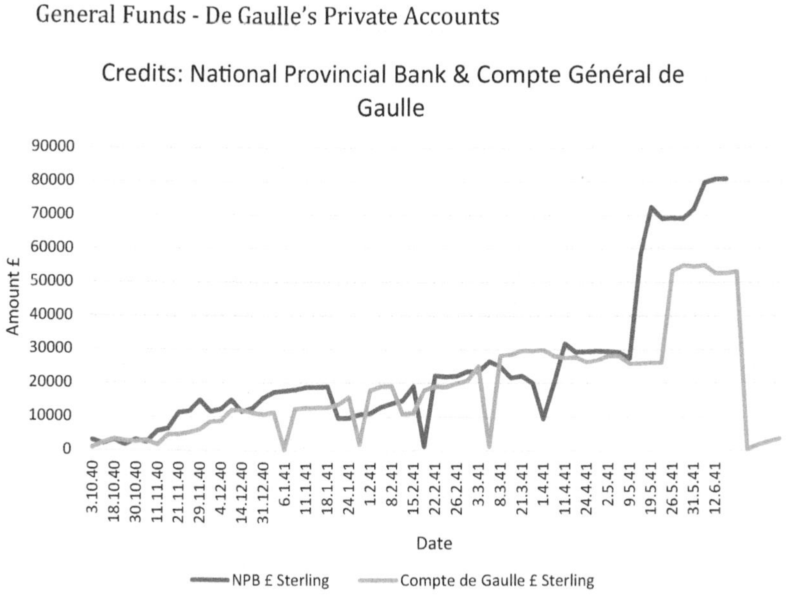


**Fig. 3.2** Credits in Pound Sterling: N.P.B. & Compte Général de Gaulle, October 1940–June 1941 (AN, 3 AG 1 301)

the confused political situation in London, the accounts do not appear to have been recorded (Figs. 3.2 and 3.3).

General de Gaulle's principal British bank account was held with the National Provincial Bank, the predecessor to the National Westminster Bank, at their Charing Cross branch.[15] This account was opened, on 20th September 1940, with an initial balance of £1,582 18s 8d and debits of £670 1s 9d. The debits included purchases of items for immediate usage, such as books, stationery and reading glasses. Equally, the donations received from abroad would be channelled through the account. It operated on the basis of double-entry bookkeeping, where each entry has a corresponding and opposite transfer.

These accounts were, by far, the most frequently used of thirty accounts that were opened by the Free French movement. The others

[15] Archives nationales (AN), 3 AG (1) 305, *Letter from Capt. François Boissière, Treasurer of Gen. De Gaulle, to Pierre Denis, Financial Attaché, CFLN*, 16/2/44.

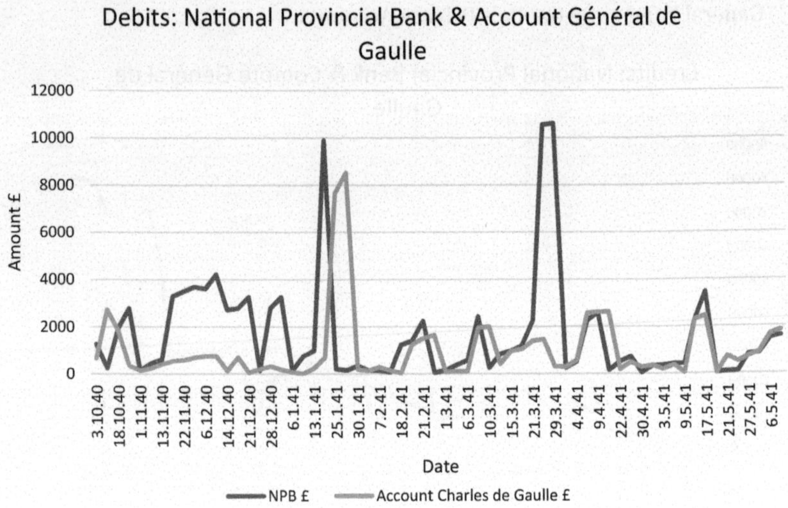


**Fig. 3.3** Debits in Pound Sterling: N.P.B. & Account Général de Gaulle, October 1940–May 1941 (AN, 3 AG 1 301)

recorded barely thirty to fifty transactions, and often saw far fewer. In contrast, entries in the credit and debit accounts of the '*Général de Gaulle*' account and the 'N.P.B.' both recorded around four hundred individual transactions: ranging from 392 events, in the 'de Gaulle' credit account, to 434 events, in the 'N.P.B.' credit account. This transactional quantity alone offers credence to the idea that these were the most important accounts and, one could plausibly hypothesise, would therefore contain the most important transactions.

Proportionally, the largest account was the 'National Provincial Bank' credit account, which was twenty times larger than the other accounts. Such a high frequency of transfers suggests that, during the period from September 1940 to June 1941, significant balances were arriving through this account. Those transfers came from committees devoted to helping de Gaulle keep the rallied French empire in the war; including the Free French Committee in Mexico, who sent £1,000, on 29th November 1940, or the Uruguayan committee, from where another £1,000 was expedited, on 20th February 1941.

The sources of many of these donations were from outside France and Europe itself. While the provenance of a cheque or mandate sent by a particular organisation was often noted, information concerning the sender of individual donations was seldom detailed. This was notably the case for the donations provided by Montréal-based Dr. Vignal, who was the son of a professor at the *Collège de France* and the head of the Canadian Gaullist delegation, when a £200 transfer was made on 26th September 1940.[16] These cheques were sent to the National Provincial Bank account and were subsequently identified in the '*Général de Gaulle*' account. However, his task was being rendered even more difficult as Ottawa "saw no advantage in promoting the 'extension of de Gaulle's movement in Canada'".[17] Courteaux wrote that the British "never considered the Free French movement to be a government-in-waiting. The Bordeaux government – soon to be transferred to the small town of Vichy – remained, for better or worse, the legal government of France".[18] Yet, this does not appear to correspond to the economic approach being taken by the Free French and British. While the Free French were not a government-in-waiting, de Gaulle was accorded powers that no ordinary citizen would have received. Examples include the fact that de Gaulle's movement had the right to train a group of foreigners on British soil, albethey lightly armed; the ability to launch an attack on a sovereign nation with full British military support, as was seen during Operation Menace and the Dakar invasions of September 1940; and the possibility of opening bank accounts with the Bank of England.

The most frequently effectuated transactions were the donations made to the movement and financial gifts sent directly to General de Gaulle. These donations were nominatively sent to both de Gaulle and to his

[16] VIATTE Auguste, *D'un Monde à l'autre: Journal d'un intellectuel jurassien au Québec (1939–1949), V. 1 mars 1939–novembre 1942*, Paris, L'Harmattan, 2001, 516p., p. 117; AMYOT Éric, *Le Québec entre Pétain et de Gaulle: Vichy, la France libre et les Canadiens français, 1940–1945*, Montreal, Éditions Fides, 1999, 365p., p. 117—"At the beginning of October (1940), General de Gaulle, at that time in French Equatorial Africa, reaffirmed the authority of Vignal: I confirm that the Surgeon General Vignal is my sole representative for the entirety of Canada stop…".

[17] COURTEAUX Olivier, *Canada Between Vichy & Free France, 1940–1945*, Toronto, University of Toronto Press, 2013, 280p., Chap. 3, Para 26 (Ebook).

[18] Idem, Chap. 3, Para 2.

movement[19] and to private individuals within the movement. The correspondence that accompanied the payments has been separated from the accounts and, therefore, the only way to assess the motivations of donors is through references in secondary literature.

Nonetheless, the relative lack of public recognition that these supporters received, from the movement or de Gaulle himself, both during the war and afterwards, remains surprising. The few references that do exist include Pierre Denis mentioning the donation of a large diamond that was worth £100,000, according to its Syrian donor.[20] At this time, French presence in Syria remained limited, with only 16,640 N.C.O.'s and enlisted men and 686 officers based in the entire Levant area.[21] This was to be the next battleground in what was to become the British riposte, after having suffered a number of defeats in 1940 and 1941. Such munificence from a Syrian would have seemed to confirm the information that the Free French were passing to the British, that, were they to invade the Levant, there would be very little in the way of Vichy resistance.[22] However, scant mention is made in the secondary literature as to the identities of donors, with only passing reference being made towards their financing activities. This propensity to underplay the role of Free French donors may reflect upon the humility of those who gifted the funds and upon contemporary distaste for discussions concerning money. People may not have necessarily wished to have details of their donations being discussed; whether they feared being decried, targeted for their perceived riches, or possibly even lauded for their generosity.

[19] TNA, FO 371 41912 1944 (French Welfare), Letter from Williams to Speaight, 18 October 1944—"It is clear that the funds of the AVF (Amis des Volontaires Français) comprised of the subscriptions and donations of i) British and French sympathisers in this country and ii) of sympathisers, French and others, from South America, and other places abroad, were given for the purpose of welfare to de Gaulle Volunteers".

[20] DENIS, *Souvenirs de la France Libre*, 1947, p. 35.

[21] ALBORD Maurice, *L'Armée Française & les États du Levant 1936–1946*, Paris, CNRS Éditions, 2000, 336p., Chap. 2, Para. 10 (Ebook).

[22] BARR James, *A Line in the Sand: Britain, France and the Struggle for the Mastery of the Middle East*, London, Simon & Schuster UK, 2011, 350p. (Ebook), Chap. 17, Para. 9—"The British did not expect resistance. They had been told by de Gaulle to expect minimal opposition from the Vichy French, whose "will to fight would very soon crumble". To ensure the goodwill of the population, the British had not only guaranteed Catroux's declaration of independence but had also secretly underwritten it with £200,000 of payments to Druze and Bedu leaders inside Syria".

As can be seen in Fig. 3.2, there was a steady increase in received funds following the opening of accounts until 18th January, after which a fifty per cent drop in transfers into the account occurred. There were two lean periods, when payments fell drastically: once during February and the second in April. However, by May 1941, there was a parabolic increase in receipts for the movement. This pattern is reflected by the debit entry into the '*Général de Gaulle*' account, albeit with more periods of penury, where incoming monies did not maintain the general upward trajectory. While these accounts are not directly linked to the Lend-Lease programme by the United States, it seems that this increase in funding could be correlated to the support that the Free French movement were receiving from the U.S. and British governments. Other events that may have contributed to this increase in credits for the Free French accounts could have been the meeting between Hitler and Darlan at the Berghof on 11th May or the mass round-up of Jews in Paris that took place on 14th May.

On 9th June 1941, however, something bizarre occurred. The large credit balance, at over £55,600 or 9.8 million francs, drops significantly. The fall in the balance is extraordinary; a 99.2% decline on the previous running total. Moreover, on this page of the account book, and those that followed, the number ~~53,238.11.5~~ is struck through. This suggests that an error was made, but, within the context of the accounts, it seems more of a retrospective correction. However, there is no indication as to why this amendment was made. Prior to this, there had been no entries struck-out. Looking at the chronology of events for the war, this corresponded with the beginning of the Syrian campaign, which began the day before. Otherwise, little else seems to explain this rectification.

During this period, the only debits of any significance were for two payments of £1,000, which were made by Tony Mayer, the future supposed 'manager' of the *Caisse centrale de la France libre*. One was made to Sir Miles Lampson,[23] the British ambassador in Cairo, who had "immediately supported" General Catroux's proclamation of Syrian and Lebanese independence.[24] The payment reference talks of reimbursement

[23] AN, 3 AG (1) 301, Account 'Compte Général de Gaulle'—"13/5/1941 - Sir Miles Lampson (paid by Mr. Tony Mayer) reimbursement of diverse fees - £1,000.8.9".

[24] *Africa, The Near East and The War—Lectures Delivered Under the Auspices of the Committee on International Relations on the Los Angeles Campus of the University of California—Spring 1942*, Berkeley and Los Angeles, University of California Press, 1943,

for diverse charges. As Catroux was authorised by de Gaulle to issue the proclamation, it may be hypothesised that this payment was made in relation to the support that Lampson offered to the Free French movement. The other recipient of £1,000 was a man named Brissay. Like Lampson, he was equally marked as being the 'agent' in Singapore. While, in the French language, the word 'agent' does not *necessarily* have the same connotations as it does in English, it is likely that Brissay, like Lampson, was the official go-between for the Gaullist movement. Moreover, the initial transfer to Lampson was followed by two further payments, in September and October 1941.[25] Lampson's influence in Middle Eastern politics, having been the ambassador who helped negotiate a treaty which saw Britain lift the military occupation of Egypt in 1936, was clear.[26] These were marked as being 'advances for payments to be regularised'. It is likely that these payments were linked to the ongoing discussions between the British government and the Free French concerning the future independence of Syria and Lebanon, as the Vichy government began to allow German aeroplanes to be based in the territory, in May 1941.[27] Quite why Lampson was being given money by the Free French is never elucidated upon, when considering that his professional costs would have been assured by the British government. One could hypothesise that it may have been linked to payment for Lampson's influence on this particularly contentious issue concerning the independence of French mandated territories. Equally, it may simply have been a legitimate consequence of the Free French financial agreement with the British

https://books.google.fr/books?id=-ttgkb7JGUkC&pg=PP1&lpg=PP1&dq=Africa,+the+Near+East+and+the+War:+Lectures+Delivered+Under+the+Auspices+of&source=bl&ots=EbxBlRsHXD&sig=ACfU3U38ZTrz0AuTo4lnpd-KEMA9-xO_ag&hl=en&sa=X&ved=2ahUKEwiZlNKbh7nnAhUixIUKHW25ANwQ6AEwAHoECAUQAQ#v=onepage&q=Africa%2C%20the%20Near%20East%20and%20the%20War%3A%20Lectures%20Delivered%20Under%20the%20Auspices%20of&f=false, Consulted 12 August 2021.

[25] AN, 3 AG (1) 305, France Libre de Gaulle 1 – Comptes 1940, *Avances pour paiements à régulariser – Balance au 30 septembre 1941*, 30 September 1941; *Avances pour paiements à régulariser – Balance au 31 octobre 1941*, 31 October 1941.

[26] 'Lord Killearn, 84, Retired Diplomat; Ambassador to Egypt as Sir Miles Lampson is Dead', *The New York Times*, 19 September 1964, https://www.nytimes.com/1964/09/19/archives/lord-killearn84-retired-diplomat-ambassador-to-egypt-as-sir-miles.html, Consulted 12 August 2021.

[27] MICKELSEN Martin, 'Another Fashoda: The Anglo-Free French Conflict over the Levant, May–September 1941', *Revue française d'histoire d'outre-mer*, Vol. 63, N° 230, 1st Quarter 1976, pp. 75–100, p. 76.

government, namely that British personnel, when working on Free French affairs, ought to be paid by the Free French. Nonetheless, the true reason behind the payments made to Lampson and Brissay remains unclear, but the 99% drop in the account is not easily explained by a thousand pounds being paid here, and a thousand spent there.

When examining both sides of the account, a pattern emerges. Expenditure, shown in Fig. 3.3, remained fairly stable, apart from two periods in January and March 1941. Meanwhile, the entries on the credit side, in Fig. 3.2, showed the account to be consistently increasing as income was growing. In short, at the beginning of the war, the Free French movement were accumulating more money than they were spending. This was due to the growth of the Gaullist movement itself. Through the development of delegations in neutral countries—in South America, and elsewhere around the world—moral and pecuniary support for the Free French was steadily increasing. However, the small numbers of rallying troops[28] meant that the Free French Forces did not yet require the same level of financing as they would by the end of the year. Subscriptions and gifts were still making their way to London via cheque and wire transfer. Judging by the cumulatively increasing amounts of donations being made to the movement, it is clear that there was more enthusiasm for supporting the Free French than there were people capable of physically joining them. This was a positive financial sign for it ensured the steady accumulation of subscriptions and other donations from those unable to reach London. The increase, in May 1941, was linked to the signing of a further financial agreement in March of that year. These settled the exchange rate at 176.625 francs to the pound, as well as organising the spending of the Free French movement into different accounts as opposed to operating on a ministry-by-ministry basis, as had previously been the case.

The expenditure, paid from the National Provincial Bank account, were the payments for the issuance of social security, including a paternity and marriage bonus; secondly, the reimbursement of fees accrued during the course of duties performed for the Free French movement and, thirdly, the payment of goods and services received, including hotel bills

[28] TNA, CAB 101 282, The Free French Movement—Origins, Development and the Organisation of its Armed Forces, p. 40—According to Streatfield, on 1st August 1940, the Free French numbered 5,719 and twelve months' later they were just 5,326.

at some of London's most prestigious hotels, including the Connaught and the Savoy.

What these debits show is the complexity of the Free French movement, even at such an early point in their existence, and the charitable measures of solidarity that were being elicited, to facilitate the continued war effort. It also provides a point of comparison for the funding efforts of other national resistance movements.

The provision of centralised social services was, at this point, still in relative political infancy around the globe. Britain would not implement its own system until the post-war reforms, championed by Beveridge. France had undertaken the experiment of the *Front Populaire* government, led by Léon Blum, after the May 1936 legislative elections, which gave increased importance to workers' rights legislation. The paternity and matrimonial bonuses served as incentives for behaviour that was considered as being beneficial towards the wider society; namely, to encourage nuclear families and, it could be argued, foreshadowing the post-war reconstruction in which these wartime babies would be required to play an active role.

It is possible to roughly calculate the numbers of beneficiaries of these bonuses. As payments were valued at £10, in both cases,[29] one simply needs to divide the totals of the debits issued by ten. As shown in Fig. 3.4, the numbers of births seem to have been smaller than those of marriages, during the period from November 1941 to December 1942. For the following year, births outstripped marriages in all but one month. This is a pattern that is to be expected. Those who had married at an earlier point in the war would begin to beget offspring in the months that followed. One example is Marcel Louis André, of the Free French Naval Forces, who married Suzanne Maerschalch on 30th October 1941, at Marylebone Registry Office. It would appear that this was to help Ms. Maerschalch, a Belgian, to acquire French nationality. This was with the full knowledge of General de Gaulle, as was made clear in Act N° 27 in the Register of Nationality, opened by the Free French Forces.[30]

[29] AN, 3 AG (1) 303, Compte personnel du Général de Gaulle caisse journalière.

[30] AN, Paris, Registres de nationalité ouverts par les Forces françaises libres à Londres 20000247/1, Premier carnet 20000247/1, Acte n° 27, MAERSCHALCH, Suzanne Marie José, https://www.siv.archives-nationales.culture.gouv.fr/siv/rechercheconsultation/consultation/ir/consultationIR.action?irId=FRAN_IR_023109&udId=RLc1a_27&details=true&gotoArchivesNums=false&auSeinIR=true, Consulted 20 September 2020.

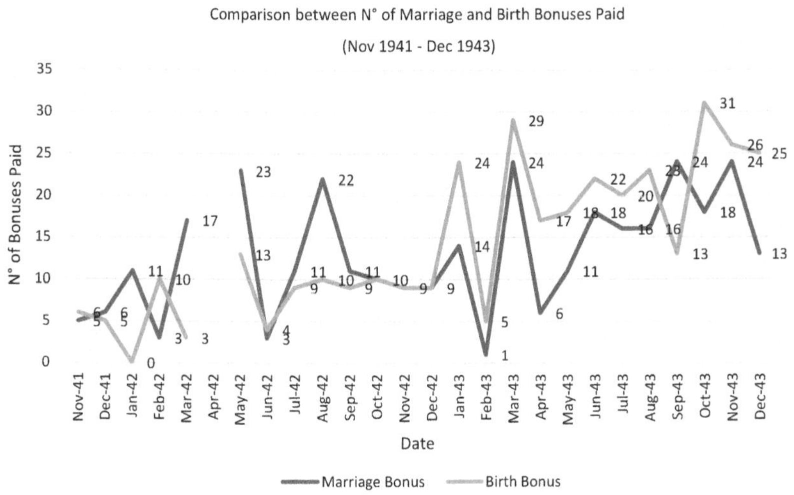


**Fig. 3.4** Comparison between Marriage and Birth Bonuses Paid (November 1941–December 1943) (AN, 3 AG (1) 303)

The 'Marriage Bonus' was paid to 'S.M. André Marcel Louis' on 6th May 1943, according to de Gaulle's personal account.[31] The title 'S.M.' means that André was a submariner. Due to the long delay between the marriage and the bonus payment, this would suggest that these bonuses were rather haphazardly managed, as it was being paid a year and a half after the marriage took place.

Over the period, there were increases in both the frequency of payments and the subsidies paid out. During this time, they grew from five births and six marriages, at the end of November 1941, to peaks of 24 marriages and 31 births, in March 1943 and October 1943, respectively. These payments reflect the Free French social security payments which were alluded to in 'Decree N° 36 on the Organisation of Social Assistants Services', or 'Ordonnance N° 19 relative to the Free French War Pension Regime', which were both promulgated on 30th December 1941. These pieces of legislation effectively extended pension payment

[31] AN, 3 AG 1 303 Compte personnel du général de Gaulle Caisse journal mai-décembre 1943, Débit, 6 May 1943.

rights to servicemen, as well as to First World War veterans and war-widows. As was seen previously, this had been unofficially effective since the movement's beginnings, as those earlier payments to Henri Marais' widow, Jeanne, showed. The payments demonstrate that the French external resistance movement was implementing a social security system for those under their governance. Clearly, the Free French were trying to portray themselves as being a government-in-waiting.

However, spending was not simply reserved for others. De Gaulle had rented a property in Little Gaddesden, at Rodinghead House, Hertfordshire,[32] but when he travelled, he took rooms at prestigious hotels, both for himself and his representatives. The receipts from the Shepheard's Hotel, in Cairo, are testament to this. A pound sterling was exchanged for Egyptian £0.975, in 1941. During his April 1941 visit to the Egyptian capital, General de Gaulle rented one of the hotel apartments at a cost of Egyptian £270 per night, where he checked-in for a two-week period.[33] The principal reason for de Gaulle's presence in Cairo was to meet with General Archibald Wavell, the British commander-in-chief for the Middle East region. Catroux and de Gaulle were attempting to convince Wavell to attack Syria and Lebanon.[34] De Gaulle stayed in this establishment, which predominantly catered for the British market, as it allowed him to be closer to those who were central to his political and military objectives and, arguably, for the prestige that it afforded him by behaving as a head of state. According to Reid, at the beginning of the twentieth century, Shepheard's catered for an Anglophone clientele.[35] While there, he frequented the celebrated Long Bar, tended by Joe Scialom, the polyglot inventor of the colourfully named 'Suffering Bastard', a concoction of bourbon, gin, lime juice, Angostura bitters

[32] 'Charles de Gaulle's time in Hertfordshire', 30 January 2017, https://www.hertfordshirelife.co.uk/home/charles-de-gaulle-s-time-in-hertfordshire-1-4865457, Consulted 24 January 2020.

[33] AN, 3 AG 1 305, France Libre de Gaulle 1—Comptes 1940–1943, *Receipt, Shepheard's Hotel, Cairo, Egypt*, 1 April 1941.

[34] ZAMIR Meir, 'De Gaulle and the Question of Syria and Lebanon During the Second World War: Part 1', *Middle Eastern Studies*, Vol. 43, N° 5, pp. 675–708, p. 681.

[35] REID Donald, *Whose Pharaohs? Archaeology, Museums and Egyptian National Identity from Napoleon to World War I*, Berkeley, University of California Press, 2003, 428p., p. 73.

and ginger ale.[36] However, de Gaulle does not appear to have ordered this; instead, preferring to stick to wine, whiskey, brandy and Martini. During the visit, he occasionally dined in the hotel's restaurant but mostly ordered from room-service, with numerous accompanying cigars, alongside. By the Second World War, Shepheard's was a preeminent hotel in the Egyptian capital, frequented by Winston Churchill and, more importantly, de Gaulle's travelling companion and head of the Spear's Mission to the Free French movement, General Edward Spears, whose bills can be found alongside those of de Gaulle.

Following his visit to Egypt, from 10th July to 15th July 1941, de Gaulle returned to Brazzaville, in French Equatorial Africa. At the same time, the British had extended their protection over the economic life of Cameroon, as a means of influencing French Equatorial Africa.[37] This involved buying the area's production, as well as providing the Free French with credit to help import goods from the sterling zone. While de Gaulle was in Brazzaville, the Armistice of Saint-Jean d'Acre was signed on 14th July 1941, which brought the Syria-Lebanon campaign to an end, with General Wilson, for the British, and General Henri Dentz, representing the Army of the Levant, acting as signatories. The Allies would take complete control over Syria and Lebanon, while the Vichy troops could keep their arms, despite being obliged to relinquish "all war materials".[38] This greatly irked de Gaulle because it meant that forces would remain under the control of Vichyste superiors; as he would subsequently decry to René Cassin, on 15th July.[39]

During August, September and October, the growth in spending, and accumulation, continued, much as it had over the previous months. The movement's assets, represented by advances, payments and cash, mirrored

[36] BROWN Derek, 'Bartenders are Liars, but It's Not Their Fault', *The Atlantic*, 2010, https://www.theatlantic.com/health/archive/2010/08/bartenders-are-liars-but-its-not-their-fault/61259/, Consulted 24 January 2020; TURKEL Stanley, 'Hotel History: Shepheard's Hotel in Cairo Known for Opulence, Famous Guests and the Military', *Eturbonews*, 2019, https://www.eturbonews.com/254665/hotel-history-shepheards-hotel-in-cairo-known-for-opulence-famous-guests-and-the-military/, Consulted 24 January 2020.

[37] 'Men of Vichy', *The Economist*, 24 May 1942, p. 676.

[38] 'The Syrian Armistice', *The Economist*, 19 July 1941, p. 71.

[39] DE GAULLE Charles, *Lettres, notes et carnets, tome 3: 1940–41*, Paris, Plon, 2014, 459p. (Ebook) 76%—*Télégramme au professeur Cassin, à Londres, Brazzaville, 15 juillet 1941.*

heavy spending in the areas of military expenditure that remained, at this point, the personal liability of General de Gaulle, for instance, the 'Spitfire Fund'[40] or the 'Action Fund'.[41] The former was opened so as to collect the donations that were destined to help contribute towards payment for the aircraft, in order to equip the Free French Air Force. The 'Action Fund' was a means of collecting money that would help to pay for the operational capacity of the Free French Forces.[42] More concerningly for the alliance, Denis also reveals that these accounts were used as a means of avoiding British scrutiny:

> The transactions made to the account of the 'President of the National Committee' are budgetary transactions which would certainly have been incorporated in the budget, had we not been preoccupied with keeping hold of certain resources that would allow us to incur expenses from outside of this budget that was being closely watched by the British authorities. On the other hand, operations sent to the 'General de Gaulle' account had an **extra-budgetary nature** to them.[43]

Above all, it should also be noted that these accounts were, for several months, balanced. However, this was not always the case.

## Opening the *Caisse*

The Free French Financial Service enabled the organisation of payments and the invoices that were received by the movement and the *Caisse centrale de la France libre* would allow the Gaullists to continue providing monetary and financial services in the rallied territories. Without such an institution, economic control over the colonies would have greatly

[40] 'Spitfire Fund', *The Times*, 6 September 1940, p. 9, Consulted 27 September 2020—"Officers and men of one of the small ships of the Free French Navy guarding the seas with the British Navy received a signal from the Admiralty on Wednesday conveying a message from Lord Beaverbrook, Minister of Aircraft Production. The message thanked the French sailors for their gift of £12 5s. towards the Spitfire Fund".

[41] AN, 3 AG 1 305 France Libre de Gaulle 1 Comptes 1940.

[42] Service des archives économiques et financières (SAEF), B0062805, *Letter from Pierre Denis to Maurice Couve de Murville, Commissioner for Finances, French Committee of National Liberation*, 25 August 1943, p. 3.

[43] SAEF, B0062805, *Letter from Pierre Denis to Maurice Couve de Murville*, 25 August 1943, p. 4.

reduced, as the *Banque de France* stopped being liable to provide banknotes once the territories had fallen under Gaullist control.

Initially conceived as the *Caisse de Défense de l'Empire français* on 16th August 1941,[44] the *Caisse centrale de la France Libre* was created in December 1941. Having evolved from being simply a manner to help fund the Free French forces, it had three objectives: to provide a hybridised central bank, a currency board and a joint colonial fund in the rallied territories.[45] A central bank is an institution which issues currency and may manage monetary policy. A currency board "combines three elements: an exchange rate that is fixed to an 'anchor currency', automatic convertibility…and a long-term commitment to the system".[46] They allow for anti-inflationary policy by ensuring sufficient liquidity enters the banking system. A joint colonial fund allowed the contracting agency to pay pensions, salaries and meet other commitments linked to loans.[47] At the time of the writing of the statutes, these territories were French Equatorial Africa, Cameroon, New Caledonia, the French Outposts in Oceania (Tahiti) and the French Outposts in India (Pondicherry). The economic trajectory of the Free French movement was clearly gaining in momentum and it showed that the formalisation of economic relations with the British was continuing unabated. Through this organisation, the money that would circulate in the colonies would be supplied and managed from London. The personnel of the Bank of England and the Treasury were in full accord, as the numerous examples of documents and correspondence attest.[48] Under British supervision, Pierre Denis and his collaborators created a system that would supply money to the colonies, who had been

[44] BoE, OV45 129, *Acte de Concession.*

[45] BoE, OV45 129, *Acte de Concession—Draft 1*, p. 4.

[46] ENOCH Charles, GULDE Anne-Marie, 'Are Currency Boards a Cure for All Monetary Problems?', *Finance & Development*, Vol. 35, N° 4, December 1998, https://www.imf.org/external/pubs/ft/fandd/1998/12/enoch.htm, Consulted 30 October 2020.

[47] SUNDERLAND David, 'Chapter 4—The Management of the Joint Colonial Fund and the Joint Miscellaneous Fund', *Managing British Colonial and Post-Colonial Development: The Crown Agents, 1914–1974*, Woodbridge, Boydell & Brewer, 2007, 312p., pp. 97–114.

[48] BoE, OV45 129, *Letter from A.S.G. Hoar to Lithiby*, 21 August 1941—"We have been working up draft Statutes with Meyer. He in turn has had to satisfy Rauzan and others at Carlton Gardens and the form of the Statutes has varied pretty considerably from time to time. We have now, however, arrived at a draft which Rauzan has accepted and which gives something solid to bite on".

separated from their metropolitan overseer, thereby ensuring monetary chaos was avoided. However, was it successful?

The principal preoccupation of the *Caisse centrale* was to respond to monetary questions. The organisation tried to ensure that the spending of the Free French was concentrated on the war effort, and that the level of spending on administrative purposes was minimised as much as possible. Such concerns were sparked by the influence that the Free French had over a growing number of territories in Africa and beyond. As colonial currency deteriorated through natural usage, the ability to mint became an increasing priority for the Free French. However, fearing the monetary rigidity of central banking structures, Denis preferred to employ the name of *Caisse*, signifying 'till' or 'fund'. The difference is fundamental. A central bank is required to stock quantities of bullion, in order to guarantee the notes that it issues. By using the term '*caisse*', the Free French could bypass this thorny issue by issuing their currency based upon the bullion stored within the safes of Threadneedle Street. This was, effectively, financing the French colonies with the confidence accorded to the Bank of England and, most importantly, its gold reserves. However, the Free French were only in cursory control of any gold extracted in their colonies, for it was necessary to send it back to London as collateral for their borrowing activities.

Within the accounts held by the *Caisse centrale*, a capital base of 100 million francs (£566,171 2s 2d) in British Treasury bonds was kept.[49] Initially, two conceptions were proposed to the Defence Council; the first by Pierre Denis, as director of the Financial Service, and the second by Tony Mayer.[50] Mayer was the manager of the *Caisse centrale*[51] and served under Pierre Denis.[52] Referred to, in his obituary, as the "Englishman's Frenchman", largely due to his Anglophile tendencies, Tony Mayer was a French Jew.[53] His faith would plausibly have had wider implications upon

[49] BoE, OV45 130 Caisse centrale de la France d'Outre-mer, *Balance Sheet 1942*, undated.

[50] BoE, OV45 130, *Tableau comparatif des projets P.R(auzan). et T.M(ayer).*, undated.

[51] BoE, OV45 129, *Letter to Mr. Bentley Front Lodge*, 12 January 1942.

[52] BoE OV45 129, *Tableau Comparatif des projets P(ierre).R(auzan). et T(ony).M(ayer)*, 15 July 41.

[53] CALDER John, 'Obituary: Tony Mayer', *The Independent*, 6 November 1997, http://www.independent.co.uk/news/obituaries/obituary-tony-mayer-1292389.html, Consulted 31 August 2017.

his experience, as his religious background was different to that of the majority of his four to five thousand colleagues.[54] Previously employed as an exchange agent at the French *Bourse*, he officially joined the movement, in London, on 1st October 1941, according to Ecochard's list.[55] However, Mayer was first mentioned in a note, dated 15th July 1941,[56] outlining the efforts that would be made to resolve the ongoing economic and financial difficulties.[57] Thus, Mayer was working with the *Caisse* long before officially signing-up with the Free French. In contrast to Denis' rallying, from within England, Mayer travelled from France, via Lisbon, to the U.K. This confirms that there were no two identical paths to joining General de Gaulle's movement and everybody enlisted differently.

René Pleven remarked that he met Mayer and his spouse in London and that Mayer was attempting to enter the Financial Service. Tellingly, he explains, "*Rauzan* (Pierre Denis) was having some difficulties finding space for him as he has quite large ambitions".[58] This reflection shows that tensions were present in this small department. It also demonstrates that there was some divergence of opinions as to motivations for joining the Free French. For Denis, who, in his memoirs, commented that the monetary question was always placed secondary to military concerns, Mayer's overt ambition may have grated. Equally, for Mayer, 38 years old at the time of his enrolment, the adventure of the situation and the danger may have stimulated an impatience that was difficult to contain. He and Denis belonged to different generations. Denis, a veteran of the Great War, whose ascetic and somewhat grey mannerisms[59] would have

[54] MURACCIOLE Jean-François, *Les Français Libres, L'Autre Résistance*, Paris, Éditions Tallandier, 2009, 425p., p. 36—«Les ralliements de l'été 1941, après l'affaire de Syrie, offrent un bel exemple de ces divergences. Selon Ecochard, ils seraient au nombre de 4,500, chiffre compatible avec les estimations antérieures d'Etchegoyen (4,070) et de Crémieux-Brilhac (5,500).»

[55] ECOCHARD Henri, 'Liste Ecochard', http://www.francaislibres.net/liste/ecochardv40.php?&lie=35187, Consulted 4 December 2018.

[56] BoE, OV45 129, *Note from T. Mayer*, 15 July 1941.

[57] BoE, OV45 129, *Problèmes financiers et monétaires*, 12 July 1941.

[58] PIKETTY Guillaume, 'René Pleven', *Français en résistance: Carnets de guerre, correspondances, journaux personnels*, 1169p., p. 969.

[59] CASSIN René, 'Rauzan' (Pierre Denis)', *Fondation de la France Libre*, 2011, http://www.france-libre.net/pierre-denis-rauzan/#2, Consulted 30 August 2017.

clashed with the debonair and cultured Mayer.[60] The contrasting characters, motivations and experiences were brought together in the differing views on the *Caisse centrale*.

Evidence of Mayer's role within the *Caisse* remains, nonetheless, limited. For a man who was appointed as the 'manager' of the *Caisse centrale*, occupying the position beneath Pierre Denis, it would be expected that Mayer would be frequently mentioned; through correspondence with other members of the *Caisse* or the British organisations with whom they interacted, in much a similar way to Pleven or Gorrell-Barnes in the Anglo-French Coordinating Committee network. However, his presence is hardly ever commented upon, suggesting either that Mayer was ineffectual, as little was produced that bore his mark, or that he was actively written out of the story. The archives seem to suggest the former, but this should be nuanced, as is often the case with interpersonal relations. As will be seen later, the Free French did seem to expunge any mention from the records of those who were not in the General's favour.

The manner in which the colonial financing worked was through a system of double transfer. Firstly, the British Treasury would pass the pre-approved required amount to the account of the *Caisse centrale*. The *Caisse* would contact its operating branch in the colony and authorise that the payment be released from their holding account. This method of transfer would allow amounts to be released as required. Due to the geographical situation of Free French African colonies, notably in their close proximity to their British counterparts, as well as to Vichy France, in French Western Africa, the Free French were compelled to print their own notes in order to contain the risk of monetary contamination. There were two reasons for this urgency. Theoretically, the pre-war parity in the Free French territories (£1:176.625F) acted as an incentive to cross the border into French Equatorial Africa.[61] Despite the two attempts to take Senegal, the Free French movement had to temporarily concede power in French West Africa to Vichy. As Thomas explained:

> Though the Vichy government and its colonial lieutenants were intent upon crushing Free French rule in Equatorial Africa, between September

[60] CALDER John, 'Obituary: Tony Mayer', *The Independent*, 6 November 1997, http://www.independent.co.uk/news/obituaries/obituary-tony-mayer-1292389.html, Consulted 31 August 2017.

[61] BoE, OV45 129, *Problèmes financiers et monétaires de la France Libre*, p. 7.

and December 1940, the administrations of French North and West Africa attached greater priority to preventing any further colonial declarations for de Gaulle.[62]

According to the Free French, "We were under an obligation to protect the Bank of England against the risk of B.A.O. (*Banque d'Afrique Occidentale*) notes being smuggled from the territory of the non-rallied colonies into that of the rallied colonies, where they might have been offered for exchange against pound sterling".[63] The Vichy-controlled *Banque d'Afrique Occidentale* notes that were in circulation in both territories could be exchanged, in French Equatorial Africa, at a far more advantageous rate than could be obtained in French West Africa.[64] From a more practical point of view, the physical separation from other French colonial territories meant that the supply of banknotes was interrupted.[65] Passing through the ever-permeable border, this clandestine traffic of notes risked the surety of the new francs that the *Caisse centrale* was introducing. This was because the B.A.O. notes had a tendency to depreciate and inflationary pressure was always a risk, due to the political instability caused by the war.

In order to anchor the *Caisse centrale* in the territory that it administrated, the headquarters were provisionally established in Brazzaville. However, it had branches that operated in the different colonies. Five departments were created: Issuing; Exchange Control; Accounting; Banking Questions and Studies and Contentions.[66] Effectively, this complex organisation proves that external French resistance was now sufficiently professionalised as to warrant an array of financial services.

The Issuing Department ensured that the used bills would be exchanged for new examples. In theory, this should have been a relatively

[62] THOMAS Martin, *The French Empire at War 1940–1945*, Manchester, Manchester University Press, 1998, 298p., pp. 61–62.

[63] BoE, OV45 129, *Problèmes financiers et monétaires de la France Libre*, p. 7.

[64] MAGUIRE Gloria, *Anglo-American Policy Towards the Free French*, London, Macmillan Press, 1995, 210p., p. 121—Although Maguire illustrates the difference in the exchange rate by using North Africa, in November 1942, as an example, the same can be said for French Equatorial Africa.

[65] BoE, OV45 129, 'Free French Banking', *Financial News*, 18 February 1942.

[66] BoE, OV45 129, *Note de T. Mayer pour le Directeur du Service Financier (Denis)*, 20 July 1940.

simple three-part process of taking in the old *Banque de France* bills that were circulating in the rallied colonies, exchanging them and allowing the circulation of the newer examples. In reality, it was a much more complex and problematic undertaking. This can be seen when, in January 1943, the cashiers of the *Banque de l'Afrique Occidentale* in Brazzaville continued to exchange old notes, 1,350 billion francs in total, long after the *Caisse centrale*'s official deadline to do so had passed on 1st October 1942.[67]

The Exchange Control responded to the need for greater clarity in the financial situation of the Free French movement. Through the centralisation of their accounts, they were able to provide concrete answers on the amount of foreign currency held within the colonial coffers, and this enabled the movement to respond more rapidly to any financial demands that may have been placed upon them. Incidentally, the main beneficiaries of the foreign exchange possibilities cited were the Free French and the U.K.[68] This reveals the thinking of the Free French leadership; notably that the *Caisse centrale* was a tool by which to advance the Free French war effort. Any foreign exchange surplus would be used towards furthering the interests of the Free French and, by extension, the British.[69] When placed into the context of a European theatre of war, this adds credence to the ideas of both Jennings and Maguire that African matters, in Free French thinking, were merely serving the fight for metropolitan independence, notably via their money and resources.[70]

The Accounting department kept the accounts of the *Caisse centrale*. Following the creation of the Free French movement, the accounts of the Financial Service were dispersed in a number of British banks, as

[67] BoE, OV100 13 Equatorial Africa, *Letter from Penton to Lithiby*, 25 January 1943.

[68] BoE, OV45 129, *Note de T. Mayer pour le Directeur du Service Financier (Denis)*, 15 July 1940, p. 4.

[69] «De plus, la connaissance précise des ressources et des besoins de change de la France Libre, permettrait de donner une solution plus nette aux questions si délicates que pose la gestion des offices, et de s'assurer que tout excédent de change se trouve utilisé au mieux intérêts de la France Libre et de la Grande-Bretagne.», OV45 129, *Note de T. Mayer*, 15 July 1940, p. 4.

[70] MAGUIRE Gloria, *Anglo-American Policy Towards the Free French*, London, Macmillan Press, 1995, 210p., p. 115; JENNINGS Eric, 'La France libre en AEF et au Cameroun: Recrutement et extraction des ressources' in CORNILL-FRERROT Sylvain (Ed.), OULMONT Philippe (Ed.), *Les Français libres et le monde*, Paris, Éditions Nouveau Monde, 2015, 241p., pp. 215–229, p. 220.

has been seen previously. Regrouping these under the aegis of the *Caisse centrale*, Denis and his staff could better ensure the financial and monetary efficiency of the movement. Five different bank accounts existed, which allowed the Free French to separate payments and their income. The increased financial scrutiny that the Accounting department offered would help to influence and form economic policy in the colonies.

However, this consultative role would also belong to a separate department, that of Banking Questions. Its role was to manage the reorganisation of banking within the colonial territories. Furthermore, it was expected to offer help and guidance for French businesses who were experiencing difficulties, having been cut-off from their customer base, and their supply lines, through the economic warfare measures in place.[71] Their representatives interacted with their American and British colleagues in the banking sector. This involved action in public and commercial relations, to increase awareness of the movement's existence and to begin to form and develop the individual members' business networks. In essence, this was an attempt to avoid and pre-empt financial difficulties that could result from a lack of confidence in the movement's economic base among potential creditors.

Lastly, the Studies and Contentions Service was a department that played two roles. They were tasked with organising and waging economic warfare, in conjunction with the British Ministry of Economic Warfare. Equally, they would play a judicial role and offer advice on the correct functioning of the other departments. Economic warfare is the means of attempting to hamper and attack an enemy's economy, both on their capacity to meet domestic demand and distribute their supply to potential consumers, whether they be military supply lines or foreign buyers. Having been introduced late into the First World War, the British and French governments were keen to collaborate as quickly as possible on aligning their economic efforts against Germany in 1939. This involved a form of international central planning, whereby the British and the French collectively organised their economies on the macroeconomic level, placing joint orders, through the Anglo-French Coordinating Committee, to avoid depleting the limited resources upon which both countries were reliant. However, following the fall of France and the Armistice of 22nd June 1940, the British turned their efforts against the

[71] See COX Nechama J., *The Ministry of Economic Warfare and Britain's Conduct of Economic Warfare, 1939–1945*, Doctoral Thesis, London, King's College, 2001, 366p.

newly occupied territories, as signalled by Arthur Greenwood's report on the consequences of the collapse of French military resistance when faced with the *blitzkrieg*.[72] While this option was viewed as being "repugnant", it was recommended that supplies and resources should be imperatively impeded from arriving in Axis-controlled territory.[73]

Furthermore, any requisitions would fall into Allied hands, thereby helping their economies with the war effort. It is this effect that was appreciated by Pierre Denis who referred to a "*gage marchand*".[74] This 'merchant's pledge' refers to the collateral that the Free French were obliged to put up in order to continue trading. Effectively, the colonial goods that were sold to the British were a means of ensuring that the colonial economies did not grind to a halt, due to the loss of their principal export markets in metropolitan France and other Vichy-controlled territories. The sales of colonial produce also meant that the Free French had access to foreign exchange, with which to pay their other debts to the British government. In short, had the British refused this 'pledge' from the Free French, they would have risked losing both their initial investment and the goods for which they had paid. The realities of war had an important impact on the ability to trade; notably once faced with the Battle of the Atlantic.

The administrative alliances that provided a funding framework for the French external resistance were beginning to bear fruit. However, it remains to be seen whether, or not, it was indeed legal to export the money that they were beginning to attract from overseas supporters.

72 TNA, CAB 67/7/5, *The Economic Consequences of a Complete or Partial Collapse of French Resistance, Memorandum by the Minister Without Portfolio*, 17 June 1940.

73 TNA, CAB 67/7/5, *The Economic Consequences...*, 17 June 1940, p. 19.

74 DENIS, Op. cit., 1950, p. 26.

CHAPTER 4

# A Few Dollars More?

*Long live France and long live de Gaulle! I think that the State Department should grant you the fullest legal and diplomatic recognition. All those who fight the Nazis are our real friends.*[1]

This enthusiastic appraisal of General de Gaulle on the part of the Republican mayor of New York reflected an opinion held by few of his compatriots, including his own president. Fiorello La Guardia became the city's first Italian American mayor, elected in 1933, and his paternal links with Europe clearly impacted upon his views of the ongoing conflict. He was a fiery character who drove through progressive reforms while mayor and rejected American isolationism, best represented by the Monroe Doctrine. It stands to reason that La Guardia would have looked favourably upon the Free French delegation that was created in the United States. However, this was a position held by a minority of American diplomats, civil servants and members of the public, as Roosevelt preferred to "refrain from the recognition of any one person or group as the Government of France".[2] Instead, the United States recognised

[1] AGLION Raoul, *Roosevelt and de Gaulle: Allies in Conflict, A Personal Memoir*, New York, The Free Press, 1988, 239p., p. 30 - Fiorello La Guardia, Mayor of New York, to Raoul Aglion, General Secretary for the Free French Delegation, May 1941.

[2] MURPHY Robert, *Diplomat Among Warriors: The Unique World of a Foreign Service Expert*, Garden City, New York, Doubleday & Company, Inc., 1964, 470p., p. 102.



D. Foulk, *The Price of Freedom*,
https://doi.org/10.1007/978-3-031-09066-0_4

Vichy as the legitimate government of France by retaining diplomatic contacts, before according full ambassadorial status to their representative in January 1941, whereas the Gaullists were virtually ignored.[3]

While de Gaulle's presence in London was acknowledged among the Francophone community of the United States, his message solicited suspicion and scorn. Alexis Léger, the former secretary-general at the French Foreign Ministry at Quai d'Orsay and exiled in the United States, "steadfastly refused" to see France "represented by a General, however heroic, who had not received a mandate from the people".[4] This suspicion was magnified among other enemies of de Gaulle, including the high-ranking former diplomat, Roger Cambon, who "carried out an incessant campaign against the General", having resigned his post at the French Embassy in London.[5] Much as they disagreed with Marshal Pétain and the policy of collaboration that was being instituted under the Vichy government, his prominence was unquestionable. Placed alongside a relatively unknown, recently promoted general who argued that his Committee would appropriate the jurisdiction over "all French citizens at present in British territory",[6] the reticence of the American-based French expatriates to rally to de Gaulle is more understandable. In order to rectify this lack of visibility, and in an effort to raise both funds and volunteers, it was decided that a form of diplomatic mission should be organised to the United States. However, the political reality in the United States was far different from the expectations that de Gaulle and the Free French assumed would be the case.

There were very few among the early members of the Free French movement in London who had as much lived experience in the English-speaking world as René Pleven. Considering his role as the European executive for an American telecommunications firm, he spoke English fluently and had a greater understanding of the Anglophone world than his colleagues. It was therefore natural that de Gaulle should rely upon him to resolve the growing number of problems that the movement

[3] WRIGHT Gordon, 'Bullitt and the Fall of France', *World Politics*, Vol. 10, N° 1 (October., 1957), pp. 63–90, p. 87; RASKIN Richard, 'CASABLANCA and United States Foreign Policy', *Film History*, Vol. 4, N° 2, 1990, pp. 153–164, p. 153.

[4] AGLION, *Roosevelt and de Gaulle…*, 1988, p. 35.

[5] Idem, p. 53.

[6] TNA, CAB 101 282, *The Free French Movement; Its Origin, Development and the Organisation of Its Armed Forces, June 1940-September 1941—Ms Y M Streatfield*, p. 4.

were experiencing when dealing with the United States. This chapter will attempt to ascertain the different stages of development of the movement's American branch, which was known as the Free French delegation to the United States. Furthermore, in contrast to many of the other delegations that sprang up in both neutral and allied countries, the French who rallied to support de Gaulle in America were largely unsuccessful in achieving their stated economic aims and goals.

## Disorganisation

The end of the Phoney War, and the fall of France, took many by surprise. The shock was exacerbated for those French who found themselves outside of France's metropolitan borders. Raoul Aglion, serving as an attaché for the French legation in Cairo, described his feelings:

> *Stunned by these almost unbelievable events, I immediately left my diplomatic post and sought out the nearest French military base, which was located in Lebanon. When I arrived in Beirut, I found a lovely, peaceful city quietly basking in the sun.*[7]

The unexpected nature of the capitulation left him searching for meaning and for a manner to best serve his country. The implementation of the Vichy state compounded this sense of loss, confusion and indignation. Raoul de Roussy de Sales, a French journalist in the United States, wrote about the uncertainty and the overwhelming sense of bewilderment on his side of the Atlantic:

> *It isn't possible any more to get a clear idea of what is happening in France. The Reynaud Cabinet has fallen and a new one under Pétain has been formed or is being formed.*[8]

René Pleven was one Frenchman who knew exactly what was happening. While serving under Jean Monnet, he was in Bordeaux when Reynaud's government held last-minute discussions on whether to accept the British offer of a Franco-British union. The same stupefaction was

[7] AGLION Raoul, *Roosevelt and de Gaulle…*, 1988, p. 2.

[8] DE ROUSSY DE SALES Raoul, *The Making of Yesterday*, New York, Reynal & Hitchcock, 1947, 310p., p. 132.

rife in Gironde as embassies desperately sought to hide their archives and personnel in different Bordelaise chateaux in and around the village of Sauternes.[9] As Monnet explained: "He (de Gaulle) confirmed to me the feeling that all was finished, any effort was pointless, and that he was coming back (to London)."[10] Pleven's first instinct was to ensure that his wife, Annette, and their two children were safe.[11] With the help of Sir Edward Bridges, he did so by sending them to Canada but, rapidly, Annette found herself in New York, assisting with the efforts to organise aid and supplies for the Free French movement. Moreover, Monnet, along with his wife, Sylvia, also travelled to the United States, after having aired his misgivings to de Gaulle about the creation of a pseudo-French government, practically under the control of a foreign power, in his letter of 23rd June 1940.[12] The Monnets joined the growing community of French migrants and more recent expatriates of every political persuasion who had crossed the Atlantic and made the United States their home, either temporarily or permanently, much as was the case for de Roussy de Sales.

In the United States, the foremost group devoted to charitable and welfare-providing activity was called 'France Forever' or '*France Quand-Même*'. This group was created by Eugène Houdry, a French-born engineer who had patented a revolutionary method for 'cracking' petroleum that allowed for twice as much gasoline to be produced from crude oil.[13] His group aimed to encourage the estimated 500,000 French in the United States to rally around the Gaullist message and to support the movement, both morally and monetarily.[14] However, as Houdry told Raoul Aglion, his association had far more American members than

[9] SOULEAU Philippe, *La Région de Langon sous l'Occupation*, Breil-sur-Roya, Éditions du Cabri, 1991, (Ed. Fenixx Réédition Numérique, Ebook), 112p., Annex 7.

[10] MONNET Jean, *Mémoires*, Paris, Fayard, 1976, 642p., p. 28.

[11] PIKETTY Guillaume (Ed.), *Français en Résistance: Carnets de Guerre, Correspondances, Journaux Personnels*, Paris, Éditions Robert Laffont, 2009, 1169p., p. 933–934.

[12] MONNET, *Mémoires*, 1976, p. 172.

[13] American Chemical Society, 'The Houdry Process for the Catalytic Conversion of Crude Petroleum to High-Octane Gasoline', 1996, https://www.acs.org/content/acs/en/education/whatischemistry/landmarks/houdry.html.

[14] LOYER Emmanuelle, *Paris à New York: Intellectuels et artistes français en exil 1940–1947*, Paris, Editions Grasset et Fasquelle, 2005, (Ebook), Chapter 2, Para 4.

**Table 4.1** Membership statistics, France forever, 1941, (AN, 560 AP 25 Dossier 2)

| *Type of Membership* | N° | $ |
|---|---|---|
| Active | 3,594 | 17,965.50 |
| Benefactor | 54 | 5,400 |
| Associate | 3,978 | 3,977.50 |
| Anonymous | 900 | |
| TOTAL | 8,526 | 27,343 |

French.[15] It is likely that Aglion, who made the estimation, was inflating their importance so as to serve his own political motivations, as the American census of 1940 had estimated the French-born population to be 102,930, according to Loyer. France Forever sought to organise events, conferences and dinners, in order to increase their subscription numbers and, by extension, their income.[16] With around 8,000 members, each of whom was obliged to pay anywhere from $5, for 'active' membership, to $100 per year, for their more well-heeled 'benefactor' category, their subscriptions were worth anywhere from $40,000 up to $800,000 per year, according to the president of the organisation, Eugène Houdry. It may have been thought that Houdry may have been exaggerating the size of the group's membership, due to the nature of the event to which he was presenting—a fourteenth of July rally at the Manhattan Center in New York.[17] Nonetheless, it is not far removed from the realms of possibility that about ten per cent of the French expatriate and migrant community could have joined. In fact, when consulting the submitted accounts for 'France Forever' for the period dating 1st January to 1st August 1941, it can be seen that there were 8,526 members (Table 4.1)[18]:

Under normal circumstances, this would appear to be a healthy subscription rate for a group supporting a rebellious general who was plotting to reject and depose a legitimate, albeit collaborationist,

[15] AGLION, *Roosevelt and de Gaulle…*, 1988, p. 20.

[16] AN, 560 AP 25 Dossier 2 Délégation de la France Libre aux États-Unis, *Letter to William E. Dreux from René Pleven*, 4, October 1941.

[17] AN, 560 AP 25 Dossier 2, *Address of Mr. Eugene J. Houdry, President of France Forever, at the 14th of July Meeting in Manhattan Center, NYC, 1941*, 14 July 1941.

[18] AN, 560 AP 25 Dossier 2, *France Forever Inter-Office Memorandum from Mr. HM Ufford to Mr. E. Gentil*, 29 August 1941.

government. Furthermore, with donations totalling $44,344.30, this far surpassed what could have been expected, had it been based solely on money acquired through their subscriptions. In all, alongside $11,763.41 from other income streams, including a loan and profit from the sale of insignia and entertainments, France Forever brought in $83,450.71. However, this is only one side of their balance sheet. On the other, their expenses were extensive, including organisational expenses, like legal and accounting fees; 'membership costs' involving travel, meeting and sustenance for their representatives and salaried staff; advertising; 'liaison work' with the colonies; their assets; taxes and general office expenses. These costs amounted to $88,805.23, which left France Forever in deficit by $5,354.52. While this may not have been too excessive of a loss to incur, it would, in the longer term, have proven unsustainable to continue spending as they were.

However, the most negative aspect of France Forever's financing is that the group were not allowed to send donations directly to their intended recipient. Due to the 1939 iteration of the Neutrality Act, which was U.S. legislation designed to limit any risk of funding foreign militias and armies from within the United States, one of the articles expressly forbade groups like France Forever from sending funds abroad. Therefore, members may have been donating money, believing that it was being sent to London, when, in fact, it was merely servicing the large expenses bill of the group. Such irresponsibility irked those within the Free French movement, as René Pleven made clear in one of his letters to his wife, Annette:

> We want the rowdy, political activity of France Forever to end...France Forever should only be a local committee, be it New York or Philadelphia and would have no power to represent the Free French.[19]

Things were little better in the official delegation of the Free French movement. For reasons known only to himself, de Gaulle issued multiple letters promising the recipients that they were his chosen representatives and accorded them the ability to speak on his behalf in the United States. This was a grave error and contributed to the extremely negative impression that the movement made upon the American government. For instance, in his letter on 11th July 1940, de Gaulle categorically told

[19] PIKETTY Guillaume (Ed.), *Français en Résistance*..., 2009, p. 977.

Captain Jacques de Sieyès, his contemporary at the military school, Saint-Cyr, and one of the few with whom he used the grammatically informal *tutoiement*:

> *I know your first-rate situation in New York and the influence that you have been able to acquire in the U.S.A. I am counting on your total friendship, which is why I am asking you to accept this additional task. On the one hand, I am asking you to be my representative in all points of view but, particularly, in all that concerns "information" and orientating the American press, and, on the other, (to handle) all that deals with the transactions that could become necessary for the purchase of different materials, including aeroplanes.*[20]

Concurrently, Maurice Garreau-Dombasle, the commercial counsellor to the French Embassy in Washington, believed that he, too, was entitled to speak for de Gaulle on "administrative or diplomatic matters", which led him to rubbish de Sieyès' claims of authority.[21] Moreover, Houdry, of France Forever, was overstepping his own boundaries too, necessitating the despatch of a London-based envoy. Pleven, when he travelled to the United States, in June 1941, also bore a letter attesting to his credentials as coming directly from de Gaulle, himself. Is it surprising that Roosevelt's government came to see the Free French movement as being little more than a disorganised rabble?

## Disfunction

The situation was becoming untenable. Based on a number of downcast telegrams from both Jacques de Sieyès and Maurice Garreau-Dombasle, de Gaulle understood that something needed to change:

> *We have received telegrams from de Sieyès and Garreau Dombasle complaining about each other in such terms that no reconciliation appears possible. Dombasle has offered his resignation that we have accepted under certain conditions that are designed to avoid personal quarrels taking the appearance of a fundamental disagreement.*[22]

[20] AN, 560 AP 25 Dossier 2, *Letter to de Sieyès from de Gaulle*, 11 July 1940.

[21] AGLION Raoul, *Roosevelt and de Gaulle*..., 1988, pp. 18–19.

[22] AN, 560 AP 25 Dossier 2, *Letter to de Gaulle from Pleven*, 1 June 1941.

It had already been made clear to de Sieyès that the Free French were dissatisfied with his performance.[23] Whether this criticism was justified is another question entirely, as the legislative difficulties being placed on him by the American system, specifically by the Neutrality Act, were far above his station and outside of his control. It was certainly not de Sieyès' fault that de Gaulle had not understood the legislative confines of the country in which he intended to raise funds. This speaks to the wider problem that the Free French movement were attempting things that were simply too far removed from their own capabilities, being that many were military personnel or civilians, rather than administrators and legislators. The consequence was that it left those who served de Gaulle's movement risking failure from the outset.

Nonetheless, de Sieyès did commit errors. The most flagrant concerned blocked funds which were being kept in the United States that belonged to the French government. Alfred Bergman, a 33-year-old New Yorker, offered to attempt to assist the Free French in unlocking American support by recovering the money. In return, he expected commission of between two and ten per cent of the total value.[24] According to later court documents, Bergman's potential windfall was valued at being in excess of $250 million![25] De Sieyès inexplicably approved this agreement, which had been made by Gérard San Andréa *alias* de Saint-André, one of de Gaulle's followers in the United States, without consulting anybody in the Free French hierarchy.[26] The two men had to be extricated from the situation, and were informed as much, by way of a mocking letter from Lord David Davies, the Welsh Liberal politician. Davies' letter underlined that the "so-called 'agreement' wasn't worth the paper it was written on and that we had not a scrap of sympathy with him in his agitation".[27] Furiously, Bergman wrote letters to both Anthony Eden and Cordell Hull, highlighting the embarrassing episode further still. De Sieyès had to

[23] PIKETTY Guillaume (Ed.), *Français en Résistance…*, 2009, p. 977.

[24] AN, 560 AP 25 Dossier 2, *Letter to Gerard de St. André from Bergman*, 3 April 1941.

[25] Congressional Record: Proceedings and Debates of the 80th Congress, Second Session, Appendix Vol. 94—Part 11, May 11, 1948 to June 19, 1948, Pages A2881 to A4174, United States Government Printing Office, Washington, 1948, p. A3727.

[26] MAGUIRE Gloria, *Anglo-American Policy towards the Free French*, London, Macmillan Press, 1995, 210p., p. 21.

[27] AN, 560 AP 25 Dossier 2, *Letter to Denis Saurat from N.B. Foot*, 19 October 1941.

be replaced, and quickly. However, he did not go far. Such was the paucity of skilled support in the United States that de Sieyès remained a member of the soon-to-be-created French delegation. This episode was written about by Arnaud Manas of the *Banque de France*.[28] However, Manas did not elucidate upon the full implications of the embarrassing episode, nor did he make further reference to the reactions of those within the British and American establishment. Through the subsequent trials in 1946 and 1948, it had major implications on American diplomatic law, laying down the precedent of immunity for diplomats who were transiting through the United States on route to a new post, as de Sieyès was served the legal documents while on his way to a new post in the Bolivian embassy. All this was caused by the attempted rush to acquire the gold of the *Banque de France*.

Considering the state of de Gaulle's support in the United States, necessity called for an effective and proven interlocuter to help organise the movement's affairs. Pleven spoke good English; he had demonstrated his capabilities through the rallying of the African colonial territories in 1940; and, above all, his judgement was trusted by de Gaulle. He was issued with orders to travel to the United States on 19th May 1941. His duties were to establish relations with the State Department; to organise the economic and financial relations between Free French Africa and their Pacific territories with the Americans; to try and arrange for the direct purchases of ordnance along similar lines to those provided to the Belgians; to create a delegation; to reinforce their intelligence collection and propaganda; and to encourage goodwill within the private sector.[29] Maguire states that the creation of the Free French delegation was Pleven's initiative, but it is clear from de Gaulle's telegram that this idea had been previously decided.[30] Pleven's wide-ranging brief meant that his time in the United States was heavily occupied.

Unsurprisingly, de Sieyès was less than thrilled at being asked to leave his role. He was even less impressed with his effective demotion. In spite of this, the new composition of the Free French delegation took shape,

[28] MANAS Arnaud, *L'Or de Vichy: L'État Français et la monnaie*, Doctoral Thesis, Université Paris I – Sorbonne, Defended 11 April 2013, 757p., p. 119.

[29] AN, 560 AP 25 Dossier 2, *Telegram to Pleven from de Gaulle*, 19 May 1941.

[30] MAGUIRE, *Anglo-American Policy…*, 1995, p. 24—"Realizing that there was no single person who had the force and reputation for such a position, Pleven decided to form a delegation".

with the introduction of a number of new faces, including Adrien Tixier, the head of the International Labour Organization (I.L.O.) in Washington; Raoul Aglion, a recently arrived military civil servant; Étienne Boegner, the son of the head of France's protestant church and representative for *Optique et Précision de Levallois*; and Raoul de Roussy de Sales, the now-critically ill journalist. De Sieyès was retained and took over the role of recruitment.

Pleven needed to choose one of the members to head the delegation and his choice was between Boegner, who was well-liked but whose political allegiances were very similar to those of the Free French hierarchy, and Tixier. While one would have thought that the preference would have been given to Boegner, it was not the case. There were a number of reasons for selecting Tixier. While he fitted in well with the London headquarters, de Gaulle seems to have preferred avoiding intentional conflict with Roosevelt, to whom he would shortly be approaching for military assistance. As Roosevelt was a Democrat, he was sensitive towards workers' concerns, and, as Tixier was a man of the left, it was hoped that he would be able to connect with the Roosevelt administration. Considering his long-standing relationship with the I.L.O., it was felt that Tixier could better empathise with the goals of the Roosevelt administration. Tixier had an extraordinary ability to work longer and harder than his colleagues, due to his damaged hypothalamus which left him needing practically no sleep at all. However, his character was abrasive, his wit sardonic and his tongue acerbic. The outspoken Tixier had escaped France to travel to the United States, having "caused a fuss" in Geneva, where the I.L.O.'s headquarters were situated, by attacking a general "who retreated with his men, having been disarmed by the Swiss".[31] Furthermore, he was well known to John G. Winant, the recently appointed ambassador to the Court of Saint James, having served as deputy director of the I.L.O when Winant was its director. Above all, Tixier was a veteran of the Great War, having lost his left arm in the Ardennes through shell damage. De Gaulle clearly favoured these criteria over those offered by Boegner, the younger, protestant, businessman, with wider-reaching connections in the United States, and Tixier was appointed to the post.[32] However, de Gaulle's

[31] Interview with Gilles Morin, 'Fenêtre sur Adrien Tixier 1893–1946', Centre d'histoire sociale du XXe siècle, CNRS, Université Paris I. 24′38, 06:12–06:35, Consulted, 2 February 2017.

[32] A. Haute-Vienne, 88 J 18, *Note signed Charles de Gaulle*, 27 September 1941.

choice contributed greatly to the abject failure of the delegation to meet its intended aims.

## Disintegration

However, the problems facing the American delegation were only just beginning. Despite receiving $15,000 on a monthly basis,[33] the issues of financing such an enterprise were evident. Foreboding permeated throughout Tixier's correspondence with Pleven. He complained of the haphazard way that the Free French delegation was financed, calling it, in no uncertain terms, "absurd".[34] The reason for this absurdity was the lack of any form of accountability on the part of the various members, notably regarding bills and receipts. They felt no need to consult the head of the delegation, nor the treasurer, before spending any money. This rendered correct budgeting practically an impossibility. Tixier's solution was to implement a provisional monthly statement for the different classes of spending, as well as a system of authorisation. He hoped that this would stop the constant overspending that blighted their revenue stream at the beginning of each month.

A further cost that the Free French were obliged to cover was the rental of properties. Contrary to the subsidies that were offered by the Bank of England for their offices at Threadneedle Street, the American delegation did not receive any governmental economic assistance. They had to rent offices, on the open market, in some of the most expensive cities in the United States. This was more complicated than anticipated. Initially, they were using de Sieyès' property.[35] As he was one of the members of the delegation, there were no costs incurred for the New York office. Understandably, as it was a perfume shop, it was far from ideal. Moreover, with the development of purchasing commissions, like those led by Monnet and Purvis, real estate was becoming difficult to acquire. Through a letting agent, Aglion visited premises at the Rockefeller Center, on Fifth Avenue, that had recently been vacated by the Italian consulate.[36] The agent was dumbfounded when he heard about

[33] A. Haute-Vienne, 88 J 18, *Letter for Pleven from Tixier*, 15 November 1941.

[34] A. Haute-Vienne, 88 J 18, *Letter for Pleven from Tixier*, 15 November 1941.

[35] AGLION, *Roosevelt and de Gaulle*..., 1988, p. 25.

[36] Idem, pp. 28–29.

the political upheaval that was occurring between London and France. Despite needing reassurance that the group would vacate the premises once the war ended, the American was ready to rent the property, but only in Aglion's name. As the Free French delegation was not a legal entity in the United States, they could not rent property. This was one of the consequences that the lack of official recognition engendered for the movement. It also highlights the discrepancy between the receptions that the Free French received in the U.K., being relatively positive, and in the United States, where the welcome was far cooler. Instead, a solution was found and, rather than rent the property to the organisation, the agent did so directly to Aglion, under his remit as the acting general secretary. It was only upon the renewal of the lease, two years later, that the text, which stipulated that the property was "Rented to Mr. Raoul Aglion", was addended by the addition of "and to his successors representing the Free French".[37] This highlights that trust and honour played an important role in the American legal system of the era. Aglion explained that the delegation only wanted part of the original office space. The rental fee was, therefore, lowered by 40% in comparison with those paid by the Italians, due to the smaller surface area being rented. Their eventual contract was for a three-year lease, taking them into 1944, at a cost of $425 per calendar month, until May 1942, and $625, thereafter.[38] This meant that the office had originally cost the Italian consulate somewhere between $1,060 and $1,560 per month. When it is considered that the average rent across the city was $50[39] and median home prices were $45,700,[40] the price that was paid by the Free French delegation was much higher than elsewhere in New York, but it was far lower than that paid by the previous occupants. This suggests that, in order to pay the fees, the members either had their own means, access to other people's

[37] AGLION, *Roosevelt and de Gaulle…*, 1988, p. 29.

[38] AN, 560 AP 25 (Dossier 2), *Letter from Raoul Aglion to René Pleven*, 18 July 1941.

[39] DALLEY Jessica, 'What Would $50 In 1940 Rent a New Yorker Today?' *Curbed New York*, 21 July 2013, https://ny.curbed.com/2013/11/21/10172014/what-would-50-in-1940-rent-a-new-yorker-today, Consulted, 9 September 2020.

[40] MARTIN Emmie, 'Here's How Much Housing Prices Have Skyrocketed Over the Last 50 Years in Every U.S. State', CNBC, 27 June 2017, https://www.cnbc.com/2017/06/27/how-much-housing-prices-have-increased-since-1940-in-every-state.html, Consulted 9 September 2020.

funds or that Aglion was an excellent negotiator. In reality, it was probably a combination of the three.

It was quite possibly for this reason that Aglion was awarded the highest salary among the 26 personnel of the American delegation, with a monthly salary of $350. This surprisingly large number of personnel was composed of people spread across the United States, either in the New York office or in the San Francisco branch. Fourteen of the staff were women, and two had yet to be hired, leaving a male demographic of ten. Their salaries ranged from $350 down to a mere $17.33, which was paid to the errand boy, Paul Fryda. The posts that these people occupied were given general office nomenclature such as 'H.R.', 'Purchasing', 'Communications', etc. This offers a comparison with those in London who were, on the whole, paid far less than their American counterparts. Pleven, Aglion's superior, had a salary of £60, or $240.[41] The cost of living, when using the average of 1935–1939 as the base, had increased slightly during the year 1941. As of 15th January 1941, all items were at 101.1 but, by 15th December, the basket had increased to 108.7, or by 7.5% in the space of a year, and 8.7% from the base price index.[42]

Life was getting more expensive in New York. The same pattern was seen in San Francisco, which grew by 9% during 1941, from 102.1, in January, to 111.3, in December. However, much the same pattern could be seen emerging in any of the belligerent powers. This was largely due to disruption of international trade that resulted from conventional and economic warfare measures that were beginning to bite:

> *The principal reasons for the advance in prices were those which ordinarily characterize a major war. Immediately following the outbreak of World War II, markets were upset by the disruption of international trade, as a result both of the blockade and of the diversion of materials and shipping to serve the needs of the belligerents. As the war spread and intensified, this disruption was steadily aggravated.*[43]

[41] Exchange rate-$1:0.25p (£1:$4) in 1940, (£60*4).

[42] HOOVER Ethel, WILLIAMS Faith, 'Cost of Living in 1941', *Bulletin of the United States Bureau of Labor Statistics*, No. 710, 41p., Table 2, p. 9, https://fraser.stlouisfed.org/title/cost-living-1941-4209, Consulted, 9 September 2020.

[43] BLAIR John, ULMER Melville, NELSON Saul (Ed.), 'Wartime Prices', *Bulletin of the United States Bureau of Labor Statistics*, No. 749, 272p., p. 1, https://fraser.stlouisfed.org/title/wartime-prices-4235, Consulted, 9 September 2020.

It would seem that, in the United States, work was simply better paid. Evidently, this was as true for those serving with the Free French, as it was for anybody else.

The functioning of the delegation was established as part of a decree ratified on 2nd December 1941.[44] The group was originally conceived with eight members in mind; however, considering the difficulties that Pleven encountered during his mission to enrol members of the French expatriate community in support of de Gaulle, the number of delegates was cut to five. These men, Étienne Boegner, Jacques de Sieyès, Raoul de Roussy de Sales, Adrien Tixier and Raoul Aglion, were responsible for different aspects of the diplomatic mission. Tixier was the delegate to Congress and the trade unions; Boegner was sent to the State Department, in Washington; de Sieyès would continue in his role as de Gaulle's personal representative at official functions; Roussy de Sales took care of press and communication issues; and Aglion acted as general secretary for the four others, operating out of New York.[45]

In Washington, Tixier's role was to manage the political and diplomatic issues that the Gaullists faced, as well as to respond for their actions. There was some overlap with the responsibilities of the other delegates, as Tixier controlled the administration of the budget; hence, he impinged on Boegner's role. A similar quandary was legislatively imposed by the document relating to Tixier and de Sieyès. As the head of the delegation, Tixier was the 'official' representative of General de Gaulle. This put him in direct confrontation with de Sieyès, who held three letters stating that he was General de Gaulle's representative in the United States. As each felt that the other was encroaching upon their domain, conflicts inevitably erupted. It could be argued that this environment was a result of the stressful wartime circumstances, but it could also be seen to have served to ensure General de Gaulle's influence and primacy over the movement. Moreover, such difficulties seem to have been relatively commonplace throughout the Free French organisation. It is likely that this was caused by the rapid establishment of their administrative structures and the difficult circumstances surrounding their inception.

[44] A. Haute-Vienne, 88 J 18, *Délégation du Comité National Français aux Etats-Unis*, undated.

[45] AGLION, *Roosevelt and de Gaulle…*, 1988, p. 39.

Consequently, tensions arose between the members, as Aglion recounted, such as when Roussy de Sales accused Tixier of behaving as though he was an "enemy of de Gaulle".[46] In order to avoid this, Aglion attempted to give as wide a birth as possible to the Capitol. These squabbles did little to improve the Americans' impressions of the Free French and their capacities for teamwork and leadership. The ill-feeling came to a head during Tixier's visit to London, in March 1942. De Gaulle tended to listen to Tixier without question. During their meeting, de Gaulle was convinced to allow Tixier to become the sole holder of the delegation's power, and that the other delegates were to become his 'counsellors'. This caused great consternation to Boegner and left de Sieyès thinking that the whole objective of the mission was to centralise even more power in Tixier's hands. Nevertheless, this course of events would hardly have troubled de Gaulle—himself in a struggle to affirm his legitimacy as the leader of the French nation-in-exile. The State Department official in London, Matthews, explained to Cordell Hull that he found Tixier "unhappy over the situation he has found here. He feels that neither the British Government nor our own 'understands' the situation in France and that General de Gaulle and his entourage at Carlton Gardens are equally devoid of all 'sense of realism'".[47] Tixier presciently predicted that:

> *France must again become a battlefield before the end of the war. The seeds of resistance which exist in France should therefore be carefully nurtured. Those seeds of resistance are only to be found in the 'people'. De Gaulle and his followers, he says, have no contact with 'the people'". Most damningly of all, "he finds the Free French headquarters, here, so occupied with 'their own petty squabbles' as to be unable to give that leadership 'devoid of self-seeking' which the movement requires".*

While Tixier impressed Matthews, marking him as both intelligent and honest, the American was sceptical about the *poilu*'s impressions on the situation in France, due to the length of time that he had been absent from the country. The result of his visit was that Tixier became the sole vector of communication with London, although this was bypassed by the other delegates who continued to correspond with the members of

[46] AGLION, *Roosevelt and de Gaulle...*, 1988, p. 43.

[47] NARA, U.S. Office of the Historian, 851.01/390: *Telegram, The Chargé in the United Kingdom (Matthews) to the Secretary of State (Cordell Hull)*, 26 March 1942.

the *Comité National*, in London, who passed information along to them in return.

These political machinations did little to foster cohesion among the members of the delegation and left them divided, not simply on a geographical basis, but on ideological and administrative grounds, too. In order to attempt to repair the relationship, Étienne Boegner decided to go to London, in an attempt to clear up any misunderstandings, but he was severely chastised by General de Gaulle. In a letter sent to Roussy de Sales, dated 3rd June 1942, Boegner wrote, "For one hour, I was insulted, as were our (American allies)… It was like a storm…de Gaulle is a phenomenon of patriotism".[48] His pro-American sentiments were anathema to de Gaulle in the wake of the crisis in New Caledonia, following the invasion of Saint-Pierre-et-Miquelon over Christmas 1941. De Gaulle told Boegner that Tixier was "a good and loyal Frenchman", meaning that he accepted the report relating to the antagonism shown by the U.S. State Department, and that he did not believe a word that Boegner said. De Gaulle's vitriol overflowed with a flourish of *ad-hominems* aimed at Sumner Welles, the under-secretary of state—calling him "a stupid idiot" (*un con*) among other things—and referring to Cordell Hull as an "old moron" (*ce viel abruti*).[49] De Gaulle accused Boegner of being a double agent for the Americans and, unsurprisingly, Boegner resigned on the spot!

Moreover, less than three weeks later, de Gaulle was clearly questioning the reliability of his own personnel in the Free French delegation. Winant, in his telegram to Cordell Hull dated 29th June 1942, recounted how "(De Gaulle) pointed out that, unfortunately, some of his local officials were not always 'reliable' and mentioned the difficulties in New Caledonia".[50] De Gaulle was rubbishing those attempting to assist him, in front of those from whom he would have liked support. Clearly, he had forgotten to whom he was talking and about whom he was gossiping.

[48] AGLION, *Roosevelt and de Gaulle…*, 1988, p. 46.

[49] MUNHOLLAND Kim, *Rock of Contention: Free French and Americans at War in New Caledonia, 1940–1945*, New York, Berghahn Books, 2005, 251p., p. 178.

[50] NARA U.S. Office of the Historian, 851.01/536: *Telegram, The Ambassador in the United Kingdom (Winant) to the Secretary of State (Cordell Hull)*, 29 July 1942.

It must be underlined, however, that the Americans were "informed", meaning that it was the British who were feeding them the information.[51]

The delegation was reduced to four members. However, within six months, it was reduced still further. Roussy de Sales passed away in December 1942, following a long battle with illness that often left him bedridden, and de Sieyès was recalled soon after and redeployed to Syria. This left Tixier and Aglion. Their personalities clashed, with Tixier regularly employing a "leftist harangue"[52] and blaming all and sundry for the problems being experienced in France. This extended to criticisms of both the Vichy regime and his own movement. In the light of these *faux pas*, it is surprising that anything was successfully organised by the delegation, when considering the conflicts of personalities, the absence of instructions from London and the increasing centralisation that was being demanded by de Gaulle. Interestingly, Aglion also belonged to S.O.E. as an informer.[53] This effectively means that the delegation was, itself, compromised by the British. It has become clear that, much as de Gaulle may have otherwise wished, from an economic perspective, separating the British interest from the French was becoming ever more difficult.

Initially, Roosevelt's administration was not inclined to offer assistance to the Free French. However, with a change in strategy, and polling statistics, this position altered to one of limited pragmatic cooperation, while enforcing strict political distancing from de Gaulle. Julian Jackson's work demonstrates that political machinations that were taking place in order to keep an interest alive with Vichy.[54] Had Roosevelt even so wished, it would not have been prudent for his administration to support the Free

[51] Ibid, "We are informed that General de Gaulle seemed quite pleased with the memorandum which Eden gave him today".

[52] AGLION, *Roosevelt and de Gaulle*..., 1988, p. 47.

[53] TNA, HS9/12/2 Aglion Raoul David Emmanuel, 7 July 1941,—"Report N° SO/176 from New York advised: 3449 is employed by us and we have given him number G.108. He is used for the organization of Syrians in the United States. He is also the ostensible head of the Near East Information Bureau, which is handling Arabic broadcasts and propaganda among the Arab press in the U.S. including Al Hoda. 3449 is also employed by de Sieyes and we are paying him too with the understanding that if he should lose his appointment with de Sieyes because of the work he is doing for us, we will make up his loss of salary to him".

[54] JACKSON Julian, *A Certain Idea of France: The Life of Charles de Gaulle*, London, Penguin, 2018, 906p., p. 235—"Since North Africa Was Strongly Vichyist, and Had Little Resistance Presence, de Gaulle No Longer Figured in American Calculations".

French in too overt a manner. However, in spite of the movement's initial attempts to ingratiate themselves in the United States, American legislation and internal bickering seem to have greatly hindered the delegation's development.

Moreover, large costs were engendered while supporting the Free French movement, as has been shown by the rental fees at the Rockefeller Center, in one of New York's most costly areas. The salary base for the Free French delegation in the United States was a heavy cost that would have to be borne either by De Gaulle, in London, or paid from their own resources. Initially, costs were limited as the delegation used their own premises. However, the political and military position adopted by de Gaulle on issues relevant to the Roosevelt administration, including Saint-Pierre-et-Miquelon, rendered much of the delegation's earlier work moot. Furthermore, De Gaulle's disparaging attitude towards some of his subordinates, and favouritism of others, also had a negative effect on diplomatic relations.

While the United States would later go on to massively support the Free French, it does not appear to have been due to the efforts of the Free French delegation. Instead, the Free French movement were seen more as a group with strategic holdings of value. Were other Free French delegations elsewhere around the world viewed from the same perspective?

CHAPTER 5

# Viva La Resistencia! Francs from the Foreign-Based French, 1940–1942

This chapter explores the financial role that was played by the French expatriate communities in supporting the Free French movement in South America, notably the delegations in Mexico, Argentina, Uruguay and Chile. It provides an overview of their relative wealth and the donations that they made to the Free French movement; something that has received little previous interest from historians of the movement.

The historiography concerning the French diaspora, during the Second World War, is limited to an isolated collection of articles,[1] edited volumes[2]

[1] ROE Teiva, 'Les Français d'Australie et la France libre (1940–1944)', *Outre-mers*, Vol. 95, n° 360–361, 2nd semester 2008, *L'Afrique des Indiens*, pp. 209–222; ROLLAND Denis, 'Jacques Soustelle, De l'Ethnologie à la Politique', *Guerres mondiales et conflits contemporains*, N° 180, October 1995, pp. 171–185.

[2] CORNIL-FRERROT Sylvain (Ed.), OULMONT Philippe (Ed.), *Les Français Libres et le Monde*, Paris, Éditions Nouveau Monde, 2015, 431p.



D. Foulk, *The Price of Freedom*,
https://doi.org/10.1007/978-3-031-09066-0_5

and monographs.[3] Studies by Jennings,[4] Munholland[5] and Thomas[6] have concentrated on the military and political history of the Free French movement within the French colonies, as opposed to investigating the members of the French community outside the colonial empire. Therefore, the financial contribution of these groups has never been investigated by historians. This is a great oversight for, as will be shown, without the Free French delegations' contributions, the movement would have been incapable of servicing its early debts and would have been wholly reliant on the British exchequer. Individual memoirs, such as the work of Jacques Soustelle,[7] who, from 1940 to 1942, was the de facto head of the Free French delegations in central America and the Antilles, provide an insight into his centralising role in enabling the smaller groups to maintain links with London. However, evidence of any donating activities in his book, or any of the other works mentioned above, is rare.

The financing of the Free French movement was a truly global enterprise, which depended on the enthusiasm and ingenuity of French expatriates and those whose families originated in France. General de Gaulle's accounts showed that donations were made from individuals and organisations across the world. Some were large, amounting to thousands of pounds, and some were small, being only a few pounds, shillings and pence. These funds were destined to support the Free French movement in acquiring ordnance, such as aeroplanes and armaments, and paying sums that were owed to personnel and other governments for services rendered.

The newly formed *Caisse centrale de la France libre* organised the Free French movement's income, in London, with assistance from the Bank

[3] ROLLAND Denis, *Vichy et la France Libre au Mexique: Guerre, cultures et propagandes pendant la Deuxième Guerre mondiale*, Paris, L'Harmattan, 1990, 443p. (Ebook).

[4] JENNINGS Eric, *La France libre fut africaine*, Paris, Perrin, 2014, 350p. (Ebook).

[5] MUNHOLLAND Kim, *Rock of Contention: Free French and Americans at War in New Caledonia, 1940–1945*, New York, Berghahn Books, 2005, 251p.

[6] THOMAS Martin, *The French Empire at War 1940–1945*, Manchester, Manchester University Press, 1998, 298p.

[7] SOUSTELLE Jacques, *Envers et contre tout: De Londres à Alger (1940–1942)*, Paris, Robert Laffont, 1947, 470p.

of England. Small payments were sent as cheques or were telegraphically wired by donors. However, delegations were not only established in belligerent nations, but also in neutral countries, thus reflecting the spread of the French diaspora across the world. Money that was raised by these overseas Free French delegations became an early, but sporadic, source of revenue.

The undertaken financial analysis shows that 32 of the 42 national delegations were sending significant proportions of the funds that they collected to London.[8] However, the amounts of the donations, made by some delegations, must be questioned as it appears that their stated contributions were inflated and, subsequently, some participants may have greatly overestimated their own bestowals to the cause.

## The Donations and the Balances

Before venturing further into the accounts of individual committees, it would be judicious to demonstrate the full extent of the various committees' funding throughout 1941 and into early 1942. The table demonstrates both the account balances that were kept by the different delegations and the donations that were sent to supplement the income of the Free French in London. Furthermore, it enables for the analysis of the most financially important of the delegations, according to their bank balances, but also allows us to ascertain which delegations were the most generous. By this, it is meant that certain delegations gifted fifty per cent of their holdings, but some gave more, and others offered much less.

Firstly, the balances of the individual delegations show an average increase in their holdings, over the five-month period, from October 1941 to February 1942. The average holding rose from £1,676, in October, to £2,386, in February 1942, thus indicating a 69% increase.[9] While this is a

[8] CRÉMIEUX-BRILHAC Jean-Louis, *La France Libre: Tome 1, De l'appel du 18 juin à la libération*, Paris, Éditions Gallimard, 1996, 818p., p. 332—"In mid-1942, there were national committees in thirty-nine countries and, counting the local committees, professional groups and welfare committees, nearly five hundred Free French Committees"; BELOT Robert, 'Les comités de la France Libre en Amérique latine pendant la guerre: enjeu symbolique, politique et diplomatique' in *De Gaulle et l'Amérique Latine*, Rennes, Presses universitaires de Rennes, 2014 (Ebook, 2019), 280p.—"In mid-1942, we note the existence of 42 national committees around the world, without mentioning the 412 sub-committees".

[9] (1160/1676)*100%.

cumulative average, it shows that the delegations grew over time. Some, such as Japan, remained static and Venezuela experienced a reduction in their balance between November 1941 and January 1942. However, most saw their balances increasing, for instance, in Egypt and Australia. The decline could be explained by a certain amount of spending being undertaken, possibly for propaganda purposes. Furthermore, it could also be due to declining memberships. The static figures could suggest that no activities of any note were being undertaken or that subscriptions remained unchanged. Conversely, the increases could reflect a growing number of donors and a wider reach being attained by the groups' propaganda, which could have encouraged more people to rally to the movement and, consequently, to donate funds.

On the other side of the table are the donations that were sent to London from each of the delegations in 1941 and 1942. Firstly, a word of explanation on the percentages; when a figure of 100% is showing, this means that the same amount of funding was donated to London as was being held by the delegation in the source country, such as Panama or South Africa in 1941. Anything greater than 100% signifies that the delegation was sending more funds than they held in their bank accounts, including Argentina's 188%, in 1942. A percentage below 100 indicates that the delegation retained more funds than those that were sent to London, such as the Dominican Republic's delegation, at 18%, in 1942.

By using this data, it is possible to identify the most financially successful delegations, through a ranking of their bank holdings. These include Argentina, Mexico, Australia, the U.K, Egypt and Chile; all of whom held thousands of pounds in their accounts. Some of these, like Argentina, had tens of thousands of pounds, but barely saw an increase in their holdings over the period. This suggests that much of their income came from stable sources, such as subscriptions. However, some, including Australia or Mexico, showed a notable evolution over the five-month period, increasing by multiple thousands of pounds. One can hypothesise that these delegations experienced increasing receipts due to the successful combinations of propaganda and subscription fee growth. Conversely, a negative percentage, shown only by Brazil, reflected the fact that Carlton Gardens credited the delegation with more funds than they had received, through credit notes, or *extourne* in French, thus giving a net negative total. A number of credit notes were written in 1942, but Brazil's case was the only one that gave a net negative total.

However, the donations show a more nuanced image. While Argentina may have sent the largest proportion of their holdings to London, specifically the 188% in 1942, several of the less wealthy delegations sent a very large part of their own resources to the Free French. This was notably the case in Uruguay and Guatemala, who sent 186% and 172%, respectively, in 1942. These delegations were not as wealthy as the Argentinian delegation, but they gave far beyond their means to support the movement. Despite their smaller fortunes, the donations made by these delegations are proportional to their smaller size. It would be just as difficult for a delegation that did not earn as much to provide the amounts shown in the table. Equally, it must be remembered that the evolution of the war itself would have greatly impacted the amounts that the delegations would have been able to send. This was notably the case for the Japanese delegation who were unable to send any money in 1942, following the beginning of the war in the Pacific in December 1941. This was because the funds had previously been sent by the head of the delegation, using diplomatic suitcases to send the money to London, but the financial link was severed along with the political ones.

A notable absence from Table 5.1 is the United States of America. While a delegation did exist in the country, they were unable to provide funds directly to the Free French. In large part, this was due to the continuing U.S. ambiguity over diplomatic relations with the Free French and, more importantly, they were simply not acquiring enough money to spare any. According to Raoul Aglion, the secretary of the American delegation, the selling of stamps was their only source of income in January 1941.[10] By August 1941, the income of France Forever, one of the main groups catering to the French diaspora, was $83,450, comprising membership fees, donations, loans and other income like profits from entertainments that they had curated. However, their expenditure was $88,805,[11] thus leaving a shortfall of $5,355. While this group were not the delegation, per se, they were one of the American groups who helped to provide support to the Free French in the United States. If such a group were not able to turn a profit, it is unlikely that the delegation would have fared

[10] AGLION Raoul, *Roosevelt and de Gaulle: Allies in Conflict, A Personal Memoir*, New York, The Free Press, 1988, 239p., p. 27.

[11] AN, 560 AP 25, Dossier 2, Délégation de la France libre aux États-Unis, *France Forever—Inter-Office Memorandum from Mr. H.M. Ufford to Mr. E. Gentil*, 29 August 1941.

much better from a financial perspective. Most importantly, the lack of diplomatic recognition for the Free French movement, by the Roosevelt administration, was the most important factor in the American's absence from Table 5.1. This was outlined in a letter from Aglion to René Pleven, who was in the United States on a mission to try and assist the delegation. The group's legal representative, presumably Frederic René Coudert Jr., advised Aglion that, in his firm's opinion, it would be "imprudent" to receive donations or to seemingly tax people. Such action risked being in violation of laws pertaining to foreign consular organisation on American soil.[12] As Frederic Coudert Jr. was a state senator for New York, at the time, his firm's legal opinion held great weight.[13] It is for these reasons that the U.S. delegation have not appeared in the table.

Cumulatively, from the end of 1941 to the beginning of 1942, the donations increased by 22.5%.[14] This suggests that the propaganda efforts and adherent drives were having a positive effect on General de Gaulle's accounts. Interestingly, when one examines the donations made in 1940 and 1941,[15] totalling £68,741, with those in the two credit accounts, of the 'National Provincial Bank' account and the 'Général de Gaulle' account, between September 1940 and June 1941,[16] to which are added the donations made in November and December 1941,[17] or £63,749, the donation tally leaves a minor shortfall in the books of £4,992. It could plausibly be argued that this shortfall could have been made up during the missing five months, from July to September 1941.

However, when comparing the figures from the first two months of 1942, in de Gaulle's two principal British accounts, £23,000 was said

[12] AN, 560 AP 25, Dossier 2, Letter from Raoul Aglion to René Pleven, 27 August 1941—"As long as we are not recognised by the Government of the United States, it seemed to MM. Coudert that it would be unwise, even for a de facto government, to receive donations or collect taxes".

[13] 'Biography of Frederic René Coudert Jr.', *History, Art & Archives: United States House of Representatives*, https://history.house.gov/People/Detail/11462, Consulted 19 May 2020.

[14] (13,345/59148)*100.

[15] AN, 3 AG 1 305 France Libre Comptes 1940–1943 –(1940) 9,593 + (1941) 59,148 = 68,741.

[16] AN, 3 AG 1 301—Livre renfermant des compte 1940–1941.

[17] AN, 3 AG 1 302—Compte personnel du général de Gaulle Caisse journal Novembre 1941-Avril 1943.

**Table 5.1** Balances and Donations from Free French Delegations, in £ sterling—Table constructed from data found within Archives nationales (AN, 3 AG (1) 305)

| | Bank balances (£) | | | | Donations (£) | | | | |
|---|---|---|---|---|---|---|---|---|---|
| | 31/10/41 | 31/11/41 | 31/01/42 | 28/02/42 | Donations 1941 (£) | As % of 31/11/41 Balance | Donations 1942 (£) | As % of 28/02/42 Balance | Net Total (1941–1942) |
| Argentina | 13,605 | 13,605 | 13,655 | 13,655 | 11,654 | 86 | 25,679 | 188 | 37,333 |
| Australia | 1,260 | 3,739 | 3,739 | 6,805 | 3,258 | 87 | 3,866 | 57 | 7,124 |
| Bolivia | 147 | 147 | 147 | 147 | 147 | 100 | 0 | 0 | 147 |
| Brazil | 750 | 1,350 | 1,650 | 3,100 | 1,150 | 85 | -2,750 | -89 | -1,600 |
| Canada | 540 | 562 | 648 | 648 | 648 | 115 | 266 | 41 | 914 |
| Chile | 4,284 | 4,284 | 5,244 | 6,244 | 4,744 | 111 | 7,378 | 118 | 12,122 |
| Columbia | 250 | 250 | 458 | 458 | 250 | 100 | 208 | 45 | 458 |
| Costa Rica | 69 | 69 | 886 | 886 | 69 | 100 | 915 | 103 | 984 |
| Cuba | 932 | 932 | 948 | 1,815 | 55 | 6 | 0 | 0 | 55 |
| Egypt | 655 | 4,400 | 5,422 | 6,422 | 4,922 | 112 | 6,200 | 97 | 11,122 |
| Ecuador | 84 | 84 | 84 | 84 | 84 | 100 | 24 | 29 | 108 |
| Far East-Singapore | 100 | 1,272 | 1,389 | 1,748 | 1,389 | 109 | 359 | 21 | 1,748 |
| Gold Coast-Ghana | 2,889 | 2,889 | 3,089 | 3,089 | 2,889 | 100 | 1599 | 52 | 4,488 |
| Guatemala | 519 | 519 | 519 | 519 | 519 | 100 | 892 | 172 | 1,411 |
| Haiti | 247 | 247 | 470 | 470 | 247 | 100 | 421 | 90 | 668 |
| Mauritius | 3,250 | 3,250 | 4,250 | 4,250 | 3,750 | 115 | 0 | 0 | 3,750 |
| India | 483 | 483 | 633 | 633 | 308 | 64 | 0 | 0 | 308 |
| Dutch East Indies-Indonesia | 1,153 | 1,153 | 1,153 | 1,153 | 1,153 | 100 | 0 | 0 | 1,153 |
| Japan | 424 | 424 | 424 | 424 | 394 | 93 | 0 | 0 | 394 |
| Mexico | 6,948 | 6,948 | 6,955 | 14,955 | 3,866 | 56 | 11,218 | 75 | 15,084 |
| Nicaragua | 347 | 347 | 313 | 411 | 313 | 90 | 323 | 79 | 636 |
| Nigeria | 2,000 | 2,000 | 2,000 | 2,000 | 2,000 | 100 | 0 | 0 | 2,000 |
| Nyasaland-Malawi | 100 | 100 | 100 | 100 | 100 | 100 | 50 | 50 | 150 |
| Panama | 337 | 337 | 387 | 387 | 337 | 100 | 250 | 65 | 587 |
| Peru | 123 | 123 | 123 | 123 | 123 | 100 | 253 | 206 | 376 |
| Puerto Rico | 2,154 | 2,228 | 2,798 | 3,244 | 2,549 | 114 | 2,672 | 82 | 5,221 |
| Dominican Republic | 321 | 420 | 667 | 790 | 420 | 100 | 140 | 18 | 560 |
| El Salvador | 401 | 401 | 525 | 624 | 523 | 130 | 0 | 0 | 523 |
| Sierra Leone | 470 | 470 | 670 | 670 | 670 | 143 | 600 | 90 | 1,270 |
| Trinidad | 2,150 | 2,150 | 2,150 | 2,150 | 1,145 | 53 | 0 | 0 | 1,145 |
| South Africa | 1,008 | 1,008 | 1,008 | 1,008 | 1,008 | 100 | 0 | 0 | 1,008 |
| United Kingdom | 5,000 | 5,000 | 6,500 | 6,500 | 5,000 | 100 | 2,000 | 31 | 7,000 |
| Uruguay | 3,761 | 3,761 | 3,958 | 5,154 | 2,782 | 74 | 9,573 | 186 | 12,355 |
| Venezuela | 239 | 239 | 41 | 1,051 | 682 | 285 | 357 | 34 | 1,039 |
| TOTAL | 57,011 | 65,203 | 73,015 | 93,071 | 59,148 | | 72,493 | | 131,641 |
| AVERAGE | 1,676 | 1,917 | 2,147 | 2,386 | 1,740 | | 2,132 | | |

*Note (1)*—Names are given with their contemporary equivalent
*Note (2)*—In 28/2/42, donations made to 'Amis des Volontaires Français' from Cuba, Venezuela, Gold Coast and San Sebastian—totalling £1,339—have been included in the month's final total

to have been received from the foreign delegations. However, when the receipts were tabulated, the delegations actually sent a total of £72,493. This shows a significant shortfall of £49,493, between the reported figures and those found in the ledgers. Furthermore, these are figures that are taken from corresponding periods, over two months, at the beginning of 1942.

From the evidence, it would seem that amounts were sent by the delegations, whose records are found within Box '3 AG 1 305', and were effectively lost during the Accounting process in London, conserved in Box '3 AG 1 302'. Where this additional money went is open to interpretation, for it represents a 215% difference over the reported figure, in the accounts.[18] In the following sections, the case studies will highlight the circumstances in which these payments were raised. This significantly alters the historiographical perspective of the Free French movement as being simply a London- or colonial-based enterprise. It will be seen that French resistance was, in fact, far larger in scope than has previously been credited. Jacques Soustelle described this groundswell of expatriate support:

> Beginning in June and July (1940), the 'De Gaulle Committees', 'Free French Committees', 'France Forever Associations' were created everywhere - without orders, without plans, without instructions. Those who began them were generally salesmen or technicians who were cut off from politics by their long absence, but confusedly felt that, in such times wherein the state abdicated its responsibilities, it was for citizens to unite to grasp the country's destiny in their feeble hands.[19]

## Mexico

French links with the Mexicans date back to the beginning of the nineteenth century, even before Napoléon III placed Maximilian Hapsburg onto the throne of Mexico.[20] Much like the Second Empire in France,

[18] ((72,493–23,000)/23000)*100.

[19] SOUSTELLE Jacques, *Envers et contre tout (1): De Londres à Alger*, Paris, Robert Laffont, 1947, 470p., (Ebook), Chap. 2, Para. 28.

[20] BARKER Nancy Nichols, 'The French Colony in Mexico, 1821–61: Generator of Intervention', *French Historical Studies*, Vol. 9, N° 4 (Autumn, 1976), pp. 596–618, Duke University Press.

the Mexican monarchy was inherently unstable and was quickly replaced by the initially enlightened autocracy of General Porfirio Díaz. Díaz was eventually overthrown in 1911, having descended into tyrannical rule, with the help of Emiliano Zapata's peasant forces, and a military-led, single-party republic was established. It was within this highly charged political context that the French expatriate community was surrounded. According to Rolland,[21] the First World War had a great impact upon the size of the French community in Mexico, having fallen by 76% between the years 1910 and 1918.[22] However, the interwar years were more propitious for encouraging emigration, with 6,000 French making Mexico their home.[23] This was despite policies which encouraged the raising of salaries for Mexican workers, much like in France.[24] According to Henri Goiran, the minister plenipotentiary in Mexico, from 1933 to 1939,[25] this had a disincentivising impact on foreign entrepreneurs who hired local labour.[26] Expatriate owners of capital in Mexico were, therefore, heavily impacted by socially progressive policies that were becoming *de rigueur* in numerous countries during the 1930s.

The French community in Mexico was smaller than those in neighbouring countries and was well-integrated into the life of the host country. As was seen in Argentina, French 'soft power' permeated through the transmission of ideas and *savoir-faire*. For instance, a small number of French-trained agronomists were responsible for changing local practices, including implementing newly discovered research into fertilisers and "sweeping land reform" which exacerbated the ongoing

[21] ROLLAND Denis, *Vichy et la France Libre au Mexique: Guerre, cultures et propagandes pendant la Deuxième Guerre mondiale*, Paris, 1990, (Ebook), Chap. 1, Para. 7; See KNIGHT Alan, *The Mexican Revolution Vol. 2: Counter-Revolution & Reconstruction*, Lincoln, University of Nebraska Press, 1990, 679p.

[22] ((3787–900)/3787)*100%.

[23] ROLLAND Denis, *Vichy et la France Libre au Mexique*, 1990, (Ebook) Chap. 5, Para. 9.

[24] BEZBAKH Pierre, *Le Petit Larousse de l'histoire de France*, Paris, Larousse, 2003 (Ed. 2011), 1023p., pp. 600/601—"Domestic demand can also grow through wage increases; but these cause costs to rise if productivity gains of the same magnitude are not achieved. France will in fact experiment with these various policies".

[25] Biographical information on Henri Goiran Papers, https://dl.tufts.edu/concern/eads/dr26z763h, Consulted 19 May 2020.

[26] ROLLAND Denis, *Vichy et la France Libre au Mexique*, 1990, (Ebook) Chap. 1, Para. 91.

financial crisis of the late 1930s and early 1940s.[27] These agronomists were some of the few French people who travelled to Mexico during the time of the Third Republic. However, the French community was deeply rooted in the country. As Rolland explained, "These French were not refugees; they were Mexicans in training, of French origins".[28] While they may have been sympathetic towards the movement, many Franco-Mexicans did not divulge their pro-Free French sympathies until May 1941 and the signature of the Paris Protocols. This agreement removed any ambiguity regarding Vichy's collaborationist position, in the eyes of the Mexican government.[29] These protocols allowed the Germans access to French military facilities in Syria, Tunisia and French West Africa, in exchange for a reduction of occupation fees and the return of some French prisoners of war.

However, in the political arena, Mexican sympathy and affinity with the Free French seems to have been present from the very beginning of the conflict. Under the presidency of General Manuel Ávilha Camacho, the Mexican authorities gave their full support to the delegation—notably by ensuring that French assets were not placed under any form of restriction, in contrast to those of citizens of the Axis powers, "whose property was sequestrated for more than ten years".[30]

In June 1940, René Dubernard, in Mexico, sent a telegram to French Prime Minister, Paul Reynaud, insisting that the war must continue.[31] Dubernard, a recipient of the Croix de Guerre for his role in the First

[27] COTTER Joseph, OSBORNE Michael A., 'Agronomía Afranceada: The French Contribution to Mexican Agronomy, 1880–1940', *Science, Technology & Society*, Vol. 1, Issue 1, 1996, Sage Publications New Delhi, pp. 25–49, p. 43.

[28] ROLLAND Denis, 'L'exil structure l'émigration (Mexique, Seconde Guerre mondiale)' *Matériaux pour l'histoire de notre temps*, n° 67, Pour une histoire de l'Exil français et belge, 2002, pp. 66–77, p. 68.

[29] *Idem*, p. 70.

[30] 'Le Comité de la France Libre du Mexique, par René Dubernard', *Revue de la France Libre*, n° 126, June 1960, 12 November 2009, http://www.france-libre.net/comite-fl-mexique/, Consulted 1 February 2020.

[31] 'Le Comité de la France Libre du Mexique, par René Dubernard', *Revue de la France Libre*, n° 126, June 1960, 12 November 2009, http://www.france-libre.net/comite-fl-mexique/, Consulted 1 February 2020.

World War,[32] had been introduced to Jacques Soustelle by Georges Pinson—who was the president of Alliance Française, a former *poilu* and victim of the Zapatista and Villista period of the Mexican revolution, in 1915.[33] Together, Soustelle, Pinson and Dubernard decided to form the Free French delegation in Mexico.

Jacques Soustelle was a graduate of the *École normale supérieure* and *agrégé* in philosophy.[34] Between November 1932 and September 1934, alongside his wife, Georgette, a fellow ethnologist, they travelled to Mexico to study the Otomi, an indigenous people who lived in central Mexico. Upon the declaration of war, he returned to France where he was mobilised as a diplomatic envoy to Mexico. In February 1940, he became the assistant to the military attaché in Mexico, Commander Signoret.[35] Soustelle's role was to provide the link between the Free French in London and the Mexican government, while encouraging the local French expatriate community to support the continued war effort.

On 22nd June 1940, four days after de Gaulle's first appearance on the B.B.C., the Mexican delegation held their first public meeting, where 250 people became supporters and donors, meaning that they agreed to make monthly contributions. These subscriptions were later supplemented by the manufacture of lapel pins and car-bumper stickers bearing

[32] 'Les frères Dubernard seront honorés, aujourd'hui, à Meymac', *La Montagne*, 11 November 2014, https://www.lamontagne.fr/ussel/vie-pratique-consommation/2014/11/11/les-freres-dubernard-seront-honores-aujourdhui-a-meymac_11214725.html, Consulted 26 May 2020.

[33] 'Georges Pinson (France) v. United Mexican States', 19 October 1928, https://legal.un.org/riaa/cases/vol_V/327-466.pdf, Consulted 26 May 2020—While serving in Europe, in February 1915, Pinson's 'Establo Higénico' was occupied by Zapata's forces. Wishing to place machine-guns on the roof of a barn, his wife duly objected. Zapata's forces acquiesced and took milk and other foodstuffs, instead. The next day, the barn was taken by Carrancista troops who accused her of being Zapatista, on the pretext that the house was not looted. They ransacked the property and removed more goods, animals and furniture.

[34] ROLLAND Denis, 'Jacques Soustelle, De l'éthnologie à la politique', *Guerres mondiales et conflits contemporains*, N° 180 (October 1995), pp. 171–185, p. 171—"Born in 1912 to a family from the Cévennes, after studying in Lyon, then École normale supérieure de la rue d'Ulm à Paris (1929), Jacques Soustelle graduated in Ethnology (1930) and was a very young *agrégé* in Philosophy (1932).

[35] ROLLAND Denis, 'Jacques Soustelle, De l'éthnologie à la politique', *Guerres mondiales et conflits contemporains*, N° 180 (October 1995), pp. 171–185, p. 174.

the 'V' for victory, in blue upon a white background, with a superimposed red cross of Lorraine, according to Dubernard.[36] These cost five piastres for the pins and one piastre for the sticker, which was a very small sum. Presumably, the pricing was intended to allow them to be spread as widely as possible, thereby increasing the likelihood of greater numbers of people supporting, and joining, the movement. By 10th October 1940, the group held their first general assembly, which attracted around 300 people. Pinson was selected as President, and Dubernard was chosen as treasurer. He subsequently wrote that:

> The financial contribution to London from the Mexican Committee was particularly important. It was on 17th October 1940 that the first sending of funds was addressed to General de Gaulle. The total transfers rose to £41,500, $17,800. Within these amounts are not included those which were sent for spending on propaganda, sending over volunteers, etc...[37]

Throughout 1941, the importance of Free French propaganda was underlined, both in Mexico City and throughout the rest of the country. This can be seen above in Fig. 5.1, showing the general trend of growth in published articles. With increasing levels of propaganda being produced, awareness of the movement began to spread. While this came with a sizeable initial outlay of printing equipment of 25,000 to 30,000 pesos ($150,000 to $180,000 at 1939 rate,[38] £37,220 to £44,665[39]), in 1940, and a monthly cost of 2,000 pesos ($12,000 at 1939 rate, £2,997), a print run of 20,000 copies per month of the Spanish-language newspaper, *Gaceta de la Guerra*, became possible.[40] According to Crémieux-Brilhac,

[36] 'Le Comité de la France Libre du Mexique, par René Dubernard', *Revue de la France Libre*, n° 126, June 1960, 12 November 2009, http://www.france-libre.net/comite-fl-mexique/, Consulted 1 February 020.

[37] 'Le Comité de la France Libre du Mexique, par René Dubernard', *Revue de la France Libre*, n° 126, June 1960, 12 November 2009, http://www.france-libre.net/comite-fl-mexique/, Consulted 1 February 2020.

[38] The Mexican peso, in 1939, was worth U.S. $6. By 1942, the Mexican peso was worth $4.85.

[39] The U.S. dollar was exchanged at a fixed rate of £1 = $4.03.

[40] ROLLAND, *Vichy et la France Libre*, 1990, Chap. 6, para 146–147.

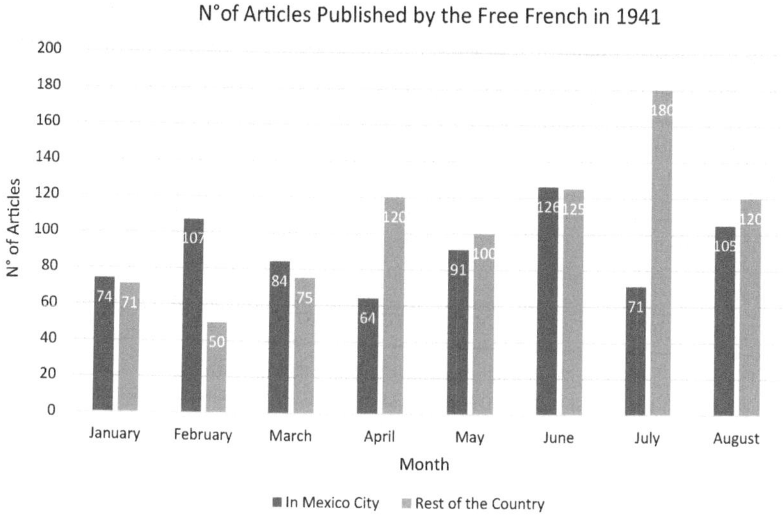


**Fig. 5.1** N° of articles published by the free French in 1941 (Adapted from ROLLAND, Vichy et la France Libre…, 1990, Ch. 6, Para. 115)

the Mexican delegation managed to achieve a circulation of 40,000 newspapers with the paper *France Libre*.[41]

In Fig. 5.1, we can see the increasing general trend in the numbers of articles written and published by the Free French delegation. When the size of the Francophone community is taken into consideration, a mere 6,000, the importance of translation and the publication of Hispanophone articles is underlined. It is highly likely that it was this decision that helped the Mexican delegation to become one of the most financially successful of all the delegations, as shown in the transfers recorded in London.

From the end of 1940, transfers began to be received, via John Lithiby, at the Bank of England. By March 1942, the delegation sent transfers of £8,000,[42] a significant sum, and equivalent to 156,960

[41] CRÉMIEUX-BRILHAC, *La France Libre*, 1996, p. 334—"The weekly, bilingual (newspaper) *France Libre* reached forty thousand examples".

[42] AN, AG 3 (1) 314 Comptes et Dons Pays Etrangers, *Telegram to Soustelle, Mexico*, 28 December 1942.

pesos. These funds, which were recorded in the summaries of the Free French accounts, were intended to help finance the movement's military spending. Instead, the money may have helped to pay for the production of propaganda articles that appeared in the aforementioned publications. Jules Romains, the president of *Pen Clubs* and a renowned author, had been invited to lecture at the *Universidad Nacional de México*, in 1942. While he did not join the Free French officially, Romains provided a number of pro-Allied articles, in exchange for payment.[43] Ten transfers were made to him between August 1942 to July 1943, which amounted to U.S. $1,400, and his pieces appeared in *Pour la Victoire* and *La Marseillaise*.[44]

Nevertheless, the sending of money was not facilitated by the imposition of governmental impediments. As has been noted, Soustelle was not simply responsible for the delegation in Mexico but was tasked with overseeing operations from various countries in Central America, including Puerto Rico, an unincorporated territory within the United States. Due to legislation designed to stymie the financing of foreign military powers, money raised in Puerto Rico had to be sent to a London-based welfare organisation, instead of directly to the Free French headquarters, at Carlton Gardens. Eventually, this additional step was circumvented, but it highlights the difficulties in fundraising for military efforts and, also, the long reach of the Roosevelt administration.

> The corresponding cheques have been sent to the Personal Service League, 41 Lowndes Square, in London, rather than the Headquarters since the laws governing this country only allow for capital exportation for charitable purposes, but the Committee wishes to specify that this does not, in any way, prevent General de Gaulle from using it in any way he so pleases.[45]

However, Soustelle's claims that the Mexican Free French delegation sent "twenty million"[46] to the Armament and Action funds seems

[43] ROLLAND, 'L'exil structure l'émigration…', p. 72.

[44] SAEF, B 0,062,836, *Transferts de fonds vers le Brésil, les Etats-Unis et le Mexique réalisés pour le journal « La Marseillaise» (1942–1943).*

[45] AN, AG 3 (1) 314 Comptes et Dons Pays Etrangers, *Telegram to the Free French Financial Service from Soustelle*, 5 July 1941.

[46] SOUSTELLE Jacques, *Envers et contre tout: De Londres à Algérie*, Paris, Robert Laffont, 1947, 470p., (Ebook), Chap. 2, Para. 27—"Considerable sums – more than

difficult to reconcile with the figures cited above. Firstly, Soustelle did not specify as to which given currency he was referring. Was it pesos, U.S. dollars, French francs or pound sterling? Using Rolland's figures, he affirms that the Mexican Free French delegation had sent £7,950 up to the date of 21st February 1942.[47] Once again, this does not tally with the money recorded in General de Gaulle's account books, in London, which recorded £14,955 as having been donated by the date that Rolland cites. Nonetheless, this figure is certainly far closer than anything approaching Soustelle's "twenty million" comment. In all likelihood, the money referred to, by Rolland, was the transfer of £8,000 that was recorded on 28th February 1942, in General de Gaulle's accounts.[48] However, this does suggest that Soustelle was prone to exaggeration in his book.

The approximate population of the Franco-Mexican community was 6,000 people. Through the year 1941, the number of members belonging to the Mexican delegation fluctuated, from around 1,500 in April 1941, up to 2,300 people, by December. This meant that over a quarter of the French community subscribed to the Free French delegation. However, this is far from the 99% whom Captain Lavergne, the special envoy of the *Comité national français* to Mexico, considered as being Free French supporters.[49] Nonetheless, it is still a healthy rate of subscription and thus helped to underline the delegation's legitimacy, in the eyes of the Mexican politicians. Moreover, using the December statistic, on a per capita basis, the £14,995 that had been sent, by February 1942, translated into around £6 10s 2d[50] being sent to London for every member.

It is impossible to know exactly what became of the Mexican money due to the still-experimental internal bookkeeping practices. Income

twenty million from the Mexican colony alone – went to fill the Armement and Action Fund, created by General de Gaulle...".

[47] ROLLAND Denis, *Vichy et la France Libre au Mexique*, 1990, Chap. 7, Para. 120 - "...the treasurer of the Central Committee paid, up to 21st February 1942, £7,950 to the bank account of General de Gaulle in Mexico, intended to support the London organisation...".

[48] AN, 3 AG 1 305, France Libre de Gaulle Comptes 1940–1943.

[49] ROLLAND Denis, *Vichy et la France Libre...*, 1990, Chap. 6, Para. 154.

[50] (14,995/2300) = £6 10 s 5d or £6.52.

was committed to a central fund, before being separated for different purposes. Undoubtedly, the money served to further the cause for which it was intended.

## Argentina

The French community in Argentina was among the largest in South America. However, significant migratory activity had occurred during the nineteenth century, when approximately 230,000 French had sailed for Argentina, with 28,000 settling in Buenos Aires.[51] As a city with 2.47 million inhabitants,[52] this represented a tiny proportion comprising barely one per cent of the entire population. In 1928, they numbered 82,000 people, but fell to 49,000 by 1942.[53] However, this French community was influential, with many belonging to the middle-classes and serving in professional posts, as architects, engineers, manufacturers and businesspeople. Moreover, it was in the cultural sphere where their impact appeared to have been most dominant, with Buenos Aires being regularly described as the 'Paris of the Southern Hemisphere' and contemporaries, including Clemenceau,[54] often commented on the city's architectural similarities with its French counterpart. The importance of the language of Molière, as Argentina's foreign language *par excellence*,[55] was underlined by the presence of Hachette, the publisher and one-time chain of bookshops, which had a large branch in Buenos Aires.[56] Moreover, despite French investments falling during the interwar years, from U.S. $450 million in 1914 to $165 million in 1938, France still remained

[51] DAUGHTON J. P., 'When Argentina Was "French": Rethinking Cultural Politics and European Imperialism in Belle-Époque Buenos Aires', *The Journal of Modern History*, 80 (December 2008), pp. 831–864, p. 844.

[52] SAS Louis Furman, 'The Spirit of France in Argentina', *The French Review*, Vol. 15, N° 6, May 1942, pp. 468–477, p. 470.

[53] RIPPY J. Fred, 'French Investments in Argentina and Brazil', *Political Science Quarterly*, Vol. 64, N° 4 (Dec. 1949), pp. 560–578, p. 561.

[54] DAUGHTON, 'When Argentina was "French"', p. 842—"Georges Clemenceau, touring in 1911, considered the Parque de Palermo to be the "Argentine Bois de Boulogne".

[55] SAS, 'The Spirit of France…', p. 476—"So far did this tendency go, so many Gallicisms were introduced into Argentine Spanish, that in 1900, the ridiculous theory was advanced that the language of Argentina no longer was Spanish but Argentinian".

[56] SAS, 'The Spirit of France…', p. 471.

an important source of foreign capital.[57] These long-established ties between the French community in Argentina and the *Hexagone* were renewed, notably with three in ten Franco-Argentines returning to fight for *la Patrie* during the First World War.[58] The dynamics that led Argentina to become the home of the leading delegation for pecuniary donations to the Free French movement are thus easier to understand. From November 1940 to February 1942, the community sent payments totalling £37,333 to the fund, as seen in Table 5.1.

The 'De Gaulle Committee' in Argentina was established in July 1940. Its President, Albert Guérin, ran the organisation from 192 Libertad, Buenos Aires.[59] He was born in Avignon, in 1893, before moving to Argentina, in 1911, to help with his father's perfume factory.[60] However, on the eve of the outbreak of the First World War, he returned to France. After having served in the military, Guérin headed both the Franco-Argentinian Chamber of Commerce and the Veteran's Association. This provided him with valuable leadership experience which later proved extremely useful in the task of leading the Free French delegation. As was seen with Adrien Tixier, the head of the U.S. delegation, Guérin's service suggests that those who led the delegations were often former *poilus*. Whether the personality and temperament of veterans meant that they were more willing to accept positions of responsibility, or whether they were simply preferred by the London-based Free French leadership over other possible choices is not clear. Nevertheless, accusations were rife that Guérin was unreceptive to the opinions of his collaborators and he was described as being "intoxicated by his success".[61] His politics were on the left, much like those of Tixier, which may have put Guérin at odds with members of the high society who surrounded him in Buenos

[57] RIPPY, 'French Investments…', p. 565.

[58] OTERO Hernán, 'Emigración, movilización militar y cultura de guerra. Los franceses de la Argentina durante la Gran Guerra', *Amnis*, 10 | 2011, https://journals.openedition.org/amnis/1137, Para. 25.

[59] AN, 3 AG (1) 305 France Libre de Gaulle Comptes 1940, *Comptes des Comités Nationaux de la France Libre—Amérique du Sud*.

[60] Biographical information on Albert Guérin, https://www.ordredelaliberation.fr/fr/compagnons/albert-guerin, Consulted 1 February 2020.

[61] PELOSI Hebe Carmen, 'Les Comités de la France Libre en Argentine et en Uruguay', in CORNIL-FRERROT Sylvain (Ed.), OULMONT Philippe (Ed.), *Les Français Libres et le Monde*, Paris, Éditions Nouveau Monde, 2015, 431p., pp. 125–151, p. 133.

Aires. Nonetheless, his diligence can be seen through the launching of a newsletter, *Pour la France libre*, in July 1940, which was available in both Spanish and French. These newsletters were printed in large quantities, beginning with an initial print run of 20,000.[62] Using his Argentinian business contacts, Guérin was able to organise activities which generated further subscriptions to the newsletter and adhesions to the Free French movement.

According to Pelosi, Guérin's delegation numbered around 3,500 to 4,000 people, which represented approximately 90% of the French community.[63] Inscriptions, in Argentina, were therefore double the number of people who joined the Mexican committee. However, Henri Pincemin, the head of Transradio,[64] suggested that the French community in Argentina was nearer to 50,000.[65] With the Argentinian delegation's subscription numbers being higher, it is understandable that their donations to London were much higher than those of Mexico, as can be seen in Table 5.1. For the historian Bruno Leroux, this was intentional as Albert Guérin sought to widen his delegation's activities far beyond Argentina's borders.[66] However, Leroux and Pelosi are not in agreement over the number of newsletters that were sent out, with Leroux stating that 25,000 copies of the first three editions were printed

62 Idem, p. 142.

63 Idem, p. 133.

64 NEWTON Ronald, 'The United States, the German-Argentines and the Myth of the Fourth Reich, 1943–47', *The Hispanic American Historical Review*, Vol. 64, N° 1 (February 1984), pp. 81–103—"Confusion was heightened by the activities of private concerns such as I. G. Farben and Transradio, which also gathered intelligence and provided cover for funds and agents being sent to the Western Hemisphere".

65 CORNIL-FRERROT Sylvain, 'Le Comité de la France Libre d'Argentine', Fondation de la France Libre, https://www.france-libre.net/comite-fl-argentine/, Consulted 21 May 2020—"I will take this opportunity to suggest that, if you happen to think that you are authorised to speak on behalf of the 50,000 French in Argentina, which, between you and I, constitutes a pure and surprising manifestation of totalitarian spirit, that you will remember, before letting yourself be carried away by the heat of your own feelings, that there are many good French people in Argentina who do not share your opinions and that it might be advisable to consult us beforehand".

66 LEROUX Bruno, 'Albert Guérin dans la France Libre' in CORNIL-FRERROT Sylvain (Ed.), OULMONT Philippe (Ed.), *Les Français Libres et le Monde*, Paris, Éditions Nouveau Monde, 2015, 431p., pp. 153–166, p. 153—"This communication will tackle the issue in another way by showing how the Committee's action has gone far beyond Argentina, at the instigation of its creator and president, Albert Guérin".

in French and 25,000 in Spanish.[67] Pelosi stated that the number was closer to 20,000.[68] Leroux argues that the reach of the newsletter grew rapidly, with 120,000 copies of the fifth edition being produced—of which 90,000 were in Spanish. Finally, a circulation of 150,000, for the seventh letter, showed that the newsletter's readership had outstripped the size of the delegation in Argentina. This confirms that Guérin had wide-ranging ambitions for the committee, especially within the wider Spanish-speaking community.

In September 1940, a telegram, signed by General de Gaulle and addressed to Guérin, requested that more subscription payments were necessary, in order to help the Free French organise war materials, such as planes, tanks and ordnance:

> In addition, (...) I indicate the essential need for the Free French Forces to receive funds quickly. Great Britain are providing advances; to be capable of intensifying our own action, we must have our own funds to be able to attend to our own needs. C. de Gaulle.[69]

The committee responded by sending £2,000 in September 1940,[70] but this does not feature in the general summary of donations.[71]

In March 1941, a further telegram thanked the delegation for having enabled the transport of numerous volunteers who had rallied to the Free French forces, from Argentina, despite the large fees involved. According to Belot, 400 volunteers joined from Argentina. This was more than double the number mobilised in 1939.[72] Unfortunately, he does not

[67] Idem, p. 154.

[68] PELOSI, 'Les Comités de la France Libre en Argentine et en Uruguay', 2015, p. 142.

[69] CORNIL-FRERROT Sylvain, 'Le Comité de la France Libre d'Argentine', https://www.france-libre.net/comite-fl-argentine/ Consulted 21 May 2020.

[70] AN, AG 3(1) 314, Comptes et Dons Pays Etrangères, *Letter to René Pleven, Commissaire national aux Finances, from Albert Guérin*, 3 December 1942.

[71] AN, 3 AG (1) 305 France Libre de Gaulle Comptes 1940, Comptes des Comités Nationaux de la France Libre—Amérique du Sud.

[72] BELOT, 'Les comités de la France Libre en Amérique latine pendant la guerre...', 2014, Para. 39, https://books.openedition.org/pur/42525?lang=en#bodyftn18, Consulted 22 May 2020,—"In Argentina, 400 volunteers were raised, more than double the number mobilized in 1939".

specify the years about which he is talking. This suggests that approximately 200 volunteers left the country at the outbreak of war. These troop movements cost the delegation $35,367.37, or £8,776.02.[73] However, the source also refers to a supplementary payment by the delegation of $34,000, or £8,436, in the *Voix de l'Argentine*, one of the country's French language newspapers.

> Around the same time (2nd March 1941), the Voice of Argentina said: Despite the heavy costs caused by the travel fees of numerous volunteers who left to join the Free French forces, which totalled $35,367.37, we have been able to send to General de Gaulle, since our last sending of funds, the sum of $34,000.[74]

Additionally, a member of the delegation's steering committee, Pierre Robertie, the president of the Mutual Aid Federation, sent a cheque of £1,000,[75] making a total of £9,436, when added to the amounts stated in the article. From November 1940 to March 1941, the totals that were recorded as having been received, or £4,500, fall well beneath £9,436. A cheque for £1,000 was, indeed, received in de Gaulle's bank account, which was sent on 12th February 1941, from Buenos Aires[76]; thereby corroborating the information in the article. According to the records, only two similar transfers of £1,000 had been received in November 1940, therefore, the amounts do not tally with the $34,000 (£8,436) that had been referred to in the *Voix de l'Argentine*. The funds received prior to March 1941, when the article was written, were significantly fewer than this amount, being closer to £3,550, according to the list made by the Free French Financial Service. Furthermore, looking at the entries directly, until 27th February 1941, in de Gaulle's account book, a total of £4,217 had been entered.[77] This suggests that payments were entered

[73] Extract of *Revue de la France Libre*, n° 126, June 1960 in 'Le Comité de la France Libre d'Argentine', https://www.france-libre.net/comite-fl-argentine/, Consulted 21 May 2020.

[74] Ibid.

[75] Ibid.—"Mr. Robertie, member of the Steering Committee, gave us a cheque of £1,000 sterling".

[76] AN, 3 AG 1 301, Livre renfermant des compte 1940–41.

[77] AN, 3 AG 1 301, Livre renfermant des compte 1940–41.

incorrectly onto the summary sheet. There are a number of possible explanations for this: either (i) *Voix de l'Argentine* were greatly overstating the amount that they had sent; (ii) they sent money before the Accounting systems were fully established; (iii) cheques had gone missing between Buenos Aires and London; or (iv) Carlton Gardens had intentionally chosen not to enter the extra transfers into their summaries.

Most peculiar, however, is a letter sent in December 1943 by Guérin to Mr. Gorse, a member of General de Gaulle's cabinet, in Algiers.[78] Guérin confirms two important details: firstly, that the accounts, on the Argentinian side, were verified by external auditors; Messrs. Santiago, Jacques Pradel and Charles Coin—the latter being a graduate of the École Commerciale, Paris—and all of whom were accountants in Buenos Aires. Secondly, Guérin goes on to explain that:

> It would be interesting to highlight that the Committee de Gaulle of Buenos Aires sent the cumulative sum of $1,116,553.85, from June 1940 to 31st December 1942. All the supporting documents, concerning the sending of funds to London and payments made to General de Gaulle's headquarters have been provided and duly verified as conforming, by the auditors – Messrs. Pradel and Coin of Buenos Aires.[79]

The $1.1 million dollars, when converted into British pounds at a rate of £1:$4.03, would have meant that the Argentinian delegation had sent £277,060 over the period. The Free French were merely showing 13% of the actual total amount that was sent by the Argentinian delegation in their summary.[80] There is no reason to doubt the veracity of Guérin's letter as it is internal correspondence, unlike the previous piece of journalism, written by *Voix de l'Argentine*.

In all probability, the donations' summaries, housed in the French National Archives, were tallied for the eyes of external auditors, rather than showing the actual income of the Free French movement. This would explain the great divergence between the two sets of figures. It

[78] AN, AG 3(1) 314, Comptes et Dons Pays Etrangères, *Letter to Gorse from Guérin*, 26 December 1943.

[79] Ibid.

[80] (37,333/277060.50)*100%.

also suggests that the Free French movement were in less dire financial difficulties than have been traditionally claimed by the participants within their memoirs, as well as historians who have hitherto accepted their affirmations on funding as being correct.

## Uruguay

The Uruguayan delegation, *Pro Francia Libre*, was founded from the amalgamation of two separate entities; a Ladies' group, founded on 31st July, and a Men's group, which was established on 2nd August 1940.[81] The Ladies' committee was formed by Mmes. Rouanet, Charrier, Cunha and Lansac and worked in tandem with the British Catholic group, the *St. Helen's Club*, which was organised by the wife of the British representative in Montevideo.[82] However, these groups acted as a meeting of friends, rather than properly defined 'committees'. The more formalised organisational undertaking occurred on 28th August, and was led by Dr. Maxime Halty, a Montevideo medical professor, who had been born to a Uruguayan mother and a French father. He was assisted by four vice-presidents, two of whom were French and two who were Uruguayan.[83] Concurrently, de Gaulle employed the services of the former secretary

[81] BELOT, 'Les comités de la France Libre en Amérique latine pendant la guerre…', 2014, Para. 21; BARBIER Colette, *Henri Hoppenot. Diplomate (25 octobre 1891–10 août 1977*, Paris, Comité d'Histoire Économique et Financière en France, 1999, 630p., p. 214—"The Franco-Uruguayan Committee for the Free French was the result of the fusion of two committees: Ladies' and Gentlemens', which were founded respectively on the 31st July and 2nd August 1940. The forming of this large committee can be traced to 28th August 1940".

[82] PELOSI, 'Les Comités de la France Libre en Argentine et en Uruguay', 2015, p. 127—The Uruguayan movement began with a Ladies' Committee, created by Mme. Rouanet and Charrier who told de Gaulle: "A women's group in the French community of Montevideo has established a Free French Committee to help the combatants and French refugees in Great Britain, in whichever way possible; this Ladies' Committee intends to merge with the Men's Free French Committee which was founded on 2nd August 1940"; BARBIER, *Henri Hoppenot*…, 1999, p. 215—"As for the French Ladies' Section, they originated in the small circle of French ladies who, from the month of July 1940, had coalesced around Mmes. Rouanet, Charrier, Cunha and Lansac, in order to provide clothes and collect donations in kind and cash for the Free French Forces".

[83] PELOSI, 'Les Comités de la France Libre en Argentine et en Uruguay', 2015, p. 133.

to the French legation, Albert Ledoux, who was also based in Montevideo. The Uruguayan supporters began to send money to London in September 1940, with the first transfer of £1,000 being made. These payments continued to be made throughout the period.

By the end of January 1941, the Uruguayan delegation had 300 members.[84] They had begun to arrange rallies aimed at levying funds, which took the form of cocktail parties. However, the Uruguayan economy was not as strong as that of its neighbours.[85] This explains why the transfers of funds, in Table 5.1, were lower than either Mexico or Argentina. One of its members, Madame Glucksmann, was commended for having organised a collection in May 1942.[86] Ledoux's wife, Geneviève, was also involved in the fundraising efforts and was personally thanked by Maurice Dejean, the commissioner for the French National Committee.[87] The funds were said to be sent to the 'Action Fund' and flown into France to support the military activities of the resistance. Both of these telegrams highlight the important roles that women played in rallying support among the French expatriate communities in their host nations and in the acquisition of funds for the continued efforts of the Free French in London. Nevertheless, by 1942, Dr. Halty and his team were forced to relinquish their positions, in large part due to the increasingly autocratic manner in which they were running the organisations.[88] However, exactly what is meant by 'autocratic' is not elaborated upon by Pelosi.

[84] AN, AG 3(1) 314, *Telegram sent from Free French Committee, Montevideo*, 29 January 1941.

[85] PELOSI, 'Les Comités de la France Libre en Argentine et en Uruguay', 2015, p. 149.

[86] AN, AG 3(1) 314, *Telegram from Ladies' Committee Montevideo to Financial Service, London*, 9 May 1942.

[87] AN, AG 3(1) 314, *Telegram from Maurice Dejean to Free French Committee, Montevideo*, 26 August 1942.

[88] PELOSI, 'Les Comités de la France Libre en Argentine et en Uruguay', 2015, p. 136—"Meanwhile, in Montevideo, Halty, the president of the committee, took his leave, while the secretaries and the treasurer resigned. The board appointed Mauricio Demoulin as his replacement. The majority of the Montevideo committee members were unhappy with the authoritarian manner in which Halty and three of the founders attempted to run its activities".

According to an article published in the *Revue de la France Libre*, the committee sent $42,500 from 1940 to 1944.[89] At a rate of exchange of $4.03 to the pound, this would have been the equivalent of £10,545. However, in the summary of delegation's accounts, during the period from October 1940 to February 1942, the Uruguayan committee had only sent £7,764. Nevertheless, this final figure only covers the period up to February 1942, whereas the article's chronology stretches until 1944 so it is very possible that extra funds were sent after the final entry in the summary.

Indeed, when scrutinising the donations in the Free French accounts, the transfers were paid into the 'Général de Gaulle' and the 'N.P.B.' accounts. From the first transfer, dated 14th October 1940, until the final recorded entry concerning Uruguay, on 9th July 1943, a total of £29,613 was entered into the accounts, in fourteen separate transactions. This is considerably more than the £7,764 that was recorded in the summary.

As with the Argentinian delegation, it is highly possible that the shortfall was a method of intentional accounting obfuscation. Arguably, this was intended to lead external auditors into believing that the movement had less money than was indeed the case. This assumes that anybody wanting to verify the figures would naturally choose to look at the summaries rather than referring to the original ledgers. Nonetheless, the payments continued unabated after 1942.

## Chile

The French population in Chile was smaller than those that have previously been discussed. Compared to Argentina, the 9,800 people of French origin, who appeared on the Chilean census of 1907, were significantly fewer in number.[90] In fact, the population spread was more commensurate to that of Mexico. Those who had left to fight in the First World War numbered around 800 or 900, which translates as being between eight and nine per cent of the community.[91] In a foreshadowing of the

[89] 'Le Comité de la France Libre en Uruguay', *Revue de la France Libre*, n° 126, June 1960, http://www.france-libre.net/comite-fl-uruguay/, Consulted 22 May 2020.

[90] CARRELLÁN RUIZ Juan Luis, DE LA LLOSA Alvar, 'L'Appel de la Patrie: Les Réservistes et les Volontaires Français du Chili pendant la Première Guerre mondiale', *Guerres mondiales et conflits contemporains*, PUF, 2018/2 N° 270, pp. 7–23, p. 14.

[91] Idem, p. 21.

Second World War, the Franco-Chilean community rallied around to raise funds for the families of those who had left to participate in the various theatres of the Great War. These included the committee 'Pro-Francia', at Concepción, who raised 25,000 pesos, or around US $68,250 at 1913 rates[92] where 1 peso was the equivalent of 2.73 dollars. Generally, their supporters were business owners, such as *Maison Etcheverry* and *Duhart frères*, who imported household products from France, including sheets, wine and wallpaper.[93] According to Fernández-Domingo, by the end of the nineteenth century, 40% of Santiago's retail sector was under French ownership.[94] However, as the new century progressed, French products' desirability was on the wane, as demonstrated by steadily declining membership of the Franco-Chilean Chamber of Commerce.[95] In 1907, it had 132 members but, by 1916, this had dropped to 110, before declining further to just 81 members in 1930. This was undoubtedly linked to the decline in trade precipitated by the outbreak of the First World War, but also attests to wider trends in world migration, with fewer migrants leaving the old continent for the new. Between 1851 and 1915, 41 million Europeans moved to South America. However, towards the end of this period, between 1905 and 1914, this had fallen to as little as 1.5 million. Between 1920 and 1929, only half a million migrants left Europe[96]! The 'Age of Mass Migration' was abruptly ending, partially as a result of worldwide conflict, but also through the growing burden that visa legislation placed upon emigrants.

[92] Monthly Summary of Commerce & Finance of the United States for the Fiscal Year 1913, Financial Tables, November 1912, Value of Foreign Coins, January 1, 1912 and 1913, p. 606—https://books.google.fr/books?id=UXT8ePT3-wMC&pg=PA606&lpg=PA606&dq=exchange+rate+chilean+peso+to+dollar+1913&source=bl&ots=sGl7hy7lDR&sig=ACfU3U1H_YJGhlX_D3bSW82RGeUBNJUPNQ&hl=en&sa=X&ved=2ahUKEwiy5tmylIfqAhUFExoKHajPDe8Q6AEwCXoECAwQAQ#v=onepage&q=exchange%20rate%20chilean%20peso%20to%20dollar%201913&f=false—$1:0.365 pesos, Consulted 22 May 2020.

[93] FERNÁNDEZ-DOMINGO Enrique, *Le Négoce français au Chili—1880–1929*, Rennes, Presses universitaires de Rennes, 2006, 379 p., Chap. 6, Para. 69—https://books.openedition.org/pur/25240, Consulted 22 May 2020.

[94] Idem, Chap. 6, Para. 50.

[95] Idem, Chap. 6, Paras. 94, 99 and 100.

[96] CITROEN H. A., 'European Emigration in the Inter-War Period', *European Emigration Overseas Past and Future*, Publications of the Research Group for European Migration Problems, vol 2., Dordrecht, Springer, 1951, pp. 17–20, p. 17.

However, numbers of those, in Chile, who identified as being French or Francophile did not fall as drastically. By November 1943, *La Liga Chilena pro Francia Libre* had attracted 2,151 adherents and 3,812 supporters.[97] Belot states that:

> The sums of money collected were not insignificant: Chile sent $900,000.[98]

Once again, this amount, cited by Belot, does not correspond to the money that was entered into the Free French summary, or £6,311 from 1940 to 1942. During 1941 and 1942, £12,122 was entered into General de Gaulle's accounts, yet when we compare that to the $900,000, or £223,325, drawn from Belot's work, the amounts entered in the account are eighteen times smaller. Regrettably, however, Belot has not cited the source of this figure.

Despite her name not appearing on a list of Chilean volunteers, Margot Duhalde was the only female pilot to be 'accepted' by the Free French, although she would not fly for France until after the war ended. Duhalde was born on 12th December 1920, in Rio Bueno, to parents from the Basque country. She was the second of twelve children born to a conservative farmer and his wife who had emigrated from France to southern Chile.[99] A passionate aviator from a young age, Duhalde trained for her pilot's licence at 16 and gained her qualification at 18. Upon hearing of de Gaulle's Call of 18th June, she resolved to join the movement and headed to the French consulate in Santiago. She arrived in Liverpool in April 1941 and attempted to sign up with the Free French Air Force. However, she was rejected as a pilot on the grounds of her gender and was, therefore, assigned more menial tasks.[100] The British Air Transport Auxiliary (A.T.A.) were not in a position to refuse a qualified pilot

[97] BELOT Robert, 'Les comités de la France Libre en Amérique latine pendant la guerre…', 2014, Para. 33.

[98] Idem, Para. 49.

[99] CHILDS Martin, 'Obituary: Margot Duhalde, Chile's first female pilot who came to Europe to help Allies fight Axis forces', *The Scotsman*, 22 March 2018, https://www.scotsman.com/news/obituary-margot-duhalde-chiles-first-female-pilot-who-came-europe-help-allies-fight-axis-forces-316718, Consulted 23 May 2020.

[100] 'Margot Duhalde, wartime ATA pilot – obituary' *The Telegraph*, 16 February 2018, https://www.telegraph.co.uk/obituaries/2018/02/16/margot-duhalde-wartime-ata-pilot-obituary/, Consulted 23 May 2020.

and, on hearing that they were accepting women and foreigners, Duhalde approached the A.T.A. and was accepted into the pool of female pilots, at Hamble, rising to the rank of First Officer, despite her limited English. Upon entering the Chilean delegation, new volunteers were paid a bonus of £3 yet, according to the *Telegraph*'s obituary, Margot did not receive hers until 5th September 1941, four days after she had joined the A.T.A. In her new role, Duhalde flew both new and repaired planes; ferrying them to wherever the Royal Air Force's Bomber or Fighter Command decided that they were most needed. By the end of the war, she had flown over 1,500 aircraft, including bombers, fighters and transport aircraft.[101]

Although Margot had had to abandon her initial plan of being in the Free French Airforce, she did not neglect to send money back home, and £5 per month were sent to her family, via the Chilean delegation. This was a task in which the Free French foreign committees participated, with transactions being noted for the months of April through to October 1942.[102] They continued into 1943, albeit more sporadically. This shows an important aspect of the Free French financial services, which allowing links to be retained with one's country of origins and with one's family.

The transfer of money, to and from London, was mirrored by funds that were sent to other French mandated territories, including Syria and Lebanon.[103] An ingenious, but ancient, system was adapted by the Chilean delegation, as a means of acquiring the support of the two communities. *Hawala* was a means of informally transferring funds from one country to another. It relied upon trust within the community. The sender takes their funds to the exchange broker who provides them with a password to be used by the other client. The broker contacts their agent, who releases the funds, minus commission, to the recipient, upon being given the agreed code. The debt is therefore incurred by the broker, who will need to settle with their fellow agent at a later point.

[101] 'Disparition du Margot Duhalde, symbole des Forces françaises libres', Délégation à l'Information et à la communication de la Défense (DICoD), 14 February 2018, https://www.defense.gouv.fr/actualites/international/disparition-de-margot-duhalde-symbole-des-forces-francaises-libres, Consulted 23 May 2020.

[102] AN, AG 3(1) 314, Relevé du Compte Avances Remboursables du Comité de la France Libre au Chili du 1er janvier 1942 au 31 octobre 1942—April 30, "To be given to the family of Mlle. Margot DUHALDE, *aviatrice*".

[103] AN, 3 AG 1 314, *Transferts Syro-Libanais Letter from A. Piraud to A. Ledoux*, 21 November 1941.

In the case of the Chilean committee, this involved the Santiago branch receiving the deposits of those who wanted to transfer funds to Syria and Lebanon. While the Lebanese and Syrian communities in South America have been the subject of academic studies for countries including Peru,[104] Argentina[105] or Ecuador,[106] there are fewer sources on their presence in Chile. According to a text produced by the *Biblioteca Nacional de Chile*, at the end of the nineteenth century, the majority of the 8,000 to 10,000 Arabs in Chile were from Palestine, or 50% of their total, with 30% coming from Syria and the remaining 20% coming from Lebanon.[107] These figures would translate into about 2,400 to 3,000 Syrian people and 1,600 to 2,000 Lebanese living in Chile, depending on whether the higher or lower end of the range is taken. Another document offers further insights into the community by suggesting that, in 1930, 6,703 people from the Middle East had migrated to Chile.[108] Mattar's *Guía Social de la Colonia Árabe*, published in 1941, found that 2,994 Arab families were in Chile; a figure that would correspond to about 15,000 people.[109] These families were composed in a very similar manner to

[104] CUCHE Denys, 'L'immigration libanaise au Pérou: Une immigration ignorée', *Journal de la société des américainistes*, N° 83, 1997, pp. 173–199, https://www.persee.fr/doc/jsa_0037-9174_1997_num_83_1_1676, Consulted 23 May 2020.

[105] COUTINHO Priscilla, *Lavoura Arcaica: Un Romain de la diaspora libanaise au Brésil*, Doctoral Thesis in Literature, Université Sorbonne Paris Cité, Universidade de São Paulo, defended on 16 January 2018, 250p. https://tel.archives-ouvertes.fr/tel-02147419/document, Consulted 23 May 2020; NANCY Michel (Ed.), PICARD Élisabeth (Ed.), *Les Arabes du Levant en Argentine*, Aix-en-Provence, Institut de recherches et d'études sur les mondes arabes et musulmans, 2014, 144p., https://books.openedition.org/iremam/2943, Consulted 23 May 2020.

[106] ALMEIDA Mónica, 'Los Sirio-Libaneses en el espacio social ecuatoriano: cohesión étnica y asimilación cultural', *Journal de la société des américainistes*, N° 83, 1997, pp. 201–227, https://www.persee.fr/doc/jsa_0037-9174_1997_num_83_1_1676, Consulted 23 May 2020.

[107] 'La inmigración árabe a Chile (1885–1950)' Memoria Chilena—Biblioteca Nacional de Chile, http://www.memoriachilena.gob.cl/602/w3-article-3523.html#presentacion, Consulted 23 May 2020.

[108] CORBINOS Lorenzo Agar, 'Árabes y Judíos en Chile: Apuntes Sobre La Inmigración y la Integración Social' in KLICH Ignacio (Ed.) *Árabes y judíos en América Latina. Historia, representaciones y desafíos*, Buenos Aires, Siglo XXI Editoria Iberoamericana, 2006, 21p., p. 9, http://www.iea.usp.br/publicacoes/textos/arabesyjudiosenchile.pdf, Consulted 23 May 2020.

[109] Ibid.

their predecessors; 51% were Palestinians, 30% were Syrians and 19% were Lebanese. Of the Syrians, virtually half came from the city of Homs.[110] These migrants showed a predilection towards itinerant selling, which entailed moving around the countryside and trading their wares, but, in 1941, 41% of the Middle Eastern community settled in Santiago. Clearly, some kept links with their places of origin, and their commercial activities enabled them to send money back to Syria and Lebanon. As these two countries fell under French mandate, it is understandable why they would undertake money transfers via the Free French delegation in Chile. The order was given to the French National Committee, in London, who would perform the transfer to the recipient via the intermediary of a Syrian bank, either in local currency or in another type of currency. The British embassy insisted that the operation should pass through them and thus they were the ones to transfer the funds to the Free French Financial Service.[111] This system invariably made use of modern telecommunications technology, in facilitating the passing of orders between one continent and the next. Ultimately, it also demonstrates the importance of relational interactions as a means of facilitating funding. However, as money is little more than a means of resource transfer, it stands to reason that allies should facilitate such actions in a time of conflict on behalf of their partners.

It has been made clear that the South American delegations who supported the Free French were financial contributors to the external resistance's early funding. While the delegations had varying degrees of wealth in their bank accounts, their financial success depended upon the political climate in which they were established, the competence of their own leadership and the sentiments of the expatriate-migrant communities on whom they relied. Unsurprisingly, it seems that the larger that this community was, the more funds that the delegations were able to acquire. According to Belot,[112] South America had an estimated French

[110] Ibid.

[111] AN, AG 3(1) 314, Transferts Syro-Libanais—V—Lettre 3L.

[112] BELOT Robert, 'Les comités de la France Libre en Amérique latine pendant la guerre...', 2014, Para. 32.

population of 274,220 so the thousands who rallied to the Free French delegations remained in a minority, nonetheless.

The important role played by the organisers of the Free French committees has been highlighted, most notably by Dr. Halty and Ledoux, in Uruguay, and Jacques Soustelle, in Mexico. The funds upon which the Gaullist movement came to rely could not have been collected without the efforts of these men and women who formed the bedrock of the delegations' support. Many of these groups were drawn to a nucleus of those who had previously fought for France, during the First World War, such as Dubernard, in Mexico, or Guérin, in Argentina. Their experiences in the trenches of Europe had a lasting impact and the resurgence of the old enemy, Germany, appears to have galvanised some of these *poilus* towards charitable actions. The financing of the delegations, during the Second World War, underlines the strong attachment that many formed to the land of their birth, or that of their parents.

It has also been shown that this funding was not entered into the account books accurately. The discrepancies between the funds that were discussed in letters and articles and those amounts which were entered in the summaries are significant. In short, the Free French had access to far more money than they claimed or insisted upon, afterwards, in their memoirs. Such claims formed an integral part of the creation of a propaganda legend around the Free French. It suggests that the Free French were the sole Gallic resistance to Vichy collaboration and Nazism; they who emerged from nothing to liberate the French from the German invaders and from traitors within.[113] It is extremely unlikely that their message would have been accorded the same level of support from their compatriots if it had been known that they were being bankrolled by the British or, in this case, French expatriates and migrants in South America.

While some volunteers, like Margot Duhalde, travelled overseas to assist in the continuation of the combat; others, including Jacques Soustelle, helped to organise the levying of funds that would support

[113] DE GAULLE Charles, *Mémoires de guerre*, Paris, Plon, 1989, 886p., p. 78—'As for me, who was trying to climb such a slope, at the start, I was nothing. At my side, not a hint of a force, nor an organisation. In France, no one who answered and no reputation. Abroad, neither credit nor justification'.

the troops. Moreover, through the adaptation of ancient financial techniques, monetary links to other parts of the colonial empire were upheld. The Free French were not only African, as Jennings argued[114]; financially speaking, they were South American, too.

114 JENNINGS Eric, *La France libre fut africaine*, Paris, Perrin, 2014, 350p.

CHAPTER 6

# Colonial Contributions to French Freedom

The final months of 1941 were moments of great change on both the military and economic front for French external resistance. The United States declared war of Japan on 8th December 1941, thus increasing the danger of attack on the Free French Pacific territories, and, on 2nd December, the Free French movement promulgated Ordonnance N° 21 which created the *Caisse centrale de la France libre*.[1] While the former remains one of the seminal moments in the history of the Second World War, the latter is all but forgotten. However, the *Caisse centrale de la France libre* has a history that continues to this day, having become the *Agence Française de Développement*. Its creation reflected the moment of the Gaullist movement's economic coming of age. Previously, the Free French had fallen entirely under the financial influence of the British government. With the introduction of the *Caisse centrale*, a veneer of monetary sovereignty was regained through the support of the colonial territories which rallied to de Gaulle's side. Furthermore, the *Caisse centrale* afforded a measure of independence to the movement and the colonies, as the British ministries, which had hitherto provided material support to the movement, could now be paid from a French-operated institution.

[1] *Journal Officiel de la France Libre*, 30 December 1941, https://gallica.bnf.fr/ark:/12148/bpt6k9616635p/f1.image, Consulted 27 May 2021.



D. Foulk, *The Price of Freedom*,
https://doi.org/10.1007/978-3-031-09066-0_6

Nevertheless, much of this was smoke and mirrors, in large part due to the British capital base which continued to back the *Caisse centrale*'s printing activities. Moreover, the inhabitants of the rallied French colonies saw the collapse of metropolitan military forces, in 1940, and yet it was they who were being subjected to ever-increasing demands for natural resources. This led to a certain amount of Germanophilia among certain inhabitants of the African colonies, as indicated by Memoli-Aubry: "This is the case, for example, of Amougou Dominique, a transporter from Yaoundé who was living in Bafia, who said: 'The French rob. On the contrary, the Germans enrich the blacks and teach them how to make money'".[2] Dominique's critiques are confirmed by a report written on the economic situation in French Equatorial Africa by 'Pelabon'.[3] The author was presumably André Pelabon, the head of the Algerian branch of the newly created *Direction Générale des services spéciaux* (D.G.S.S.). The document made scathing criticisms of both the administrative and personnel management of the rallied colony: the indigenous workers were "too often treated as a beast of burden: wages extremely low, starvation rations, excessive work".[4] Pelabon qualified exactly what he meant by citing the example of a particular administrator with whom "the price of the day…is reduced to nothing, sometimes to less than nothing" as the administrator "(took) back from (the workers) by way of tax or tithe the few cents which (they were) able to earn and, if (they) could not pay, he put (them) back to work".[5]

The Free French movement sought to bring about two outcomes: firstly, helping to liberate metropolitan France and, secondly, continuing to oppose Germany and her Axis allies. Their *raison d'être* had never been intended as that of a government-in-exile but, rather, as a military force. However, at the end of 1941, they controlled tiny islands and mandated territories in the Pacific, the Atlantic and in the heart of Africa. This rendered communication and military collaboration convoluted and

[2] MEMOLI-AUBRY Crécence, 'Le Mbam dans la Seconde Guerre Mondiale: contribution d'une région administrative du Cameroun à l'effort de guerre français', *Outre-mers*, Vol, 96, N° 362–363, 1er quarter 2009, L'Atlantique Français, pp. 241–266, p. 242.

[3] ANOM, 1AFF-POL 873, Affaires Politiques, Carton 873, Dossier 12 – Affaires économiques 1943–1944, *Rapport M. Pelabon sur l'Économie de l'A.É.F.*, 1 November 1943.

[4] Idem, p. 2.

[5] Ibid.

seriously hampered efforts to run a centralised system of government, while also leaving Free French representatives in the rallied territories with a great degree of autonomy. Such a style of management proved successful in providing resources to the Allied war effort but failed some of those whom it governed, as seen in Pelabon's report. By comparing the economic contributions afforded by and to certain colonial territories, a clearer picture of how, and what, contributions were provided by those rallied French colonies and territories towards internal resistance in France can be seen.

Syria and Lebanon, collectively known as the Levant, were two countries that had previously fallen under Ottoman rule. They were subsequently mandated to France by the League of Nations, in 1923. While heavily reliant upon French economic support, notably to produce enough wheat to feed the population, the strategic importance of the territories rendered them vital to the war effort.[6]

French Equatorial Africa and Cameroon proved more prepared to accept Free French rule. Through the example shown by Félix Éboué—the first black, high-ranking, official in the French colonial administration—Chad, Cameroon, Congo and Ubangi-Chari rallied to the Free French, in August 1940.[7] Gabon was later conquered, in November 1940.[8] These territories brought both significant manpower to the Free French Forces and prized natural resources, such as rubber, gold and palm oil. However, it proved difficult to simultaneously provide troops and continue with industrial and consumer production activity.

In the Pacific Ocean, the island of New Caledonia was not heavily populated but held strategic value in the region and had plentiful access to natural resources, such as nickel which was used in the manufacturing of alloyed nickel-steel plates, the production of armour plates and which had the capability of withstanding "the corrosive effects of salt

[6] BARR James, *A Line in the Sand: Britain, France and the Struggle for the Mastery of the Middle East*, London, Simon & Schuster UK, 2011, 350p. (Ebook), Chap. 18, Para. 12.

[7] CAPDEPUY Arlette, *Félix Éboué, 1884–1944: mythe et réalités coloniales*, Doctoral Thesis, Université Michel de Montaigne—Bordeaux III, 2013, 509p., p. 114—"His rallying to the Free French had important local repercussions due to the moral authority that he held with his colleagues and the local population".

[8] THOMAS Martin, *The French Empire at War 1940–1945*, Manchester, Manchester University Press, 1998, 298p., p. 75.

water".[9] However, the arrival of American forces, in March 1942, led to a weakening of the traditional economic system in the colony—one best evidenced by negligible wages and indentured labour. When the New Caledonian miners realised that they could provide services to the American troops stationed on the island, by selling imported consumables or launderette services, many abandoned their usual work, in favour of the new opportunities which had just presented themselves.[10]

This chapter highlights the role played by the extraction of raw materials, the difficulties in communication over vast, inhospitable country and the diversity of products that were traded in wartime. The continuing economic support that was offered to the Free French, by the Allied powers, was vital for financial and monetary stability in the rallied colonies. The compulsory buying of entire yields by the British government; the provision of Lend-Lease aid to the Free French colonies; the American forces requisitioning large swathes of New Caledonia, all demonstrate the economic weakness of the Free French empire and its reliance upon the assistance of the Allied powers. Moreover, similarly to the expatriated French in neutral and Allied countries, a successful campaign, which raised hundreds of millions of francs in the final few months of 1943, was launched. This was directly aimed at supporting those opposing the Germans in France. Funding French resistance was a truly global undertaking.

## The Levantine Crossroad

Syria and Lebanon, and their coastlines, "occup(ied) an important position in the Eastern Mediterranean" where, according to a contemporary source, "they command(ed) ancient and important trade routes east and west between the Levant and the Middle East, and north and south

[9] SUDOL Stan, 'Nickel Closest Thing to a True 'War Metal', *Republic of Mining*, 13 February 2009, https://republicofmining.com/2009/02/13/nickel-closest-thing-to-a-true-%E2%80%98war-metal%E2%80%99-by-stan-sudol/, Consulted 31 July 2020.

[10] MUNHOLLAND, *Rock of Contention*..., 2005, p. 131—"The Americans hired labour to work in these establishments, and they also employed native Melanesians and Asians to assist them with the unloading of equipment and supplies. These employees received generous salaries by local standards, much to the dismay of certain Caledonian business leaders who now faced competition for labour services".

between Anatolia and Egypt".[11] Rail and freight ports served to distribute Iraqi petrol that was destined to be sent to Western Europe and further afield. Their other main exports included wool, olive oil and raw cotton, while the two countries imported goods like coal and rice. Regional transportation was facilitated by a railway line that passed through Hama and Homs, running from Aleppo to Damascus. Beirut and Tripoli, in the north and centre of Lebanon, were also linked to this trainline. The Baghdad Petroleum Company, operating in British-mandated Iraq, was directly connected to the north of Syria. While this connection would eventually fall foul of Turkey's decision to remain neutral, the two countries' connectedness demonstrated their geostrategic importance.

Syria and Lebanon had a combined surface area of 200,000km$^2$. In July 1939, this sizeable territory was under the control of just 686 officers, 16,640 non-commissioned officers (N.C.Os) and combat troops. Furthermore, 312 officers and 1,319 N.C.Os and troops served on bases or were used as service personnel. In addition to these regular troops, there were 455 officer-reservists and 2,090 reserve troops. Furthermore, 311 officers and 16,000 N.C.Os and troops, belonging to Lebanese and Syrian auxiliary forces, were serving with the occupying forces.[12] As the Free French movement controlled a total population of 6.25 million inhabitants,[13] of whom three million lived in Syria, it would have been difficult for only 37,813 armed forces personnel to control a population of this size. Effectively, there would have been 12.6 members of the armed forces for every 1,000 Syrian inhabitants, but clearly not all of these could be devoted to policing civilians.[14]

The cultural impression that France attempted to imprint upon its colonies was fully implemented in the Levant. According to Ouahes,

[11] M.B. & H.G.L., 'Syria & Lebanon: The States of the Levant under French Mandate', *Bulletin of International News*, July 13th 1940, Vol. 17, N°14, pp. 841–851, p. 841.

[12] ALBORD Maurice, *L'Armée Française & les États du Levant 1936–1946*, Paris, CNRS Éditions, 2000, 336p., Chapter. A, Para. 7 (Ebook).

[13] Middle East Centre Archives, St. Antony's College, Oxford, GB165-0269 Sir Edward Spears BOX 2 Files 5–7, Information Booklet 'The Free French Movement', p. 9, Para. 37,

[14] ((37,813/3000000)*1000); As a comparison, using 2017 data, average numbers of police officers in member-states of the European Union are 3.2 per thousand inhabitants. 'Police, court and prison personnel statistics', Eurostat, July 2018, https://ec.europa.eu/eurostat/statistics-explained/index.php/Police,_court_and_prison_personnel_statistics, Consulted 31 July 2020.

the encouragement of Francophilia via education, and the press and control of patrimonial heritage were fundamental vectors of control in the mandated countries.[15] However, the use of such methods only succeeded in recruiting new adherents to the local nationalists' cause. Furthermore, linking Syrian and Lebanese pounds to the French franc was becoming untenable, due to the arbitrary weakening of the Vichy franc. Inflation was exacerbated by the wheat producers' hoarding their grain and the actions of speculators.[16] Both contributed to the increasing of prices, as grain was removed from the market and, thus, the price of wheat became artificially inflated. This information came from the Spears Mission, which was led by Major-General Edward Spears, a close friend of Churchill and de Gaulle's guide within the British administration. In July 1941, "Spears became head of the British Mission (to Syria and Lebanon) and, in February 1942, he became the first British Minister to the two republics"[17] as well as continuing to serve on his mission to the Free French. While Spears would later fall out with de Gaulle, his published work confirms the archival evidence concerning the difficulties surrounding the production of wheat.

Nearly two months after Operation Exporter had finished, on 12th September 1941, Syria and Lebanon were welcomed into the Sterling Area by an exchange of letters between de Gaulle and Churchill. In an extension to the financial agreements that had been signed on 19th March, the two countries' currencies were pegged to pound sterling, at a fixed exchange rate of 176.625 colonial francs to the pound.[18] This was a renewal of the Franco-British Monetary Agreement that had been signed on 4th December 1939.[19] The only noticeable difference between the

[15] OUAHES Idir, *Syria and Lebanon Under the French Mandate: Cultural Imperialism and the Workings of Empire*, London, I.B. Tauris, 2018, 320p.

[16] SPEARS Edward, *Fulfilment of a Mission: The Spears Mission to Syria and Lebanon, 1941–1944*, London, Leo Cooper, 1977, 311p., p. 173.

[17] SPEARS, *Fulfilment of a Mission*, 1977, Introduction—VIII.

[18] Middle East Archive Centre, St. Antony's College, (N1) GB165-0269 Sir Edward Spears BOX 2 Files 5–7, '*The Free French Movement*', The Foreign Office, December 1941.

[19] A.J.B., 'The Sterling Area', *Bulletin of International News*, Vol. 21, N° 24, November 1944, pp. 1000–1005, p. 1003; MIKESELL Raymond F., 'Sterling Area Currencies of the Middle East', *Middle East Journal*, Vol. 2, N° 2 (April, 1948), pp. 160–174, p. 164—"Before World War II the sterling area consisted of a loose association of countries which had close economic ties with Britain, maintained a fixed exchange rate

two agreements was the lack of a stipulation to keep the *Caisse*'s reserve in London. Syria joined Egypt, Sudan, the Faroe Islands and the other Free French and Belgian colonies within the sterling area, where "payments were, at least partly, free from restriction".[20] Despite the loss of monetary sovereignty that such action entailed, the Free French were able to organise payments to London in a far more effective manner. Furthermore, most members of the sterling bloc left their sterling balances in London, thereby helping to keep much-needed liquidity running through the London financial system.[21] By joining, it became much easier for Syria and Lebanon to effect transactions with other countries in the bloc, including with their immediate neighbours, Palestine and Iraq. This was part of a wider scheme to coordinate the industrial and productive efforts of the Allies. By founding the *Caisse centrale de la France libre*, there was a move towards the full mobilisation of Free French resources, as a means both to centralise payments to the British government and to enlarge the sterling bloc, so as to include rallied French colonial territories.

However, this did little to counteract the Nazi and Vichy propaganda smears that the Gaullists were 'paid up' and in hock to the enlarged British empire.[22] If anything, it may have been one of the kernels of truth in the Axis propaganda. In March 1942, MI5 was cognisant of claims being levelled against the *Caisse centrale*, including that it was organised in such a manner as to facilitate the manipulation of the French colonies and mandated territories by elements within the City of London.[23] Politically and temperamentally, Churchill and de Gaulle had an oscillating relationship.[24] From an economic perspective, the administrative collaboration

between their currencies and the pound, and tended to keep all or a large part of their foreign exchange reserves in London".

[20] A.J.B., 'The Sterling Area', 1944, p. 1004.

[21] Ibid.—"Far the most important aspect of the Sterling Area since 1939 has been, however, the way in which the member countries have been content to pile up balances in the United Kingdom in return for goods and services supplied to her".

[22] "Sir, Madam, With that 'de Gaulle', there, you will catch nothing"—Propaganda image, edited by the *Ligue Française Antibritannique*, 1940, BnF Gallica, https://gallica.bnf.fr/ark:/12148/btv1b9013935t/f1.item, Consulted 12 June 2021.

[23] BoE, OV45 129, *Letter to J. Lithiby from Trade Control and Investigations Office*, 13 March 1942.

[24] Contrast the relationship as shown in TNA, CAB 66 39 41, Relations with General de Gaulle, *An Outline of Relations between His Majesty's Government and General de Gaulle between June 1940 and June 1943*, 7 August 1943, p. 1—"During this period

forged between the British and the Free French helped to ease the severance of ties between the Free French and Vichy France. However, this also left them open to monetary coercion by the British government, as a War Cabinet report states:

> During the protracted negotiations between de Gaulle and Giraud, which occupied March, April and May (1943), our relations with de Gaulle were again disturbed by the persistence of Free French propaganda against the French leaders in North and West Africa and against the policy of the United States. This caused protests to us from the United States Government, and it was difficult to convince the Americans that we were really unable to stop it, since de Gaulle remained dependent on us financially.[25]

Furthermore, it helped to impose an Allied monetary union within the French colonies and mandated territories.[26] The inherent danger of keeping the Free French and Vichy francs tied would have been that, as a means of economic warfare, one side could attempt to flood the enemy's economy with excess money, thereby compounding the existing cost-push inflation with demand-pull inflation.

The direction of trade between certain Middle Eastern countries shows the importance of the trade flows between Lebanon, Syria and their neighbouring countries.[27] In 1938, Syria and Lebanon only imported 16% of the total trade value and exported 45%. In 1943, the two countries imported 51% of their total trade value from other Middle Eastern countries and exported 71% to them. However, in 1946, imports had

(August 1940) de Gaulle was held in the highest esteem by His Majesty's Government…"; TNA, CAB 66 18 14, *Record of a Meeting between the Prime Minister and General de Gaulle at N° 10 Downing Street on Friday, September 12, 1941*, 16 September 1941—"The Prime Minister said that he had witnessed with very great sorrow the deterioration in General de Gaulle's attitude towards His Majesty's Government"; and Churchill Archives (CHAR) 20/128/39, *Prime Minister to Foreign Secretary (Eden)*, 21 May 1943—"He (Alexis Leger) warned me of the evil effects of the De Gaullist propaganda… He said De Gaulle was thoroughly unfriendly both to Britain and the United States and that while affecting Communist sympathies had Fascist tendencies. This again tallies with my own feeling".

[25] TNA, CAB 66 39 41, *Relations with General de Gaulle,* 7 August 1943, p. 6.

[26] BoE, OV45 129, 'Free French Banking', *Financial News*, 18 February 1942.

[27] See Table III in WILMINGTON Martin, *Economic Regionalism in the Middle East during World War II (The Middle East Supply Center)*, Doctoral Thesis, New York University, 1960, 448p., p. 379.

once again fallen to 19% and exports had also receded to nearly their pre-war level, at 48%. This increase in wartime trade was greatly facilitated by belonging to the sterling area. Prior to this, the exchange controls that were in place for Syria and Lebanon meant that they were commercially and financially isolated from their closest neighbours.[28] The Syrian and Lebanese cases objectively show that it was easier to resupply from nearby countries, or those with whom they shared a currency. Equally, the fact that trade fell back to pre-war levels emphasises that the increase, seen in 1943, was principally due to the British and Free French collaborative effort. While the proposed Franco-British Union of June 1940 may have failed to materialise, the enlargement of the sterling area, to include certain French colonies and mandated territories, was an economic *rapprochement* that would not have been undertaken had the circumstances not called for deeper cooperation between the Allies. The increased flow of goods, between the Middle Eastern mandated territories, is even more surprising when one considers the state of near famine which existed prior to the imposition of Allied control.[29] From an economic perspective, the collaboration between the Free French and the British, in the Middle East, saved the Syrians and Lebanese from starvation.

The most important contribution towards the Syrian and Lebanese economies was the 'Wheat Fund', which was introduced to provide producers with an acceptable return on their grains. In peacetime, both Syria and Lebanon were exporters of cereals, particularly to Palestine. However, the fear of famine, such as the one experienced during the First World War, was further compounded by failed harvests in 1939, 1941 and 1942, which forced the pressing issue of food supply to the fore as the price of grain was rapidly increasing. Consequently, the temptation for producers and intermediaries was to hoard stocks, sitting and waiting for

[28] 'Syria in the Sterling Area', *The Economist*, 20 September 1941, p. 360.

[29] DAVET Michel-Christian, *La Double Affaire de Syrie*, Paris, Fayard, 1967, 356p. (Ebook), Chap. 5, Para 25—"It was necessary to increase wheat by 50% in order for the stocks to emerge from their hiding places. Prices rose to such an extent that part of the population was on the verge of famine"; WILMINGTON Martin, *Economic Regionalism in the Middle East during World War II (The Middle East Supply Center)*, Doctoral Thesis, New York University, 1960, 448p., p. 296—"no call would be made on Allied shipping for imported wheat and flour during the first six months of 1943, by the two countries which, in 1941, on the brink of famine in the cities, had absorbed more than a hundred thousand tons of Allied grain and shipping space within a few months".

inflation to increase their eventual realised profits. In response, the Middle East Supply Centre and the Spears Mission, which was the liaising organisation between the British government and the Free French, agreed to establish a Wheat Commission.[30] This allowed the authorities to prevent hoarding and price gouging that would have been more economically and socially costly than simply paying the farmers a fair price. At the Commission's behest, the issuance of permits to move grain around was introduced and collectors were employed to travel across the country to pay the producers, at a fixed rate, for their yield. The farmers could thus pay off their debts or rental costs and would be less likely to hoard, at least in theory. In Fig. 6.1, the amounts shown were accounted as being credited to the *Caisse centrale* to pay to the Syria Wheat Fund. The graph shows that, from June 1942 to June 1943, advances were made to fund the purchase of grain in Syria, as had been stipulated in the statutes of the *Caisse centrale*.[31]

The provision of advances for buying wheat is confirmed when it is compared to the shipments of cereals received from abroad, cited by Wilmington.[32] Between 1942 and 1943, the total tonnage of wheat received across the Middle East dropped by 64%.[33] This was linked to the ongoing battles that were occurring between merchant navy vessels, the Allies' navies and the U-Boat packs. With increasing efforts to support the grain producers, importing wheat from elsewhere became less essential, as the domestic market helped supply Syria and Lebanon, instead. In Spears' memoir, he indicates that, for the years 1942 and 1943, 365,000 tons

[30] WILMINGTON, *The Middle East Supply Center*, 1960, p. 295—"Instead, MESC and the Spears Mission obtained from the new governments of Syria and Lebanon approval for the formation of a Wheat Commission (Office des Céréales Panifiables) in whose hands was placed a total state monopoly for the purchase, transport and distribution of bread crops in the country".

[31] AN, 382 AP 32 René Cassin, *Statuts—Caisse centrale de la France libre*, p. 3—"VII—To make: Treasury advances, either to the Free French, or to one of the territories concerned in paragraph I-1 of the present article".

[32] Table 1, WILMINGTON, *The Middle East Supply Center*, 1960, p. 377.

[33] (((465.7–169)/465.7))*100 = 63.7%.

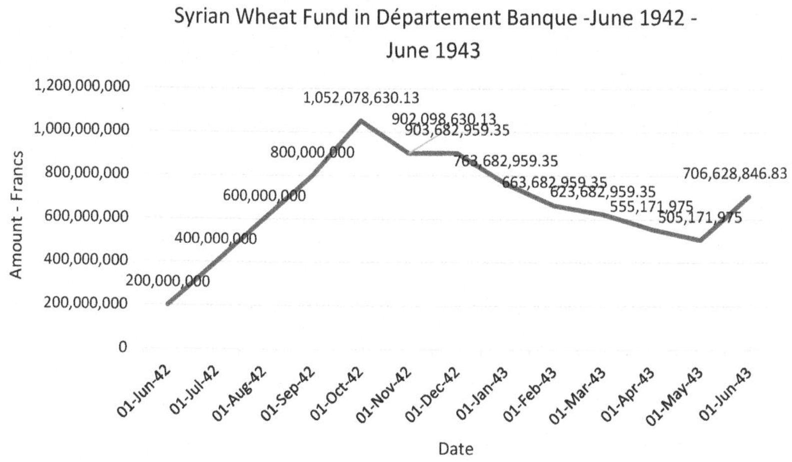


**Fig. 6.1** Syrian wheat fund, June 1942–June 1943 (Journal Officiel de la France Libre)

of material were imported into the Middle East.[34] However, Wilmington's figures[35] show that 982,100 tons of imports were received, meaning that there was a disparity between Wilmington's and Spears' statistics of 617,100 tons.

The decrease in imports represents an example of a supply-side shock, which would have caused a contraction in G.D.P. and increased the general price level. One method of countering the negative effect was to import more. However, as was shown by the American statistics on exports of domestic merchandise for 1942, there were relatively few goods entering Syria.[36] The total dollar value of American exports was

[34] SPEARS Edward, *Fulfilment of a Mission: The Spears Mission to Syria and Lebanon, 1941–1944*, London, Leo Cooper, 1977, 311p., p. 174—"The magnitude of the problem of feeding the people of the Levant is shown by the fact that imports for 1942–43 were 365,000 tons for the whole area of the Middle East, including Palestine, and only 95,000 tons of this was for the forces. In 1942, Damascus, alone, received, from British sources, 117 tons of cereals a day. (In 1943, I had this down by ten tons)".

[35] Table 1, WILMINGTON, *The Middle East Supply Center*, 1960, p. 377.

[36] *United States Exports of Domestic Merchandise Under the Lend-Lease Program—Calendar Years 1942, 1944, 1945 & 1946*, Washington, DC., United States Bureau of the Census, 2015.

$969,542 and included items and equipment such as trailers, freight carriages, tin plate, wire and inner tubes. These are examples of industrially produced goods that would have been almost impossible to obtain in the country. When compared to the U.S. export figures, from 1944, the dollar value of goods that were sent to Syria was $258,532, or practically a quarter of the 1942 value.

These figures confirm that there was falling strategic importance in the Levant, by evaluating the value and quantities of ordnance and civilian goods that were shipped. In 1942, the invasion of North Africa, or Operation Torch, required the two countries to be as stable as possible, thus necessitating the transfer of material. By 1944, the military situation had drastically altered. The invasion of metropolitan France was being prepared, the Red Army was advancing on Germany, and the Americans had launched operations in the Pacific. Imports from the Lend-Lease programme for both Syria and Lebanon, in 1944, had decreased as the risk of invasion had fallen.

Throughout the war, Syria and Lebanon were net beneficiaries of British and American contributions. However, rather than providing tangible economic benefit in return, the countries were important in geostrategic terms. Their proximity to the Suez Canal and other British mandated territories meant that it was paramount to bring Syria and Lebanon safely into the Allied camp. The two countries represented an early Allied attempt at providing supplies to a stricken population. It would certainly not be the last.

## Gaullist Gold and African Airports

Prior to 1943, French Equatorial Africa was the largest rallied French territory. It was composed of four constituent colonies: French Gabon, French Congo, Ubangi-Shari and Chad. Under the leadership of Félix Éboué, the governor-general of Chad, French Equatorial Africa rallied to de Gaulle over the period from 26 to 28th August 1940, with the exception of Gabon.[37] Gabon fell to Free French troops on 12th November, when the Vichy troops based in Port-Gentil agreed to lay down their

[37] JENNINGS Éric, 'La France libre en AEF et au Cameroun: Recrutement et extraction des ressources' in CORNIL-FRERROT Sylvain (Ed.), OULMONT Philippe (Ed.), *Les Français libres et le monde*, Paris, Éditions Nouveau Monde, 2015, 241p., pp. 215–229, p. 220.

arms.[38] From 1939 to 1944, Gabon lost 477 indigenous soldiers of the 2,140 who were sent to fight for France. From a population that numbered 455,000, in 1936, before falling to 421,000, in 1946,[39] the losses represented 0.5% of the 1946 population.

As Nnang Ndong has indicated, "Economic aid that was provided by Gabon can be summed up in two words: produce and pay".[40] Economic order was what René Pleven had attempted to achieve, as the general secretary for French Equatorial Africa, from the summer of 1940 until the beginning of 1941.[41] While French Equatorial Africa may have represented the first territorial acquisition for the Free French movement, it was also rich in natural resources. However, it desperately required functioning administration, governing hierarchies and personnel to run the resource extraction sites. This remained the most pressing concern, as it was for many of the other Free French colonies. If the Free French recruited the male workforce for their armed forces, they could no longer pan for gold or pick cocoa beans, thereby effectively limiting the size of the potential domestic workforce. Women, usually accompanying their husbands, cultivated the land around the camps. As the Pelabon Report underlined, this type of work was underpaid and dangerous due to the prevalence of the Tsetse fly and sleeping sickness. The report also notes that those working in the mines "would earn 3.50 per day and an extra ration of food, as his wife would work in the food plantations".[42] Furthermore, under wartime conditions, there was the additional concern of knowing exactly who would be capable of transporting the commodities to the markets, and by what means?

[38] '1940: Gabon', Amicale de la 1e Division Française Libre, https://web.archive.org/web/20161124075631/http:/1dfl.fr/-1940-Gabon-.html, Consulted 5 August 2020; CORNIL-FRERROT Sylvain, 'Le ralliement du Gabon à la France Libre', *Fondation de la France Libre*, http://www.france-libre.net/le-ralliement-du-gabon-a-la-france-libre/, Consulted 5 August 2020.

[39] NNANG NDONG Léon Modeste, *L'effort de guerre de l'Afrique: Le Gabon dans la Deuxième Guerre mondiale (1939–1947)*, Paris, L'Harmattan, 2011, 286p., (Ebook), Ch. 1, Paras 50 and 54.

[40] NNANG NDONG, *L'effort de guerre de l'Afrique*..., 2011, General Introduction, Para. 31.

[41] DENIS, *Souvenirs de la France Libre*, 1947, p. 39.

[42] ANOM, 1 AFF-POL 873, Affaires Politiques, Carton 873, Dossier 12, *Rapport M. Pelabon sur l'Économie de l'A.E.F.*, 1 November 1943, p. 2.

The solution began with the two agreements signed between the Free French and the British government, in March 1941. These accords established the official franc-sterling exchange rate of 176.625 francs to the pound. In the context of French Equatorial Africa, the most important clauses related to the offering of any gold produced by the Free French territories directly to the Bank of England. The Defence Council of the French Empire, as the Gaullists' administrative organisation was called, would be responsible for controlling the importation and exportation of the precious commodity.[43] During the eighth meeting of the War Cabinet Committee on Foreign (Allied) Resistance, on 7th February 1941, it was decided that any excess gold production would be pooled with general Allied resources.[44] There is a discrepancy between the 1940 production and export figures for gold extracted from French Equatorial Africa by Jennings[45] and Nnang Ndong.[46] Overall, the peak of production and exportation was reached in 1941.

When these quantities of gold are valued in U.S. dollars (Table 6.1), using Green's *Historical Gold Price Table*,[47] they show a similar pattern. In 1939, the gold that was expedited was worth 1.9 million dollars. By 1941, French Equatorial Africa's largest wartime production year, it had reached 3.25 million dollars. However, by 1945, this had fallen back to 2.6 million dollars.

[43] TNA, FO 892 101 1941–1942 Commercial and Economic Relations between the U.K. and the Cameroons and French Equatorial Africa, *I—Memorandum of Credit Agreement, Art. 7, II—Memorandum of Credit Agreement, Art. 4a) & 4b)*, 21 March 1941.

[44] TNA, CAB 85 29 War Cabinet Committee on Foreign (Allied) Resistance, *Minutes from Eighth Meeting* N° 5, 7 February 1941.

[45] JENNINGS Eric, *Free French Africa…*, 2015, Chap. 6, Para. 62—"Statistics confirm the rapid rise in gold production in FEA (French Equatorial Africa). While the federation only produced 668.4 kg of raw gold in 1937 and 1,738.1 kg in 1939, it reached the following levels under Fighting France: 2,476.4 kg in 1940, 2,993.2 kg in 1941, 2,943 kg in 1942, 2,772.8 kg in 1943 and finally 2,580.3 kg in 1944. Within FEA, Gabon led the way, followed by Oubangui-Chari until 1943, at which point Moyen-Congo vaulted into second place. Cameroon's totals mirrored those of Oubangui-Chari, rising from 544.6 kg in 1940 to 710 kg in 1941, 717 kg in 1942 before dipping to 678 kg in 1943".

[46] NNANG NDONG, *L'effort de guerre de l'Afrique…*, 2011, Table 21, Chap. 3, Para. 8.

[47] PIKETTY Thomas, 'Historical Gold Prices—1833 to Present', http://piketty.pse.ens.fr/files/capital21c/xls/RawDataFiles/GoldPrices17922012.pdf, Consulted 5 August 2020.

**Table 6.1** Gold Production (Kg) and Value in $ and Francs, 1939–1945, (Adapted from NNANG NDONG, Chap. 3, Para. 8)

| *Year* | *Total (kg)* | *Total ($)* | *Total (Fcs. At Rate 47,000 Frs. / Kg)* |
|---|---|---|---|
| 1939 | 1793 | 1,984,185 | 84,271,000 |
| 1940 | 2276.4 | 2,477,412 | 106,990,800 |
| 1941 | 2993.2 | 3,257,508 | 140,680,400 |
| 1942 | 2943.8 | 3,203,746 | 138,358,600 |
| 1943 | 2772.8 | 3,017,646 | 130,321,600 |
| 1944 | 2580.3 | 2,808,148 | 121,274,100 |
| 1945 | 2366.4 | 2,640,790 | 111,220,800 |
| 1946 | 2225.7 | 2,483,775 | 104,607,900 |
| Total | 19,952 | 21,873,210 | 937,725,200 |

The noticeable decline suggests that a political decision was taken to reduce supply. This could have been caused, most plausibly, by an increase in troop numbers being drawn from French Equatorial Africa. However, when the enlistment statistics for French Equatorial Africa are considered, this does not seem to be the case, either. Using Jenning's figures,[48] enlistment numbers were greatest in 1940, with 5,270 people joining the armed forces. This dropped significantly, to 2,516, in 1941, before halving, again, to 1,384, in 1942. Finally, in 1943, recruitment was as low as 516 people.

Instead, the reductions in the value of exported gold suggest a shift away from gold production. Firstly, the tedious work necessary to extract gold was backbreaking.[49] In the context of total war, such work was hardly the most productive task that could be being undertaken. Gold is both a medium of exchange and a store of wealth. It helps to buy other resources but, if those commodities have not been extracted, gold serves

[48] JENNINGS Eric, 'La France libre en AEF et au Cameroun: Recrutement et extraction des ressources' in CORNILL-FRERROT Sylvain (Ed.), OULMONT Philippe (Ed.), *Les Français libres et le monde*, Paris, Éditions Nouveau Monde, 2015, 241p., pp. 215–229, p. 217.

[49] JENNINGS Eric, *Free French Africa*..., 2015, Chap. 6, Para. 64—"The governor of Gabon recognized in January 1941: "One cannot count on the natives for seeking out gold. They have an insurmountable repugnance for this form of work. It is indeed very difficult since miners must spend the whole day semi-immersed in muddy and often nauseatingly disgusting water. The washing techniques presently used do not allow for any other solution. One can readily understand why natives would want to avoid this work".

little other purpose than as a store of wealth. Furthermore, considering the stipulations of the Free French and British accords, any gold extracted needed to be sent to London, from where it would be resold. However, economic warfare prerogatives would not necessarily have allowed for such a use of shipping. If the British government was going to risk sending merchant sailors to face the U-Boat packs, then, strategically, it made more sense that it should be for a product that could actively contribute to the war effort. This is possibly the reason that gold exports began to decline while French Equatorial Africa, concurrently, experienced a falling level of enlistment. Therefore, the question as to the most significant products provided by French Equatorial Africa remains.

In order to know the most valued commodity that a country produces, from the perspective of its government, one of the most useful indicators is to look to those sectors that receive governmental support and subsidies. In the 'Memorandum of Agreements' that were signed in 1941 and 1942, the British government agreed to buy a number of products from the Free French rallied colonies. Some of these were sold in their entirety, notably the cocoa crop. Furthermore, Britain agreed to ensure the economic stability of Cameroon under French Mandate and to facilitate their trade with the U.K.[50] This was a consideration that was foremost in the minds of the war planners. When one considers the gradually falling levels of imports to Cameroon, between 1937 and 1940, in Fig. 6.2 as well as the population statistics, the territories were seeing their domestic market being greatly tested by the war.

The graph, Fig. 6.2, shows the total quantity, in kilograms, and the value of imports, in francs, during the period from 1937 to the second quarter of 1941. In order to correct this decline in imports, the British government decided to relax the quotas of Navicerts, which were certificates that attested to a ship's right-of-passage, which had been issued by H.M. Government. This scheme allowed the ship to continue its journey unhindered, in the case of a spot-check by Allied naval forces. By attempting to increase imports, it also indicates a reasoning behind the acquisition of the colonial produce by the British. If the British government bought the stocks of commodities in French Equatorial Africa, this

[50] TNA, FO 892 101 1941–1942 Commercial and Economic Relations…, *Exchange of Letters between the Secretary of State for Foreign Affairs (Anthony Eden) and General de Gaulle concerning Commercial and Economic Relations between the United Kingdom and the Cameroons under French Mandate*, 21 January 1941.

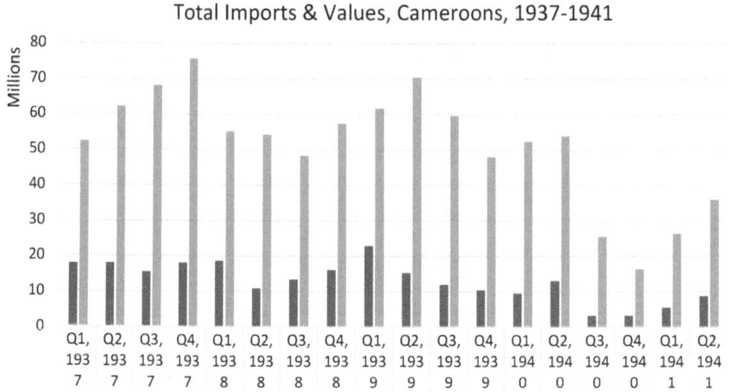


| | Q1, 1937 | Q2, 1937 | Q3, 1937 | Q4, 1937 | Q1, 1938 | Q2, 1938 | Q3, 1938 | Q4, 1938 | Q1, 1939 | Q2, 1939 | Q3, 1939 | Q4, 1939 | Q1, 1940 | Q2, 1940 | Q3, 1940 | Q4, 1940 | Q1, 1941 | Q2, 1941 |
|---|---|---|---|---|---|---|---|---|---|---|---|---|---|---|---|---|---|---|
| ■ Quantity (Kg) | 17,7 | 17,8 | 15,4 | 17,9 | 18,5 | 10,8 | 13,3 | 16,0 | 22,7 | 15,2 | 11,9 | 10,3 | 9,49 | 13,0 | 3,30 | 3,25 | 5,52 | 8,76 |
| ■ Value (Fcs.) | 52,2 | 62,0 | 68,0 | 75,5 | 55,1 | 54,2 | 48,3 | 57,4 | 61,5 | 70,4 | 59,5 | 47,9 | 52,3 | 53,8 | 25,5 | 16,3 | 26,4 | 35,9 |

Quarter, Year

**Fig. 6.2** Total Imports (Kg) and Values (Fcs.), Cameroons, 1937–1941 (TNA, FO 892 101)

would provide the country with foreign exchange, which could be then used to increase their imports from neighbouring British colonies. Moreover, with an increase in imports, rising levels of exports were also to be expected. A cargo ship's voyage entails a great deal of financial risk and in a time of war, to leave port without a full cargo load would have rendered the highly dangerous exercise inefficient.

It is also possible to see the most valuable colonial products from the total price that was attributed to their eventual purchase. The four products that commanded the largest minimum purchase, in the Memorandum of Agreement, were rutile—a mineral used in the manufacture of titanium metal—peanuts, wild rubber and palm oil. Furthermore, Table 6.2 shows the products that were attributed the greatest importance within the domestic economy of French Equatorial Africa. The palm almonds and oil required a considerable workforce to harvest, employing 49,350, in 1939, which increased to 72,400, in 1940, and, finally, 87,164, in 1941.[51] These products served to ease the wartime

[51] NNANG NDONG, *L'effort de guerre de l'Afrique*..., Chap. 3, Para. 27.

**Table 6.2** Table of commodities, their price per ton, the minimum purchase by the British and the total price, French Equatorial Africa, (TNA, FO 892 101)

| *Resource* | *Price per Ton (Fcs.)* | *Minimum purchase (Ton)* | *Total price (Fcs.)* |
|---|---|---|---|
| Palm Almonds | 850 | 23,000 | 19,550,000 |
| Palm Oil | 1,200 | 5,000 | 6,000,000 |
| Peanuts (Garoa) | 825 | 10,000 | 8,250,000 |
| Peanuts (Douala) | 1,350 | 2,000 | 2,700,000 |
| Sesame | 1,425 | 1,000 | 1,425,000 |
| Wild Rubber | 8,500 | 750 | 6,375,000 |
| Rutile | 8,600 | 1,200 | 10,320,000 |
| Maize | 600 | 3,000 | 1,800,000 |

shortages of oil and fat. They had many uses, particularly in the production of soaps, grease and oil. The British Food Programme used the oil, and "in certain countries, its yellow color is considered to make the oil particularly suitable as an ingredient in margarine".[52]

While Britain agreed to buy the entire production of certain commodities, the United States played a vital role in supplying the armed forces of French Equatorial Africa. This assistance came in the form of Reciprocal Lend-Lease. The Free French had been declared eligible for its precursor, Lend-Lease, on 11th November 1941. This was as a direct consequence of the enlarged territorial acquisitions that the movement had been making throughout 1940 and 1941. The Reciprocal Lend-Lease Agreement was signed on 3rd September 1942.[53] Ultimately, these were emergency measures, provided without many stipulations and conditions, in order to facilitate America's allies with continuing the war against the Axis powers. Over the next few years, the programme increased in scope and a wide range of American products, ordnance and materials were provided.

In 1942, French Equatorial Africa and the Cameroons were two of the largest Free French recipients of Lend-Lease aid. As has been seen, French

[52] DRAKE HALL Marian, 'The Belgian Congo as a Fats-and-Oils Source', *Foreign Commerce Weekly*, Vol. 24, pp. 3–5, 24 August 1946, p. 3.

[53] Vere Harmsworth Library, Rothermere American Institute, Oxford, *11th Report to Congress on Lend-Lease Operations for the Period Ended July 31, 1943*, Appendix IV, p. 41.

Equatorial Africa was a colony and the French part of the Cameroons had been mandated to them, in 1922, after having been taken from Germany.[54] This is as indicative of the state of the countries' economies as it is of their status within the movement. A great deal of time and expertise was expended to keep these lands under Free French control. It has been seen that levels of imports were also progressively decreasing. As the two countries were dependent on foreign imported foodstuffs, this was a particularly worrying development. Furthermore, as can be ascertained by the types of export stock that Britain was buying from the two countries, in 1941, there was very little heavy industry. In many ways, this was similar to the situation in Syria and Lebanon. Largely, it was by the design of the French colonial administration, who viewed the African colonies as being places from which resources were to be extracted, rather than transformed into consumer goods. The types of American products, and produce, that were imported into French Equatorial Africa included condensed milk and cream, vegetable seeds, reinforced concrete bars, nails, wire, a limited number of trucks and parts for firearms. The U.S. exports that were made to Cameroon were in much a similar vein, but also included building materials, such as galvanised steel sheets, and administrative equipment, like typewriters or paper (Fig. 6.3).

As shown in Fig. 6.4, the dollar value of the goods that were sent to French Equatorial Africa, Cameroon and Syria was similar. Syria, at 52%, acquired the majority of the total goods sent to those parts of the French empire that were receiving American material support. A small quantity of goods was sent to French West Africa, which remained part of the Vichy French empire until Operation Torch, in November 1942, under the governorship of Pierre Boisson. The reason for the discrepancy between the two groups of territories, notably Syria, Cameroon and French Equatorial Africa, and the rest of the territories, was one of size, in both the geographical and demographic sense. The populations of Saint-Pierre-et-Miquelon, New Caledonia and Madagascar were considerably smaller than those of Syria or French Equatorial Africa. This meant that Syria and French Equatorial Africa required greater levels of material

[54] NZUME Anastasia Nlende, *British and French Administration of Peoples on the Southern Borderlands of Cameroon: The Case of the Anglo-French Inter-Cameroons Boundary, 1916–61*, Doctoral Thesis, School of African and Oriental Studies (S.O.A.S.), University of London, 2004, 410p., p. 49—https://eprints.soas.ac.uk/29199/1/10731294.pdf, Consulted 30 October 2020.

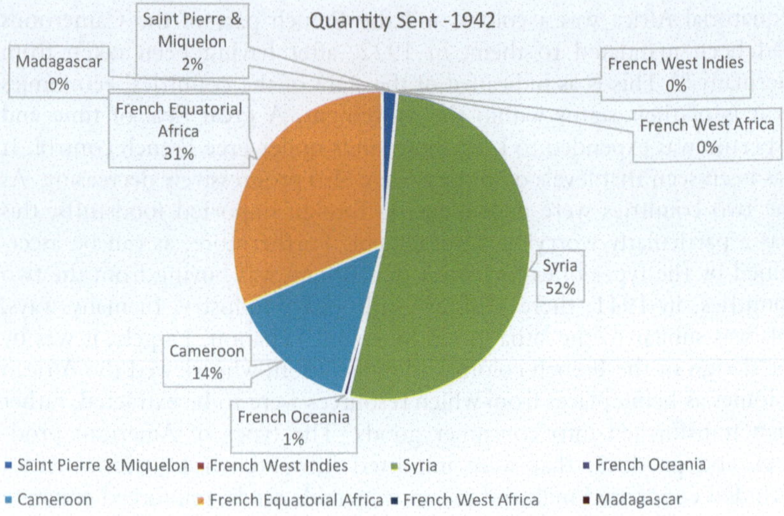


**Fig. 6.3** Lend-Lease Aid as a % of Quantity Sent, 1942, ('United States Exports of Domestic and Foreign Merchandise under the Lend-Lease Program: Country of Destination by Commodity' U.S. Bureau of the Census, 2015)

support to feed and house their larger population, as can be seen in the charts above.

In order to manage these imports, improved communication links were required. The Free French needed to transport goods between their territories and, considering the ongoing war, the safest, and quickest, transport route was by air. Discussions began in July 1942 concerning the enlargement of the airport, and the installation of oil storage facilities at Pointe-Noire, on the coast of French Congo, by American forces. According to René Pleven, while in conversation with Lieutenant-Colonel Merrick, one of the American representatives, de Gaulle insisted that the Fighting French were merely stewards for the future French government and, as such, did not have the authority to relinquish control over a proposed oil installation.[55] This was a double pique that was aimed

[55] NARA, 313 76 10, *Note: Meeting at the Office of Mr. Pleven at Fighting French Headquarters*, 5 October 1942—"Mr. Pleven replied, in essence, that Fighting France was not a Government de jure but was merely acting as an interim administration prepared to do everything possible to promote the war effort... Mr. Pleven felt that he must leave the

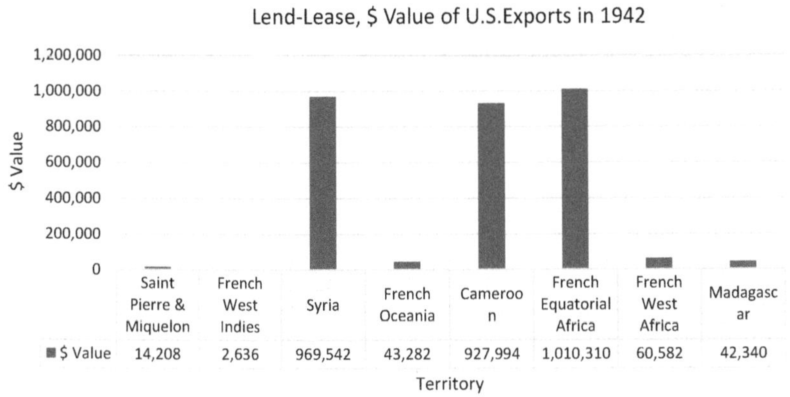


**Fig. 6.4** Lend-lease aid sent to French colonies and mandated territories in 1942, ('United States Exports of Domestic and Foreign Merchandise under the Lend-Lease Program: Country of Destination by Commodity' U.S. Bureau of the Census, 2015)

directly at the White House, as Roosevelt's government refused to accord his movement any form of legitimacy, while concurrently complaining about the Frenchman's authoritarian tendencies. De Gaulle's refusal to acquiesce to the Americans over the oil installation showed that the Free French were prepared to endure hardship and privation to ensure French sovereignty remained unaltered. Furthermore, General de Gaulle demonstrated his negotiating abilities, by acquiring twenty transport planes, Lockheed Lodestars, that were delivered using Britain's Lend-Lease account.[56] These discussions led to an agreement that would allow a post-war French government to keep control of the oil storage unit. On 6th August, de Gaulle sent a formal letter giving the approbation of the French National Committee to the American request to land troops at the Pointe-Noire airport, as well as to station a small contingent of troops

post-war government a completely free hand to deal with the situation as it then might exist".

[56] NARA, 313 76 10, *Memorandum for Admiral Stark: Subject: Negotiations with Fighting French (General Dahlquist and Major Walker)*, 24 August 1942—"A despatch from the War Department (August 22) indicated that a British Lend-Lease Requisition of 20 transport planes for Fighting French Equatorial Africa liaison and communications had been approved in July".

nearby.[57] As the installations were to be operated by an independent contractor, Socony-Vacuum Oil Company, third-party legal and contractual needs would have to be considered as part of any eventual agreement. The company's authorisations, licences and contracts were issued on 9th October.

It was impressed upon the Fighting French that the Americans were using the airbase as a necessity of the war effort. Any assistance, or equipment, being provided under the Lend-Lease programme was to be handled as a separate issue. This enabled them to keep the different streams of goods and money apart. Communication links across Africa had been badly disrupted by the war and the fragmentation of the French empire into opposing camps only exacerbated matters. It did not need to be worsened by logistical difficulties and duplicated requests. Irrespective of minor issues that may have arisen, the usefulness of the programme was highly praised in the American reports:

> The money cost of reverse lend-lease aid, great as it is, is in no sense a measure of the help we receive from our allies. Our principal allies have contributed fully in proportion to their resources.[58]

Ultimately, the United States recognised that "we furnish lend-lease aid in order to help ourselves".[59] By providing resources to countries that needed them, there were two direct benefits. Firstly, the production from industry had an outlet that was not previously available to them. This enabled American industry to continue growing. Secondly, it created new demand in those markets that were being supplied. By bringing American products to a country, it allowed for its inhabitants to recognise the quality of U.S. production and thus demand grew further still. This was a longer-term benefit. While victory remained the prime objective, such goals drove the Lend-Lease scheme, the gold production, the enlargement of the Pointe-Noire airport and the agreed futures purchase of French Equatorial African production. In this comparatively underdeveloped corner of the Free French territory, the wide range of economic

[57] NARA, 313 76 10, *POINTE-NOIRE AIRPORT*, undated.

[58] Vere Harmsworth Library, Rothermere American Institute, Oxford, *13th Report to Congress on Lend-Lease Operations*, Chap. 1, p. 15.

[59] Vere Harmsworth Library, Rothermere American Institute, Oxford, *18th Report to Congress on Lend-Lease Operations*, Chap. 1, p. 8.

activity helped to advance the strategic objectives of the Allies and ensure the continued provision of vital raw materials, including palm almonds. The same pattern was to be seen in New Caledonia, in the South Pacific.

## Production in the South Pacific

For a period of approximately two years, New Caledonia was situated directly within one of the principal theatres of the Second World War. This contrasted greatly with its reputation as being one of France's forgotten territories. A former penal colony that housed French exiles, following the Commune of 1871, the 220 miles-long and thirty-one to forty-three miles-wide island, *Grande Terre*, was home to a population of between 50,000[60] and 70,000.[61] Munholland estimated that the demographic of the islands' inhabitants was composed of 29,000 Melanesians, 17,000 European settlers and 11,000 Asians.[62] The Asian diaspora was constituted of 7,000 indentured Tonkinese and Javanese labourers, who worked in the mines, and 1,100 Japanese.[63]

Geographically, New Caledonia is far removed from metropolitan France. However, it had valuable, tradeable raw materials on its territory. Unfortunately for the New Caledonians, the profits from these natural resources disappeared to pay dividends to absentee shareholders; gross profits for the island's largest mining company, *Société Le Nickel*, totalled 186 million francs in 1938–1939, but the entire budget for the New Caledonian government was a mere 50 million francs.[64]

The islands' natural resources, which include metals such as nickel, iron and chrome, were vital constituents of industrial products, from automobiles to electroplating and in munitions manufacture. As it was home to the "world's only important producing area outside of Canada", the

[60] NARA, 313 76 1, *Fighting France in the Pacific—Translation from a Lecture given by Admiral Thierry d'Argenlieu*, 9 March 1943.

[61] HENNINGHAM Stephen, 'The French Administration, the Local Population and the American Presence in New Caledonia, 1943–1944', *Journal de la Société des océanistes*, 98, 1994, pp. 21–41, p. 22.

[62] MUNHOLLAND, *Rock of Contention*..., 2005, p. 87.

[63] MUNHOLLAND Kim, 'The Trials of the Free French in New Caledonia, 1940–1942', *French Historical Studies*, Vol. 14, N° 14 (Autumn, 1986), pp. 547–579, p. 549.

[64] FEUER Lewis, 'Cartel Control in New Caledonia', *Far Eastern Survey*, Vol. 15, N° 12 (June 19, 1946), pp. 184–187, p. 186.

nickel produced in New Caledonia made up "one-eighth of the world output" in 1940.[65] However, their position had been steadily declining since the beginning of the twentieth century, largely due to the "substantially higher costs of production" in New Caledonia.[66] Nonetheless, the total production of nickel ore from 1937 to 1939 grew by 48.5%, from 249,000 tons to 370,000 tons.[67] Three mining companies operated the nickel mining on the island: '*Le Nickel*', '*Les Petits Mineurs*' and the '*Société de l'Océanie*'. *Le Nickel* ran two production centres, with one situated at Voh-Kone and the other at Thio-Ouenghil. The company extracted 201,881 tons at the two sites in 1939.[68] Japan and Germany were buying as much of the ore as they could,[69] as it was a vital component that was used in military production.[70]

The production of low-grade iron ore also increased from 90,000 tons, in 1939, to 150,000 tons, in 1940. This represented 67% growth over one year[71] and suggests one of three things: firstly, that innovation had occurred in the mining process; secondly, that more miners were mining; or, thirdly, that the existing personnel were working more productively or longer hours. Had it been showing incremental improvements to the growth rate, this final reasoning may have been the case. However, with such growth in production, it is more likely that the extraction techniques were either becoming more efficient or the use of improved technology was having a significant effect on production, or possibly both. As it was

[65] 'New Caledonia and the United States', *The Economist*, 2 May 1942, p. 600.

[66] FEUER Lewis, 'Cartel Control in New Caledonia', 1946, p. 184.

[67] TNA, FO 892 79—1941 Economic Position of Free French Colonies in the Pacific, *Letter to F.R. Cowell (Spears Mission) from A.H. Lincoln (Ministry of Economic Warfare)*, 5 May 1941, p. 3.

[68] TNA, FO 892 79, *Letter to F.R. Cowell (Spears Mission) from A.H. Lincoln (Ministry of Economic Warfare—M.E.W)*, 05 May 1941—Voh-Kone—159,919 tons; Thio-Ouenghil—41,962 tons, p.3.

[69] TNA, FO 892 79, *Letter to F.R. Cowell (Spears Mission) from A.H. Lincoln (M.E.W.)*, 5 May 1941, p. 4.

[70] SUDOL Stan, 'Nickel Closest Thing to a True 'War Metal'', *Republic of Mining*, 13 February 2009, https://republicofmining.com/2009/02/13/nickel-closest-thing-to-a-true-%E2%80%98war-metal%E2%80%99-by-stan-sudol/, Consulted 7 August 2020.

[71] NARA, 313 76 1, *Note on Production of Iron Ore in New Caledonia*, 25 July 1942, p. 1.

a metal used in the production of stainless steel, which served in arms, ammunition and vehicles, demand had greatly increased.[72]

There were many rich veins from which iron ore could have been mined, but only one was being exploited, on the south-eastern coast of the island, known as Goro. This belonged to the company '*La Fer*', which was established using five million francs of Franco-Japanese capital. '*La Fer*' was a branch of the '*Société Anonyme des Mines en Nouvelle Calédonie*'. With a low iron content, not exceeding 52%, it was this iron that would go on to help the Japanese war effort. The company had envisaged increasing production at the site in 1940, to 500,000 tons annually. However, the final result fell a long way short of their goal. In November 1940, 650 miners were employed at the Goro mine. Many of the miners were of Japanese or Javanese origins, or were Kanaks, who are the indigenous population of the island. The site was run by Ley, a New Caledonian of French descent, but the technicians and engineers were from Japan.[73] Ward shows that, on 1st January 1941, New Caledonia's Japanese population numbered 1,126, of whom 52 were women and 1,074 were men.[74] However, by 24th November, this had fallen to 1,104, with 1,047 men and 57 women.[75] Once the island was controlled by the Free French, the mine was sequestered and handed over to a trustee, Jean Andrain, a French accountant, who was responsible for closing the enterprise.[76]

The economic uncertainty continued into 1941. By this point, there was virtually no trade occurring between the New Hebrides and New Caledonia.[77] As was the case in the other mandated territories, the main

[72] OSTENDORP Peter, 'Nickel: Hidden in Plain Sight', Dartmouth Toxic Metals, National Institute of Environmental Health Sciences Superfund Research Program, Dartmouth College, Undated, https://sites.dartmouth.edu/toxmetal/more-metals/nickel-hidden-in-plain-sight/, Consulted 4 March 2021.

[73] NARA, 313 76 1, *Note on Production of Iron Ore in New Caledonia*, 25 July 1942, p. 2.

[74] WARD Rowena, 'Repatriating the Japanese from New Caledonia, 1941–46', *The Journal of Pacific History*, 51:4, pp. 392–408, p. 394.

[75] WARD Rowena, 'The Internment and Repatriation of the Japanese-French Nationals Resident in New Caledonia, 1941–1946', *PORTAL Journal of Multidisciplinary International Studies*, Vol. 14, N° 2, September 2017, pp. 55–67, p. 58.

[76] NARA, 313 76 1, *Note on Production of Iron Ore in New Caledonia*, 25 July 1942, p. 4.

[77] TNA, FO 892 79, *Letter from British Resident Commissioner to Secretary of State for the Colonies*, 7 May 1941.

difficulty with exporting was in procuring shipping. During 1941, the British Ministry of Shipping had been expecting to carry 35,000 tons of chrome.[78] The London Chrome Company, whose subsidiary, *Société le Tiebaghi*, owned the largest chrome mine on the islands, had contracted a Greek ship, the S.S. 'Constantinos Louloudia', to transport one shipment of ore across to the United States.[79] However, the ship was requisitioned by the Greek government.[80] Payment would also be made in dollars, underlining the importance of American currency reserves for the Free French movement.

In the months preceding the outbreak of hostilities, chrome and its ore were being blocked from being sent to Japan, by order of the Free French, and were instead being diverted to the United States.[81] However, this decision does not appear to have been entirely of the Free French's own volition. War Cabinet Committee notes suggest that, due to the "considerable economic assistance" afforded to the islands, the British government felt entitled to request that local authorities should "prohibit exports to Japan in excess of quantities exported in previous years".[82] Moreover, Japan was no longer wanting the low-quality iron ore that was being produced in New Caledonia.[83] As a result, unemployed iron miners were transferred to the construction of the islands' defences, before the declaration of war with Japan, in December 1941, provoked the internment of the Japanese personnel.[84]

1942 was the year in which the war monopolised the economic life of New Caledonia. Munholland explains that: "At first, de Gaulle seemed willing to cooperate with the still neutral Americans, as seen in

[78] TNA, FO 892 79, *Letter to A. Willoughby (Spears Mission) from John Penton (Treasury)*, undated, p. 2; TNA, CAB 85 29, Annexes, *New Caledonia—Chrome*, 1 January 1941.

[79] FEUER Lewis, 'Cartel Control in New Caledonia', 1946, p. 185.

[80] TNA, CAB 85 29, Annexes, *New Caledonia—Chrome*, 1 January 1941.

[81] NARA, 313 76 1, *Note on Production of Iron Ore in New Caledonia*, 25 July 1942, p. 4.

[82] TNA, CAB 85 29, War Cabinet Committee on Foreign (Allied) Resistance, *7th Meeting*, 4 February 1941.

[83] TNA, CAB 85 29, War Cabinet Committee on Foreign (Allied) Resistance, *7th Meeting*, 4 February 1941.

[84] TNA, FO 892 79, *Letter to A.H. Lincoln from Lt. R.M. Galsworthy (R.N.V.R)*, 8 January 1941, p. 2.

his offer to allow American air forces to use bases in Africa and the Pacific".[85] This was prior to the Saint-Pierre-et-Miquelon incident, in December 1941, which considerably cooled Gaullist-American relations, after Admiral Muselier's Christmas Eve 'invasion' brought the war close to the U.S. sphere of influence. Relations would not truly thaw for the remainder of the conflict, either politically or economically.

Yet, barely three months later, the disembarking of American troops onto New Caledonia suggested that the pressing necessity to win the war had dampened the effect of any perceived diplomatic slights. Defending the island's natural resources, and helping to protect Australia, took precedence. 40,000 American troops were to be sent to New Caledonia and, on 12th March 1942,[86] an initial force of 17,000 arrived in Nouméa's harbour.[87] The impact on the urban environment was immediate. The disembarkation of ordnance onto the small docks necessitated alterations to Nouméa's infrastructure,[88] such as one-way streets having their direction changed. Henningham, citing John Lawrey, an Australian diplomat who was serving as a junior official in New Caledonia at the time of the arrivals,[89] observed:

> The American presence was overwhelming. The local population, both white and Melanesian, was increasingly and profitably absorbed into the various American work forces, and relations between Americans and locals were, on the whole, remarkably good.[90]

When compared to the 1,400 Free French troops and 2,000 militia who were ordinarily stationed on the island, it is understandable as to why the Americans' presence would have seemed staggering.[91] The arrival of

[85] MUNHOLLAND Kim, 'The Trials of the Free French...', 1986, p. 559.

[86] MUNHOLLAND, *Rock of Contention*..., 2005, p. 89.

[87] LAWREY John, *The Cross of Lorraine in the South Pacific: Australia and the Free French Movement 1940–1942*, Canberra, *The Journal of Pacific History*, 1982, 152p., p. 93.

[88] MUNHOLLAND, 'The Trials of the Free French...', 1940–1942', 1986, p. 564.

[89] HENNINGHAM, 'Some Australian Official Views of New Caledonia's Melanesians, 1941 to 1953', *Journal de la Société des Océanistes*, 141/2015, pp. 323–336, p. 324.

[90] HENNINGHAM, 'The French Administration...', 1994, p. 21.

[91] MUNHOLLAND Kim, *Rock of Contention*..., 2005, p. 90—"In addition to the twenty members of the d'Argenlieu mission, there were only fourteen hundred men, including Kanak, who had been called up or had volunteered for active duty and some

the U.S. troops virtually doubled New Caledonia's population overnight. An agreement was reached between the U.S. Government and the Free French, in which the Roosevelt administration defined its policy towards the French National Committee, by recognising the French National Committee's authority over the French Pacific territories, as well as cooperating in the defence of the islands.[92] The Americans had arrived, but they needed the cooperation of the Free French and the islanders for this cohabitation to succeed.

The impact on the local economy of this explosive population growth completely changed the service sector, as the G.I.'s came with significant disposable income. Their arrival entailed an increase in the quantities of both goods and services that could be sold to the troops. Considering the difficulties with importing products, due to the war and the islands' isolated geography, it became necessary to introduce rationing on certain everyday items including shoes, clothes, meats and sugar.[93] Petrol was also rationed for the local population, but not for the American troops. This led to the G.I.'s searching for supplies outside the main centres of billeting. Through the increased demands being placed on the islands' economy, the arrival of American forces helped to raise levels of inflation. The risk of demand-push inflation came to pass. Local businesses and the French administration regularly complained about the newly created snack bars and canteens that were springing up to satisfy this excess of demand. These were operated on a not-for-profit basis, so they paid their employees higher wages and were not taxed.[94] Consequently, in New Caledonia, the dollar was elevated to the position of hegemonic currency.[95] This de facto changing of the currency underlines the importance that variable factors, such as individual spending behaviour, had on the economic system.

two thousand Caledonians, mostly Broussards, who had been organised into a militia under the command of Captain Dubois".

[92] NARA, 313 76 10, Agreement: US and Free French, *Agreement between the United States of America and Free France*, p. 1.

[93] MUNHOLLAND, *Rock of Contention*..., 2005, p. 136.

[94] HENNINGHAM, 'The French Administration...', 1994, p. 23.

[95] VAISSET Thomas, 'Maintenir et défendre la France Libre aux Antipodes' in CORNIL-FRERROT Sylvain (Ed.), OULMONT Philippe (Ed.), *Les Français Libres et le Monde*, Paris, Éditions Nouveau Monde, 2015, 431p., pp. 75–88, p. 84.

To facilitate the arrival of goods and troops, on 14th August 1942, an agreement was reached between Maurice Dejean, the French National Committee's commissioner for Foreign Affairs, and Admiral Stark of the U.S. Navy. The airline, Pan-American, operating under the control of the U.S. Navy, was allowed to establish a transport base in New Caledonia and to open an air and ferry service between the United States and Australia.[96] As Lawrey recognised, from his diplomat's vantage point:

> American high command, traditionally extremely conservative on the uses of strategic aviation, became extraordinarily air-minded as it contemplated the possible role of an island war of the Army Air Forces' excellent new bomber, the B17 Flying Fortress, now coming off the production lines in fair numbers.[97]

These aircraft would require a facility that could accommodate a 5,000-foot runway, which was the length of runway necessary for the American B17.[98] However, by July, the Nouméa airbase was under risk of attack from the Japanese air force, who were building new landing strips on Guadalcanal.[99] Nouméa's geographical position, opposite the Solomon Islands, forced this battle, as the strategic location of the French territory meant that the Americans wanted to secure New Caledonia. The capturing of the Japanese airfield, known as Henderson Field, would help to ensure that the ongoing battle for supplies in the Pacific would remain firmly on the side of the Allies.

> But in the six months' struggle on Guadalcanal, the Japanese had not only lost two-thirds of the 36,000 ground troops committed there, but also their lead in air power, and above all the strategic initiative, which they were never to regain.[100]

96 . NARA, 313 76 1, *Memorandum for Admiral Stark by T.B. Kittredge (U.S.N.R.)*, 13 August 1942; *Letter, to H.R. Stark from M. Dejean*, 14 August 1942; *Letter to M. Dejean from H. R. Stark*, 14 August 1942.

97 LAWREY John, *The Cross of Lorraine…*, 1982, p. 82.

98 Idem, p. 88.

99 Idem, p. 116.

100 Idem, p. 118.

On the islands, warehousing was at a premium.[101] The provisions and *matériel* that were to be transported to New Caledonia required secure storage facilities. Consequently, the Free French placed eight public-sector warehouses at the Americans' disposal and an additional 29 buildings that were in the hands of private enterprise.[102] These included the *Grand Hôtel du Pacifique*, the *Hôtel de France* and the deserted Japanese consulate building.[103] However, these spaces were insufficient for the needs of the U.S. military. A building campaign was begun to erect housing for the military staff, and base personnel, who were stationed on the islands. Governor Montchamps had, hitherto, refused the Americans permission to requisition buildings. However, on 26th October 1942, General de Gaulle cabled him and insisted that "the military requirements of the American Army and Naval staffs must be given priority over the administrative requirements of the civilian government of New Caledonia".[104] Clearly, the balance of economic power did not favour de Gaulle and the Free French.

French recriminations continued into 1943. Admiral Thierry d'Argenlieu complained as to the lack of drive and vigour being demonstrated by the Americans with their building programme.[105] Commander William 'Bull' Halsey responded to these critiques by ordering a thorough investigation to ascertain the true scope of the U.S. building efforts on New Caledonia. The report, dated 8th May, indicated that the Americans had built 2,186 individual buildings and 271 warehouses that offered a total floor space of 409,284 square feet.[106] Furthermore, for every thousand

[101] MUNHOLLAND, *Rock of Contention…*, 2005, p. 125—"Warehouses to store the vast amounts of goods and equipment were needed, and empty spaces in Nouméa was leased by the military for the construction of Quonset huts. Open spaces also became storage depots for ammunition and military equipment. An extensive construction program began in late 1942 and early 1943 that was to transform the landscape of New Caledonia".

[102] NARA, 313 76 1, *Locations put at the Disposition of the American Command at Nouméa*, 22 March 1943.

[103] . NARA, 313 76 1, *List (Made from memory) by Some Local People of the Buildings Occupied by the American Authorities at Nouméa*, 12 March 1943.

[104] NARA, 313 76 1, *Memorandum for Admiral Stark, Colonel Waite—Facilities for U.S. Staffs, Nouméa, New Caledonia*, 26 October 1942.

[105] MUNHOLLAND, *Rock of Contention…*, 2005, p. 127.

[106] NARA, 313 76 1, *Construction and Use of Buildings by U.S. Forces in New Caledonia*, 8 April 1943.

**Table 6.3** Tabulation of buildings constructed by or for U.S. Forces in New Caledonia, 1 May 1943 (NARA, 313 76 1)

| | *Quonset Huts* | *Other sheet metal* | *Portable wood* | *Thatched native type* | *Other type* | *Total* |
|---|---|---|---|---|---|---|
| Barracks | 100 | 14 | 395 | 93 | 86 | 688 |
| Offices | 91 | 14 | 50 | 24 | 67 | 246 |
| Storage | 82 | 257 | 44 | 83 | 119 | 585 |
| Other Purposes | 67 | 108 | 69 | 73 | 350 | 667 |
| Total | 340 | 393 | 558 | 273 | 622 | 2186 |

American troops on the island, 905 of their number were housed in tents, ninety were in American-built buildings and only five, mostly from the officer class, stayed in buildings which had been vacated by the French. The billeting of Americans was far from being an imposition on the local population, but it is clear to see that relations were strained under the Franco-American cohabitation.

From the statistics in Table 6.3, it can be seen that the majority of the American-built structures were made from wood and most served as barrack blocks for the troops. Quonset huts were semi-cylindrical tunnels of corrugated steel that served either as barracks, offices or storage. The Americans also used thatched buildings that had been built for them by the Kanaks—the Melanesian people of the island—using traditional building methods. It was by performing tasks, including assisting and serving the troops, that helped the local population to acquire the higher wages on offer to those who worked for the Americans. Furthermore, the report's construction figures refuted d'Argenlieu's baseless accusations about the American building programme in New Caledonia.

On 6th June, an American request to increase the number of Melanesian personnel working in the Nouméa docks, from 500 to 800, was declined by Jan Bourgeau,[107] the secretary-general of the colony since March 1941.[108] The refusal was on the grounds of the difficulty in acquiring labour on the island. Bourgeau insisted that the potential workforce would serve a better purpose, in the fields, by ensuring that the island's food supply did not dwindle. This was a pressing concern

[107] HENNINGHAM, 'The French Administration…', 1994, p. 29.

[108] LAWREY John, *The Cross of Lorraine…*, 1982, p. 53.

because inflation was steadily eating into the wealth of those who were on fixed salaries. With the influx of demand, primarily from the American troops, the business opportunities opened to those who were enterprising. However, the increasing revenues entering the island's limited commercial sector risked depleting the stocks of consumer goods available on the island and thus raise inflation ever higher. As a means of responding to these criticisms, a postal exchange was set up and the Red Cross opened a canteen from which they sold consumer goods to the armed forces.[109] This helped to keep the products, and profits, out of general circulation. Controlled distribution allowed demand to fall and prices to return to a more reasonable level.

By 1944, Lend-Lease figures show that American troops, stationed in North Africa, West Africa and New Caledonia, had received war supplies and industrial material worth an estimated $46.75 million. This was a percentage increase of 56% on the services provided by those territories, under reciprocal Lend-Lease, up to the end of 1943.[110] While these do not identify individual countries, the money demonstrates the scale of the assistance that was afforded to the Free French movement, and the territories that they controlled. As Mulholland explains, when the Americans left New Caledonia, they left the island with far better infrastructure, services and, ultimately, richer than when the first U.S. troops disembarked in 1942.[111]

## Subscriptions to Help the French Resistance

As the above considerations were in the economic sphere, they did not have a direct implication on the financing of French resistance as such. Instead, the contributions of the Levant, French Equatorial Africa and New Caledonia acted as a means for providing the Free French movement with an increased level of importance in the eyes of Allied strategists. The most direct colonial contribution to funding French resistance was through donated money, notably via funding drives and the organisation of social, sporting and cultural events within the colonies. This was money

[109] MUNHOLLAND, *Rock of Contention…*, 2005, p. 154.

[110] Vere Harmsworth Library, Rothermere American Institute, Oxford, *14th Report to Congress on Lend-Lease Operations—For the period to December 31, 1943,* 11 March 1944, p. Chap. 3, p. 29—(((46,750,000–30,000,000)/30000000)*100%).

[111] MUNHOLLAND, *Rock of Contention…*, 2005, p. 227.

that was provided by expatriated French citizens as well as donations from colonial subjects and foreign workers, in much a similar way as to those funds sent to the movement from the Free French delegations around the world.

These funds were intended to pay for arms and ammunition. Any purchases would be sent to France, thereby directly helping the *réfractaires* and those actively participating in the fight for French freedom. The money was to be sent to Algiers and kept in an account that required the express authorisation of General de Gaulle to be used. While it was not presumed that the amounts that would be collected from the fundraising would be particularly significant, they would serve as a useful propaganda tool for the Fighting French.[112] Moreover, these funds were raised from people of all ethnic origins and the contributions were not to be imposed but were, instead, to be solicited. Great care was taken to avoid these donations appearing as though they were simply another level of taxation.[113] The campaign ran from 20th September to 11th November 1943. As this was in the middle of the Italian campaign, which saw the liberation of Corsica, it is likely that these events helped to raise the level of donations even further. The amounts have been tallied in Table 6.4.

These donations are classed in terms of their size, from largest to smallest, and the total raised was close to 229 million francs. The greatest contribution came from French West Africa, which had rallied to the Allied camp in December 1942, whose donors offered around sixty per cent of the funds raised. It may suggest that their population was very generous, or hint at the efficacy of those leading the funding drive in the country. From Cogneau, Dupraz and Mesplé-Somp's work on fiscal capacity and dualism in colonial states, it is clear that, while Europeans made up only a tiny minority of the population share in French West Africa, their average income per capita was far higher than those of either the indigenous poor or non-poor.[114] Similar conclusions could

[112] ANOM, 1AFF-POL 879, Souscription Aide à la Résistance, 'Donnons des Armes à la Résistance', *Combat*, 11 September 1943.

[113] ANOM, 1AFF-POL 879, Souscription Aide à la Résistance, *Projet d'Appel*, Undated (1943).

[114] COGNEAU Denis, DUPRAZ Yannick, MESPLÉ-SOMPS Sandrine, 'Fiscal Capacity and Dualism in Colonial States: The French Empire 1830–1962', *Paris School of Economics Working Paper*, N° 2018–2027, 2019, 126p., p. 50, https://hal.archives-ouvertes.fr/halshs-01818700v3/document

**Table 6.4** Results of the national subscription to help the resistance, 6 December 1943 (ANOM, 1AFF-POL 879)

| Country | Amount | % |
|---|---|---|
| French West Africa | 141,314,029 | 61.90 |
| Madagascar (Civilians) | 34,700,000 | 15.20 |
| French Equatorial Africa | 21,000,000 | 9.20 |
| French India | 7,500,000 | 3.29 |
| Martinique (Civilians) | 6,600,000 | 2.89 |
| Martinique (Army) | 6,600,000 | 2.89 |
| New Caledonia (Civilians) | 4,529,411 | 1.98 |
| Cameroon | 4,101,053 | 1.80 |
| Oceania | 3,110,000 | 1.36 |
| Guadeloupe | 2,200,000 | 0.96 |
| Somalia | 2,091,488.65 | 0.92 |
| French Guiana | 602,084.50 | 0.26 |
| New Hebrides | 445,309 | 0.20 |
| Saint-Pierre-et-Miquelon | 351,386 | 0.15 |
| Belgian Congo | 230,000 | 0.10 |
| Madagascar (Army) | 111,318 | 0.05 |
| Seba in Fezzan | 28,390 | 0.01 |
| **Total (Francs)** | **228,306,819.10** | |
| Actual total (Francs) | 228,914,469.15 | |
| Total in £ (1:176.625) | 1,292,607.61 | |

be reached about the funds that were raised by Malagasy civilians, who donated fifteen per cent of the total. Therefore, seventy-five per cent of these donations came from these two countries alone. Neither of their populations would be classed as 'rich' by any conventional standards. French West Africa had limited population numbers of around 15.6 million inhabitants, in 1910, and covered a wide geographical expanse of 4.7 million $km^2$.[115] While G.D.P. is difficult to calculate for the African colonies, largely due to a paucity of data, estimations have been made by McLeary showing that these fluctuated between $1575 and $1898 per capita.[116] The donations in Table 6.4 show that around 9 francs were donated per head of population, in French West Africa. To offer some form of comparison, the figures will need to be compared with those of another colonial territory; in this instance, New Caledonia shall be used.

Unlike other countries cited in the above table, detailed analysis was kept of those New Caledonians who gave to the cause. While the 4.3 million francs donated do not tally *exactly* with those cited above, they fall within an acceptable margin of error. It is shown that 1.8 million francs were donated by 'Europeans', or Caucasians who supported de Gaulle's movement; 1.2 million francs were donated by 'companies'; 747,000 francs were raised at fêtes and dances; 186,000 francs were gifted by the indigenous Kanaks; 139,000 francs came from the Asian community; and 103,000 francs were given by members of the armed forces.[117] According to Henningham, around 70,000 people lived on the islands prior to the arrival of the American task force in 1942.[118] This means that, per capita,

[115] COGNEAU Denis, DUPRAZ Yannick, MESPLÉ-SOMPS Sandrine, 'African States & Development in Historical Perspective: Colonial Public Finances in British and French West Africa', *Paris School of Economics Working Paper*, N°2018–2029, 2018, 37p., p. 5, https://horizon.documentation.ird.fr/exl-doc/pleins_textes/divers18-07/010072984.pdf

[116] McLEARY Luke, *Rethinking Africa's GDP, 1796–1950*, Master's Thesis, Universitat de Barcelona School of Economics, 2018, 40p., p. 16, http://diposit.ub.edu/dspace/bitstream/2445/125521/1/TFM-ECO_McLeary_2018.pdf

[117] ANOM, 1AFF-POL 879, *Résultat complet et détaillé de la souscription du 20 septembre 1943 au 11 novembre 1943 pour venir en aide aux Combattants et Patriotes de France*, 22 December 1943.

[118] HENNINGHAM Stephen, 'The French Administration, the Local Population and the American Presence in New Caledonia, 1943–1944', *Journal de la Société des Océanistes*, 98, 1994, pp. 21–41, p. 22.

the New Caledonians donated a total of 61 francs. Using the population estimates in Munholland, it would appear that the Europeans gave 105.88 francs per head, while the Asians offered 12.63 francs and the Melanesians donated the least, with 6.41 francs being given, per capita, to the funding drive.[119] There were, therefore, marked differences between the donations gifted by the different communities on the islands. When considering the social, professional and cultural distinctions, this is hardly surprising. The Kanaks tended to work the land or in industry, whereas the more well-to-do 'Europeans' tended to work in the administration or commercial enterprise. However, this must be nuanced as many of settler descent also eked out a living working the land on the western side of the island and were known as *Broussard*—which is taken from the French word for 'bush'—or served as supervisors in the mines.[120] Concerning the Asian community, many served as technicians, but their incomes remained limited in comparison with those of European descent. Nonetheless, these funds translated into tangible military support that was received by resistance members in metropolitan France.

The colonial contributions that the Free French territories made towards the war effort were numerous but were not easily quantifiable, either economically or monetarily. Instead, it was their geostrategic position and the provision of raw materials that were vital to the Allied armaments industries.

Syria and Lebanon helped to facilitate a successful Allied invasion, which was inestimable from the perspective of morale. Furthermore, its proximity to the shipping lanes allowed Britain to continue sending ships to the Indian Ocean and the Pacific, through the Suez Canal. This objective meant that the British and the Free French needed stability in the countries. The creation of a 'Wheat Fund' allowed for the purchase of stock, which helped to keep grain prices stable and avoided farmers hoarding their produce. Between 1942 and 1943, the Middle East region reduced imports of wheat by 63%. This was an immense success, when considering the challenging circumstances, and was a credit to those who performed the rural collections of wheat and paid the farmers. It was

[119] MUNHOLLAND, *Rock of Contention*..., 2005, p. 87; Calculations: Europeans—1,800,000frs/17,000; Asian—139,000frs/11,000; Melanesian—186,000frs/29,000.

[120] Ibid.

also a testament to the policymakers who succeeded where generations of previous tax and tithe collectors had failed.

In French Equatorial Africa, the rising gold prices of 1940 and 1941 were followed by declining production in the final years of the war. While African gold was a boon to the Free French movement, from the point of view of refuting the Vichy and Nazi propaganda efforts, it was not as vital to the war effort as other raw materials, such as groundnuts, for making oil, or natural rubber. However, one of the major difficulties experienced in colonial Africa was with resource transportation. The U.S. armed forces attempted to resolve the problem through the enlargement of the airport at Pointe-Noire. However, this risked provoking further intractability on the part of the Free French, vis-à-vis the future of any Allied war *matériel* that was to be installed on French territorial possessions.

Similar issues occurred on New Caledonia, in the Pacific. The nascent American military-industrial complex was remarkably efficient at building vast facilities and transporting armies across the world. However, their dealings with local authorities seemed less diplomatically astute, even if their presence was popular and very profitable for the local people. In truth, clashes of personalities progressively worsened logistical difficulties. Nevertheless, the importance of the nickel mines on the island and its geography, in geostrategic terms, meant that the economic and military collaboration between the Gaullists in the South Pacific and the Americans resulted in a viable and working relationship.

However, the most tangible, and quantifiable, contribution towards funding French resistance was the direct subscriptions that were paid to the Fighting French in 1943 and which were to be transferred to France in ever-increasing increments. The funding drives were never expected to be particularly successful, so even the small amounts that were raised should be viewed as being a victory. Furthermore, these subscriptions were not exclusively from European expatriate communities but were also contributed by local minority ethnic communities too. This shows the diversity of support that the Fighting French movement solicited and illustrates the strength of feeling against Axis tyranny that was felt in far-flung parts of the French empire.

The colonial contributions were based upon reciprocity and good faith between the Allies, which rendered the economic collaboration a successful one. However, the exploitation of indigenous labour was troubling even for contemporaries, as was shown in French Equatorial Africa. Ultimately, however, these case studies underline the relative impotence of the Fighting French movement to act of its own initiative. In Syria, the funds that were provided for the purchase of wheat were not from French sources. In New Caledonia, the sheer weight of the Patch's forces doubled the population overnight and even the subscription payments, intended for French resistance, necessitated British assistance in order to be sent into France.

Nonetheless, the economic contributions from the rallied territories were a much-needed demonstration of collective support for the Gaullist movement. Britain benefitted from the natural resources that the Fighting French rallied territories provided, as a means to help bolster the economic stability of her own imperial territories. For the United States, the strategic importance of the Fighting French territories served both to infuriate them, as was the case with the Saint-Pierre-et-Miquelon incident of 1941, and also helped them to launch the counterattack against the Axis powers, most notably in New Caledonia and, later, from North Africa. It only remains to be seen exactly how this colonial monetary and economic assistance went on to serve French resistance efforts in France, through the actions of people like Jean Moulin, the former prefect of Eure-et-Loir, and his secretary, Daniel Cordier.

CHAPTER 7

# Of Pay and Parachutes: Mission *Rex* and the Financial Activity of Jean Moulin's Network

> Max…the capital role that he played in our combat will never be recounted by himself…[1]

Jean Moulin served as General de Gaulle's representative in metropolitan France from January 1942 until his death on 8th July 1943, following torture at the hands of Klaus Barbie. The former prefect of Eure-et-Loir's mission was to bring the disparate networks in the non-occupied zone and, eventually, throughout France, under one aegis. The financial aspects of this role fell under the responsibility of the B.C.R.A., the Central Bureau of Intelligence and Action, and of André Dewavrin, nom-de-guerre *Colonel Passy*.

This chapter aims to explain the difficulties that Daniel Cordier and Jean Moulin faced when helping to finance resistance activity, and the innovative solutions that were found to counteract them. With a network that grew from the industrial heartlands of Lyon and crossed the Line of Demarcation, the team that they assembled were able to finance clandestine activities and fund the underground existences of their collaborators. From 1942 to 1944, most of the funding came via two sections of the S.O.E. (Special Operations Executive), known as Section 'RF' and

[1] MOULIN Jean, *Premier Combat*, Paris, Les Éditions de Minuit, 1983, 169p., préface de Gén. Charles de Gaulle (1946).



D. Foulk, *The Price of Freedom*,
https://doi.org/10.1007/978-3-031-09066-0_7

Section 'F'. Essentially, 'RF' was a combined British and Free French effort and 'F' was purely organised by the British. By demonstrating that the financing of resistance activity acted as a centralising vector around the Free French, more so than any other, with the possible exception of the receipt of arms and ammunitions, the constraints that were placed upon resistance activity in France become clearer to see.

Previously, no study of the Gaullist or S.O.E. account books have been undertaken; despite sociological,[2] military[3] and administrative[4] studies having all been conducted. Binot and Boyer briefly considered the sources of the funding, but they stopped at simply confirming their initial hypothesis on funding being sourced in the U.K., having relied solely upon the use of French archival sources.[5] While laudable in its scope, Albertelli's work on the B.C.R.A. neglects to consider the funding that facilitated the covert action in France. This chapter concentrates on the financing of a single mission, the REX mission, and has been clarified through the reflections of one of those most heavily involved; Daniel Cordier, nom-de-guerre *Alain*, who served as the mission's secretary after parachuting into France in June 1942. As one of the most experienced political operators to reach London by the end of 1941, an important aspect of Moulin's mission was financial in nature. It represented the connection of the internal French resistance and the external Gaullist movement, both politically and financially.

By channelling the administrative capability and political structures of the movements, Moulin was able to help organise a supply chain of both money and arms that served the fight for French liberation. While the movements may not necessarily have agreed with de Gaulle's policy, the donations provided did generate a certain level of influence by the Free French, as the financing effectively supported their propaganda, intelligence collecting and military actions. Without the strong ties and organisational network established by Moulin and his colleagues, French

[2] MURACCIOLE Jean-François, *Les Français Libres, L'autre résistance*, Paris, Éditions Tallandier, 2009, 424p.

[3] ALBERTELLI, *Les services secrets du général De Gaulle…*, 2009.

[4] OULMONT, *Pierre Denis*, 2012.

[5] BINOT, BOYER, *L'argent de la Résistance*, 2010.

resistance would have been in a markedly more precarious position, both monetarily and in terms of preparedness, for the trials that would be presented to them throughout 1943 and 1944.

## *Régis* and the Financial Support of General de Gaulle

In June 1940, Jean Moulin was serving as prefect of Eure-et-Loir. His *département* seat, at Chartres, was overrun and he fell victim to the German army. He was imprisoned and was left to attempt suicide, having been subjected to attempts at forcing him to issue spurious proclamations as to the identities of those who had committed a massacre, nearby.[6] Leaving his administrative post a few months later, on 1st December, he travelled to the south of France to visit his mother at Saint-Andiol. Over the course of the next few months, he travelled to Marseille where he began to meet others who wished to take direct action against the invaders. He collated the information into a report, written in Portugal, from where he wanted to try and cross to Britain.[7] Clearly, Moulin was too great a draw for the British and the Free French to be left languishing in Lisbon. On Sunday, 19th October, he was flown out by seaplane and arrived, the next day, in Poole.[8]

Undoubtedly, Moulin's political reputation helped him to arrange a meeting with General de Gaulle, on 25th October 1941, but his presence in London also represented an opportunity for the Free French movement; as a former prefect, he would prove invaluable to the movement. The movements that Moulin represented—*Libération*, *Libération nationale* and *Liberté*[9]—needed money to function. It was in their name that he came to request de Gaulle's assistance, as well as to offer his own

[6] MOULIN Jean, *Premier Combat*, Paris, Les Éditions de Minuit, 1983, 169p., p. 109.

[7] CORDIER Daniel, *Jean Moulin: La République des Catacombes*, Vol. 1, Paris, Folio, 2011, (Ebook), Chap. 2, Para. 111 & 113—"Finally, on 9th September 1941, after having examined resisting France, Jean Moulin left Metropolitan France... After having traversed Spain, Jean Moulin arrived in Lisbon on 12th September 1941".

[8] LEVISSE-TOUZÉ Christine, 'Faux Papiers de Jean Moulin', http://museedelaresistanceenligne.org/media3331-Faux-papiers-de-Jean-Moulin, consulted 31 October 2020.

[9] TNA, HS 910106, *Extracts from M. Jean Pierre Moulin's interrogation report after arrival in England, 20th October 1941*, 23 October 1941.

to the nascent external resistance.[10] They had to pay for the increasing costs of specialised printing that newsletters and underground newspapers demanded; the payment of salaries to those employed on a full-time basis; the rental of property. All represented heavy fixed costs, which would only increase due to the rampant inflation that Vichy was trying to quell.[11]

Initially, he requested three million francs per month, which was to be doubled by the end of the year,[12] as Daniel Cordier confirmed.[13] As the largest movement, which had been formed from the fusion of Henri Frenay's *Mouvement de Libération nationale* (M.L.N.) and *Liberté*,[14] *Combat* had been incapable of raising more than 400,000 francs since the fall of France.[15] It was thus clear that the movements' aspirations for growth would have been complicated, without external assistance. The report underlines Moulin's commitment that any funds that were awarded to him would serve to support propaganda efforts, as opposed to any acts of violence. Public support and influence were of fundamental importance in ensuring growth for a developing internal movement. Unfortunately, as Frenay remarked, printing presses were expensive pieces of equipment to run and were extremely difficult to acquire.[16] Nonetheless, their aim was to reach the masses, despite their "derisory means".[17] Moulin had

[10] TNA, HS 910106, *Liberté, Libération Nationale, Libération*, 25 October 1941.

[11] GRENARD Fabrice, LE BOT Florent, PERRIN Cédric, *Histoire économique de Vichy*, Paris, Perrin, 2017, 500p. (Ebook), Chap. 5, Para. 50—"Shortages and the black market fuelled an inflationary surge, the most violent in France in the twentieth century and in Europe during the same period - Greece and Italy excepted... Inflation peaked in 1945 and 1948: averaging 19% per year from 1938 to 1944".

[12] TNA, HS 910106, *Rapport sur l'activité, les projets et les besoins des groupements constitués en France en vue de la libération du territoire national*, Undated, p. 9.

[13] CORDIER Daniel, *Jean Moulin*..., 2011, Chap. 4, Para. 174 (Ebook)—"3) On money – Initially, a sum of three million per month for the three movements – this sum should be doubled at the end of the year".

[14] Biographical information on Henri Frenay, https://www.ordredelaliberation.fr/fr/compagnons/henri-frenay, consulted 14 August 2021.

[15] TNA, HS 910106, *Rapport sur l'activité, les projets et les besoins des groupements constitués en France en vue de la libération du territoire national*, Undated, p. 8.

[16] FRENAY, *La nuit finira*, 1973, p. 76—"We cannot acquire a new machine, but are able to find a very old, used model".

[17] Idem, p. 77—"With derisory means, it was a mass that we aimed to reach progressively, in order to make use of the men, whom we would need to perform particular tasks in the clandestine battles".

therefore proposed to act as the intermediary who would seek to arrange British and Free French funding for the heads of the movements, in exchange for the vital on-the-ground information that they could provide.

Moulin's mission as de Gaulle's representative in France began with two parachuting tests in England, on 31st October 1941.[18] These went well and, during Moulin's actual jump, back into France, on the night of 1st January 1942, he took with him 1,500,000 francs, meaning half a million francs for each of the represented movements.[19] While it remained a risky venture, this was only half of the three million francs that had initially been requested.

Parachute jumps were incredibly dangerous events for the crews of the aircraft, the passengers and the welcoming committee. The risk was exacerbated by the fact that most of the people organising these actions were relatively inexperienced, in terms of the technical acumen required to arrange major logistical operations. Money transportation took place concurrently with the transfer of people. The bills would be bundled into 100,000-franc amounts, with violet bands indicating the amount.[20] When a transfer needed to be made to one of Moulin's intermediaries, the bundle would be secreted within a copy of a newspaper which would be passed from one person's hand to another. As operational security dictated that Moulin should meet his contacts as rarely as possible, it became necessary for him to form his own general staff, in order to facilitate these quotidian tasks.

## The Secretariat

The first person to be recruited was Daniel Cordier, *Alain*, a member of the *Bureau central de renseignement et d'action* (Central Bureau of Intelligence and Action), who was parachuted, on 26th July 1942, close

[18] TNA, HS 910106, *Parachute Training Report*, 3 November 1941.

[19] TNA, HS 910106, *Air Transport Form N° 5, Air Transport Operation Report, Signed W/Cmdr. J.E. Benham.*

[20] Interview conducted with Daniel Bouyjou-Cordier, Cannes, 11 May 2017—"The notes were held with a violet wrapper which meant that we could skip recounting the money. They were stacked in 100,000 francs or in a million. If one needed 400,000 francs, therefore, one needed four stacks".

to Montluçon.[21] Much of the equipment that Cordier carried during his parachute jump was bought from shops around London. Each operative was free to choose clothes that corresponded with their character and which were fitted to their measurements. He wore his suit underneath the R.A.F. jumpsuits with which they were issued, made from heavy linen to avoid any damage to their clothes upon descent.[22] Originally, Cordier was supposed to work as wireless operator for Georges Bidault, head of the *Bureau d'Information et de Presse* (Bureau of Intelligence and Press). However, necessity intervened and, on 1st August, Cordier met Moulin for the first time. It was a meeting that would have lifelong consequences for both men.

The duties of the secretariat were much like those of other, non-clandestine, administrative organisations—notably report-writing, letter production, accounting, organisation of meetings[23]—to which were added tasks that would not have been within the remit of an ordinary secretarial body, including the encoding and decoding of clandestine correspondence or the organisation of secure letter-drop locations and hide-outs.

Cordier was tasked by Moulin with organising an administration, with whom he could liaise to ensure that all the necessary duties were covered. Early contacts proved invaluable, such as Paul Schmidt, a B.C.R.A. liaison officer who ensured the provision of weapons and equipment, as well as organising parachute drops and supply dumps; Anne-Marie Bauer, *Claudine*, who participated in all aspects of the organisation, including wireless transmissions, under the codename *Eureka*; or the Moret family, whose city-centre house became an ideal base for Cordier, and upon whom he would rely for the acquisition of material that was difficult to obtain.

[21] CORDIER Daniel, *Alias Caracalla*, Paris, Gallimard, 2009, 929p., p. 321—"Daniel Cordier, parachuted on Sunday 26th July (1942), at 2 a.m., near to Montluçon".

[22] Interview, Cordier, 11 May 2017—"We were dressed, and we were given the suits to put over the top, and also a revolver or a knife. It was a jumpsuit in heavy linen because if we fell into a tree, we could not very well be half-naked, holes in the trousers or a ripped jacket".

[23] CORDIER Daniel, *Jean Moulin*…, 2011, Chap. 6, Para. 151 (Ebook)—"type notes, letters and reports, coding and decoding of texts, archiving important sheets, accounting, distribution of funds, prospecting for secure locations, organisation of meetings with the service chiefs and other people of responsibility."

These people helped to support resistance activities through their technical capabilities or their free labour. They must also be classed as being integral parts of the resistance economic system.

Laure Diebold was one of Cordier's earliest collaborators in the underground network that they created. Diebold, alias *Mado*, was a secretary from Alsace and, having been a member of the '*Mithridate*' network as a liaison officer, her skills were highly valued.[24] Despite her arrest, alongside her husband and fellow refugee, Eugène, Diebold was released, in July 1942, through a lack of evidence. They went to Aix-les-Bains, in order to escape the increasing scrutiny under which they had fallen. It is at this time, on 9th August 1942, that Diebold was introduced to Cordier, for whom she would become secretary. The initial meeting took place over lunch with the Moret family, where Cordier explained her future duties, including the drafting of telegrams, letters and reports; accountancy and the coding of classified messages.[25] Binot and Boyer state that she was paid 1,200 francs per month for her copywriting skills[26] which was the same wage that Cordier was paid by Moulin[27] They were both trusted lieutenants for Moulin and Cordier acknowledged her as being the "corner stone of his secretariat".[28] However, due to difficulties involved with finding an office, Diebold was forced to work from home. This became a continual concern, as operational security dictated that one should separate clandestine work and homelife.

Almost immediately, Cordier came to rely on the false ration papers with which he had been provided. He also began to realise the true value of the home-cooking that he had eaten with the Moret family, who had insisted that Cordier dined alongside them on his first evening

[24] Biographical information on Laure Diebold, *Ordre de la Libération*, https://www.ordredelaliberation.fr/fr/compagnons/laure-diebold, consulted 20 November 2019.

[25] CORDIER, *Alias Caracalla*, 2009, p. 377—"I explained the work – typing telegrams, letters and reports, keeping accounts and helping me to encode and decode the texts exchanged with London".

[26] BINOT, BOYER, *L'argent de la Résistance*, 2010, p. 14—« Recrutée en août 1942, Laure Diebold, alias *Mado*, touche 1 200 francs par mois pour se charger de la frappe des lettres et rapports de Jean Moulin»

[27] CORDIER, *Alias Caracalla*, 2009, p. 378—"I announce to him that she received, as I did, 1,200 francs".

[28] Idem, p. 414—"Much as Mado became the cornerstone of my secretariat..."

in their home.[29] It allowed him to avoid making the potentially fatal mistake of looking quizzically at the ration slips that he had brought over from London, when paying in a restaurant, which would, undoubtedly, have raised suspicion. Moreover, when the fare served in such restaurants consisted of little but virtually inedible vegetables, fruit and bread, the Moret's home cooking served as a welcome alternative, which helped to welcome Cordier back into an environment which had changed greatly since he left, in June 1940.

During the period of mission's activity, the Moulin network grew from Moulin, Cordier and Diebold to include fifteen people. Payroll began to accrue, and the spending increased, from 30,000 to 40,000 francs.[30] For typists, a salary of 800 francs per month was paid. These wages remunerated copywriting and encoding tasks, holding packages and may have been used to pay bribes for the acquisition of information. Cordier remarked:

> I ate little and could not go on the black market with those prices. I remember, one night, accompanying Moulin to his lodgings…Passing under the light, he looked at me and said, "Are you eating enough?". I told him: "Well, I eat with what you have told me that I am able to spend, but to eat sufficiently costs a lot more than that, so I don't really have the means". He responded: "Well! You will take what you need and tell me how much it'll cost. For those around you, too. The couriers…"[31]

This attitude corresponds to the left-wing convictions that Moulin professed to Cordier, and the relationships that he had previously kept,

[29] Idem, p. 329—"I understand, at once, that this refined meal, offered by our hosts, had cost them much".

[30] Interview, Cordier, 11 May 2017—"I believe that, in the accounts that I published, the secretariat went from spending little - 30,000 to 40,000 francs - to nearly 200,000 francs for fifteen people"—The figure of 200,000 francs split between fifteen personnel would indicate a salary of about 13,300 francs per person, per month which, while possible, seems implausible, when considering Moulin's reputation for frugality.

[31] Interview, Cordier, 11 May 2017; Similar views are expressed in CORDIER, *Alias Caracalla*, 2009, p. 436.

with Pierre Cot among others.[32] It could be argued that Moulin should have already realised that menu prices, on the black market, would have rendered it virtually impossible to live on such a salary, week-after-week. Henri Frenay[33] the leader of Combat, said that a 'reasonably-priced' bistro meal cost fifteen francs.[34] Over the course of a month, this would have cost between 425 and 475 francs per meal. Any extra meals would have further eaten into their monthly salaries. As a former prefect, Moulin's decisive response reflected the actions of an experienced manager and leader. It demonstrated a level of practicality, notably in his recognising of the need for those who facilitated his own mission to eat correctly, at the very least, and, therefore, to maintain their operational readiness. Managing eighteen-hour days, waking at 06:00 and sleeping at midnight—until the imposition of a curfew in 1943[35] interrupted this rhythm—fuelled by meagre rations, operating under great stress; it is unsurprising that his personnel were more prone to succumbing to illness. However, Moulin was fundamentally opposed to any demonstrations of largesse with the public purse and thus kept a close watch over the spending.[36] Such difficulties and considerations were both banal in their ordinariness and yet were tactically vital. Without keeping a tight rein over the network's finances, periods of penury would have become ever more frequent. Resistance required regular financing as it involved living on the peripheries of society and those participating in such activity could not even receive the meagre rations that were being provided to the other members of society. As Gildea explained, city dwellers themselves began to take their bicycles further afield to procure scarce farm products and

[32] Interview, Cordier, 11 May 2017—"He was a man of the left, and I explained that, due to my family, I was of the right"; TNA, HS 910106, *MI5 Minute Sheet 15/10/1941—Jean Moulins (Sic.)*, 29 November 1941—"His ideas are slightly 'left' – was believed to have been friendly with Pierre Cot".

[33] FRENAY, *La nuit finira*, 1973, p. 66—"...Concerning cheap restaurants with fixed prices, without surprise. I retain two, at Perrache".

[34] BINOT, BOYER, *L'argent de la Résistance*, 2010, p. 32—"eating in 15-franc restaurants".

[35] 'Couvre-feu pendant la Seconde Guerre mondiale', *Mémoire Alpine*, https://web.archive.org/web/20200807220144/http:/www.memoire-alpine.com/couvre-feu-pendant-la-seconde-guerre-mondiale_pat325.php, consulted 20 November 2019.

[36] Interview, Cordier, 11 May 2017—"I simply knew that if one needed 100,000 or 200,000 francs, I would ask Moulin before. I never spent a centime without the express word of Moulin".

rural families could make a killing on the long-distance black market.[37] Clearly, for clandestine forces, the economic and financial problems were amplified from the very beginning of their missions and only improved incrementally over time.

## Pay & Penury

In order to better understand the efficacy of the monetary transfers to Moulin's organisation, Table 7.1 offers an overview of the money sent from the beginning of the mission until the final deliveries of Moulin's clandestine career, showing the monetary flows from London to France from March 1942 to June 1943. However, this summary does not show the initial transfer of 1.5 m francs that De Gaulle made to Moulin, during his first visit to London, in October 1941.

Distinct periods in the financial evolution of Mission REX can be seen. The initial period lasted from October 1941 to August 1942. During those months, the expedited funds remained relatively limited, at around one million to two million francs per month. This was the time that Moulin was operating alone in unoccupied France, cultivating contacts through the clandestine world in Lyon and the Rhône-Alpes region. This meant that he would have had far fewer chances to organise the reception of parachutes which, therefore, limited the funds that could have been sent into France.

The second period, which began slightly after Daniel Cordier arrived in June 1942, showed an increase in funds. From August to September 1942, the growth was 150% and, from September to October, by 300%. This stabilised at seven million francs per month, an increase from the August 1942 figure by 250%. Here, the quantitative impact of the secretariat becomes apparent. With the commissioning of Daniel Cordier as secretary and his fledgling organisation, the increased administrative capacity meant that the deliveries could become more frequent. This money was to be split between the representatives of the different movements whom Moulin was supporting. However, this variable was not operating in isolation. The tide of the war had begun to shift following the entry of the United States and the ill-fated German invasion of the

[37] GILDEA Robert, *Marianne in Chains: In Search of the German Occupation 1940–45* (London, Macmillan, 2002), (Ebook, Picador, 2011), 465p., Chap. 1, Para. 36.

**Table 7.1** Funds paid to Mission REX, (AN, AG3 (2) 277—171 MI 109 BCRA)—Dark blue are author's own calculations

| Month | Transfer in Fcs. | Transfer in $ | $ rate | $ Value in Fcs. | Monthly Total in Fcs. | N° of Resistance Members Potentially Funded by REX Mission (1,500 Fcs. pcm) |
|---|---|---|---|---|---|---|
| March 1942 | 550,000 | 5,000 | 100 | 500,000 | 1,050,000 | 700 |
| June 1942 | 1,000,000 | | | | 1,000,000 | 666 |
| | 2,000,000 | | | | 2,000,000 | 1,333 |
| July 1942 | | 20,000 | 100 | 2,000,000 | 2,000,000 | 1,333 |
| August 1942 | 2,000,000 | | | | 2,000,000 | 1,333 |
| September 1942 | 3,500,000 | 15,000 | 100 | 1,500,000 | 5,000,000 | 3,330 |
| October 1942 | 15,000,000 | 35,700 | 140 | 5,000,000 | 20,000,000 | 13,320 |
| December 1942 | 1,000,000 | 42,850 | 140 | 6,000,000 | 7,000,000 | 4,666 |
| January 1943 | 1,400,000 | 40,000 | 140 | 5,600,000 | 7,000,000 | 4,666 |
| February 1943 | 2,000,000 | 25,000 | 200 | 5,000,000 | 7,000,000 | 4,666 |
| March 1943 | | 100,000 | 200 | 20,000,000 | 20,000,000 | 13,320 |
| April 1943 | | 100,000 | 200 | 20,000,000 | 20,000,000 | 13,320 |
| May 1943 | | 176,500 | 170 | 30,000,000 | 30,000,000 | 20,000 |
| June 1943 | 42,025,000 | 217,000 | 175 | 37,975,000 | 80,000,000 (+2,000,000) | 54,666 |
| **TOTAL** | **70,475,000** | **777,050** | - | **133,575,000** | **206,050,000** | **137,319** |

U.S.S.R., Operation Barbarossa, which meant that the tactical nightmare of fighting on multiple fronts became a reality for the Axis powers.

By October 1942, the financial channels were becoming more established with the developing secretariat. The arrival of Cordier, as a wireless operator, meant that communications could be resumed with more regularity. Joseph Monjaret (*Hervé*), the radio operator who parachuted into

France alongside Jean Moulin and Raymond Fassin (*Sif*) on New Years' Day 1942, had his movements noticed and was initially ordered to return to London[38] However, he asked Moulin to assign him elsewhere and he returned to the shadows as a liaison officer, with the *Franc-Tireur* movement, in the unoccupied zone. Despite the loss of an experienced wireless operator, the arrival of Cordier and the establishment of the secretariat meant that Monjaret's communication duties were assured.

The three principal movements—*Combat*, *Libération* and *Franc-Tireur*—began to receive regular monthly payments. *Combat* was accorded the most money and, thus, it may be assumed that they were the most important to the efforts of the B.C.R.A. On 15th October 1942, a message was sent which stated that, for the month of September, *Combat* were issued 1.2 million francs, *Libération* received 400,000 francs, whereas *Franc-Tireur* were allocated only 120,000 francs.[39] When it is taken into account that Moulin was authorised, at the beginning of the month, to spend ten million francs in the occupied zone and the same amount for the unoccupied zone, this meant that the totality of September's spending amounted to only 12% of the overall authorised total.[40] Of this 12%, nearly 70% went to Combat. The sum of 20 million francs, in October, was a double count, intended to provide a contingency 'float' in the event of an impossibility to transport funds from one month to the next.[41] The remaining 30% was split between *Libération* and *Franc-Tireur*.

Since the war ended, it has been virtually impossible to accurately compare the sizes of the various resistance movements in terms of their memberships, as written archives were few and far between. However, by using their monetary receipts, comparison becomes a possibility. The same

[38] 'Entretien avec Joseph MONJARET', *Magazine 39–45*, N° 88, October 1993, http://www.memorialjeanmoulin.fr/articles.php?lng=fr&pg=495#mainContent, consulted 21 November 2019.

[39] AN, AG 3 (2) 277—171 MI 109 BCRA—Dossier 1—Jean Moulin and Rex Mission, *Extrait du câble N° 88 et 89 de REX à Etat-Major Forces Françaises Libres*, 15 October 1942.

[40] (1,200,000/10,000,000)*100% = 12%.

[41] AN, AG 3 (2) 277, *Letter from Colonel Passy, B.C.R.A., to Lieutenant-Colonel Billotte, chief of staff*, 10 December 1942—"Following telegrams and conversations with the heads of *Combat* and *Libération*, we have decided to send to the President of the Coordinating Committee, a total sum of 20,000,000 francs which will provide the necessary reserve of funds for the smooth running of the resistance's work in France".

pattern is present for the figures for July 1942. In July, *Combat* received 800,000 francs as opposed to the 430,000 francs awarded to *Libération* and 55,000 francs for *Franc-Tireur*, meaning that the amount that had been given to *Combat* was practically double that awarded to the other movements.[42] The growth in the funding to *Combat* is clear, with a 50% increase between July and September. The funding for *Libération* actually dropped by 7%. *Franc-Tireur* received an increase, of 118%, on their July funds. This meant that *Franc-Tireur*'s coffers grew by the greatest proportion over the quarter, but it remained significantly underfunded in comparison with the other two. This puts Frenay's complaints about the lack of funding into context, when he decided to seek money from Allen Dulles of the Office of Strategic Services (O.S.S.) in Switzerland.[43] In fact, *Combat* received more than the other movements supported by Jean Moulin. It also confirms that Moulin was financially supporting the largest right-wing movement to the greatest degree and was not favouring the more left-wing groups.

One would naturally assume that French resistance members would have transacted in francs, as this was the legal tender of the country. However, the use of francs had two major inconveniences. It meant either acquiring the notes that were to be despatched along with the agents who left Britain, from within France itself, or by counterfeiting them. The former was rendered difficult by the severing of trade and the latter was an inexact art and risked the lives of those who carried the counterfeit notes, meaning that the copies would have needed to be beyond reproach. One answer was to use foreign currency and the U.S. dollar was favoured. The largest transfer occurred in October 1942, to the tune of 20 million francs. It was, in reality, two payments; the first was expedited on 10th November 1942, in which Moulin acknowledging having received seven million francs and fifteen thousand dollars.[44] The second payment, for ten million francs and 30,700 dollars, was sent on 27th November.[45] Overall, these totalled seventeen million francs and 45,700 dollars.

[42] AN, AG 3 (2) 277, *Extrait du câble N° 57458 de Rex du 4.8.42 arrivé le 8.8.42*, 16 October 1942.

[43] FRENAY, *La nuit finira*, 1973, p. 311—"By cutting our budget, you wanted to strangle us, but at the same time, you were strangling the Maquis, while they called for help. We need money, and more, not less, than the previous month".

[44] AN, AG 3 (2) 277, *Message from Rex, Receipt for October*, 10 November 1942.

[45] AN, AG 3 (2) 277, *Message from Rex, Receipt for November*, 4 December 1942.

After this increase, the invasion of the unoccupied zone by German forces, on 11th November 1942, had a negative impact on the amounts being sent to the REX mission. In Cordier's account, Fassin handed him the ten million francs and 30,700 dollars.[46] The following month, however, one of the recurring issues in financing resistance came to the fore. With Moulin having left Lyon for the Midi region on 4th December, and Cordier having fallen ill and confined to his lodgings, Henri Manhès (*Frédéric*) came to collect the money for the northern-based movements. Manhès was an infantryman in the First World War but transferred to the Air Force prior to the Second, reaching the rank of commander before resigning in 1940.[47] Cordier decided, against his better judgement, to issue the requested money, taken from the 'safe' which was concealed in a fake-bottomed bin—several hundred thousand francs, in all—instead of sending it on, once he had acquired Moulin's approbation. This demonstrates the emotional toll that money in resistance circles engendered, as Manhès is reported to have said, "The Resistance is not an administration. We are at war, damn it!"[48] Through this outburst, it shows the overtaking of the 'civil' by the 'military' prerogatives and, above all, demonstrates that, when it came to money in clandestine activity, some were prepared to do anything, including intimidating colleagues, to get what they deemed as being necessary.

The third phase for the finances of the REX mission could be described as being the time at which funds were the most plentiful, from January 1943 onwards, as the organisation was expanding. In the formerly unoccupied zone, an increasing volume of transfers meant that funds were beginning to enter the coffers with more regularity. However, this also meant an increasing workload. Moulin's plans to bring the major movements of both zones under Gaullist military organisation meant that expansion into northern France was inevitable.

[46] CORDIER, *Alias Caracalla*, 2009, p. 531—"I drive him to the station at the end of the afternoon, then hurry to a meeting with Raymond Fassin: he hands me over 10 million francs and 30,700 dollars in bills, as well as the rest of the mail".

[47] 'Henri Manhès', https://www.ordredelaliberation.fr/fr/compagnons/henri-manhes, consulted 13 June 2021.

[48] CORDIER, *Alias Caracalla*, 2009, p. 549.

In April 1943, Moulin tasked Cordier and his team with going to Paris and to create a new secretariat in the city.[49] The acquisition of information and the organisation of guerrilla troops in occupied territory greatly contributed to the war effort. Not only did it help to generate a climate of fear among the occupiers, but it offered a point of reference around which those who disagreed with the pervading politics of the day could begin to group. From these transfers, conclusions can be made concerning the relative strength and success of the mission; with increasing efficiency and organisation, the more money that could penetrate the Atlantic wall, the more effective that the underground war could become.

Figure 7.1 shows the authorisations to send money to agents, issued by the B.C.R.A., against those authorisations that were given specifically to the REX mission, with the actual amounts that arrived in France, from the period November 1941 to July 1943. The trajectory of their fundraising was reflective of the increasing interconnectedness of the movements and the B.C.R.A. It also reflected the development of Jean Moulin's war, which mirrored those of the movements that made up the Gaullist internal resistance movement. It is important to underline that Special Operations Executive were running their own networks simultaneously. Through the release of financial documentation, it is possible to assess the effectiveness of the resistance organisation with a degree of objectivity that has previously been unavailable to historians.

B.C.R.A. transfer authorisations were lower those being awarded to the REX mission. Although money was being sent into France, the B.C.R.A. did not appear to be entering these in their accounts. One hypothesis could be that the amounts entered in the main B.C.R.A transfer authorisations reflected money "lost" during transportation as well as those that were successfully transferred. More likely was that the B.C.R.A.'s reported figures were to be shown to other organisations, notably the British government, and, therefore, these were intended to show that the Free French were running missions of less monetary importance than was actually the case. The Free French were certainly not experiencing difficulties in acquiring financing in the fourth quarter of 1943, after Moulin's capture and death.

In Table 7.1, the transfers were not only made in francs, but also in American dollars. Dollars were far more accessible in the U.K. than

[49] CORDIER Daniel, *Jean Moulin*..., 2011, (Ebook), Chap. 6, Para. 163.

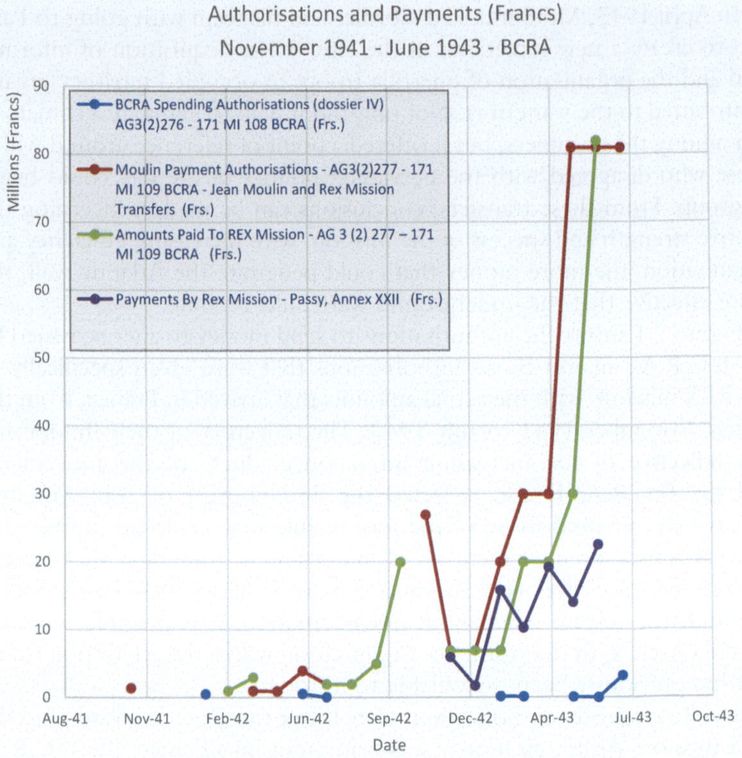


**Fig. 7.1** BCRA authorisations and payments to mission REX from 1941 to 1943, data sources appear on legend

used francs. Following the declaration of war, the gold trade had been forbidden. As dollars were worth significantly more than francs, more value could be transported in each trip by sending fewer dollars. The difficulty was finding somebody willing to change them. This problem was solved by Cordier's contacts with the Moret family. He states that they found a son of a Lyonnais banker who was able to change the London-sent dollars for French francs.[50] However, Cordier's comments also demonstrate much about the perception of value and quantity:

[50] Interview, Cordier, 11 May 2017.

> I do not remember the exact numbers, but they were not huge; a few million dollars, to be fair. it was nearly always in francs.

Quantitatively, he was quite correct. The received dollars did only amount to $777,050. When compared to the nearly 70.5 million francs that passed through his hands, it must have seemed triflingly insignificant. The bills were packed in bundles of 100,000 so the totality of American funds, seven stacks in all, would have looked miniscule when compared to the 705 bundles of francs. However, from a point of view of purchasing power, the two were practically incomparable. The dollar was, for much of the period, from March 1942 to June 1943, worth anywhere from 100 to 200 francs. This meant that the $777,050 were, in fact, worth the equivalent of 133,575,000 francs, nearly double the nominal value of the actual francs that were sent. Those seven bundles of bills did, in fact, hold great value. The fact that they were not controlled by the *Reichskreditkassen*, the issuing bank for the occupied territories, was a significant reason behind the dollar's retention of value in occupied Europe. However, the question remains as to how these dollars actually arrived in France?

## Pecuniary Politics

Moulin's impact on the wartime resistance went much further than simply providing liquidity; the administration that he and Cordier built would outlive the ex-prefect. Moulin's republican role testifies to the acquired experience that his educative and professional path had provided, as much as it indicates his political qualities. Through personal interactions with the heads of the main movements, dating back to 1941, and experience of the administrative construction of supply and communications lines to London, Moulin and Cordier helped to provide the hub around which a tentative centralisation of metropolitan resistance could occur. As Christian Pineau, the founder of *Libération Nord* and the *Phalanx* network, stated:

> He was the one who pulled the strings and to reattach them would be difficult.[51]

[51] PINEAU Christian, *La Simple Vérité 1940–1945*, Paris, Julliard, 1960, 632p., p. 121.

Centralisation offered an external link that helped to finance the resistance movements for a year and a half. The concerns of the resistance leaders were greatly increased following Pierre Laval's announcement of the '*Relève*' on 22nd June 1942.[52] Its extension was confirmed by the 'Law of 4th September 1942' which required that all adult men, up to the age of 50, and women, from 21 to 35 years-old, should acquiesce to doing work that was required by the Vichy government. This was addended by the second *Action Sauckel*, named after Fritz Sauckel, the Nazi general plenipotentiary for Labour Deployment, which implemented the *Service du Travail Obligatoire* (S.T.O.) on 16th February 1943.[53] The S.T.O. succeeded in encouraging a wave of young people to take to the mountains and forests in the lowly-populated regions of the Massif Central and the Vercors, in order to escape being pressganged into serving the Reich. In spite of the motivated manpower that this generated for the groups of *Maquis*, their needs deleteriously impacted upon the already precarious finances of the movements.

For the period between January and May 1943, shown in Fig. 7.1, the amounts authorised by the B.C.R.A. for the REX mission and those actually received in France differ. The figures quoted in Passy, showing the payments made by the REX mission, closely reflects the payments that were made to the mission. Where there was an overspend, during the month of February 1943, the amounts authorised for the following month are corrected.

In March, two major changes occurred; firstly, the transfers began to be marked as being destined for either the northern zone or the southern zone, as opposed to being combined, as was previously the case; secondly, a regrouping of the three large movements—*Combat*, *Franc-Tireur* and *Libération*—under the aegis of the *Armée secrète* had repercussions on payment destinations.

The payments being made to the movements did fall, from February to March 1943, as Frenay remarked in his book, *La nuit finira*.[54] *Combat*

[52] SERRE Robert, 'Relève et S.T.O.', *Musée de la Résistance 1940–1945 En Ligne*, http://www.museedelaresistanceenligne.org/expo.php?expo=2&theme=6&stheme=24&sstheme=47#English, consulted 19 November 2020.

[53] AGLAN, *La France à l'envers…*, 2020, p. 319.

[54] FRENAY, *La nuit finira*, 1973, p. 300—"I noticed that his March 1943 budget was inferior to that of February but certain "stakeholders", unknown to either the B.C.R.A., I believe, or *Libération* kept the preceding months' payments".

had received four million francs in February, and this fell by 800,000 francs in March. *Libération* remained static on 1.5 million francs, for both months, and *Franc-Tireur* fell from 950,000 to 650,000 francs. This represents a cumulative drop for the main movements of 1.1 million francs.

However, payments from REX for the month of February had seen an increase on January's spending by 7.9 million francs, before dropping, once again, by 5.5 million francs in March. The trend was increasing. Furthermore, the fact that spending vastly outstripped the receipt of funds for that month may also explain the difficulty for Moulin and Cordier to meet the demands of the movement heads. Whether this corresponded to the increased financial needs being required to feed and equip *Maquis* forces is debatable but Frenay's comments on the financing of the *Montagnards* appear exaggerated when he spoke of Moulin refusing all subsidies to the Maquis, despite paying the *Montagnards* in the Vercors.[55] In fact, Yves Farge, a personal friend of Jean Moulin and organiser of this mission, only received 1.2 million francs, in financing, over the two-month period.[56] With manpower of approximately 350 *maquisards*, according to Gildea, this would have meant that each *maquisard* had been allocated over 3,400 francs for the two months,[57] therefore revealing that they were allocated 1,714 francs per month. This is only slightly above the rate of funding that had been envisaged for members of the Maquis, which was 1,500 francs per month.[58] In contrast, Frenay's movement, *Combat*, were receiving 3.2 million and four million francs, at this point. Using 1,500 francs as a base assumption, the 7.2 million francs that had

[55] FRENAY, *La nuit finira*, 1973, p. 300—"I also noticed that when Max refused us any subsidy for the Maquis, he had one which at the same time he was funding. Like the others, this one was still in its infancy. However, it alone received a budget equal to a third of the entire "Combat" budget".

[56] FRENAY, *La nuit finira*, 1973, p. 300—"Its instigator was Yves Farge, personal friend of Jean Moulin. We will speak again of this *Maquis*, whose conception was madly dangerous but which was one of the highest points of the Resistance: that of the Vercors"; GILDEA, *Fighters in the Shadows*..., 2015, (Ebook) Chap. 10, Para. 9, "'From now on,' said Delestraint for security reasons, 'we will forget that name (Vercors). Your plan will be called the *Montagnard* plan". Early in April 1943, Delestraint himself visited the Vercors, where about 350 men were grouped in nine camps, and held a meeting of the organising committee".

[57] 1,200,000/350 = 3,428 francs.

[58] AN, AG 3 (2) 276—171 MI 108 BCRA, *Note for Fl/F*, 17 July 1944.

been provided by the REX mission would have funded around 2,400 members of *Combat* for a month.[59] Moreover, if the same calculation is extrapolated to take account of the entirety of the funds despatched to the REX mission during the fifteen months that Moulin was leading it, or a total of 206,050,000 francs, the number of resistance members who could have been funded per month would have been around 9,157.[60] Clearly, this is subject to certain caveats notably that different roles were paid at different rates, such as the 800 francs paid for typists as opposed to the 1,200-franc salary that Daniel Cordier initially received. Quoting the work of Granet and Michel, Ruby indicated that, in June and July 1943, the *Armée secrète* had around 50,000 members.[61] Based on the estimations made in Table 7.1, the funding situation appears to confirm Granet's and Michel's hypothesis, by demonstrating that money was potentially available for 54,666 resistance members in the month of June 1943.

However, in March 1943, there was little love lost between Frenay and Moulin. Cordier later wrote that "exasperation was growing between the heads (of the movements) and Rex, or more precisely between Frenay and Rex".[62] In *L'Affaire Suisse*, the point is made about how, during a meeting of the Committee of the *Mouvements Unis de la Résistance*, the three heads of movement attacked London's responses to their requests for extra funds:

> The crisis exploded during a meeting of the Directing Committee of the MUR which took place after Moulin's return from London on Tuesday 23rd March 1943. According to Jacques Baumel, the general secretary of the Directing Committee, who was at the meeting, together, the three heads attacked London as doing nothing significant to diffuse the timebomb which the Refractaires and the Maquisards represented.[63]

Their complaints seem to have been taken to heart by Daniel Cordier, who sympathised with their position and saw the seeming hypocrisy of

[59] ((7200000/1500)/2).

[60] ((206050000/1500)/15).

[61] RUBY Marcel, *Résistance civile et résistance militaire*, Lyon, Éditions L'Hermès, 1984, 156p., p. 105.

[62] CORDIER, *Alias Caracalla*, 2009, p. 633.

[63] BELOT Robert, KARPMAN Gilbert, *L'affaire suisse: La Résistance a-t-elle trahi de Gaulle?*, Paris, Armand Colin, 2009, 432p., p. 44.

the one that he was obliged to adopt by withholding the money.[64] However, in the light of *Combat*'s attempts to solicit ten million francs per month from the American O.S.S., represented by Allen Dulles at Berne,[65] Frenay's attempts to acquire the money from Cordier were heavy-handed.[66] In reality, the lack of available aircraft in Europe for running supply missions and the overspend in February 1943 meant that the coffers were empty. Moulin learnt from these difficulties. The following month, he contacted André Philip, national commissioner for the Interior, to request thirty million francs to ensure that he would have enough to continue the financing streams.[67]

Cordier left Lyon for Paris on 24th April 1943,[68] leaving Anton de Graaff in charge of the Lyon branch and the southern zone.[69] His first

[64] CORDIER, *Alias Caracalla*, 2009, p. 683—"A doubt ran through my mind: Was Frenay not right to demand his two million? Am I not guilty of 'refusing to obey' if I place the Resistance in peril? Rex confirmed to me the transfers to the Vercors; why he would not do the same for the refractaires?"

[65] BELOT, KARPMAN, *L'affaire Suisse*..., p. 120—"Jean-Pierre Azéma cites a telegram, from Jean Moulin to London, on 25th April 1943, which states that the Americans have promised ten million per month, and twenty airdrops to Frenay, which would already be considerable for anyone who had only fifteen million for the entirety of the southern zone".

[66] CORDIER, *Alias Caracalla*, 2009, p. 682—"In reality, Henri Frenay fixed a meeting with me on each of the following days. Without a doubt, he hoped that I would cave into the threats. I don't know if I was courageous, but, for nothing in the world, would I have betrayed my boss".

[67] CORDIER Daniel, *Jean Moulin*..., 2011, Chap. 14, Para. 70 (Ebook)—"Moulin pragmatically drew the lesson of the Resistance's claims on a purely financial level. Upon his return from London, and before the discovery of this affair, he had cabled Philip: "Due to increase budget Z.O. and spending fight against *relève* necessitates sending moon April important sum of thirty million".

[68] CORDIER, *Alias Caracalla*, 2009, p. 731—"As soon as I knew that I was to be stationed in Paris, I had *Germain* reserve a sleeping car. The night trip offered the best security since the cancelling of *Ausweis* (*laissez-passer*): at the start of the journey, the handing of I.D. cards to the conductor would, in theory, avoid all checks during the trip. The Germans undertook their rounds at around 1 in the morning at Chalon-sur-Saône, but did not systematically search the compartments".

[69] TNA, KV6 24 Rex, *Biographie Antoine Daniel DE GRAAFF*, p. 3—"De Graaff served under '*Alain*' until April 1943, when Alain was sent off to Paris to organise Rex's secretariat there. De Graaff then replaced him as private secretary to REX for the southern zone".

mission in Paris was to find accommodation,[70] having travelled with Laure Diebold (*Mado*), Hugues Limonti (*Germain*), Georges Archimbaud and Laurent Girard.[71] Suzette Olivier-Lebon was to act as the intermediary with the Lyonnais team, led by de Graaff. De Graaff's father, Louis-Henri, a banker of Jewish Dutch origins, converted the London-sent dollars into francs. The family's bank, Wellhoff, had been established by Louis-Henri and his brother, Pierre Wellhoff.[72] This position allowed Louis de Graaff to operate a transnational *bureau de change*—accepting dollars, sent from Britain, which were exchanged for francs.

The importance of multinational financing towards resistance action in France is underlined by the contributions which were made by the British, the Americans and the Fighting French and were destined for French union movements. The payments made to the *Confédération générale du travail* (C.G.T.), which was established in Limoges in 1895, came from these three sources. The support for unionism and resistance by the working classes initially stemmed from the solidarity of British colleagues, notably the Trade Unions Council, through their sending of 800,000 francs in November 1942.[73] Interestingly, the C.G.T. refused to employ the funds until January 1943, as they could not be sure that they were sourced from a fellow union. It was through the B.B.C. that the message "The Earth orbits the Sun" was broadcast, which confirmed the provenance of the funds. This was, however, the only documented example of such a transfer from one union to another. The funds which appeared

[70] CORDIER, *Alias Caracalla*, 2009, p. 735—"As for me, Suzette lodges me with one of her childhood friends, who was married to a lawyer. This household longed to serve the Resistance. They have a large apartment on the Place des Ternes. I can stay there while I find my feet".

[71] CORDIER, *Alias Caracalla*, 2009, p. 716—"I take *Mado*, *Germain*, Georges Archimaud and Laurent Girard and affected the intrepid Suzette on the daily liaison with Paris. Once there, I met Jean-Louis Théobald, the Parisian friend of Suzette whom she finally recruited under the pseudonym of *Terrier*. I fix my departure for the night of 24$^{th}$ into 25$^{th}$. My colleagues would leave on the 23$^{rd}$, in order to be up and ready as soon as I arrived".

[72] 'Tony de Graaf', https://www.memoresist.org/resistant/antoine-de-graaff/; 'Pierre Wellhoff', http://www.memoresist.org/resistant/pierre-wellhoff/, consulted 24 November 2019.

[73] AN, AG 3 (2) 277—171 MI 109 BCRA, Note for the Head of the B.C.R.A., 06/05/1943—"The result of the meeting was that, in November 1942, 800,000 francs were sent to the C.G.T. by the T.U.C., which was organised by this group".

with more regularity were those financed conjointly by the British, the Americans and Fighting French movement. However, the U.S. unions and their British counterparts had trouble with raising the required funds in francs and, therefore, it was requested that the payments should be made in pound sterling, which would allow supplementary withdrawals to be made available to those in France.

There were a number of particularities to the union clandestine activity, as opposed to other military, intelligence or evasion movements. Resistance actions were conducted concurrently to members' work supporting the labour movement. According to Louis Jouhaux, the C.G.T. had drastically reduced in membership, down to only 750,000, in February 1940, following the dissolution of unions, federations and departmental unions on 26th September 1939.[74] However, despite this considerable loss of subscriptions, their structuration and established hierarchy rendered their support helpful to both the British and Free French. Nonetheless, the unions remained reticent to follow either group too closely, as they were afraid to relinquish too much of their independence. Aglan writes:

> On his return from London, carrying a declaration from General de Gaulle, the messenger felt the coldness of the trade unionists, which was even greater. Charles Laurent (a founder of Libération-Nord and general secretary of the C.G.T.) asked Christian Pineau to let London know that they wanted "to keep their independence and above all not to (get involved) politically".[75]

The C.G.T. were blamed for exacerbating "moral tensions", as "vectors of the defeat" by a certain part of the population.[76]

However, they too were beneficiaries of the increasing level of funds entering France, provided by London (Fig. 7.2). These funds were also handled by Cordier and the REX mission. Payments were made to both

[74] LE CROM Jean-Pierre, 'Syndicalisme et Résistance' in DOUZOU Laurent (ed.), FRANK Robert (ed.), PESCHANSKI Denis (ed.) et VEILLON Dominique (ed.), *La Résistance et les Français: villes, centres et logiques de décision*, Actes du colloque de Cachan—IHTP, pp. 395–413, 1995, p. 1; POGGIOLI Morgan, 'La CGT et la répression antisyndicale (août 1939 – décembre 1940): Entre légalisme et apprentissage de la clandestinité, *Vingtième Siècle. Revue d'histoire*, 2016/2 N° 130, pp. 149–162, 152.

[75] AGLAN Alya, 'Des syndicalistes dans la résistance', *Vingtième Siècle, Revue d'histoire*, n° 67, Juillet-septembre 2000, pp. 119–127, 122.

[76] LE CROM, 'Syndicalisme et Résistance', 1995, p. 3.

branches of the C.G.T., in the former non-occupied zone, represented by Julien Forgues,[77] and the occupied zone, by Louis Saillant,[78] the representative of the C.G.T. on the National Resistance Council.[79] This funding demonstrates that Moulin recognised the support of left-wing groups. While the right was consistently well-represented among the senior Free French and within the internal resistance, the support of the unions, through their sabotage operations, industrial action and protests against forced work schemes, should also be highlighted. The C.G.T. issue and the problems generated by the *Combat* movement seeking additional financing from Switzerland were two of the final concerns that would occupy Moulin, prior to his arrest. The increasing efforts required to establish the *Conseil National de la Résistance* (*C.N.R.*), and to find a replacement for General Charles Delestraint, the head of the Secret Army, led to a fateful meeting at Caluire, a suburb in Lyon, at the house of Dr. Dugoujon, on Monday, 21st June 1943.

## Life After REX

Much has been written on the *rendez-vous* at Dr. Dugoujon's house, which ended in the arrest of all eight men who had gone to attend the meeting.[80] The pressing necessity to find a replacement for Delestraint brought them together. The recently appointed head of the *Armée secrète* had been arrested on 9th June. His loss was a major destabilisation for the internal resistance and its organisation throughout France, which

[77] AN, AG 3 (2) 277—171 MI 109 BCRA, Note for the Head of the BCRA, 5/3/43—"The suggestion is that the sending of English and American money must be done with the bills that they will provide us (800,000fr) to the destination and handed over to Mr. Jules F"; DREYFUS Michel, PENNETIER Claude, 'FOURGUES Julien', *Le Maitron*, https://maitron.fr/spip.php?article50708, consulted 2 November 2020.

[78] CORDIER, *Alias Caracalla*, 2009, p. 685—"Two cables arrived, yesterday. In the first, Rex asked me to advise Frédéric to give 500,000 francs to Louis Saillant, the head of the C.G.T. in the northern zone".

[79] LE CROM, 'Syndicalisme et Résistance', 1995, p. 10.

[80] AZÉMA Jean-Pierre, *Jean Moulin: Le politique, le rebelle, le résistant*, Paris, Perrin, 2006, 596p., p. 472—"The arrest at Caluire, above the judicial and mediatised exploitations that have been made, produced a geostrategic context which provoked a wave of arrests among members of the resistance."; PÉAN Pierre, *Vies et morts de Jean Moulin*, Paris, Fayard, 715p., (Ebook) Chap. 30, Para. 41—"Monday morning, on 21st June, Aubry met Moulin next to Perrache station…Lassagne indicated them to take tramway n° 33 and to alight at Place Castellane, from where he would lead them to the meeting".

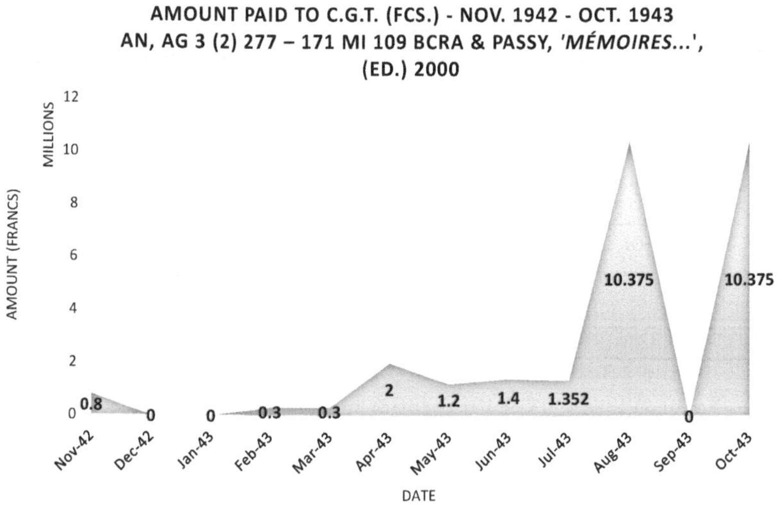


**Fig. 7.2** Amount paid to C.G.T. (Fcs.)—November 1942–October 1943, (AN, AG 3 (2) 277—171 MI 109 BCRA; Passy, 'Mémoires...', 2000)

would, in itself, precipitate the arrest of Moulin and his high-ranking co-attendees. By 14:30, the Germans had arrived at the surgery and arrested the attendees. This would be the end of the REX mission.

Meanwhile, confusion reigned in Paris and London as a result of Moulin's arrest.[81] With Moulin gone, Claude Bouchinet-Serreulles, alias *Sophie*, assumed responsibility for the C.N.R., the organisation that brought together the different movements under the same aegis. He was assisted by Cordier in his duties as interim leader.[82] They were joined, as of August 1943, by Jacques Bingen, the delegate for the French Committee of National Liberation (C.F.L.N.). The payments and parachutes continued to be deployed. The provisional budgets for the month of October and November 1943 show that, rather than slowing, the pace of financing continued to increase dramatically.

[81] TNA, KV6 24, *Rapport S.O.E. sur la mission REX*, 28/07/1943—"On 14/06/1943, CLAUDE heard that Rex's adjoint, ALAIN, who had succeeded Colonel FREDERIC after his arrest in March, had been arrested in Paris".

[82] CORDIER Daniel, *La victoire en pleurant: Alias Caracalla 1943–1946*, Paris, Éditions Gallimard, 2021, 310p., p. 34.

Through the work of the scholars belonging to the Historical Division of the War Department Special Staff, in 1945, the Americans recognised that one of the principal results of the REX mission was the creation of the *Mouvements unis de la Résistance* (M.U.R.). It is for this unifying act that Moulin is usually remembered. However, equally as important to the U.S. historians was the "3) Revival of a union of all working classes within C.G.T. (*Confédération Générale du Travail*) (March 1943)" and "4) Creation of a liaison between C.G.T. and C.F.T.C. (*Confédération française des travailleurs chrétiens*)".[83] On 19th September 1943, Pierre Brossolette was sent into France to introduce the new representative of the French Committee of National Liberation,[84] Émile Bollaert, or *Beaudoin*,[85] to the resistance heads. At this crucial juncture of the war, the C.F.L.N., in Algiers, were most interested in gaining control over the internal resistance movement[86] and it would appear that the C.G.T., among the other funded groups, seem to have been one of the vectors by which they envisaged so doing.

The amounts, shown in Table 7.2, are from the provisional budget for the months of October and November 1943. In contrast to the amounts in Fig. 7.1, these were provisional and did not necessarily represent money that was actually parachuted into France. There was a continuation of funding for the C.G.T. through the collaborative efforts of British and American union members, alongside the Fighting French movement. Nonetheless, when compared to Fig. 7.1, it can already be seen that the amounts sent to France were superior to those presented in this provisional budget. For instance, for the month of October 1943, in Table 7.2, the required budget was estimated to be around six million francs, with an allowance for fluctuating exchange rates. However, the actual

[83] NARA, RG 331 314.7 Vol 1 to 314.7 Vol. II, *The French Forces of the Interior: Their Organization and Their Participation in the Liberation of France, 1944*, Chapter 1, p. 28.

[84] PIKETTY Guillaume, *Pierre Brossolette: Un héros de la Résistance*, Paris, Éditions Odile Jacob, 1998, 416p., p. 312.

[85] NARA, RG 331 314.7 Vol 1 to 314.7 Vol. II, Chapter 1, p. 46—"In September 1943, BROSSOLETTE (alias BRUMAIRE, pseudo BRIAND) was sent to the CNR to introduce the new representative from the French Committee of National Liberation, Mr. BEAUDOIN"; 'Émile Bollaert' *Ordre de la Libération*, https://www.ordredelaliberation.fr/fr/compagnons/emile-bollaert, consulted 3 November 2020.

[86] NARA, RG 331 314.7 Vol 1 to 314.7 Vol. II, Chapter 1, p. 64.

**Table 7.2** Provisional budgets, October and November 1943 (francs and dollars)—(AN, AG 3 (2) 277—171 MI 109 BCRA)

| Organisations | October 1943 | November 1943 |
|---|---|---|
| *C.G.T.* – C.F.L.N. | 1,000,000 | 1,000,000 |
| *C.G.T.* - British unions | 1,000,000 | 1,000,000 |
| *C.G.T.* - American unions ($) | $25,000 (4,375,000 frs. – exchange rate $1 : 175 frs.) | $25,000 (4,375,000 frs. – exchange rate $1 : 175 frs.) |
| *Front National* | 1,480,000 | 1,500,000 (Zone Nord), 500,000 (Zone Sud) |
| *Franc-Tireur et Partisans* (F.T.P.) | 3,000,000 | 3,000,000 |
| *Ceux de la Résistance* | 1,300,000 | 1,700,000 |
| *Ceux de la Libération* | 1,400,000 | 1,800,000 |
| *Libération* | 1,500,000 | 1,500,000 |
| *Comité Central des Mouvements* | 2,300,000 | 3,850,000 including Maquis |
| *Mouvements Unis de la Résistance* | 11,500,000 | 12,500,000 |
| *Parti Socialiste* | 400,000 | 400,000 |
| *Coopérative* | | 1,500,000 |
| (Jean) Brodier | 66,000 | |
| *Voix du Nord* | 150,000 | 150,000 |
| *Service Prisonniers* | 200,000 | |
| **TOTAL (Fcs.)** | **29 671 000** | **34,775,000** |

sums despatched to France were closer to ten million francs, according to Fig. 7.1.

Figure 7.3 shows the information in Table 7.2 in graphical form. It outlines the transfers that were envisaged for French resistance groups. Understandably, as they incorporated the majority of non-communist movements, the *Mouvements unis de la Résistance* were to be awarded a large amount in October. However, as can be seen above, there were a number of groups who either fell outside their remit or were receiving supplementary funds. This is notably the case for *Libération*. Normally, they were founding members of the M.U.R. However, they were to

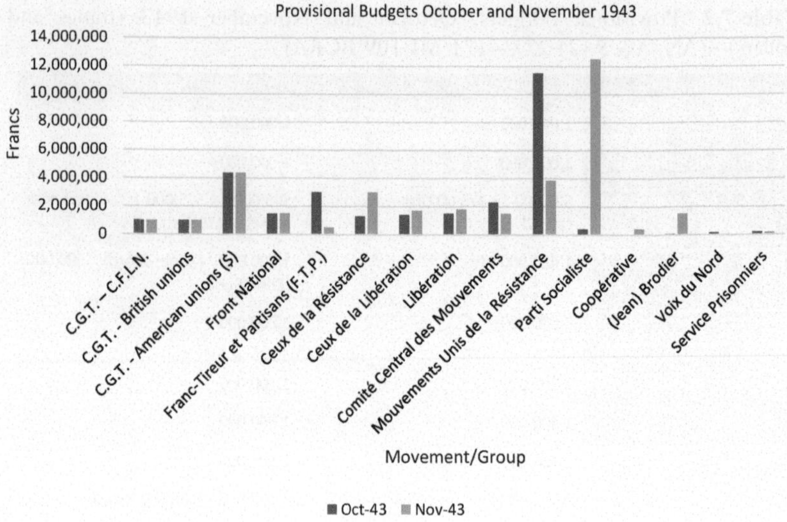


**Fig. 7.3** Provisional budgets, October and November 1943 (francs and dollars), (AN, AG 3 (2) 277—171 MI 109 BCRA)

be paid outside the cadre of the M.U.R. too. Furthermore, a marked increase in the funding allocated to the *Parti Socialiste* can be seen, notably in November 1943. This represented the increasing politicisation of the resistance, insofar as the unions and the political parties were concerned.

With the successful landings in Sicily by Allied troops, in August 1943, the invasion of continental Europe was beginning. In France, largely thanks to the efforts of Moulin, the REX mission and the *Conseil National de la Résistance*, the disparate groups were beginning to coalesce and centralise. With the altering of the strategic context and the loss of Moulin, the REX mission's direction would change; but exactly how so, nobody really knew:

> Jean Moulin has been temporarily replaced by Claude Serreulles (Sophie) who, during the Caluire tragedy, was on a mission in France. An officer in

> General de Gaulle's cabinet, he had everything to learn about the Resistance. He's very young. What will he be able to do? What will his role be? He is neither president of the C.N.R. nor of the M.U.R.[87]

As the funds for the REX mission came from London, it is understandable as to why leaders, such as Henri Frenay, may have felt aggrieved by the strict control of funds. However, it has also become clear that many of the movements would not have gained the importance that they later came to hold, had it not been for Moulin's clandestine financial activity. Nonetheless, according to Frenay, Bouchinet-Serreulles and Bingen were plagued by a lack of funds:

> And Bingen, in his monthly report, made allusion to the lack of funds, writing: 'Consider how tragic it is. It's no longer a question of providing a living for a respectable permanent staff or central services, but of feeding, dressing, etc. In short, it is to prevent starvation or the shooting of the young men of whom we have taken charge in your name.'[88]

However, the British S.O.E.'s official history of Section 'RF', aside from severely castigating Serreulles for his lack of operational security,[89] the capture of his group's archives[90] and far worse besides, explained that:

> Money was not reaching the lower resistance echelons (78) and was still not reaching them in February 1944. It is probable that these two [Bingen and Serreulles], as well as Manuel's brother Doyen (verbal report...from Major Cardozo) were keeping the funds for future electoral purposes. They put up a most specious and vigorous defence.[91]

It is for this reason that a financial investigation has been necessary for Mission REX. Through Moulin, as the organiser of Gaullist attempts to assert hegemony over the resistance in France, links with London were

[87] FRENAY, *La nuit finira*, 1973, p. 345.

[88] FRENAY, *La nuit finira*, 1973, p. 371.

[89] TNA, HS7 124 RF Section History 1943, p. 23; CORDIER, *La victoire en pleurant*..., 2021, p. 25—"I am frightened when he announces that he will come every morning at 09:00 to this apartment: he intends to hold his appointments here because he finds the place pleasant and spacious! Almost overwhelmed, I didn't say a word".

[90] TNA, HS7 124 RF Section History 1943, p. 49.

[91] Idem, p. 50.

established. Cordier, and his secretariat, acted as the intermediaries for any financial interactions that occurred with the major resistance movements.

This hegemony passed through the use of money as a lever to encourage clandestine activity and to ensure that any information arrived via the services of the Fighting French. As *L'Affaire Suisse* demonstrated, it was not always possible to ensure that this was respected. Dissension among the resistance leaders occurred on the grounds of money, or its lack thereof, as much as it did on the grounds of political differences, as is often underlined in the historiography of French resistance. As has been shown here, Henri Frenay, even when receiving the lion's portion of the funds sent to Moulin, still felt aggrieved that he was being 'short-changed'. It may be suggested that money was not the be all and end all of their relationship, but Frenay himself did attribute much of his movement's growth to Moulin's financial links:

> If, since January (1942), in less than six months, "Combat" has grown greatly, it is due to the resources that Max places at our disposition, each month.[92]

For better or worse, his movement was tied to Moulin by monetary constraints.

Moreover, the fact that dollars were arriving, as of March 1942, shows the level to which the American currency had taken precedence. Through the clandestine bureau de change, run by Louis-Henri de Graaf in Lyon, these dollars would be exchanged into French currency, thus allowing it to flow into the local money supply. Clearly, the levels were not enough to cause any great risk of inflation, by flooding the market with external money, but it shows the level to which the dollar had become the hegemonic currency, even above that of the pound sterling. Firstly, it was a currency that could be readily exchanged and whose value was tied to the country that was the productive centre of the war. Secondly, Britain's financial clout was greatly affected by the military losses that had occurred since the beginning of the war. The value of a currency is heavily linked to confidence in its convertibility and whether it can be exchanged against other currencies. If so, its value will increase. If it can be exchanged against Treasury notes and bonds, its value will rise even further, and so on. The dollar's premium was due to practicalities, namely the difficulty

[92] FRENAY, *La nuit finira*, 1973, p. 193.

of obtaining the correct French francs in either the U.K. or the United States, and the necessity of sending much of the currency into occupied territory, thus requiring it to be as compact and convertible as possible.[93] As some of these dollars came through donations from union members in the United States, the idea of transnational finance for the resistance is therefore confirmed.

Moulin, Cordier, Diebold and the other members of the REX mission undoubtedly performed exceptionally dangerous and highly important work. Without these international links, resistance in France would have been economically hampered and, at worst, may have been snuffed out entirely, by the combined efforts of the Vichy and German counterespionage services. With an increasing number of transfers being made, it became possible to support more troops, or to ensure that those who had already rallied could be trained, in better conditions, for the ongoing guerrilla action and to prepare for the insurrection to come.

93 BLOCH-LAINÉ François, 'Le financement de la Résistance', *Revue d'histoire de la Deuxième Guerre mondiale*, 1ère année, N° 1 (Novembre 1950), pp. 6–19, p. 10—"It is because these notes were rare and difficult to sell that the B.C.R.A. resorted to sending dollars. These dollars, much appreciated in the parallel currency market, could be quite easily exchanged against francs".

CHAPTER 8

# Converting the *Caisse*: Competition and Collaboration

Table 8.1 and graph (Fig. 8.1) show the most detailed and comprehensive analysis of French resistance financing to date. No previous works, including Michael Foot's *S.O.E. in France*,[1] Binot and Boyer's *L'Argent de la Résistance*[2] and Albertelli's *Les Services Secrets du Général de Gaulle*, have performed direct comparisons between the two branches of British-supported secret services operating in wartime France. Rather than being the poorer cousin to S.O.E.'s British-led operation, the B.C.R.A.-supported Section 'RF' networks were provided with far more funding than Section 'F', whose networks were often prefixed by the name of their commanding officer, Maurice Buckmaster.[3]

Where did this injection of money come from? This strikes at the heart of the question as to exactly 'how French was French resistance funding'? The majority of the funds came from French and Francophile people abroad or from the British government, with relatively little emerging from within France itself. By this point of the war, in summer 1943, France had been subjected to three years of occupation, with the occupiers remaining intent on extracting as much money and as many

[1] FOOT Michael, CREMIEUX-BRILHAC Jean-Louis, *Des anglais dans la résistance, Le SOE en France*, Paris, Tallandier, 2014, 816p.

[2] BINOT, BOYER, *L'argent de la Résistance*, 2010.

[3] BUCKMASTER, *They Fought Alone*..., 1956 (Ed. 2014), 320p., p. IX.



D. Foulk, *The Price of Freedom*,
https://doi.org/10.1007/978-3-031-09066-0_8

**Table 8.1** Comparison between Amounts (Francs) Sent to France by SOE Section 'F' and 'RF' with BCRA, (TNA, HS7 121f; AN, AG3 (2) 276—171 MI 108 BCRA; AN, AG3 (2) 277—171 MI 109 BCRA.

| DATE | F Section | BCRA/RF | REX - Moulin |
|---|---|---|---|
| Jan-42 | | | |
| Feb-42 | | 91,195 | |
| Mar-42 | | | 1,050,000 |
| Apr-42 | | | |
| May-42 | | | |
| Jun-42 | | | 3,000,000 |
| Jul-42 | | | 2,000,000 |
| Aug-42 | | | 2,000,000 |
| Sep-42 | | | 5,000,000 |
| Oct-42 | | | 20,000,000 |
| Nov-42 | | 9,040,000 | |
| Dec-42 | | 9,370,000 | 7,000,000 |
| Jan-43 | 9,930,000 | 18,052,500 | 7,000,000 |
| Feb-43 | 1,025,000 | 39,220,000 | 7,000,000 |
| Mar-43 | 14,185,000 | 22,100,000 | 20,000,000 |
| Apr-43 | 10,663,000 | 24,425,000 | 20,000,000 |
| May-43 | 8,685,000 | 31,950,000 | 30,000,000 |
| Jun-43 | 27,353,000 | 31,950,000 | 82,000,000 |
| Jul-43 | 11,251,000 | 95,500,000 | 81,000,000 |
| Aug-43 | 10,026,000 | 110,000,000 | |
| Sep-43 | 18,666,000 | 134,000,000 | |
| Oct-43 | 14,587,000 | 107,000,000 | 29,671,000 |
| Nov-43 | 7,250,000 | 148,000,000 | 34,775,000 |
| Dec-43 | 10,100,000 | 139,500,000 | |
| Jan-44 | 7,108,000 | 395,000,000 | |
| Feb-44 | 13,604,000 | 432,400,000 | |
| Mar-44 | 24,480,000 | | |
| Apr-44 | 18,537,000 | 259,301,875 | |
| May-44 | 31,025,000 | 282,350,000 | |
| Jun-44 | 43,675,000 | 551,550,000 | |
| Jul-44 | 58,306,000 | 202,350,000 | |
| Aug-44 | 49,095,000 | 575,000,000 | |
| Sep-44 | 32,507,000 | 178,000,000 | |
| TOTALS | 422,058,000 | 3,796,150,570 | 351,496,000 |

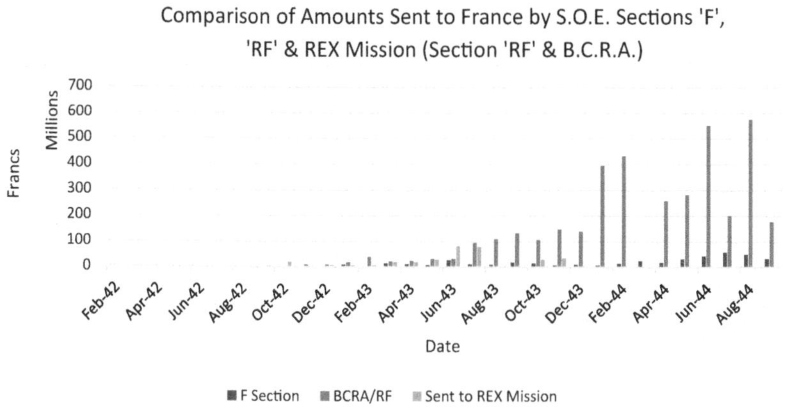


**Fig. 8.1** Amounts (Francs) Sent to France by SOE Section 'F' and 'RF' with BCRA and REX Mission, (TNA, HS7 121f; AN, AG3 (2) 276—171 MI 108 BCRA; AG3 (2) 277—171 MI 109 BCRA)

resources from the population as possible.[4] While 600 million francs that would eventually be raised by the C.O.F.I. (*Comité Financier*), following their creation in February 1944, money was still in short supply for those in France who may have been ready to support resistance activity by donating.[5] Effectively, prior to November 1943, a great deal of the funding that was received by resistance members in France came from the delegations in the rallied territories. Moreover, between November 1943 and January 1944, French citizens, subjects and Francophile foreigners across the world contributed large amounts to General de Gaulle's movement through schemes such as the Subscription Fund to Help the Resistance. The 228.9 million francs received from this colonial subscription, at the end of November 1943, were a vital source of the funding that was subsequently despatched by the B.C.R.A. This can be seen above, shown by the orange 'BCRA/RF' coloured bars in Fig. 8.1, from the beginning of September 1943 to January 1944.

Comparatively, the more frugal nature of Section 'F' becomes apparent. Payments made to them were sent on a more regular basis, in

[4] GRENARD, LE BOT, PERRIN, *Histoire économique de Vichy*, 2017, Chapter 5, Para 32.

[5] BLOCH-LAINÉ, 'Le financement de la Résistance', 1950, p. 16.

smaller amounts, without the exponential growth that characterised the Section 'RF' authorisations. This suggests that, while Section 'F' were paid lower amounts, they were also more organised and professionalised. It is important to underline that Section 'F' were much more heavily influenced by the British military. As the end of the war in France approached, the Fighting French continued to receive funding from both the U.K. and, to a more limited degree, the United States.

> Of this total—278,338,000—approximately 139,000,000 was supplied by E.M.F.F.I. from French Sources in July, August and September. Of the remainder approximately 14,000,000 was supplied by O.S.S. and 123,000,000 by S.O.E. 18,832,000 was returned by agents coming back from the Field after the liberation and a further 8,535,000 was spent in settling debts of agents who were not able to liquidate their affairs before returning to the U.K.[6]

July 1944 was the month that saw the greatest despatching of funds to the Section 'F' agents. Moreover, it corresponds to the period in which the Fighting French took over the funding of these agents. Although it is usually assumed that the two sections were distinctly separate, by July 1944, the financing for both was provided almost entirely by the General Headquarters of the *Forces Françaises de l'Intérieur*. This amounted to approximately 139 million francs. Beforehand, S.O.E. had paid for the majority of their costs, to the tune of 123 million in 1944, with the Office of Strategic Services, the American special operations section, providing 14 million.[7] However, as was shown in Table 8.1, which is constructed from the actual receipts by each network, the table does not correspond with the executive summary provided in the above quotation. Moreover, this error was replicated in the work of Michael Foot, the foremost historian of S.O.E., who used the executive summary as the basis for his conclusions on S.O.E. Section 'F' funding, as opposed to relying on the raw data.[8] This explains the discrepancy between the 278.3 million cited above and the recalculated total of 422.0 million in Table 8.1.

[6] TNA, HS7-121 F Section History and Agents, F Section History and Agents—F Section—*Francs sent to the field—1943, 1944 Mission Table Finances.*

[7] TNA, HS7-121, *1944 Mission Table Finances.*

[8] FOOT Michael, *Des anglais dans la Résistance, le S.O.E. en France*, Paris, Tallandier, 2014, 816p., Appendix C.

These comparative accounts challenge historians' and resistance members' perceptions concerning the financing of the resistance networks. Henri Frenay, the leader of *Combat*, heavily implied that the British-supported networks were better funded than those assisted by the B.C.R.A., at least in his area of influence, in the south of France:

> During this time, Carte (nom-de-guerre of André Girard) and their friends were largely supplied by the SOE; so largely, in fact, that, on the Côte d'Azur, they said to our groups: "With de Gaulle and his services, you'll never have the supplies that you're asking for. Come over to us and you'll get all the money and the materials that you need."[9]

The money that was sent to the *Combat* movement, via transfers through Jean Moulin and the REX mission, varied from 250,000 francs, in cash, at the beginning of 1942, to 800,000 francs, in July 1942. *Combat*, therefore, received double the amount allocated to the other movements. In September, 1.2 million francs were issued to Frenay. This grew to four million francs by February 1943. Conversely, for the *entire year* of 1943, the *Carte* network, aided by 'F' Section, received 1.4 million francs.[10] By June 1944, this had increased to two million francs.[11] Arguments about greater levels of financing being awarded to S.O.E. networks, as opposed to those B.C.R.A.-supported movements, seem to be without foundation.

Two competing financial philosophies were being impressed upon the movements inside France; one being continuous and steady, and the other sporadic and exponential. However, these were not adopted through conscious choice but were imposed upon the groups arbitrarily, according to whomsoever was financially supporting them. Funding links were inherently unstable, despite the best efforts of the personnel in France and Britain. This is shown in Fig. 8.1, when 'RF' networks received no funds in March 1944, ostensibly due to a decision taken in Algiers.[12]

[9] FRENAY, *La nuit finira*, 1973, pp. 219–220.

[10] TNA, HS7-121 F Section History and Agents, F Section History and Agents—F Section—*Francs sent to the field—1943, 1943 updated.*

[11] AN, AG 3 (2) 277—171 MI 109 BCRA Dossier, Colis envoyés, June 1944, 30/05/1944.

[12] AN, AG3 (2) 276—171 MI 108 BCRA, *Section AFN & Colonies—Télégramme de PELABON*, 24/03/1944.

At that time, this lack of funds had an extremely deleterious effect on the 'RF' networks.[13] Moreover, it was noted that: "...the sorry state of local resources in money and stores, such as boots and clothing became daily more apparent. Everywhere the same complaints were made".[14] Either funds were being secreted away, as was previously alluded to when concerning Serreulles and Bingen, or the number of Maquis fighters was far greater than the distributed funds permitted. Wieviorka, citing Marcot, estimated that there were around 300,000 to 500,000 men and women who made up the *Armée des ombres*.[15] The BCRA archives offer two different figures: the first, dating from 17th July 1944, supposes that there were approximately 400,000 members[16]; the second, written in a projected budget by General Koenig, from 21st July, posits that there were around 280,000, but he admitted that it was probably an underestimation.[17] In truth, if either are even vaguely accurate, it does mean that resistance forces were greatly underfunded. Were Section 'RF' closer in size to the first estimation of 400,000, this would translate into spending of 506 francs per member, using the July 1944 figure; if they approached Koenig's estimate of 280,000, it would be closer to 723 francs. In both cases, this is far below the 1,000 franc per resistance member in a rural setting that was envisaged.[18]

Once the money arrived in France, it became a matter of life and death. For instance, if caught with any notes that were not sufficiently 'worn',[19]

[13] AN, AG3 (2) 276—171 MI 108 BCRA, *Note pour le Général Koenig a/c du Colonel Passy*, 09/05/1944.

[14] TNA, HS7 124, *RF Section History 1944*, p. 42.

[15] WIEVIORKA Oliver, *L'histoire de la Résistance*, Paris, Perrin, 2013, 536p. (Ebook), Chapter 15, Para 58.

[16] AN, AG3 (2) 276—171 MI 108 BCRA, *Note pour F.1/2*, 17/07/1944.

[17] AG 3 (2) 278—171 MI 110 BCRA, Août 1944, *Général Koenig to Emmanuel d'Astier*, 21/07/1944.

[18] AN, AG3 (2) 276—171 MI 108 BCRA, *Letter from Col. Vernon to Commandant Lejeune*, 04/07/1944.

[19] BUCKMASTER, *They Fought Alone...*, 1956 (Ed. 2014), p. 82—"I sent Yveline off to get some oil and grease, meanwhile I undid the elastic bands round each bundle and flung the 1000 and 5000 franc notes abandonedly into the air. "Get busy", I ordered. (81) "Rub them in your hands, scribble on them, fold them and generally muck them up. We've got to have old notes for new." Yveline returned and we all set to, spattering the notes with ink, bending the edges, greasing them, rolling them into tight balls and then trying to straighten them out".

the holder risked being arrested. Buckmaster suggests that newly printed notes were being used by S.O.E. 'F' Section. One of the recurring issues experienced by the Free French and the British was with the acquisition of used notes. It was far easier to send legitimate currency than it was to produce passable counterfeit bills, due to the lack of information about their changing designs as the war progressed. However, it was not always possible for S.O.E. to acquire 'used' notes. Acquisition of 'fresh' franc notes was thus necessary for future clandestine use in France. This posed its own difficulties as the balance of payments for goods, from metropolitan France, was virtually neutralised through the imposition of wartime economic policies and the requirement to ship French goods to support the Reich's war effort. In order to acquire those francs, purchases would need to be made from the colonies, or as part of the limited trade that appears to have continued with Vichy.

A better understanding of the relationship between the number of transfers and the amounts transported into France helps to show the efficacy of the Section 'F' operations that were conducted. In Fig. 8.2, the majority of the transfers sent to 'F' Section networks fell beneath the 2-million-franc level. The average transfer amounted to 1.8 million francs, which was the equivalent of £10,297. On average, for those 'F' Section networks who were supplied with funds, monetary transfers occurred 3.1 times over the course of 1943. Generally, the higher the number of transfers, the greater the amount of funds that were dispatched. In Fig. 8.2, there was an anomaly, with the twenty-one-million-franc payment. These four transfers were made to the 'Donkeyman' network and assisted in their sabotage and agent-transfer activities (Fig. 8.3).[20]

However, in 'RF' Section, many networks were not the direct recipients of funds from London. This is illustrated by the B.C.R.A. transfers to Jean Moulin and the REX network. Daniel Cordier was tasked with distributing and safeguarding the funds, received from the U.K., while they undertook clandestine activities in Lyon, and Paris, from his infiltration in 1942 until Moulin's arrest in June 1943. One example was the transfer which occurred in October 1942, and which was split between

[20] BOURRÉE Fabrice, 'Plaque en Hommage à Henri Frager, dit « Paul»', *Musée de la Résistance en Ligne*, http://museedelaresistanceenligne.org/media5261-Plaque-en-hommage-A, Consulted 03/04/2021.

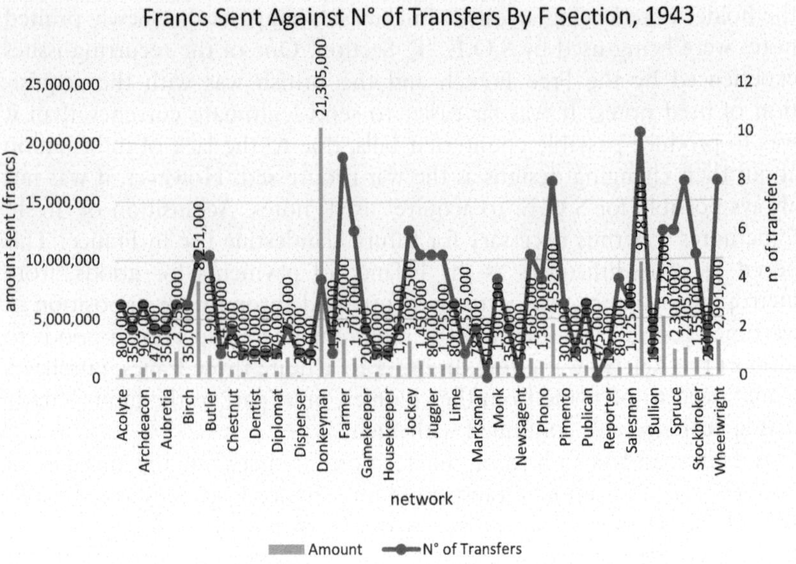


**Fig. 8.2** Francs sent against the n° of transfers by F Section, SOE, 1943, (TNA, HS7-121)

*Combat*, *Libération*, *Franc-Tireur* and other groups.[21] These transfers have been shown in the previous chapter in Table 7.1 as well as in Table 8.1.

## Liquidity for the *Libération*

Meanwhile, with the move to Algiers over the course of 1943, the economic situation between the Fighting French movement and the British government altered irrevocably. Already, on 14th July 1942, the movement changed their name to reflect the alteration of their wartime objectives. This rebranding, from Free French, or *France Libre*, to

[21] AN, AG3 (2) 277—171 MI 109 BCRA Mission Rex, *Telegram*, 1942, November 10—"Without date, arrived on 1942, November 10—From REX—Received October 7,000,000 francs and $15,000—transfers effectuated in October—Combat monthly payment 1,550,000—LIBER monthly 1,100,000—Purchase transportation business 1,600,000, Boat Purchase 45,000—TIRF monthly 200,000—Motorcycle Purchase 12,000—Petrol 74,000—Solidarity TOULOUSE, 40,000—Z.O. 240,000...

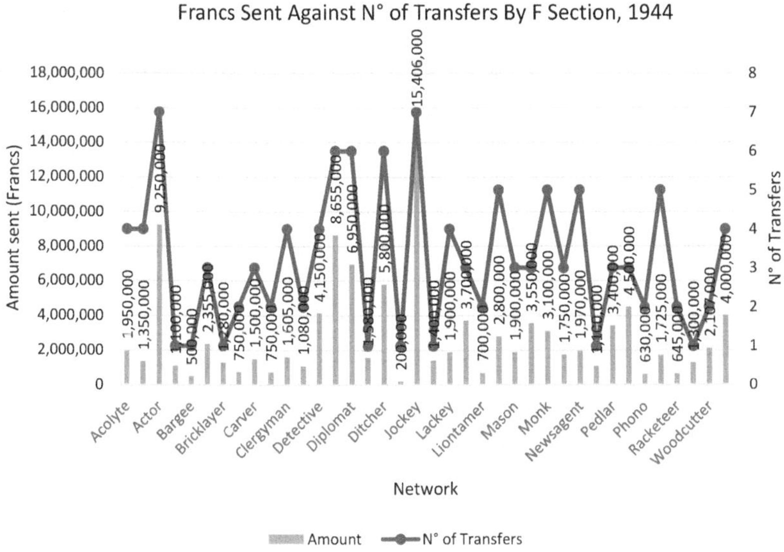


**Fig. 8.3** Francs sent against the n° of transfers by F Section, SOE, 1944, (TNA, HS7-121)

Fighting French, or *France Combattante*, was intended to show that Free France and occupied France were both fighting to liberate the country and her imperial possessions from the Axis powers.[22] By narrowing the movement's physical distance to the French colonies, they could begin to adopt the role of governing power more fully. However, as they accepted more Lend-Lease ordnance, they left themselves open to American influence.

The Algerian period, marked by the creation of the *Comité français de Liberation nationale* (C.F.L.N.), was coloured by political intrigue between the two generals: Giraud, supported by the American government, and de Gaulle, the chief *résistant de la première heure*, as they struggled for supremacy before Giraud returned to his military preoccupation, leaving the Gaullists to appropriate power. The political history of the Churchill-de Gaulle relationship is well known, but this work intends

[22] 'Communication relative à l'appellation « France Combattante', *Journal Officiel de la France Combattante*, 1942, August 28.

to examine the economic repercussions of the breakdown of their wartime relationship, which had held firm since June 1940.

Following the acrimonious split in the relationship with the British premier, de Gaulle arrived in Algiers on 30th May 1943. Three days later, on 3rd June 1943, the C.F.L.N. had been established.[23] However, the severance of the banking and financial links that had supported the rallied Free French was a process that would continue throughout 1943. Furthermore, unlike the political difficulties that arose between Churchill and de Gaulle, the economic relationship between the British government and the Fighting French movement was obliged by circumstance to continue, in some manner or other.

The continuity of pecuniary supply; market provision for colonial goods; durability in banking relations with the various representatives in the U.K., all these issues obliged the presence of Fighting French financial personnel in the country. However, the majority of those who dealt with such questions were moved to Algiers over the course of 1943 and 1944. These included André Postel-Vinay (*Duval*), the assistant director of the *Caisse centrale*, who became Pierre Denis' understudy as of 19th December 1942.[24] Those who remained in London fell under the authority of Allen Bartholomew, the elderly British accountant, who had served as the *Caisse*'s 'chaperon' in Whitehall and the City's corridors of power. Such relationships acted as the principal vectors through which economic legislation and war financing would be imposed upon the Fighting French colonies. While direct oversight of the Fighting French Financial Service by the Treasury and the Bank of England ceased, their technical expertise and advice continued to be sought, irrespective of the political quarrels occurring in the higher political echelons.

Postel-Vinay's appointment as Pierre Denis' successor followed his escape from captivity. Postel-Vinay had fled to Britain at the end of September 1942 with the personal help of '*Pat O'Leary*', pseudonym for Count Albert-Marie Guérisse, a Belgian who participated in resistance activity in France, after whom an escape network was named.[25]

[23] 'The French National Committee', *The Economist*, 1943, June 12, p. 753—"The Committee of National Liberation was established on June 3rd by virtue of an Ordinance signed by General Giraud and General de Gaulle".

[24] SAEF, B 0,062,801, *Letter from Denis (Rauzan) to Digo*, 19/12/1942.

[25] POSTEL-VINAY André, *Un fou s'évade: Souvenirs de 1941–1942*, Paris, Éditions du Félin, 1997, 248p., p. 150—"Roland Farjon knew how to reach Patrick O'Leary. He

As an Inspector of Finances, Postel-Vinay was immediately tasked with assisting Pierre Denis at the *Caisse centrale*. A highly centralised system had been created, much akin to that of a military organisation, where power was accorded by the head of the organisation to trusted lieutenants. Nonetheless, the pool from which these personnel could be chosen was dependent upon those who rallied to de Gaulle's side, especially during the early London days of the movement but which also continued well into their Algerian period. Such a system of management enabled the creation of trust between the participants, but their reliance upon the British Treasury and the Bank of England left the Fighting French in a difficult political bind. Through the adoption of protestant financial rigour, reflecting Denis' religious principles,[26] the *Caisse centrale* and the Financial Services were trusted to act in the best interests of the rallied colonies and were accorded the help of the British central bank and the moneymen in Whitehall, including John Lithiby at the Bank of England.

The importance of this bilateral economic cohesion was marked through papers and articles being passed around Carlton Gardens and the new sites in Algiers. The type of operation initially envisaged for the *Caisse centrale de la France d'Outre-mer* was a continuation of its predecessor, the *Caisse centrale de la France Libre*, but the organisation decided to change its name, in February 1944. Functionally, all remained largely the same. Bank notes continued to be printed; currency exchanges continued to be effectuated. André Postel-Vinay remarked that "the name of the *Caisse centrale de la France Libre* was not particularly adapted to the new era". However, "the role of the *Caisse centrale* had not changed much".[27]

The issuance of bank notes to the rallied colonies continued from London, replacing well-used notes that had previously been issued by the *Banque de France*. The internal *Caisse centrale* correspondence concerning dealings with Bradbury, Wilkinson and Company, the printers

sent my request to him. I needed, nonetheless, fifteen days or so to organise my trip to Marseille, where Patrick's command post was located".

[26] OULMONT, *Pierre Denis*, 2012, p. 293.

[27] POSTEL-VINAY André, PACQUEMENT François (Ed.), *La passion du développement—32 ans de Caisse centrale: Mémoires d'André Postel-Vinay*, Paris, Agence Française du Développement, 2019, 314p., p. 40.

in New Malden, Surrey, demonstrates as much.[28] Such close economic collaboration between the British and the Fighting French was made possible through the highly centralised political arrangements that such extraordinary circumstances demanded, in much a similar way as to Monnet's Coordinating Committee from four years earlier. Effectively, it also underlined that de Gaulle's movement was sufficiently in need so as to allow a foreign power to print French colonial money on their behalf. This is one of the principal aspects of monetary sovereignty, namely the ability to issue one's own currency. It also demonstrates the level of reliance that the Fighting French movement had upon the British government. One could argue that while the rejected Franco-British Union of 16th June 1940 had floundered; another, more economically based union had succeeded. Once again, this calls into question the 'Frenchness' of French resistance funding. In reality, as has been shown, it was a veritable transnational effort, driven by Gallic effort but which was fuelled by international liquidity. The Gaullists took inspiration, and advice, from the British economic and financial establishment, and the model that they chose to follow was heavily dependent on British assistance and cooperation to function effectively.

However, the increasing importance of close British and American links in dictating Allied strategy, driven by a reliance upon the Atlantic lifeline, meant that the political balance between the Fighting French movement and the British government began to fracture. This change of situation caused a strategic realignment between the Allies. The British government may have withdrawn much political support from the Fighting French movement, but the economic situation remained nominally separate, even if credit lines from the Bank of England may have been cut. For instance, many important resources, including phosphates and ground nuts, whose oil served as ersatz cooking oil, in lieu of butter or other oils,[29] came, in large part, from the French African colonies. Moreover, colonial manpower provided the Fighting French with one of its most

[28] SAEF, B 0062801, *Compte du Représentant à Londres pour le mois de janvier 1944*, 01/01/1944—"Bradbury, Wilkinson & Co. Ltd. Caisse for sending notes to Algiers £1.12.6".

[29] TNA, CAB 109 83, North Africa Economic Questions, *Letter from Maj. Desmond Morton to Brig. E. Ian Jacob: West African Oil Seed Exports*, War Cabinet Offices, 1943, October 30.

vital acquisitions: an army with which to offer support to the Allied war effort. It is within this context that the move to Algiers came to pass.

## Continued Convergence

One of the major difficulties with any economic study of the Second World War and French resistance is a lack of official documentation. André Postel-Vinay referred to the manner in which meetings would occur with the British representatives—including John Penton, of the Treasury, and John Lithiby, of the Bank of England—wherein there were "never any instructions written".[30] While this is not technically correct, judging by records conserved within the Bank of England and the National Archives on the subject, it is true insofar as written instructions are indeed rare. However, telegrams, letters and reports were kept. It is for this reason that network analysis is highly effective within this context, as these maps illustrate the most 'important' intermediaries, whose previously underappreciated links helped to apply economic policy. As has been shown, the policy was highly centralised and enacted with the full cooperation of the British state. It is clear that much help and advice were sought from, and accorded by, the British establishment. Naturally, this led to influence being exerted by dint of the financial and monetary experience that Penton, Lithiby, Bartholomew and other colleagues held. Nonetheless, the lack of notetaking appears highly irregular, especially when concerning a subject as potentially contentious as the national economy of countries at war. Furthermore, considering the highly technical nature of monetary and fiscal policy, combined with the purchasing of entire stocks of colonial produce, such a lack of notetaking seems even more astonishing. While one can empathise with the difficulty and dangers of record-keeping behind enemy lines, as Moulin and Cordier experienced, the same does not ring true for those who remained within Allied countries, especially once the immediacy of threats of a German invasion had begun to fade in 1941. Ultimately, through the use of social network analysis, the informality of relations between the British and the Free French is clarified. It was understood that both groups of bureaucrats were on the same side, economically speaking, and that compromise and

[30] POSTEL-VINAY (ed. PACQUEMENT), *La Passion du Développement*..., 2019, p. 36.

discussion were a far more effective *modus operandi* than administrative officiousness.

One hypothesis for the absence of notetaking is that the complicity between the British authorities and their French counterparts, in matters of economics, was far greater than previously imagined. While the early simplicity of the accounting system is often remarked upon, notably by Pierre Denis, such an approach rendered practical difficulties almost inevitable once the reality of wartime life struck.[31]

Had there been less collaboration among the participants, a complete economic collapse of the rallied Fighting French colonies would likely have occurred, once decision-making had entirely shifted to Algiers at the end of 1943. However, this did not happen. Instead, things continued much as they had before. It also suggests that the Free French and British wartime economies were far more converged than previously understood. It also suggests that the acrimony of the political split between the head of the Fighting French and his British hosts had relatively little impact on the economies of the rallied territories. Therefore, the question must be asked as to why this was so?

General de Gaulle was a military and a political leader, above all else, who delegated a great deal of power and influence to those ostensibly more competent in the economic domain than he. The economic and financial archives are conspicuous in their absence of mentions of de Gaulle, except occasionally in the third person or relating to issues pertaining to his own accounts. Seemingly, he did not intervene in the major questions faced by the colonies which had rallied to his cause. These included important issues such as arbitrage between the African rallied territories and their Vichy counterparts.[32] However, his delegates were often lacking in formal experience of central banking and the type of economic problems that were likely to be experienced in a colonial setting.

[31] POSTEL-VINAY (ed. PACQUEMENT), *La Passion du Development*..., 2019, p. 34—"The accounting mechanism, as far as I can remember, was extremely simple"; DENIS, *Souvenirs de la France Libre*, 1947, p. 217—"For me, this trip (Brazzaville, 1941) was a difficult test, for two reasons. Firstly, it was my initial contact with a treasurer-payer and (secondly) with French public accounting".

[32] BoE, OV45 129, *Problèmes financiers et monétaires de la France Libre*, p. 8—"We have the obligation to protect the Bank of England against the importation of contraband Bank of West Africa notes from non-rallied colonies, in the rallied colonies where they can be presented in exchange against the £".

Pierre Denis had served on the Macedonian front during World War One as an intelligence officer, for a period of two years,[33] before briefly returning to academia, after having been offered a chair in Geography at the University of Strasbourg. He briefly worked on monetary problems in Poland and Romania for the Society of Nations and served as an advisor to the Venezuelan government, as of 1936. His French colonial experience was, therefore, non-existent. André Postel-Vinay[34] had only recently finished his studies and passed the test to become an *Inspecteur des Finances*, just prior to the break-out of hostilities. The only member of the *Caisse centrale* and the Financial Service who had prior professional experience in the French colonies was André Diethelm,[35] having managed Indochina's finances, before serving as the head of George Mandel's cabinet prior to the war. Nonetheless, this is not to suggest that their competence was in question. They did the jobs given to them, by de Gaulle, under circumstances that would have made even the foolhardiest think twice. Moreover, they were handling problems with which they had virtually no experience and were responsible for working within the framework of a foreign banking system.

From an economic standpoint, the rallied colonies were extremely diverse, with populations relying on different productive sectors and finding themselves at varying stages of economic development, in different corners of the world. It is difficult to see how the jobs of fishermen in Saint-Pierre-et-Miquelon, or nickel miners in New Caledonia, could have been even remotely comparable to those of diamond miners or groundnut farmers in French Equatorial Africa.

To further complicate matters, the economic control with which the Gaullist movement governed the colonial empire differed from area to area. This was especially true for the French-mandated countries of Syria and Lebanon. Following the countries' capture from Vichy, under Operation Exporter in July 1941, they nominally fell under Fighting

[33] OULMONT Philippe, *Pierre Denis: Free Frenchman and Citizen of the World*, Paris, Éditions Nouveau Monde, 2013, (Ebook), Chapter 6, Para 12.

[34] POSTEL-VINAY André, *Un fou s'évade: Souvenirs de 1941–1942*, Paris, Éditions du Félin, 1997, p. 7—"In June 1940, I was 29 years old. I was single, an Inspector of Finances, mobilised as a lieutenant in the 70th Artillery Regiment. Having been taken prisoner, I escaped on the 24th".

[35] TURPIN Frédéric, *André Diethelm 1896–1954: De Georges Mandel à Charles de Gaulle*, Paris, Les Indes Savantes, 2004, 278p., p. 84.

French political control. Yet, concurrently, the two countries began to be inducted into the sterling group. This meant that they used the Syrian pound, instead of the franc. This second currency replacement, having converted from Turkish pounds to French francs before eventually turning to British sterling, antagonised both local traders and nationalists alike.[36] Nonetheless, as was seen earlier, this helped to increase trade with their nearest neighbours and to quell the threat of famine,[37] it was therefore difficult to envisage another course of action. A similar situation occurred between New Caledonia and the New Hebrides. In New Caledonia, the franc operated hermetically but the islands still relied on trade links with the New Hebrides, where the pound sterling and the franc were both used interchangeably.[38] This meant that there was no clear possibility for Exchange Control between the two territories. Such controls were necessary, especially in wartime, to ensure that imports were only allowed if they were in the best interests of the war effort. Various methods of facilitating their implementation were used, including direct intervention, like pegging the two currencies together[39]; altering the value of exchange between two currencies[40]; or by forcibly restricting

[36] M.B. & H.G.L., 'Syria & Lebanon: The States of the Levant under French Mandate', *Bulletin of International News*, 13/07/1940, Vol. 17, N°14, pp. 841–851, p. 848.

[37] WILMINGTON Martin, *Economic Regionalism in the Middle East during World War II (The Middle East Supply Center)*, Doctoral Thesis, New York University, 1960, 448p., p. 60—"The services rendered directly and indirectly to the civilian population were praised both by Allied and independent Middle Eastern spokesmen; one of the many eulogies credited the Center for having saved "millions of human beings" from starvation" (Speech by Sir. Francis Joseph, acting chairman of the United Kingdom Commercial Corporation (The New York Times, Dec. 18, 1943).

[38] BoE, OV45 129, *Free French Finance*, 1941, July 28, p. 2—"In New Caledonia, the existing circulation can be continued, with over stamping to avoid export of capital to the New Hebrides, where the notes are interchangeable with sterling notes".

[39] A.J.B., 'The Sterling Area', *Bulletin of International News*, Vol. 21, N° 24, November 1944, pp. 1000–1005, p. 1001, "moreover, some countries which are not generally regarded as members of the pre-war Sterling Area (Japan, the Argentine, France, Bolivia, Uruguay, Yugoslavia, and Greece) pegged their currencies to sterling…".

[40] BoE, OV100 13, Equatorial Africa, *Letter to National Commissioner of Finance, London, from Fighting French Financial Delegate, Brazzaville*, 18/01/1943—"I have suggested putting BAO notes into circulation in this territory, giving them an exchange rate in relation to the Fighting French notes".

money leaving or entering a market.[41] In areas where two currencies were concurrently circulating, this process became virtually impossible to enforce. Moreover, these issues did not merely affect the Pacific island territories but those in Africa too. When confronted with such difficulties, it is understandable that the leaders of the Fighting French economic services were closely linked to their British homologues, even if written instructions were rarely issued.

Close collaboration between the British and the Fighting French continued into 1943 and beyond. This convergence was significant as it refutes traditional historical analysis of the Franco-British wartime relationship, which has tended to emphasise the unravelling of ties with London and concentrated upon the political impact of the relationship between General de Gaulle and Winston Churchill, before the battle of the two generals—Giraud and de Gaulle. This is not to lessen the importance of relational ties, but it is necessary to underline that, economically speaking, the working relationship continued well into 1944.

## "Voler de ses propres ailes"[42]

However, while the Franco-British economic collaboration continued to hold firm, thanks in large part to the efforts of Allen Bartholomew, Pierre Denis and André Diethelm, separation did indeed occur between the British banking establishment and the Free French Financial Services.

This is best demonstrated by the increasingly important role adopted by André Postel-Vinay within the *Caisse centrale*. By December 1942, he appeared on the *Caisse centrale*'s books, as receiving a salary of £60 per month.[43] This was on the same salary grade as Pierre Denis, indicating

[41] BoE, OV45 129, *Statutes of the Caisse*, Undated (August 1941) "Article 2) 1A i) It will take charge of the notes and coin circulating in Free French territories, ii) and issue notes and coin—the notes being legal tender only in the territory of issue, but exchangeable".

[42] DENIS Pierre, 'Les finances de la France libre (juin 1940 à juin 1943)', *Revue de la Deuxième Guerre mondiale*, PUF, N° 1, novembre 1950, pp. 20–27, p. 22—"This regime was maintained until the end of 1943, when the British Government, following the formation of the National Liberation Committee in Algiers, denounced the March 1941 Agreement, and left the Committee to, financially, fly with its own wings".

[43] SAEF, B 0062801, *Letter to Mr. Mouy, Paymaster of Free French Headquarters, from unsigned* (Context suggests that the author is Pierre Denis), 1942 December 9.

Postel-Vinay's position as a decider within the *Caisse*. The pay received by Denis and Postel-Vinay was fifteen pounds more than their colleagues, Auguste Léopold Brusset[44] and Philippe Etlin,[45] both of whom were *chargés d'études* which roughly translates as 'report managers'. Curiously, Brusset's wife is referred to in documents concerning his service, stating that she also served in the *Caisse centrale*.[46] However, she received no mention in either Henri Ecochard's list,[47] or that of the Administrative Dossiers of the *Service Historique de la Défense*.[48] In all likelihood, Madame Brusset was one of the typists to whom reference is periodically made, but never by name.

Operations in London were already beginning to be wound-up in May 1943. Through a study of the general costs that were incurred by the *Caisse centrale*'s branch, at 4, St. James's Square, there were very few outgoings in that particular month. Transactions included an advertisement being taken in 'The Times' at a cost of £1 3s 6d and the £1 0s 4d spent on different transport methods being used by the personnel. In all, for the month of April 1943, the branch cost £3 19s 6d to run.[49] This fell to £1 17s 11d for the month of June. Furthermore, concerning the Prince's Street branch of the *Caisse centrale*, this downward trend was echoed by their spending figures, which also fell in June, from £2 5s 5d to £1 6s 10d in August 1943.

From a banking perspective, the spring and summer months of 1943 were indicative of this move away from the influence of the Bank of England and the British Treasury. On 1st July 1943, an account was opened in the name of the *Comité Français de la Libération Nationale*,

[44] 'Auguste Brusset', http://www.francaislibres.net/liste/fiche.php?index=58514, Consulted 2019, September 12.

[45] 'Philippe Etlin', http://www.francaislibres.net/liste/fiche.php?index=67621, consulted 2019, September 12.

[46] SAEF, B 0062799, *Letter to Commander de Boislambert, from unsigned, Representant à Londres* (Allen Bartholomew), 1943, November 5 "Madame Brusset, who is also part of our personnel, must also be sent to Algiers".

[47] Liste Ecochard, http://www.francaislibres.net/liste/ecochardv40.php?&pr=1&lie=8547, Consulted 2019, September 12.

[48] Dossiers GR16P du SHD, http://www.francaislibres.net/liste/gr16p.php?&pro=1&cot=95581, Consulted 2019, September 12.

[49] SAEF, B 0062799, *Frais généraux—Caisse centrale de la France libre, Succursale St. James*, 1943, May 11.

in francs.[50] This was a clear indication of the Fighting French's lessening reliance upon the British financial system as, during the same month, credits that had been made to the Gaullists from British sources ceased.[51] The account which had been established, in pound sterling, to allow the transfer of assets from one currency into the other, was closed in November 1943.

The beginning of July 1943 was marked by reports indicating the importance of monetary hermeticity in the African colonies. Following the 'Torch' invasions and the progressive move to Algiers, more information was becoming available to the personnel of the *Caisse*. Reports sourced in North Africa were beginning to suggest the impracticability of continued differentiation between rates of exchange in the former Vichy territories and those that had rallied to de Gaulle.[52] In the former Vichy colonies, the exchange rate (200 fcs: £) meant that their francs held a lesser value than those in the rallied Fighting French colonies (176.625 fcs: £). On the black market, the rate was closer to 700 francs to the pound.[53] In practice, this meant that one would need to spend far more francs for each pound, thereby costing the buyer and benefitting the seller.

Another difficulty concerned the transfer of bullion that had been deposited, in 1940, prior to the fall of France, in colonies like Martinique. This problem arose from the fact that $40 million-worth of bullion was envisaged as being transferable to Algiers, but the U.S. State Department decided to intervene "in no uncertain manner".[54] This embargo is hardly surprising, when put into the context of the Gaullist-American relations. Diplomatic difficulties had been rife since the initial attempts to acquire U.S. support during the Pleven mission of 1941 and the issues encountered by the Free French delegation in the United States, led by Adrien Tixier. The State Department's main complaint was that the United States had not, at this point, recognised the C.F.L.N. as a

[50] SAEF, B 0062801, *Rapprochement des Comptes de la Caisse Centrale avec ceux du Service Financier de Londres au 30 octobre 1943*, p. 2.

[51] BdF, 1,064,198,804 *Caisse centrale de la France d'Outre-mer*, *Conférence faite par M. Denis*, 1946, June 25, pp. 5–6—"The conditions in which the new French Government found itself were in fact profoundly transformed by the sudden cessation, at the end of June 1943, of the British credits which had financed the movement of free France".

[52] 'Uniting Francs', *The Economist*, 1943, July 10.

[53] *Ibid*.

[54] 'French Gold', *The Economist* 1943, July 24.

government and, as such, they insisted on keeping a supervisory eye over the gold in Martinique. Such treatment was not being inflicted upon the other governments-in-exile. This obtuse diplomacy was designed to do little more than frustrate the Gaullists and followed other slights that Roosevelt's State Department, led by Cordell Hull, inflicted upon French external resistance. Hull went as far as to claim that "De Gaulle had the unhappy faculty of alienating most of those of any nationality with whom he came into contact, while at the same time undoubtedly inspiring millions of Frenchmen who were far removed from him".[55] Nonetheless, the peculiarity of the wartime relationship between the United States and the Free French was that, in spite of the issues, economic relations continued to be facilitated between the two. According to Hull, this was intentional, largely to ensure that they remained appraised of the situation in North Africa.[56] As he put it, "The advantages of intimate contact with French North Africa clearly outweighed the disadvantages".[57] Economic considerations seemed to trump diplomatic slights, from the American point of view.

The *Caisse centrale* had, at this point, more than doubled its note issuance. Normally, this would need to be backed by bullion, which explains the increased efforts to acquire the gold that was housed in distant territories. However, this was primarily prompted by the necessity to reissue worn, tattered banknotes that had not been reissued since the territories' separation with Vichy and the *Banque de France*. This included Equatorial Africa, Somaliland and Saint-Pierre-et-Miquelon. As of 30th April 1943, the Issuance Department of the *Caisse* had gold backing (5.7%) for the notes they issued, as well as those notes that they, themselves, had already issued (11.4%). The other liability that acted as a backing for their issuance practices was old notes (82.9%) which had been withdrawn from circulation but, due to the gold standard remaining in operation, the *Banque de France* would have been able to convert at the end of hostilities.[58] Such issuance practices showed that, despite the move

[55] HULL Cordell, BERDING Andrew H.T., *The Memoirs of Cordell Hull*, New York, Macmillan Co., 1948, 1804p., p. 1159.

[56] HULL, *Memoirs...*, 1948, p. 1162.

[57] *Ibid.*

[58] BoE, OV45 130, *Caisse Centrale: Note prepared for John Lithiby*, 1943, July 9.

to Algiers, the development of independent economic policy continued unabated.

The majority of the members of the *Caisse centrale* were moved to Algiers at various points throughout 1943. The *Caisse centrale* closed its doors on the main London office at Prince's Street, on Saturday 30th October 1943.[59] Alexis Laferrière travelled from London to 21 rue d'Isly,[60] where the six-roomed offices of the *Caisse* would come to be housed.[61] Coming from a family of legal professionals, Laferrière was the president of the *Banque de Syrie et du Liban*. Having left Syria to return to France, according to Postel-Vinay, he was not a Gaullist by conviction but rather was attracted by the possible adventure.[62] Once in Algiers, Alexis Laferrière got to work by assisting Postel-Vinay.[63] He was helped by a number of staff, including a chief accountant, an inspector from *Crédit Foncier d'Algérie*, as well as another accountant from the same institution. These personnel were viewed as being sufficient to handle the task-at-hand, but they would need to be helped by the hiring of new staff. However, it was well understood that there were great difficulties in hiring qualified help, during wartime, and they continued to operate to the best of their abilities. The wings of the *Caisse centrale*.

The network above, Fig. 8.4, shows 278 separate edges, or correspondences, between 115 nodes, and includes institutions as well as individuals, including CAIFOM, FRANCAISSE and *Caisse* Princes St. These represent the *Caisse centrale de la France d'Outre-mer*, in Algiers, the *Caisse centrale de la France d'Outre-mer*, in Paris, and the *Caisse centrale* branch at Princes Street, in London. The sub-dossiers, from which the network is drawn, cover the period from 1941 to 1945. This is a result of the manner in which French archives collate related folders into a larger dossier, in contrast to British archival technique which

[59] BoE, OV45 130, *Report on Caisse centrale de la France d'Outre-mer addressed to Cameron Cobbold (HM Treasury) from John Lithiby*, 1943, October 29.

[60] SAEF, B 0062799, *Letter from Pierre Mendès-France (Commissaire aux Finances) to Auguste Brusset, Director of Requisitions*, (no date specified) February 1944.

[61] SAEF, B 0062799, *Letter to M. l'Intendant Dusset (sic.—Auguste Brusset) from unsigned*, 10/02/1944.

[62] POSTEL-VINAY (Ed. PACQUEMENT), *La Passion du Développement…*, 2019, p. 34.

[63] SAEF, 0062801, *Letter to Allen Bartholomew from Pierre Denis*, 1943, November 17.

prefers to separate the dossiers into their constituent parts. All concern various aspects of the *Caisse*'s day-to-day business in London, Algiers and, eventually, Paris.

When a comparison is drawn between the network map constructed on the basis of French data, housed at the S.A.E.F. at Savigny-le-Temple, with this above map, Fig. 8.5, showing interactions that occurred between the personnel of the *Caisse centrale de la France libre*, the Bank of England and H.M. Treasury, during the years 1941 to 1943, great differences are apparent. The central actor is John Lithiby, the assistant advisor

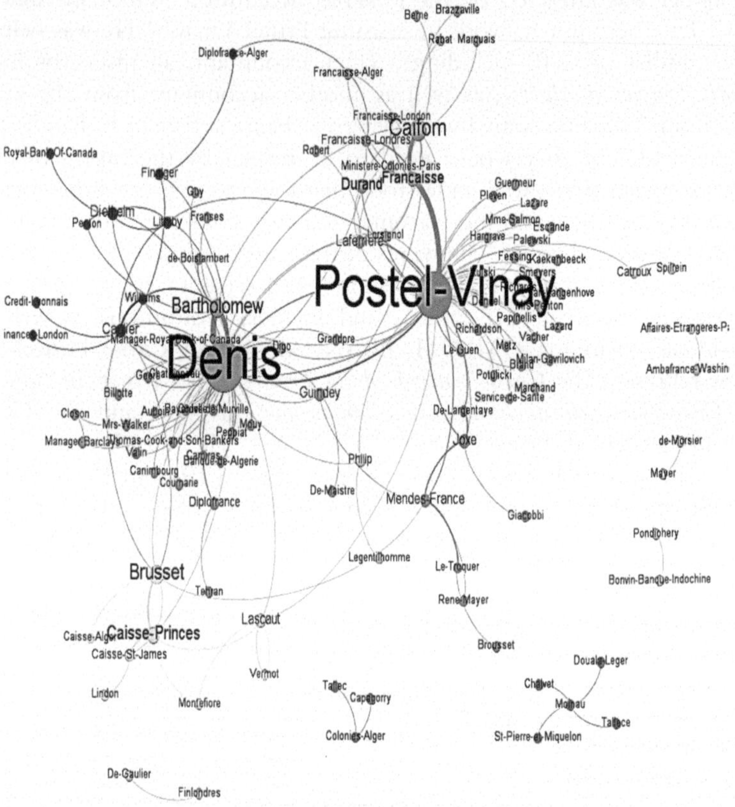


Fig. 8.4 Caisse Centrale Network, 1941–1945, (SAEF, B 0062799 and B 0062801)

to the governors of the Bank of England, as of June 1940.[64] Lithiby, a decorated veteran of Gallipoli, was not French and was, instead, a British functionary. Linked to him are people including W. Lionel Fraser, the "outsider" who was brought into the Treasury.[65] Having always had a "penchant for foreigners", Fraser was tasked with leading 'The Allies Division', where he helped to guide the finance ministers of the various governments-in-exile with British bureaucracy.[66] On the night of 5th June 1944, he was with René Pleven, by then the Commissioner for the Colonies in the C.F.L.N., dining at N°67 Cadogan Place.[67] Pleven struck Fraser as being "exacting and impatient at times – perhaps naturally – when his demands were not fully granted". Remembering Raoul de Roussy de Sales' comments on Pleven, his tenacity had clearly not abandoned him in the intervening years of the war. As the many British names show, this map was mostly dominated by Britons. The difference with the later network map, Fig. 8.4, is the personnel who are present and their nationalities. This shows that the *Caisse centrale* had developed its focus, from one centred on Britain back towards the French colonial territories and, notably, Algeria.

As shown in Fig. 8.4, the most important actors in the network are Pierre Denis and André Postel-Vinay. This is represented by the size of their names, relative to others in the network. The thickness of the line, or 'edge', that links the actors is a representation of the number of correspondences between them. The secondary hubs, such as Francaisse, Allen Bartholomew and Émile Durand, provide links to outer hubs, such as André Diethelm; Louis Joxe, the general secretary of the C.F.L.N.[68] and the Provisional Government; Auguste Brusset; and the *Caisse* at

[64] BoE, M5/533, *Advisors to the Governors of the Bank of England 1939–1945*, p. 5.

[65] FRASER W. Lionel, *All to the Good*, Kingswood, Heinemann, 1963, 275p., p. 118.

[66] *Idem*, p. 121.

[67] *Idem*, p. 132.

[68] 'M. Louis Joxe est nommé secrétaire général du Comité de la libération', *L'Écho d'Alger*, 1943, October 14, https://www.retronews.fr/journal/l-echo-d-alger/14-octobre-1943/30/1295515/1—By decree, dating 2nd October, the French Committee of National Liberation has decided that a general secretary, named by decree, will be present at committee meetings; will perform the duties of a secretary for the meetings, under the direction of the President; and give notification of any decisions adopted. Mr. Louis Joxe, Committee Secretary, has been named General Secretary, by decree on 9th October.

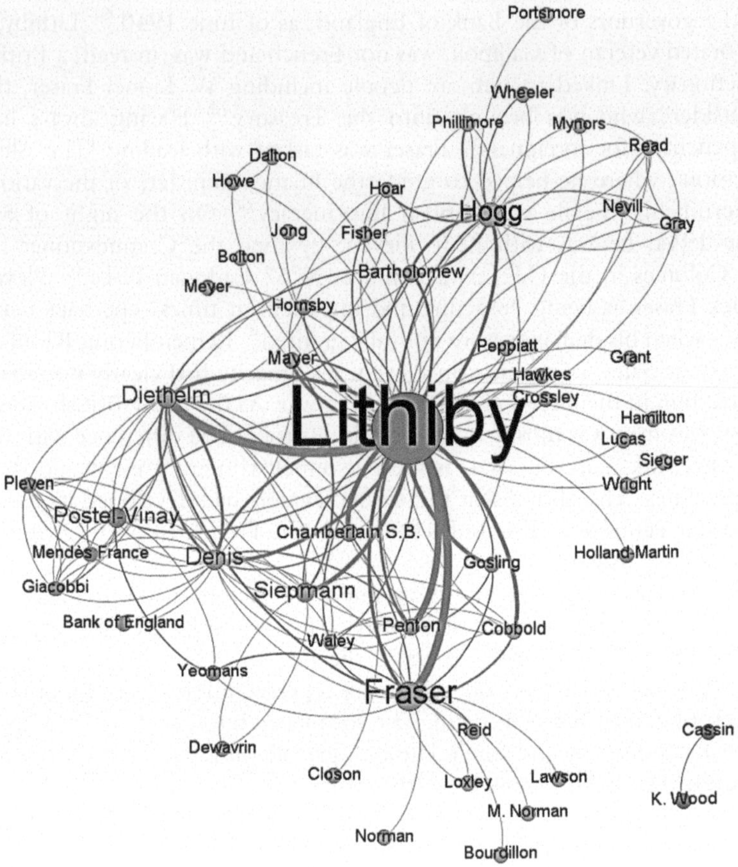


**Fig. 8.5** Network Map—Caisse centrale de la France libre, H.M. Treasury & Bank of England (>1 Interaction), 1940–1943, (BoE, OV45 129, OV45 130, OV100 13)

Princes Street. What can be seen from these different groupings are the important roles played by those who moved from London to Algiers in 1943, notably Pierre Denis and André Postel-Vinay. Knowing the stature of these individuals, within the context of French external resistance, it appears that the majority of the conserved sources stem from those who appear towards the centre of the network. Nonetheless, as Granovetter posited, the strength of weak ties is indeed present[69]; meaning that one should not ignore the lesser connected individuals in networks, for it is often they who act as conduits between different organisations. This is particularly the case with André Diethelm and John Lithiby; both of whom act as important connectors in the earlier of the two networks, Fig. 8.5. However, by the later iteration, Fig. 8.4, they have become more marginalised—appearing in the blue clique to the top-left—as their roles had clearly changed. Diethelm had moved to become Commissioner for Production and Supply for the C.F.L.N., in June 1943, before becoming Commissioner for War in April 1944. He was, therefore, far less involved with the financial concerns of the movement. Likewise, Lithiby, who had previously been the go-between for the Bank of England, was supplanted due to the decreasing importance of British money for the Free French and the increasingly active part played by Allen Bartholomew, who served as the *Caisse centrale*'s representative in Britain. These maps show the parts that intermediaries played in the financial and economic interactions between the British and the French external resistance, but they go beyond, showing interactions between the colonies and Algiers, too. These are represented by the red clique on the left of the map. This is a different manner of using historical sources, making use of computational power to underline specific ties between different organisations and their representatives who may not have necessarily been apparent from a cursory glance. It is with such network maps that the development of the influence exerted by Pierre Denis, John Lithiby, André Diethelm and André Postel-Vinay has been underlined.

## D-Day, Pay Day?

1944 will be remembered as the year of D-Day, and, in France, as the year of the *Libération,* when the *Années sombre* came to an end. It is also the year in which the Provisional Government appropriated control over the French republic and its colonial possessions. The outsiders of the previous four years returned to become the new French establishment. Collectively, they had gained a great deal of governing experience and acquired many experienced governors, both from within Vichy and from London, thus creating a reinvigorated political class. People such as Maurice Couve

69 GRANOVETTER Mark, 'The Strength of Weak Ties', *American Journal of Sociology*, Vol. 78, N° 6 (May 1973), University of Chicago Press, pp. 1360–1380.

de Murville rallied to de Gaulle's side, in 1943, after having served, for the previous three years, as director of External Finances in Pétain's Vichy governments. In parallel, long-standing critics of the Vichy regime, including Guillaume Guindey, who had fled France following the Allied landings of 1942 in Africa, became the head of the Service of External Finances. Tellingly, the *Agence Française de Développement*, the modern iteration of the *Caisse centrale*, highlighted the pre-Fighting French roles held by Guindey, but neglected to do so for Couve de Murville.[70] Collaboration remains a very contentious word in French, and its effects have seemingly outlived those who participated.

Through such acts of reconciliation and the level-footing upon which the former opponents were placed within the C.F.L.N., the democratising element that de Gaulle and his movement were attempting to push to the fore did indeed come to pass. This was vastly different approach to that taken in the earlier days in London, where loyalty and ideological purity were valued above all else. Such a change was likely prompted by the altering circumstances of the war and an increasing politicisation of de Gaulle who, at the beginning of the conflict, was more concerned with military survival than with the later preoccupations of liberation that came to characterise the Fighting French move to Algiers.

Already, change was on the way. For instance, in late December 1943, due to the difficulty of hiring capable 'European' administrators at such a crucial juncture of the war, a reform was introduced to increase the numbers of indigenous personnel in the C.F.L.N. administration.[71] De Gaulle bowed to pragmatism, as opposed to blindly following the preconceived expectations for French politicians. When it is seen in the context of a world war, this can be interpreted as Gaullist realpolitik in action. Nonetheless, in the archives, there is very little mention of administrative personnel of Algerian Muslim descent.

With the beginning of the war's end approaching, a regularisation of relations between the C.F.L.N. and the American government was quickly becoming a necessity. Having hitherto refused to do so, the Roosevelt administration could no longer avoid placing de Gaulle's organisation on a similar footing to that of other governments-in-exile. American support

[70] POSTEL-VINAY (Ed. PACQUEMENT), *La Passion du Développement*..., 2019, p. 154.

[71] 'Reform in Algeria', *The Economist*, 1943, December 18, p. 808.

for Giraud had evaporated upon de Gaulle's accession to become the undisputed head of the C.F.L.N.[72] As has been shown previously, the French delegation of the Gaullist movement had long suffered from this lack of official 'recognition' by the American government. Cordell Hull explained the American reticence:

> It was De Gaulle's constant insistence on political recognition, however, that excited so much suspicion against him. If he, as an Army general, had thrown himself wholeheartedly into the fight against the Axis in a military sense, if he had actually led French troops against the enemy wherever possible instead of spending most of his time in London, he could have rallied far more support to himself among the French and among the United Nations. Instead, his own dictatorial attitude, coupled with his adventures in the political field, inevitably inspired the thought that he was trying to develop a political standing that would make him the next ruler of France.[73]

Nonetheless, Hull disregarded military operations led by de Gaulle at the head of the Free French movement, including the abortive invasion of Dakar in 1940. The Roosevelt administration seemed to fear that, by according him full political recognition, this may have ended with the creation of another authoritarian in the heart of Europe. Yet, if this were truly the case, why did the Americans provide them with economic support and ordnance at all? There is no comprehensive answer to this question, other than to suggest that Roosevelt and Hull were uncommitted to either Vichy or the Gaullists. They recognised that the Fighting French movement, much as they may have disliked its leader, were successfully rallying territories that would prove useful to the American war effort, including New Caledonia, as well as being aware of the growing support from within internal resistance movements in France. The U.S. government could not afford to ignore de Gaulle entirely but,

[72] MURPHY Robert, *Diplomat Among Warriors: The Unique World of a Foreign Service Expert*, Garden City, NY, Doubleday & Company, Inc., 1964, 470p., pp. 184–185—"Churchill nevertheless decided to recognize for all practical purposes the French Committee of National Liberation as the Government of France and he attempted at the Quebec Conference in August to persuade Roosevelt to do likewise. The President finally yielded somewhat on this point and agreed to assign an American representative, with the rank of ambassador, to work with the committee".

[73] HULL, *Memoirs...*, 1948, pp. 1163–1164.

while there remained a chance that a legitimate alternative French government could be formed, they preferred to hedge their diplomatic bets. This attitude began to change, incrementally, throughout 1944. While the Americans understood that the C.F.L.N. was the "leading body of French resistance", this did not constitute the diplomatic recognition that the C.F.L.N. required.[74]

Another step involved the acknowledgement of the franc as an Allied currency. Following martial logic, troops needed payment in a currency that was usable and accepted in whichever area they found themselves. The alternative was a retreat towards methods that would have provoked an unsavoury reaction, but which are an ever-present risk during wartime—pillage and looting. Such methods would have alienated the local population and risked the loss of any semblance of moral high ground. The choice, for all Allies involved, seemed to be between running the American printing presses and attempting to acquire as many French notes in as short a time as possible. This decision would either entail printing the francs in Surrey or in Washington—a time-consuming task, at a point where speed was of the essence. The decision taken by the Supreme Headquarters of the Allied Expeditionary Force (S.H.A.E.F.), in preparation for the Allied Military Government of Occupied Territories (A.M.G.O.T),[75] was to design a French franc along similar lines to those used in the United States. Printed in the United States, by the Bureau of Engraving and Printing, these notes were printed from February to May 1944.

The important question is how would these invasion notes correspond and exchange with the different colonial francs that were traded at different rates of exchange, and how best to use them if they were issued by a foreign power? The answer indicates exactly where the true balance of sovereignty lay—with those who were the most able to enforce their usage. It was decided that the various francs would be harmonised, around an exchange rate that seems to have been accorded more relevance for the invading troops than for the people for whom it was ostensibly meant to serve.

[74] 'The Status of Algiers', *The Economist*, 1944, February 12, p. 207.

[75] 'Billet de banque AMGOT Recto-Verso', *Musée de la Résistance En Ligne*, http://museedelaresistanceenligne.org/media.php?media=811&expo=&sens=recto, Consulted 1944, September 18.

> The Allied Governments, especially the United States Treasury, favour round figures for territories occupied by their troops, in order to simplify the conversion of sterling and dollars into local currency. (It may be noted, for instance, that the dollar-lira rate of 100 makes the lira equivalent to one cent).[76]

The British pound to franc convertibility rate meant that one received 200 francs to the pound, and, for the Americans, the rate was fixed at 50 francs to the dollar. With the use of round-numbers, it was intended that the troops would have an easier time of judging the value of goods. However, this was a double-edged sword. While such a rate would have allowed for easier convertibility, the inflated rate would have also meant additional francs for those who converted their pay from sterling and dollars, thus according them greater purchasing power. Alternatively, it was a devaluation for people in France, as imported goods would become much more costly. Even without the need to loot and pillage, such a decision effectively accorded the franc less worth and would, *ceteris paribus*, have engendered inflation, as the troops could "corner supplies, and send prices rocketing up".[77] In the interests of avoiding economic woes from spoliation, it was necessary, according to *The Economist*, that such a course of action did not occur:

> It is imperative that the liberating troops should not appear to the French as worse despoilers than the Germans.[78]

Paradoxically, the invasion provided a form of economic cleansing fire. With the arrival of Allied troops on Europe's shores, the C.F.L.N. would be free to do as they saw fit with the tainted Vichy franc. *The Economist* suggested that this formed a "part of the process of *epuration* and would provide the opportunity for partial or complete sequestration of liquid assets acquired by suspect means".[79] This was not without risk, as it tarred all with the same brush of guilt. Those who had acquired their wealth by nefarious means would be punished, just as would be the case for those who had merely happened to belong to the right profession. However,

[76] 'French Financial Unification', *The Economist*, 1943, August 14, p. 215.

[77] 'Freedom for France', *The Economist*, 1944, April 15, p. 491.

[78] Ibid.

[79] 'The New Franc', *The Economist*, 1944, May 13, p. 652.

it is questionable whether this situation would have represented much of a quandary for those in the external resistance who had already been dispossessed, disenfranchised and seen their citizenship revoked by the Vichy regime. In the long run, the need to cleanse the stain left by Vichy and Nazi occupation mattered far more.

In reality, the conditions in Normandy rendered things far from clear. Even in the immediate aftermath of the invasions, arrangements for currency were still being negotiated. The use of invasion currency by the Allied forces, one that was different to that issued in France and was operating on a preferential exchange rate, was viewed as a great slight towards the newly established *Gouvernement provisoire de la République française*, which had been created on 3rd June 1944.[80] The American invasion forces brought Allied Military Government of Occupied Territories (A.M.G.O.T.) francs, which risked aggravating the local populace, while British troops had been supplied with old *Banque de France* notes, extracted during the Dunkirk evacuation. However, both were in very short supply and were, therefore, only temporary solutions. British forces made up any shortfall through use of the A.M.G.O.T. francs.[81] However, in *The Economist*'s view, American unwillingness to discuss the recognition of the new Provisional Government meant that these currency clashes became unavoidable. Unsurprisingly, this was not a view shared by Churchill and Roosevelt. On 9th June, Churchill wrote to Roosevelt, explaining that he needed to know whether the backing of A.M.G.O.T. francs would be the responsibility of the British and American Treasuries and, if so, whose government should redeem them? The balance of power is clearly shown by the final paragraph of the communication:

> Shall we get de Gaulle to take responsibility for these notes as President of the Provisional Government of France, in which case the French Nation will ultimately face the problem of redeeming them? Or shall we say the United States and Great Britain assume responsibility for these notes and will fix the ultimate responsibility at the Peace settlement?[82]

[80] 'Ordonnance du 3 juin 1944 substituant au nom du Comité français de la Libération nationale celui de Gouvernement provisoire de la République française', https://mjp.univ-perp.fr/france/co1944.htm#3/06/44, Consulted 2019, September 20.

[81] 'Invasion Currency', *The Economist*, 1944, June 10, p. 787.

[82] CHAR 23/13, Image 76 of 135, *Communication from Winston Churchill to F.D. Roosevelt*, N°696, 1944.

The following day, Churchill added an addendum in which his tone was more equivocal. Having seen examples of the A.M.G.O.T. notes, he described them as not striking him as "very reassuring. They look very easy to forge. Nothing is said on whose responsibility they are issued and who is responsible for redeeming them. Surely there must be some authority behind them".[83] In response, Roosevelt replied that he was fully in agreement with Churchill's estimation that they were being railroaded into a decision over full recognition of de Gaulle's *Comité*. He went on to say that "de Gaulle should be informed" that the supplementary currency would be used in the same manner as had been understood by Jean Monnet and Pierre Mendès-France. Once again, the unequal balance of power was on display. Roosevelt also warned that:

> If de Gaulle incites the French people into refusing to accept supplementary francs then the Comité would have to bear the full responsibility for any bad effects resulting from the use of the yellow seal notes and BMA notes in France. One of the certain consequences will be the depreciation of the French franc in terms of dollars and sterling in the black market which will accentuate and reveal the weaknesses of the French monetary system.[84]

As the name suggests, the yellow seal notes were dollar bills which bore a yellow seal instead of the usual green one. These were even closer in style to the actual dollar bills, bearing all the hallmarks of American monetary authority, including the images of bygone American presidents and 'The United States of America' featuring prominently upon them. Equally, the British Military Authority (B.M.A.) notes bore the British lion seated atop a crown, and the denomination was in sterling rather than francs. Nonetheless, this note was slightly less contentious, by dint of the large, capitalised 'FRANCE' that was stamped in the top-centre of the note's face. Should Roosevelt have been willing to inflict a bigger insult to Gallic pride, it is difficult to imagine one. Yet, it only took until the next page of the communication, where Roosevelt stated that "Provided it be clear that he (de Gaulle) acts entirely on his own responsibility

[83] CHAR 23/13, Image 76 of 135, *Communication from Winston Churchill to F.D. Roosevelt*, N°697, 10/06/1944, June 9.

[84] CHAR 23/13, Image 76 of 135, *Communication from F.D. Roosevelt to Winston Churchill*, N°559, 1944, June 13.

and without our concurrence, he can sign any statement on currency in whatever capacity he likes, even that of the King of Spain". This diplomatic insult is completed in the final line where he commented that "It seems clear that Prima Donnas do not change their spots".[85] Such a dismissive response from Roosevelt makes patently clear the hierarchy of power within this trio of leaders. Clearly, de Gaulle's proclamations and actions held little truck in the corridors of the White House. However, such intransigence was not without risk, as inflation, through the introduction into the money supply of 80,000 million francs, in addition to the 500,000 million francs already in circulation, risked exacerbating matters.[86] Provoking a type of invasion-induced hyperinflation, driven by rising food costs and stagnant economic activity, would have further crippled the French economy and risked the Allies being blamed for any ensuing chaos.

The positive relationships formed between the economic decision-makers in the provisional French government and British were clearly not being reflected within the higher echelons of power. The D-Day invasion was only the beginning of the liberation of France. With tensions already running high, concerning questions of strategy, the financial issues that were facing the Allied powers seem to pale in comparison. However, when considering the effect of such questions on the lives of everybody in France, as opposed to those simply within the immediate vicinity of the invading forces, these issues of multiple currencies circulating concurrently in the French money supply grew in importance, even at the highest levels of state. Under a draft agreement between the British and French, the military francs would be used in France, but their issuance was under the management of the French authorities. This meant that they remained informed of the circulating money supply in France and, therefore, remained capable of coordinating their price and wage policy.[87] These episodes, throughout 1944, show that the economy was inescapably linked with the management of the state. In much the same way that the military was the reflection of a country's hard power, its economy was a representation of domestic control and a method of

[85] CHAR 23/13, Image 77 of 135, *Communication from F.D. Roosevelt to Winston Churchill*, N°559, 1944, June 13.

[86] 'Invasion Currency', *The Economist*, 1944, June 10, p. 787.

[87] 'Monetary Agreement with France', *The Economist*, 1944, July 8, p. 56.

coercion through which a senior partner in the alliance could exert great influence over a junior. However, when the junior partner did not recognise its place and role within the hierarchy, diplomatic friction was the inevitable result.

CHAPTER 9

# Planes, Loans and Bank Robbery

1944 was the culmination of efforts for resistance forces within France. It began with the country still under the yoke of the German occupation and yet, less than nine months later, the capital and four-fifths of the *Hexagone* were freed. While this was undoubtably achieved through the blood, sweat and tears of the men and women who fought, and died, for the liberation of the country, the funding and equipment drops were the tools that allowed them to help the Allies. Through acquired experience and better-organised logistical operations, a growing level of professionalisation had begun to appear within the *Maquis* and the intelligence, escape and action networks. It was also the year in which the majority of the money that was obtained by the resistance came not from without, but from within France itself. Up to this point, the most consistent income was provided by the containers and agents who transported money on their person. However, these methods were eclipsed by money that was 'liberated' from the Vichy- and German-controlled institutions, including the Post Office and private banks, such as the *Banque de France*. Furthermore, loans were also taken out with supportive local business leaders. Whereas D-Day served to advance the war from a military perspective, it is important to underline that the financing of resistance activity had been prepared far in advance.

One of the most fundamental issues affecting financing was logistics. Transporting notes—either with an agent, or as part of a consignment of



D. Foulk, *The Price of Freedom*,
https://doi.org/10.1007/978-3-031-09066-0_9

containers—was complicated by factors that fell outside of the control of those who sent the money, whether they were entirely British-run operations or those organised in conjunction with the B.C.R.A. The losses within the leadership of the Section 'RF' networks, following the arrests of Jean Moulin and Charles Delestraint, had a significant impact on clandestine operations in 1943. This forced a wholescale change in tack from the B.C.R.A., who had hitherto operated on a centralised basis. When the organisational heads were arrested, the imperative to decentralise became obvious. Albertelli argued this point in his work on the B.C.R.A.:

> Until the end of spring 1943, the B.C.R.A. favoured a centralised organisation in France to deal with the emergency and compensate for the lack of suitable volunteers. Everything was organised around several men: Jean Moulin, General Delestraint and a few who were in charge of communications and operations. This front, of whose fragility everyone was aware, crumbled in the early summer of 1943.[1]

The official British history of Section 'RF' decried Moulin's successors, Claude Bouchinet-Serreulles and Jacques Bingen, accusing the latter of having been told to hoard money, in order to use it in forthcoming political battles.[2] The trickle of money that was reaching the groups in France was compounded by an absence of stores and the organisational shake-up that their appointments heralded.

To combat this, the decision was made to send money along with consignments of clothes, brassards and other supplies that were parachuted in containers. Two or three cells, or compartments, of the H-type container were used to allow the sending of money without needing to have an accompanying agent carry it on their person. However, this also meant that the unaccompanied payment was less secure than had it been transferred directly, as it was more liable to being discovered. The advantage of transferring money in such a manner was that it allowed for a considerable increase in the quantities of francs, and dollars, being despatched to France. Occasionally, even '*Lager Geld*' were sent, which were the notes used in German prison camps.[3] As a means of spreading

[1] ALBERTELLI, *Les Services secrets de la France libre*, 2012 (Ed. 2017), p. 187.

[2] TNA, HS7 124 RF, RF Section History 1943, Chapter 30.

[3] TNA, HS7 124, RF History 1943, *Notes on the Stores Sub-Section RF Section History, Appendix A*, p. 10.

the risk of what was, effectively, tipping money out of plane hatches, the cash payments would be separated and sent in different aircraft. Through skilful packing, ten million francs could be interspersed with chocolate, corned beef or tobacco. The money-laden container was marked with the letters 'C.O.', in black type over a white label, thereby allowing the head of the reception committee, the *Chef d'opération*, to know which ones were exclusively for them to open.

In total, from November 1943 to the end of July 1944, 1.35 billion francs, or the equivalent of £19 million, were sent into France by Section 'RF' in containers. This was accompanied by a further $75,000.[4] To put these amounts into context, during this period, the total amount of francs sent was four times greater than the authorisations that had previously been accorded to the REX mission, of 380 m francs. The REX mission received their funds over twenty-one months—from November 1941 to July 1943—but the November 1943 to July 1944 transfers only covered a period of nine months. Moreover, considerably fewer American dollars were sent than was previously the case. This was likely due to the decapitation of the REX network, following Jean Moulin's arrest. Without the same level of access to those who had previously changed money before, like the de Graaffs, this would have rendered the conversion of dollars back into francs far more convoluted and difficult.

The expedited money came in the form of 1,000-franc notes, in bundles of 1 million, and 70 million francs were sent from North Africa into France, destined for those areas controlled by S.O.E. 'RF' Section organisers.[5] While these North African notes were significantly fewer in number than those sent to France from England, it demonstrates that, in 1944, Algeria served as an important staging post for operations taking place in the south of France. As the unnamed author of the 'RF'-Section history wrote:

> If money be the sinews of war, it may be said to be the framework of Resistance and the punctual despatch of the very large sums needed to keep an Underground Movement, or Secret Army, in being was one of the greatest and, in every sense of the word, heaviest, preoccupations of the Sub-Section.

[4] *Ibid.*; 1.35 billion francs do not tally with the figures shown in Table 9, which suggests that 2.2 billion francs were authorised and expedited by Section 'RF'. Table 9 was constructed using documents from AN, AG 3 (2) 276—171 MI 108 BCRA.

[5] *Idem*, p. 9.

Many bitter arguments were caused by a lack of money and, without external funding, the movements' growth would have been significantly hampered. Henri Frenay[6] Christian Pineau[7] and Passy[8] all explained as much, in their respective war-memoirs. However, there were also artificial bottlenecks, which were ostensibly caused by the heads of the movements who were becoming embroiled in political machinations in both France and Algiers. This compounded the problem of excess demand, on the parts of the groups, with a reduced supply of funds; neither of which abated in 1944. Following the establishment of the Secret Army, the dissemination of decision-making responsibilities to a regional level ensured that the same precarity continued to reign after Moulin and Delestraint were arrested. This also meant changes for the manner in which money was sent to France.

In July 1944, the regional military delegates (*D.M.R.*) were given the responsibility for sharing the money among the heads of the F.F.I. (*Forces Françaises de l'Intérieur*). This funding activity was supplemented with payments made directly to the D.M.R. for their administrative spending and the services that they would use[9]. General Marie-Pierre Koenig, the head of the F.F.I., in a letter to Emmanuel d'Astier de la Vigerie, the C.F.L.N. commissioner for the Interior, said that they estimated needing about 420 million francs to cover the expenses of 280,000 troops. However, this was caveated by suggesting that the troop numbers

[6] FRENAY, *La nuit finira*, 1973, p. 299—"Aid to the Maquis is a vital necessity. Failure to provide it would destroy their confidence in the Resistance. Are we going to force these men to come down from their mountains and go to Germany? We need additional resources and, first of all, money."

[7] PINEAU, *La Simple Vérité*, 1960, p. 223—"Charles Laurent is a perfect honest man; he is also a meticulous finance official; he ran such risks with his methods that I cannot help but protest. He misunderstands the meaning of my reply, gets angry - so much so that I reluctantly give him the envelope that I had prepared. Meeting ends in an unenthusiastic atmosphere".

[8] PASSY Colonel, *Mémoires du chef des services secrets de la France Libre*, Paris, Éditions Odile Jacob, 2000, 801p., p. 276—"The arguments of each varied according to the phases of the moon or the hygrometric state of the atmosphere; that is to say that, in truth, they were only a function of the personal interests of such and such a leader of the movements. The slightest imprudent word aroused rowdy sensibilities and unleashed violent incidents".

[9] AN, AG 3 (2) 276—171 MI 108 BCRA, *Dispositions relatives au Budget Mensuel*, Colonel Vernon (Henri Ziegler), p. 1.

**Table 9.1** Table showing spending justification given by Colonel Ravanel (R4) and calculations (in red), (AN, AG 3 (2) 277–171 MI 109 BCRA, Dossier 9)

| | Unmarried (francs per month) | Unmarried x N° of troops | Married (francs per month) | Married x N° of troops |
|---|---|---|---|---|
| Soldiers and Corporals | 1,500 | 52,500,000 | 3,500 | 122,500,000 |
| Non-Commissioned Officers (N.C.O.) | 2,500 | 12,500,000 | 4,500 | 22,500,000 |
| Subaltern Officers | 4,000 | 10,000,000 | 6,000 | 15,000,000 |
| Superior Officers | 7,000 | 17,500,000 | 9,000 | 22,500,000 |
| TOTALS | | **92,500,000** | | **182,500,000** |

were simply estimates and that, in all likelihood, there was a much larger contingent who would require support.[10]

A table of salaries was produced by one group in the South West, in Region R4.[11] Table 9.1 demonstrates a potential budget for the *Maquis*, led by Col. Serge Ravanel.[12] Knowing that, under Ravanel's command, there were 35,000 soldiers and corporals, 5,000 N.C.Os and 2,500 officers of both levels, subaltern and superior, it is possible to analyse the payroll for this group. Unfortunately, Ravanel, the youngest colonel in France, at only 24 years old in 1944, did not leave a more detailed analysis of the marital status of those under his command.

As a means of offering a wage comparison, it shows that if all members of Ravanel's *Maquis* were unmarried, a total of 92,500,000 francs would have been needed that month. Equally, had they all been married, the total of 182,500,000 would have been required. Richard Heslop, alias *Xavier*, of Section 'F', made reference to the wives of *maquisards*

[10] AN, AG 3 (2) 278—171 MI 110 BCRA—*Letter from General Koenig to Commissioner d'Astier*, 21 July 1944.

[11] AN, AG 3 (2) 277 - 171 MI 109 BCRA, Dossier 9—*Budgets et Finances Zone Sud 1944.*

[12] 'Serge Ravanel', https://www.ordredelaliberation.fr/fr/compagnons/serge-ravanel, Consulted 18 March 2020.

receiving 1,800 francs per week along with a further 500 francs for each child in the household, up to the third child,[13] for those members of the group run by Henri Jaboulay, *Belleroche*, in Lyon.[14]

The budget requested was for 150 million francs. Ravanel suggested that this fell short of his estimations, as it did not take into account any administrative personnel. Nonetheless, the budget included a form of social security, with a bonus being paid per child—from one infant up to a maximum of three, which amounted to 200 to 500 francs per child. Were it hypothesised that the soldiers and N.C.Os were single and the officer class were married, this would give a salary base of 102.5 million francs, leaving around fifty million in child benefits. This also shows that life under the Third Republic had clearly altered people's expectations concerning social security.[15] It also suggests that a large proportion of those who served in the *Maquis*, despite their tender age, were already married and heads of families. With a budget of 150 million francs, split between 42,500 troops, the average payment per capita was around 3,500 francs.

Moreover, in comparison with agents in the field, the costs engendered by *Maquis* troops and corporals were seemingly much higher than those that were accorded to the secretaries for the networks, and slightly more than was drawn by Daniel Cordier, who had earned 1,200 francs per month, when serving under Jean Moulin. While all were risking their lives, it is difficult to understand the logic of supplying more money to those who were living in the wilds, separated from civilisation, than to those who were living in towns, when the latter were subject to the heavy additional costs of wartime urban life.

However, there is nothing to suggest that this was an official policy which was applied across the entirety of France. All groups seemed to have been operating under their own rules, relative to their own budgets

[13] HESLOP, *XAVIER: A British Secret Agent*..., 1970 (Ed. 2014), p. 227.

[14] 'Henri Jaboulay', https://www.ordredelaliberation.fr/fr/compagnons/henri-jaboulay, Consulted 20 March 2020.

[15] DORMOIS Jean-Pierre, *The French Economy in the Twentieth Century*, Cambridge, CUP, 2004 (Ed. 2010), 156p., p. 61—"Piecemeal assistance schemes introduced earlier by the Third Republic were generally limited in coverage and economical in provision; they included free medical assistance (the 'poor man's doctor'), the creation of orphanages (1904), and asylums for the destitute (1905) and the introduction of child benefit (from the fourth child) in 1932".

and finances. In Brittany, members of resistance groups were paid 1,500 francs per month, in towns and cities, whereas those based in the countryside received 1,000 francs.[16] The monthly spending on these Breton forces was 1.2 million francs per thousand troops. With an estimated 36 million francs being spent, they were thus budgeting for a force of around 30,000 troops. Colonel *Vernon*, Henri Ziegler, was the leader of the headquarters of the French Forces of the Interior (E.M.F.F.I.). Having been an engineer, graduating from *École Polytechnique,* a test-pilot and founder of Airbus,[17] Ziegler was already an important member of the French aviation community, even before the war broke out. His comment that "We are, therefore, generally reduced to a very arbitrary system concerning the regional budgets" carries a great deal of significance, in such a context. While one can understand the reasons behind this randomness, in terms of funding, it did not help when budgeting for the troops in France. Most concerningly:

> The budget of the F.F.I. (for troop numbers) is currently a peacetime budget. It must be transformed into a war budget, on the following basis: 1) 1,500 francs per man mobilised and per month; this sum comprises food, a small payment, family benefits. 2) A reserve amounting to 50% of the total budget which allows to combat unforeseeable needs: the influx of sleeper cells in a region, indemnities for civilian populations who have been tested by German reprisals, replacement of stolen or lost funds. 3) A reserve allowing us to handle the needs of liberated zones such as the Ain or the Vercors.[18]

This proposed policy underlines several things. Firstly, French resistance provided a basic form of social security to the families of people who joined and, secondly, it provides another example of the cost that each soldier required in order to be supported. However, it appears that the figure of 1,500 francs included all aspects of the cost per soldier—food, social security and pay. Members of the F.F.I. and the *Maquis*

[16] AN, AG 3 (2) 276 - 171 MI 108 BCRA, *Letter from Colonel 'Vernon' (Henri Ziegler) to Commandant Lejeune,* 04 July 1944.

[17] TAGLIABUE John, 'Henri Ziegler, Aviation Figure, Is Dead at 91', *New York Times,* 28 July 1998.

[18] AN, AG 3 (2) 276 - 171 MI 108 BCRA, *Note for F1/F,* 17 July 1944.

were receiving more, per month, than agents who came from England, irrespective of whether they were French or not.

Much as in 1943, packages continued to be sent via the Lysanders of 161 Squadron. Flight Lieutenant Charles Peter Clark was tasked with the holding and packing of 53 packets of notes, “alleged to contain 109,500,000 francs”.[19] Three weeks before the beginning of the new moon, the regional heads would submit their budgetary requirements, in order to allow for their money to be prepared in time for the optimal flying period. These covered all aspects of spending—notably personal and administrative spending, wireless operator costs and special missions.[20] The month of December 1943 had proven a particularly costly month, in terms of mission success and losses among the crews. Hugh Verity—161 Squadron’s temporary squadron leader—explained that seven sorties were attempted but only one proved successful. Of the four operational pilots in ‘A’-Flight, three had been killed in action.[21] This meant that the moon-period, in January 1944, was heavily exploited to send in both money and supplies. Of the above total, 100 million francs, or 91%, were destined for various missions that were led by Jacques Bingen, alias *Cléante*.

The remaining nine percent was split between thirteen other resistance members. Two million francs were reserved for Louis Mangin[22] who, at that time, had been serving as Regional Military Delegate (*D.M.R.*) since September 1943, when he arrived in Jura aboard Wing Commander Hodges’ Hudson. Mangin’s assistant, Jacques ‘*Chaban*’ Delmas, would go on to participate in the *Comité financier de la Résistance* (C.O.F.I.).[23] This committee was formed by Bingen and Georges Bidault, alias *Bip*—the man who was originally supposed to have been Daniel Cordier’s boss, a couple of years before, had Cordier not been employed by Jean Moulin.

[19] AN, AG 3 (2) 278 - 171 MI 110 BCRA, *Cash Handed to Ft./Lt. CLARK for despatch during January*, 24 January 1944.

[20] AN, AG 3 (2) 276 - 171 MI 108 BCRA, *Dispositions relatives au Budget Mensuel*, 24 July 1944.

[21] VERITY Hugh, *We Landed by Moonlight: Secret RAF Landings in France 1940–1944*, Manchester, Crécy Publishing, 1978 (Ed.2013), 272p., p. 154.

[22] ‘Louis Mangin’, http://www.francaislibres.net/liste/fiche.php?index=83142, Consulted 19 March 2020—Louis Mangin, formerly a commandant in the 24$^{th}$ Alpine Hunter Battalion, had, as his liaison officer, Lucien Cambas (*Trapeze*).

[23] ‘Jacques Chaban-Delmas’, http://museedelaresistanceenligne.org/media3347-Jacques-Chaban-Delmas, Consulted 20 March 2020.

The rest of the transfers, during the January 1944 moon-period, are shown in Table 9.2.

While Bingen and Mangin were the largest recipients of funds, smaller sums were allocated to other D.M.Rs, including Raymond Fassin, Valentin Abeille and Pierre-Camille Rayon. Rayon, alias *Archiduc*, was the leader of 2,000 Maquis in the Vaucluse. He spoke of having seen a marked increase in parachute landings, including up to fourteen drops in one night![24] Using the data about his group and knowing the finances that he received, it is possible to see a discrepancy having occurred between the payments and the requested funds per combatant.

Whereas leaders had been asking for sums ranging from 1,000 francs up to 1,500 francs per person, Camille Rayon was sent only 250 francs per person during the month of January. His payments would often be collected by André Charlot, alias *Diacre*. On 15th November 1943, a mission was flown to Charentes by the R.A.F.'s 161 Squadron, using the operational codename 'Albatros', which had brought Rayon another half a million francs in one packet of notes.[25] Rayon was operating within the 'R2' area, which incorporated the Vaucluse, in southern France.

In both January and February 1944, 500,000 francs were sent to Rayon. This was increased, in March, to 800,000 francs, which were delivered as part of operation 'Marquis' by 161 Squadron. He sent a message back to London, on 12th March, explaining that his troops were dispersed and demoralised—as well as reporting "acts of banditry" which were primarily due to a lack of available funds.[26]

By the end of the month, the financial situation in R2 had clearly degraded and Rayon sent word asking for a monthly budget of 1.7 million francs. This amount, split between the two thousand troops that he had under his command, would have represented a total of 850 francs per person. As it was, the transfer of 800,000 francs gave Rayon a budget of merely 400 francs per person.

[24] 'Alias « ARCHIDUC», Terroriste à la retraite', https://vimeo.com/67803592,Con sulted 20 March 2020.

[25] AN, AG 3 (2) 278—171 MI 110 BCRA, *Sommes expédiées directement (Novembre 1943) Zone Sud*, 10 January 1944.

[26] AN, AG 3 (2) 277 - 171 MI 109 BCRA, *Telegram from Archiduc*, via *Ambassadeurs Noir*, 12 March 1944—"Financial situation serious STOP from Archiduc No 3 1 of 10 March following the 30 STOP Given teams dispersed demoralised STOP Some commit acts banditry fault lack of money STOP Promis your name remedy quickly".

**Table 9.2** 'Cash Handed to Ft/Lt. CLARK for Despatch during January 1944' alongside Identity of Agents, (AN, AG 3 (2) 278—171 MI 110 BCRA)

| *Amount (francs)* | *Network* | *Name* |
|---|---|---|
| 45,000,000 | CLÉANTE Lutte contre déportation et Maquis SUD/SEC | **Jacques Bingen** alias Cléante |
| 15,000,000 | CLÉANTE Mission Civile en Mouvement SUD/SEC | **Jacques Bingen** alias Cléante |
| 25,000,000 | CLÉANTE Lutte Contre déportation et Maquis SEC/NORD | **Jacques Bingen** alias Cléante |
| 15,000,000 | CLÉANTE Mission Civile en Mouvement SEC/NORD | **Jacques Bingen** alias Cléante |
| 2,000,000 | LOSANGE | **Louis Mangin** alias Grognard DMR Zone Sud) |
| 500,000 | APOTHESE | **Jean Rosenthal** alias Cantinier alias Apotheme? |
| 500,000 | ARCHIDUC | **Pierre-Camille Rayon** alias Archiduc |
| 500,000 | POLYGONE | **Maurice Bourgés-Manoury** alias Polygone |
| 750,000 | MARQUIS | **Paul Rivière** alias Galvani, Reception SAP R1 |
| 1,000,000 | MARIN | **André Boulloche** alias Doneau alias Marin alias Segment alias Armand |
| 500,000 | SEIGNEUR | **Albert Toubas** alias Seigneur |
| 500,000 | DIAGONALE | **André Schock** alias Diagonale |
| 750,000 | GAUSS | **Michel Pichard** alias Pic alias Gauss |
| 500,000 | PIQUIER | **Raymond Fassin** alias Piquier alias Sif DMR A |
| 500,000 | GALILEE | **Jean-François Clouët des Pesruches** |
| 1,000,000 | FANTASSIN | **Valentin Abeille** alias Fantassin alias Meridien pseudo Victor Amoult DMR M—Normandie, Bretagne & Anjou |
| 500,000 | GRAMME | **Pierre Deshayes** alias Rod alias Gramme pseudo Jean-Pierre Lebert |
| 109,500,000 | **TOTAL** | |

However, for his supposed temerity, Rayon received a severe dressing-down from Algiers, via the intermediary of Louis Burdet, alias *Circonference*. Rayon had asked Burdet to request a budget of 1.7 million francs, who duly transmitted Rayon's message to Algiers. Burdet was asked his opinion on the matter.[27] Eight days later, the response to Rayon was given; Algiers was categorical that they would accept neither a budget that was triple to those that had been awarded to other individual networks, nor would they acquiesce to Rayon's ultimatum.[28] Moreover, this was commented upon in the 'RF' Section History, which recognised that:

> The distribution of funds was scandalous, and the heads of the various Maquis camps and the departments never received the money they were entitled to and were always short. CIRCONFERENCE, D.M.R. of R2 had, himself, been obliged to borrow money from the Mission.[29]

During April 1944, an additional payment of 300,000 francs was made to Rayon, dating from January which had yet to have been sent, thus bringing the total received over the course of the month to 700,000 francs. He had, at that point, not yet begun his work.[30] Nonetheless, this was clearly not sufficient for Rayon, when he could see the sorts of figures being sent to other groups. He wrote back to London complaining that 800,000 francs were being reserved for 'political' usage. What such use entailed was never fully elaborated upon by Rayon. The behaviour of those awarded politically motivated funds did seem to have grated on those *Maquisards* who were stuck in the countryside when "certain elements waft 1,000-franc bills around, looking to corrupt them".[31] Rayon's telegram continued by saying that they did not need to worry about his group neglecting to do their duty, but stated menacingly that

[27] AN, AG 3 (2) 277 - 171 MI 109 BCRA, *Telegram to Circonference* via *Algiers*, 09 April 1944.

[28] AN, AG 3 (2) 277 - 171 MI 109 BCRA, *Telegram to Circonference* via *Algiers*, 17 April 1944—"...Citation we cannot accept your budgetary project triple that of other regions STOP Have cabled *Circonference* on this matter STOP It is inadmissible that you issue ultimatum as means of pressure STOP...".

[29] TNA, HS7 124, RF Section History 1944, Chapter 6, p. 16.

[30] AN, AG 3 (2) 278—171 MI 110 BCRA, *Tableau des dépenses d'ordre militaire pour le mois d'avril 1944*, 29 March 1944.

[31] AN, AG 3 (2) 277 - 171 MI 109 BCRA, *Telegram from Archiduc*, via *Ambassadeurs Violet*, 17 April 1944.

those who had besmirched his troops' reputation would pay. This was the final monetary transfer that was made to Rayon for several months. The next one came in August 1944, for two million francs. Half of this was destined for Rayon and the other half was to be sent into the Drôme and Ardèche departments, in order to support their *Maquis* forces. This was less money per month than had previously been requested in March and April 1944. This shortfall continued into May, as was explained to General Koenig and Passy, when it was pointed out that, during the month, the "financing of the French Interior Forces (has been) absolutely inadequate for the current situation".[32] They had, by this point, sent 150 million francs as opposed to the 180 million that would have been necessary.

Rayon's threat seems to have had long-term consequences on the official recognition of his role in the liberation of France. He was not awarded the Order of Liberation, nor does he appear in Ecochard's list of members of the Free French. In fact, all history seems to recall about Camille Rayon is that he was the creator of a port model, taken from his port in Antibes, which spread around the Mediterranean, in the post-war years.[33] On economic grounds, Rayon was written-out of the history of French resistance.[34] Clearly, there were difficulties in getting money to where it was most needed, but his wartime experience is just as important to highlight as those of any other D.M.R.; many of whom received far greater political recognition in the post-war period.

## Black-Market Borrowing

Expediency and making-do were two aspects that best reflected the funding of French resistance. Wartime constraints were to be expected, and operational problems simply had to be overcome. This was especially reflected in the financial and logistics domain. With airdrops often

[32] AN, AG 3 (2) 276—171 MI 108 BCRA, *Note for Koenig and Passy from Vernon*, 09 May 1944.

[33] 'History', *Port Camille Rayon*, https://www.portcamillerayon.net/en/history/, Consulted 20 March 2020.

[34] 'Camille Rayon bâtisseur de port est décédé à l'âge de 101 ans', *France 3, Provence Alpes Côte d'Azur*, 18 September 2014, https://france3-regions.francetvinfo.fr/provence-alpes-cote-d-azur/alpes-maritimes/cannes/camille-rayon-batisseur-de-port-est-decede-l-age-de-101-ans-553258.html, Consulted 20 March 2020.

missing their intended drop-site and raids being conducted on properties, the funds of French resistance groups were constantly under strain. In addition to direct cash injections through the parachuting of notes, another of the methods that was used to slake this lack of liquidity was through borrowing. However, the important question was from whom?

Maurice Buckmaster, the head of Section 'F', encouraged agents to take loans from local businessmen and leaders. Buckmaster explained that absolutely nothing was given to the prospective creditor in guise of a receipt, for this would have been extremely dangerous were they to have been found with any such document. Messages from the B.B.C. served to offer legitimacy to the potential transaction, as it provided confirmation that a parachute drop would take place. The prearranged phrase would be transmitted to London who would broadcast it, over the B.B.C., as a form of guarantee to the relevant creditor, who was informed beforehand as to when to listen. Buckmaster stated that, following the end of hostilities, it was his job, personally, to reimburse those to whom money was still outstanding. The debt was paid "without question".[35]

It seems that these loans may not only have been sought, but certain business owners also looked to provide help in any way that they could:

> An industrialist offered credit to us that could increase in increments of 5 million up to 25 million. Withdrawals have already been taken from this credit line. The industrialist is directly participating in the resistance; he hides weapons and people and puts his cars at our disposal for certain operations that we have to do; operations in which he insisted on personally participating. On the other hand, the British authorities are looking for capitalists in France who are likely to advance them French francs and, in return, offering them credit, in pounds, in London.[36]

In Switzerland, attempts were made to establish links with French groups that would have allowed money to be safeguarded in the country, thus providing a reserve from which French resistance members would be able to draw, in case funding difficulties persisted.[37] However, as shown in

[35] BUCKMASTER, *They Fought Alone...*, 1956 (Ed. 2014), 320p., p. 165.

[36] AN, AG 3 (2) 276—171 MI 108 BCRA, *Letter from Passy to de Gaulle*, 27 March 1943.

[37] BELOT, KARPMAN, *L'affaire Suisse...*, 2009, p. 216—"Already, the English Treasury accepted to constitute a reserve from which the French could draw in the lack of flight operations; an equivalent of 150 million francs in frozen pound sterling credits".

Table 9.2, one month's payments constituted 109.5 million francs. This is slightly above two-thirds of the value of the frozen sterling credits, of 150 million francs, mentioned by the historians, Belot and Karpman. However, these Swiss funds would have proven most useful to those groups near to the border, notably within Jura and Ain. Nonetheless, it was not a funding mechanism that could have been easily replicated elsewhere. Geographical situation was very important in ensuring that the French groups' funding lines remained intact. Furthermore, this plan also underlines the role played by neutral countries in wartime, as a means of bypassing economic warfare measures. As the Americans explained: "Circuits on the border of the Swiss frontier and, more generally, those created in the east of France were completely organized, in the absence of wireless communications, by the BERNE-LONDON link".[38] In March 1944, Pierre Mendès France wrote to Jacques Soustelle, by now the head of the Information and Action Service, explaining how the Swiss banking links could help to provide the much-needed foreign exchange that was vital to resistance efforts:

> Loans in Switzerland for Action in France - The Delegation of the Resistance in Switzerland has carried out an operation to buy French francs credits to be used with French banks against Swiss francs in Geneva. This operation concerned 5 million French francs and it had been requested that the equivalent value be paid in pounds sterling, taking into account the exchange rate fixed for the operation and the commission for pounds: 6,600 to the Midland Bank of London for the Credit Suisse de Genève. This payment was made, on my instructions, on February 10th in London.[39]

However, the Swiss link was not the only one that existed for providing liquidity to resistance members in France. In fact, it merely represented a sixth of the total value of loans that were eventually arranged by the personnel of 'F' Section with businessmen in France. This began in 1941,

[38] NARA, RG 331 (Allied Operational and Occupation Headquarters, World War II), Supreme Headquarters Allied Expeditionary Forces (SHAEF) General Staff, G-3 Division, Organization and Equipment Section Project Decimal File Feb 1944-Jan 1945, 314.7 Vol. I to 314.7 Vol II, *Part 1—Chapter II—French Resistance and Allied Services (S.O.E.—O.S.S.—S.F.H.Q.)* p. 355.

[39] AN, AG 3 (2) 276—171 MI 108 BCRA, *Letter from Mendès France to Soustelle*, 14 March 1944.

**Table 9.3** Summary of Monies Expended by S.O.E. Section 'F' from 1941 to September 1944, (TNA, HS7-121)

| | *Cash* | *Franc-Sterling loans* | *D/F* | *Berne* | *Total* |
|---|---|---|---|---|---|
| 1941 | 10,000,000 | 55,000 | - | - | 10,055,000 |
| 1942 | 25,000,000 | 6,733,000 | 2,120,000 | - | 33,853,000 |
| 1943 | 40,649,000 | 31,777,500 | 4,700,000 | 2,300,000 | 79,426,500 |
| 1944 | 241,298,000 | 24,074,000 | 4,550,000 | 8,416,000 | 278,338,000 |
| TOTAL | 316,947,000 | 62,639,500 | 11,370,000 | 10,716,000 | 401,672,500 |

with agents taking out 55,000 francs-worth of loans, before increasing dramatically, growing to a peak of nearly 32 million francs, in 1943 and reducing to 24 million francs in 1944. These figures are shown in Table 9.3.

On the other hand, the money loaned from Berne represented a mere 2.3 million francs, in 1943, and 8.4 million, in 1944, respectively. The difference between the loans issued in France and money sent from Switzerland is clear. While Swiss-originated money undoubtedly assisted in efforts to finance resistance activity in the east of France, it certainly did not supplant loans contracted within the Hexagon. The contrast is even starker if we compare these figures to the money that was sent into France through S.O.E. Sections 'F' and 'RF'—422 million and 3.79 billion, respectively, between 1942 and 1944, as was shown previously in Table 9. The S.O.E. Section 'F' figures, from Table 9, do not exactly correspond to the above summary, shown in Table 9.3, but the author, I.D. Lloyd, admitted that 1941 and 1942 were inaccurate, due to insufficient data and that the only reliable figures that he had at his disposal were for 1943 and 1944.[40] This present work has rectified the amounts sent by both Section 'F' and 'RF'. Money was sent through the Franco-Swiss link, via Allen Dulles of O.S.S., in Berne. However, the main conclusion is that the vast majority of money was sent from England by aeroplane, either being parachuted in containers, or landed with agents. Otherwise, it was directly loaned or stolen within France.

Binot and Boyer have indicated that chits were given to the creditor by the borrower, alongside a double of the telegram that had been

[40] TNA, HS7-121, *Report from Mr. I.D. Lloyd to Group Captain Venner*, Undated; See also FOOT, *Des Anglais dans la Résistance...*, 2014, Appendix C, Table 6.

addressed to Algiers. This was to ensure that, should the borrower have been arrested, their loan remained proven.[41] However, operational security would have been compromised by such action. According to the B.C.R.A's own archives, the explanation given by Binot and Boyer resembled the methodology employed for Treasury Bonds.[42] In a telegram addressed to Guy Cettour Baron, a radio operator, on 30th March 1944, the following message was sent:

> First guarantee security Second Finances ask aid immediately from trustworthy person STOP We guarantee reimbursement franc for franc by following means STOP The lender gives you a phrase to broadcast over three days on the B.B.C. read B.B.C. Send us phrase to broadcast and amount sum borrowed STOP Our 15 of 2 night March STOP Besides take action to help yourself out STOP To ensure payment send us lender name and address using method indicated to Auvergnat to follow Marcel[43]

When money was to be solicited in France, the message was sent to the U.K. and retransmitted, over a fixed period, via the B.B.C, thereby satisfying the potential lender of the borrower's trustworthiness and good faith. The importance of confidence between clandestine economic actors is clear. In wartime, there was an inverse correlation between the number of guarantees given to lenders and the weight of the burden of proof required, in order to attest to the borrower's trustworthiness. While the number of guarantees available decreased, the difficulty of providing any proof that was required to attest to one's credentials became much more onerous. In peacetime, there are far easier ways of ensuring repayment, but, in war, trust is lessened. Effectively, this demonstrates the high price

[41] BINOT, BOYER, *L'argent de la Résistance*, 2010, p. 75—"The lender is obliged, in theory, to trust them for the repayment. The only 'guarantee' consists of a duplicate of the telegram addressed to Algiers, which accompanies a receipt, given by the borrower on the spot, in case the latter is placed under arrest or disappears. The accounts, we understand, are not opened under the true surname of the lender, but only with a first name and date of birth".

[42] AN, AG 3 (2) 276—171 MI 108 BCRA, *Instructions pour l'émission de bons du Trésor en France*, 24 March 1944—"Every month: the issuing agents will send a telegram to London giving the numbers of the vouchers issued and the signature on the vouchers".

[43] AN, AG 3 (2) 277 - 171 MI 109 BCRA, *Telegram to Gascon* via *Tetouan*, 30 March 1944.

of acquiring somebody's confidence in a time of war and that the process is very different to that in peacetime.

Loans clearly helped to fund resistance activity. Nonetheless, when compared to the cash sent via air delivery, the amounts loaned in France pale in significance, standing at less than twenty percent of the overall total for Section 'F'. It does not appear possible to identify individual lenders, but the amounts that were borrowed underline the limited level of loans that were taken within France. Donations for French resistance operations appear to have passed through the Fighting French accounts and were, instead, sent into France as part of the 'RF' Section transfers. In a cash-strapped society, it was important to acquire banknotes by any means necessary.

## Wartime Withdrawals

The map above, Fig. 9.1, shows the 'patriotic hold-ups' which hit *Banque de France* branches and sub-branches. Those are shown in purple, while the red marks denote branches that were not subject to any armed coercion by the fleeing German forces or members of the French resistance. Groups from both camps, Axis and Allied, extorted money from the *Banque de France*. French resistance forces took nearly 4.4 billion francs, the Germans withdrew almost 2.8 billion francs, and members of the *Milice*, who were Vichy's political paramilitary organisation, misappropriated 155 million francs.[44]

Firstly, it should be noted that action on the part of the F.F.I., or the *maquisards*, took place in areas that were not provided with many Lysander missions.[45] This indicates that forces who were financed by external sources did not need to rely upon deviant behaviour, such as robbing banks, to financially secure their operations. Secondly, the two areas in which practically no thefts can be seen as having occurred were in Brittany, which was a constituent part of the Atlantic Wall, and Alsace-Lorraine, a department which had been incorporated into the German Reich. Finally, the majority of incidents occurred in the southern part

[44] BdF, 1,069,199,410 1 – Prélèvements—Généralités, *Note*, 19 October 1944.

[45] FOULK David, 'Homeward Bound: Mapping Clandestine Transportation into France during the Second World War', *War in History*, November 2021, pp. 18–20.

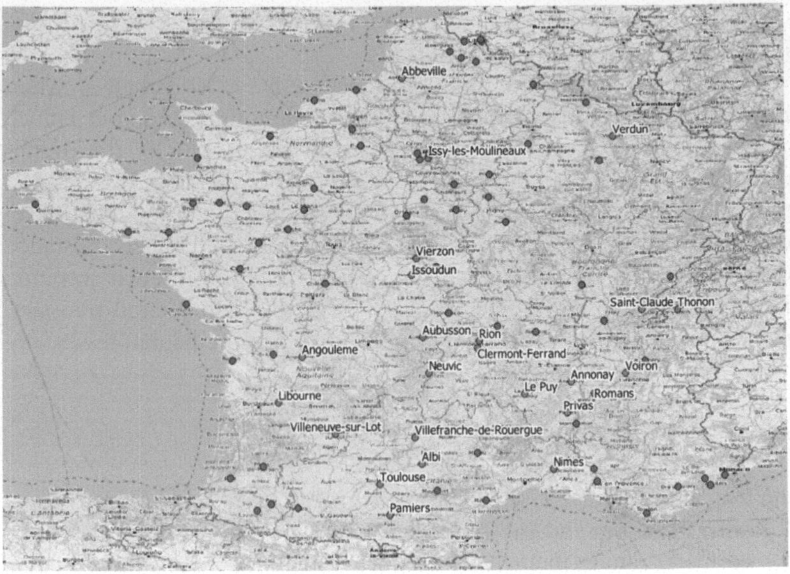


**Fig. 9.1** Map Showing 'Patriotic Hold-Ups', constructed from data (Banque de France, 1069199410 1—Prélèvements—Généralités); Map Layer—© OpenStreetMap contributors

of France. This suggests that there was relatively little conventional military activity in the areas where 'hold-ups' were most propitious or that resistance groups, in those areas untouched by the 'hold-ups', were acquiring funds from elsewhere. Around the Swiss border, money passed over the mountainous regions and it is clear that the country's priority remained protecting their neutrality, rather than hindering resistance financial activity.

The absence of 'patriotic hold-ups' in certain parts of France can be seen through the activity of Special Air Service (S.A.S.) troops, who were present in Brittany and were experiencing difficulties obtaining money. Their first request for funds was received by London on 29th June 1944. This had to be repeated a further three times before a response was finally given to Commander Pierre Louis Bourgoin.[46] London agreed that additional funds were required and that they would provide a monthly stipend of 1,200 francs per capita, notably in a telegram sent on 9th July 1944.[47] However, by 11th July, they had only managed to dispatch twelve million francs to the S.A.S. over two separate operations. These delays in sending funds to the British troops in France were caused by the awful weather during that period. A further transfer of six million francs was to be sent to one group, but this had to be diverted elsewhere when the intended recipient was arrested. An S.A.S. brigadier commented on the importance of restoring confidence, by stating that it could only come through the resumption of fluid supply lines.[48] Once again, the close links between morale and financing are underlined.[49]

The foremost of these *Banque de France* hold-ups was the Neuvic train robbery. Near Périgueux, on 26th July, a group of F.F.I. hijacked a train that was heading towards Bordeaux. The bills that were sequestrated were all crisp, having not yet been entered into the *Banque de France*'s ledgers. At 2.28 billion francs, the haul was astronomical; 250 million francs in 5,000-franc notes, 1.4 billion francs in 1000-franc notes, 500 million in 500-franc notes, 120 million in 100-franc bills and 10 million in 50-franc notes were seized.[50] Astonishingly, because these stolen bills had yet to have been entered into the *Banque*'s books, they never appeared in *Banque de France* weekly reports. Unsurprisingly, news of the heist was withheld from publication until, at the end of December 1944, the French Treasury took responsibility for 'irregular withdrawals'. By June 1945, no measures to find the lost notes had been taken (Fig. 9.2).

When a patriotic hold-up at a *Banque de France* branch occurred, the method of 'withdrawal' involved groups of armed troops bursting

[46] 'Pierre Bourgoin', https://www.ordredelaliberation.fr/fr/compagnons/pierre-louis-bourgoin, Consulted 21 March 2020.

[47] AN, AG 3 (2) 277 - 171 MI 109 BCRA, Dossier 3 'Buckmaster', *Appendix 'A' to HQ SAS, Message N° 9.*

[48] AN, AG 3 (2) 277 - 171 MI 109 BCRA, *Issue of Money to Troops and Resistance in BRITTANY*, undated.

[49] The literature on the importance of morale in warfare is abundant. Among the most pertinent is POPE Arthur Upham, 'The Importance of Morale', *The Journal of Educational Sociology*, Vol. 15, N° 4, Civilian Morale, December 1941, pp. 195–205.

[50] BdF, 1,069,199,410 1—Prélèvements—Généralités, *Prélèvement irrégulier opéré à Périgueux le 26 juillet 1944 par les Forces Françaises de l'Intérieur.*

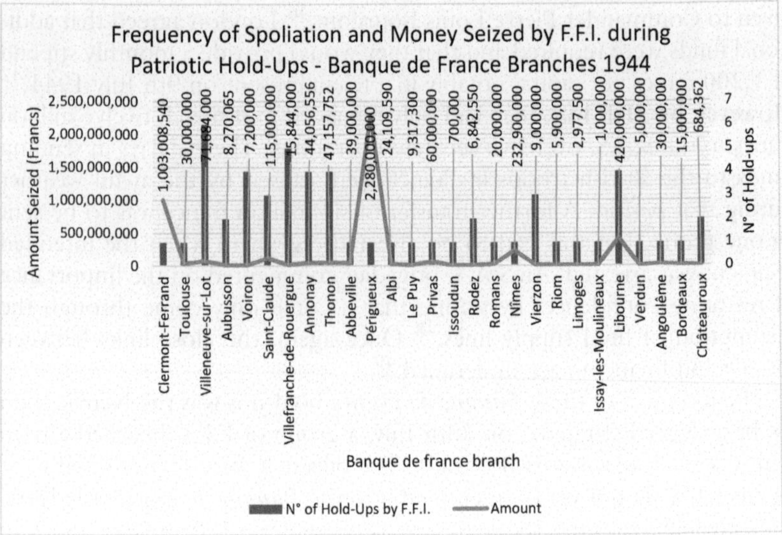


**Fig. 9.2** Frequency of Spoliation and Money Seized by FFI (BdF, 1069199410 1)

into the branch and demanding money, often holding the personnel at gunpoint. For instance, at 10:35, on 1st August 1944, four men in khaki, with sub-machine guns, crashed into the offices of the *Banque de France* branch at Annonay. The group's leader, a junior officer, without any form of identification, asked for the contents of the till.[51] When told by the manager that there was only 800,000 francs, they were taken aback but decided to take the money. This was handed over against the issuance of a receipt, marking the name of the group responsible for the requisition, the 'F.T.P'. These were groups of predominantly communist persuasion who also accepted those of other political leanings into their ranks.[52] Furthermore, as the S.O.E. Section 'RF' History confirms, when discussing Front National (F.N.), a rival communist group:

[51] BdF, 1,069,199,401 2 Prélèvements irréguliers - Comptoirs A-G, *Prélèvements effectués à nos Caisses par les F.F.I.*

[52] TNA, HS7 124 RF Section History 1944, p. 22—"The FTP contained numbers of men who were not communists, and even if there were dangerous and disciplined groups elsewhere, they were well in hand in R1".

> The Communist Party is directly subordinated to Moscow. However, as Moscow does not contribute any financial assistance, the party is, at present, dependent upon us for funds, which gives us a powerful lever.[53]

This would explain the group's need to turn towards banditry for their funding. When it is remembered that, in October and November 1943, both groups, F.N. and F.T.P., were forecast to receive around 4.5 million francs via the REX Mission, from British-based sources, the above quote appears to ring quite true. Moreover, break-ins at the *Banque de France* would have been likely to appeal to the anti-capitalist sentiments that were shared by members of the F.T.P. This explains the presumed astonishment at 'only' finding 800,000 francs in the coffers.[54] However, 'only' is a relative term, when one considers that monthly salaries, in France, among people involved in clandestine work, were anywhere from a few hundred to a few thousand francs. Using the previously cited figure of 1,000 francs per month for those in rural settings, such a sum would have covered a month's spending for around 800 *maquisard*. The same band continued by going to the other private banks in the town, later that very afternoon, including the Bechetoille bank who were twice robbed over the course of the summer, losing 130,000 francs in total.[55]

Things were not yet finished for the *Banque de France* branch in Annonay. A second requisition was made on the very same day. Two officers led a group of a dozen or so khaki-wearing troops to conduct another shakedown. Jean Jarret, leader of the 'Sixes' and 'Dozens' within the *Armée Secrète* (A.S.), was at their head.[56] He agreed to leave his men outside, on the understanding that the door remained wide open. The demands were much larger than those issued beforehand. At ten million francs, it was an astronomical figure, suggesting that Jarret was envisaging paying a monthly wage to more than 10,000 troops! He was argued

[53] TNA, HS7 124 RF Section History 1943, p. 4.

[54] BdF, 1,069,199,401 2 Prélèvements irréguliers - Comptoirs A-G, *Compte rendu annexe à ma lettre du 2 août 1944 relative aux réquisitions à main armée du 1er août 1944.*

[55] BINOT, BOYER, *L'Argent de la Résistance*, 2010, p. 105—"Established in Annonay (Ardèche), the Bechetoille Bank was visited twice by guerrillas, who took 130,000 francs in the summer of 1944. The authors and their units are well-known".

[56] BONNAUD Pierre, '*Notice Annonay (Ardèche) et sa région: les fusillés de l'été 1944*', 16 March 2020, https://maitron.fr/spip.php?article222028, Consulted 22 March 2020.

down to two million. This represented a daily loss to the *Banque de France* of 2.8 million francs. By performing a calculation of X = Amount stolen/Monthly Cost of *Maquisard*, where 'X' represents a presumed size of troop who could be financially provided for by the theft; it can be calculated that a troop 'weight' of 2,800 could have been supported, for a month, with the money that was stolen during the raids.[57]

The story of Annonay is one of workers' resistance. The town is approximately forty kilometres to the south-east of Saint-Étienne, which was, at the time, a heavily industrialised area. The potential labour force was sufficiently large as to support the creation of recruiting offices for both the F.T.P. and a separate one for the Secret Army, adjacent to the Town Hall. Moreover, a group of local union members, who belonged to the C.G.T., created their own resistance group. This union group would, in all likelihood, have been one of the intended recipients of funds that had been handled by the REX mission, stemming from United States, British and French sources, in the months that followed Moulin's arrest, in 1943. However, on 19th July 1944, the reprisals from the Germans, the *Milice* and 'reserve mobile guards' were swift and brutal. They forced their way back to the centre of town and reinstated the Vichy-backed mayor, thereby forcing the F.T.P. and A.S. volunteers to flee, before regrouping in the surrounding countryside. It was in this position that the groups of Annonay found themselves at the time of the hold-ups, and this would explain their urgent need of funds. Having not been financially supported since leaving the town, they were desperate for funds which would allow them to feed their troops. However, the amounts that were being requested of the *Banque de France* branch seem excessive. Bonnaud's article suggests that "many hundreds" of youth signed up to the two resistance groups.[58] This does not seem to correspond with the ten million francs for which Jarret asked, but 2.8 million francs would be enough for the monthly payroll for around 1,800 to 2,800 troops, depending on their salaries, which are far more realistic estimations of the potential forces in the area, in the light of Bonnaud's comments.

[57] (X = 2,800,000/1,000).

[58] BONNAUD, '*Notice Annonay…*', 2020—"Many hundreds of young people signed themselves up to the A.S. and F.T.P. between the 6$^{th}$ and 19$^{th}$ June".

The Annonay branch of the *Banque de France* lost a total of 44,056,556 francs, after being held up on six separate occasions.[59] The personnel were never harmed, and money was usually relinquished with little need for coercion. This seems to point towards one conclusion; the personnel of the *Banque de France* were, in all likelihood, supportive of the driving principle behind the 'patriotic hold-ups': freedom. It only remains to be seen how the personnel of the *Banque de France* participated in the liberation of the country to bring this history of monetary and economic resistance to its conclusion.

## The Liberation of the *Banque De France*

The *Banque* ostensibly operated as a private concern for the duration of the Occupation.[60] However, under the centralising effect of wartime control, the *Banque de France* effectively became the central bank of the metropolitan French state, as Michel Margairaz has affirmed.[61] The board of governors became political tools, to be manipulated, and thus assist with the controlled and systematic monetary pillage of France. A measure of control was still required to avoid France becoming an economic hindrance to the German war effort. However, this system began to disintegrate once the full impact of the disastrous Barbarossa campaign began to filter through, from the German economy, into France. As domestic consumption largely ground to a halt, the *Banque* played a regulatory role,[62] by injecting money into the economy through increased use of public-sector purchases. This intervention helped them to better weather the consequences of the monetary crisis in September and October 1943, where the money supply increased dramatically, up to sixteen billion francs being minted per month. The monthly average circulation, from March

[59] BdF, 1,069,199,401 2 Prélèvements irréguliers - Comptoirs A-G, *Prélèvements effectués à nos Caisses par les F.F.I.*

[60] See Loi n° 45–15 du 2 décembre 1945 relative à la nationalisation de la Banque de France et des grandes banques et à l'organisation du crédit, https://www.legifrance.gouv.fr/affichTexte.do?cidTexte=LEGITEXT000006072686&.

[61] MARGAIRAZ Michel, 'La Banque de France et l'Occupation' in MARGAIRAZ Michel (Ed.), *Banques, Banque de France et Seconde Guerre mondiale*, Paris, Albin Michel, 2015, 208p., Chap. 2, Para. 2 (Ebook)—"The years 1940–1944, one suspects, appears the time when the Bank essentially became the State Bank in wartime…".

[62] Secrétariat d'Etat à l'Économie Nationale et aux Finances, *L'Action économique en France depuis l'armistice*, Macon, Protat Frères, 1941, 181p.

1943 until March 1944, was, therefore, raised to around ten billion francs. The inflationary danger that this posed was counteracted by the issuance of short-term advances to other banks. This led to decreased lending, as the banks had to repay those advances and were thus disinclined to offer the money to clients, in the form of loans. The franc was pegged, using a highly favourable rate to the invader, at twenty francs to the Reichsmark.[63] When this was coupled with the forced sale of goods to Germany, the French economy contracted. The illusion of monetary policy choice was upheld through the continuation of the *Banque de France*'s role as an emitting agent for French currency. However, the collaboration with the occupier continued to weigh heavily on the consciences of some of the *Banque*'s personnel.

The *Forces françaises de l'intérieur* (F.F.I.) of the *Banque de France* were composed of two groups: active members and supporters. The active members numbered 135, and there were 254 people who were described as supporters.[64] From a perspective of the genders of the members and adherents, there were important differences between those taking 'full' membership, of whom only three were women, and 'adherents', a group which included many women. Members in the *Banque de France* offices in Paris, who belonged to the F.F.I., used their positions to glean information, disseminate disinformation, forge documentation and sabotage German industrial material. Their role in the liberation of the city, and in defending the economic security of the war-torn country, is indicative of the merging of economic and military resistance.

On the night of Friday 18th August 1944, eight members of the *Banque*'s F.F.I. detachment remained in the bank's foyer.[65] They belonged to the *Front National* (F.N.), a resistance movement created by Jacques Duclos and Pierre Villon, which most closely identified, politically, with the French Communist Party. It is, therefore, understandable that their role in the liberation of Paris would be underplayed by the returning Gaullist forces, who refused their homologation. The lack of recognition for their efforts led the group to point the finger towards

[63] MOURÉ Kenneth, 'Spearhead Currency: Monetary Sovereignty and the Liberation of France', *The International History Review*, 42:2, 2020, pp. 278–297, p. 280.

[64] BdF, 1,069,200,401 267 Guerre 1939–1945, *Front National, Comité Parisien de Libération, Sous-Groupe de la Banque de France.*

[65] BdF, 1,069,200,401 267 Guerre 1939–1945, *Journal Résistance Paris Témoignages 18 août—7 septembre 1944*, p. 1.

the investigation team, and their leading representative, Lt. Col. Robert Pedoussaut[66] for declining to interview the *Banque*'s personnel in the days after Paris' liberation.[67] In the midst of the political instability, any ostensive reliance upon the help of communists was anathema, notably due to lingering ill-feeling over their support of the Molotov-Ribbentrop pact and the deliberate ambiguity of their positioning as the outsiders of the resistance.

It was suggested that the F.F.I. members should remain in the *Banque*'s foyer, under lock and key, but there was a violent reaction against such an idea. Consequently, the keys remained in their possession. The following day, on 19th August, a breakfast was prepared by the wife of the governor, Mme. Boursault, who delivered coffee as well as '*Diplomate*'-brand cigars. These items were extremely difficult to obtain under the rationing system that had been in place since 8th January 1940 and, after summer 1942, they had become practically impossible to acquire.

The gifting of such luxury items demonstrated the gravity of the circumstances, and the generosity that living through such difficult times could engender. The high value was largely linked to the risks involved in acquiring the item. Such exchanges cannot be judged by the same metric as a simple economic transaction. This is well demonstrated with the example of tobacco. Under the system of tobacco rationing, introduced in 1941, smokers were required to go to a tobacco office, from where they would draw a weekly allowance—a grey paper parcel of 40 g of poor-quality tobacco, known as *gris*, and a packet of cigarettes, for which they would be charged an additional six francs.[68] The war economy

[66] Nom-de-guerre 'Suchet', Armoured cavalry officer during the 1939–40 campaign who, in 1944, was tasked with organising the northern section in the Seine area, under the orders of Commandant Macary, 'Latour'. For more information, http://museedelaresistanceenligne.org/media4851-Plaque-commA, Consulted 07 May 2019.

[67] Association Nationale des Anciens Combattants de la Banque de France, 'FFI à la Banque' - The website containing this information was discontinued in 2019. Nonetheless, it can be accessed through WayBackMachine at the following link, https://web.archive.org/web/20181220173856/http:/www.anac-fr.com/f_2gm.htm, clicking through to 'Liste des récits' and, under (F—Résistance à la Banque), the article 'FFI à la Banque' is consultable.

[68] BOUGEARD Christian, 'La vie quotidienne des Bretons pendant la guerre: Quelques aspects', *Annales de Bretagne et des pays de l'Ouest*, Vol. 92, Issue 1, 1985, pp. 79–102, p. 97.

meant that European access to the main tobacco producers was heavily restricted. This was further compounded by the fixing of the exchange rate, which rendered the transport of the Brazilian leaf and the Sumatran or Cameroonian wrapping paper impossible. Before the war, *Diplomate*-brand cigars were sold at two francs, having been rolled at Morlaix, in Brittany.[69] However, the Allied economic warfare measures meant that production became an impossibility. The extreme rarity of such cigars greatly increased both their price and value. It showed a continuation of ancient martial traditions, on the eve of the battle, where plans were shared, weapons prepared, and brews imbibed. Maussian ritual gift-giving was occurring in circumstances of war-induced penury.[70]

A further symbolic gesture that was adopted was the unfurling of the *tricolore* alongside the Lorraine cross, to highlight the repatriation of authority from the crumbling Nazi administration. This represented the culmination of a highly successful propaganda campaign, led from London. The adoption of the Lorraine cross as a symbol for the Free French, and the F.F.I., was a masterstroke of political marketing. It gave the organisation a type of brand recognition that combined both religiosity and historical resistance in three brushstrokes. On Monday 21st August 1944, a conversation took place between the heads of the *Banque de France* and the resistance leaders of the 1st arrondissement as to whether to lower the flags but, eventually, it was decided to leave both flying.[71] The support for de Gaulle's provisional government, demonstrated by the flying flags and participation in resistance activities, proved that a number of the *Banque*'s personnel were willing to demonstrate their overt support for the insurrection. The F.F.I. of the *Banque de France* were attempting to protect the bank's central Parisian properties, as well as to provide useful information to other local units. The manner in which they planned to do this manifested itself by reconnoitring the city and reporting on the ongoing situation on a street-by-street basis.

[69] BRIDGE Joe (John Steer, 1886–1967), 'Cigares Diplomates' poster, Ateliers Joe Bridge, Paris, 1930, 120 × 159.4 cm, https://auctions.posterauctions.com/lots/view/1-HG2MO/cigares-diplomates-1930, Consulted 8 May 2019.

[70] MAUSS Marcel, *The Gift: The Form and Reason for Exchange in Archaic Societies*, London, Routledge, 1990, 200p., https://libcom.org/files/Mauss%20-%20The%20Gift.pdf, Consulted 12 May 2019.

[71] BdF, 1,069,200,401 267 *Guerre 1939–1945, Journal Résistance Paris Témoignages 18 août–7 septembre 1944*, p. 2.

The lack of oil in occupied France meant that most Parisian transport occurred by foot and bicycle, including through the adoption of the Parisian *vélo-taxi*, a wartime innovation that continues to be seen around French cities to this day. Beginning in May 1944, the Americans began a concerted effort to destroy the German oil refineries and those raids had a severe impact on the availability of petrol. It was on a bicycle that an unnamed member of the Bank's F.F.I. was sent to scout the areas around the *Banque*'s two sites; the original, at 31 rue Croix des Petits Champs, in the *Hôtel de Toulouse*; and the satellite building, at the *Théâtre Ventadour*. The importance of self-powered transportation, in wartime France, must be highlighted.[72] A bicycle costs the equivalent of a month's salary and spare parts, including chains, tyres, inner tubes and cogs, were highly prized by black marketeers.[73] The bicycle's usefulness was underlined during the reconnaissance operations that were performed by the F.F.I. of the *Banque de France*. The rider could quickly escape skirmishes and make use of the smaller side-roads and cut-throughs in central Paris.

The finished report was dated 30th August 1944 and describes life within a city that was awakening from four years of occupation and stirring with revolutionary fervour.[74] The bicycle reconnaissance was conducted on both sides of the Seine, but the majority took place on the *rive droite*, to the north of the river and closer to the *Banque*. The report's author appears to have been in the immediate vicinity of the combat. Having delivered their version of the events, the person simply signed the document, without printing their name.

As shown in Figs. 9.3 and 9.4, the first day of the cyclist's mission, Sunday 20th August, was spent on the *Rive droite*, in the vicinity of the *Banque de France*[75] The points correspond to G.P.S. localisation of areas identified in the report and surround the Tuileries and the Louvre, which were major sites of skirmishes. Furthermore, the area was

[72] AGLAN, *La France à l'envers…*, 2020, 720p., p. 179.

[73] TAYLOR, Lynne, 'The Black Market in Occupied Northern France, 1940–4', *Contemporary European History*, Vol. 6, N° 2 (Jul. 1997), pp. 153–176, p. 162.

[74] BdF, 1,069,200,401 267 Guerre 1939–1945, *Journal Résistance Paris Témoignages 18 août–7 septembre 1944*.

[75] Graphical representations of the trip have been created using - QGIS Development Team, QGIS Geographic Information System, Open Source Geospatial Foundation Project, 2009, http://qgis.org.

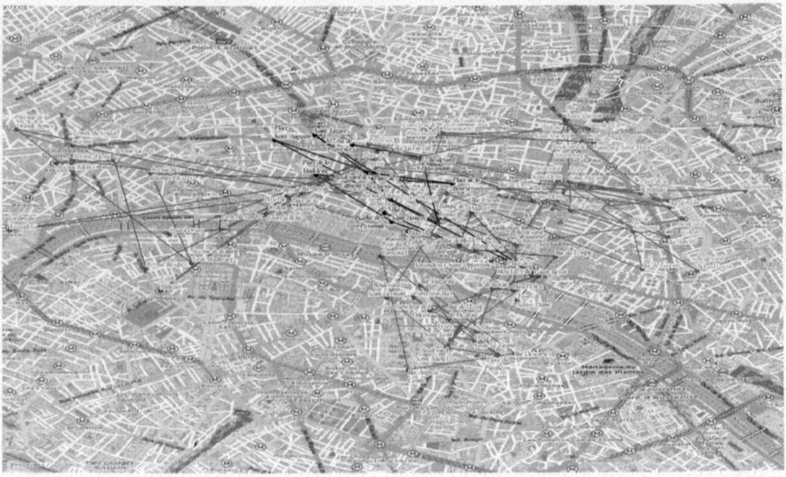

**Fig. 9.3** Bicycle Reconnaissance—Banque de France—Sunday 20th August—Thursday 24th August 1944 Legend—Day 1—Black, Day 2—Green, Day 3—Red, Day 4—Blue, Day 5—Orange; Map Layer—(© OpenStreetMap contributors)

heavily barricaded. The shops, restaurants and cafés, around the *Banque*, were all closed. Around *Gare Saint-Lazare*, the *Café Garnier*, which had previously served as an establishment that was open exclusively to Germans, had torn down the German-language signs. The obligation to hang a certain type of sign, and the extreme rapidity with which they were removed, tangibly shows the economic constraints that the Occupation had placed upon the French service sector. These signs served as both a constant reminder of the military loss and France's subjugation. Removing them was as telling of the public mood as the painting of the *Croix de Lorraine* or the overt hanging of *tricolores*.

The rout began to become visible as the Wehrmacht abandoned vehicles, having blown their tyres and lacking the spares and time to perform repairs. The vehicles were further immobilised by destroying the tyres and axles to ensure that the wrecks could not be easily moved. They acted as an impediment for the Allies' armoured vehicles and mired the liberators with a clean-up operation, thereby diverting additional resources from more strategically valuable work, such as the neutralisation of anti-tank and anti-personnel defences. Concrete *chevaux de frise* were placed across

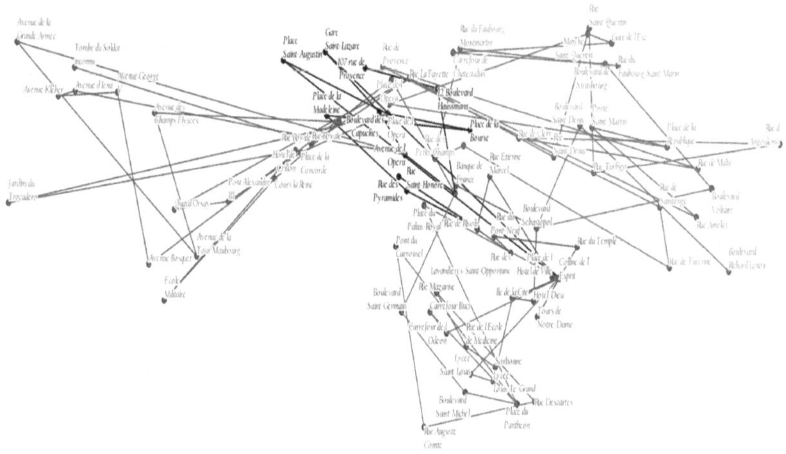


**Fig. 9.4** Bicycle Reconnaissance, 20/8/44—24/8/44—Legend—Day 1—Black, Day 2—Green, Day 3—Red, Day 4—Blue, Day 5-Orange

strategic points throughout the city, notably across rue de Rivoli and rue Saint-Honoré. These protected the German tank pool, which was housed in front of the *Hôtel Maurice*. The mood remained anxious and anticipatory. A few isolated Allied flags had been raised, but the main offensive was yet to come.

On Monday 21st August, representatives of large Parisian banks were encouraged to hang *tricolores* from the porticos of their establishments, including *Société Générale*. However, they chose not to adopt the same stance as the *Banque de France*, on the advice of the local Central Committee for the Liberation. The avoidance of reprisals by the retreating German forces was paramount. News of the atrocities at Oradour-sur-Glane, committed on 10th June 1944, where 642 inhabitants of the village were massacred by Waffen SS troops, had reached Paris[76] Provoking another such reaction was greatly feared.

[76] BdF, 1,069,200,401 267 Guerre 1939–1945, *Journal Résistance Paris Témoignages 18 août—7 septembre 1944*, p. 10, "Fearing for his life, because he surrendered to "Franc-Tireurs", he threw his weapons without shooting, which is confirmed to me by our two comrades. I reassured him as best as I could about his fate, telling him that it was not the French who were barbarians, but the supporters of Hitler, and I cited the odious massacre at Oradour-sur-Glane as proof".

The heat, on Tuesday 22nd August, was stifling. A day of skirmishes in the well-heeled areas of Paris awaited the cyclist, who stayed in the 7th and 16th *arrondissements*, through which the Avenue des Champs-Elysées is to be found. Due to the fighting, the shops on the 'most beautiful avenue in the world' were closed. Few people were in the streets and most economic life, in the centre of the city, had ground to a halt as the combat raged. Heavy patrolling gave the impression of activity but, in reality, the Germans were simply ensuring that the routes remained clear for retreating troops. Many previously occupied buildings were deserted, including the barracks on the corner of Avenue de la Tour Maubourg and the triage centre at the *École militaire*.

The *système D*, for *débrouillage*, is a quality that is often evoked when considering French resistance.[77] This translates as 'making-do', reflecting the efforts that individual agents and networks undertook, in order to ensure that their operating costs and equipment needs were met. The cyclist continued to encounter F.F.I. members, armed with German weapons. This 'system' was put to great effect at the *Banque*, through the construction of the barricades that were installed by the F.F.I., whereas the Germans built concrete *chevaux de frise* to block routes, the French used sandbags, piled high around a foundation of cars, beds, sewing machines and trolleys. These were a physical manifestation of *système D*, which offered a corollary to the operational 'make-do-and-mend' attitude that was cultivated among the S.O.E. and B.C.R.A. operatives. Nonetheless, the inexperienced and haphazard approach left room for errors, including the wrongful imprisonment of French Lorrainers, mistaken for being spies, by overzealous F.F.I. troops.[78]

By Wednesday 23rd August, the makeshift protective measures around the *Banque*'s perimeter were installed and ready to be defended from the retreating German forces. These were two lines of sand, spread across the road, 30 to 40 cm in diameter by 20 cm in height. A message was daubed

[77] BINOT, BOYER, *L'argent de la Résistance*, 2010, p. 31—"System D, dear to the French, was working at full capacity"; GILDEA Robert, *Fighters in the Shadows: A New History of the French Resistance*, London, Faber and Faber, 2015, 608p., Chap. 2, Para. 5 (Ebook)—"This was the famous *système du débrouillage* or *système D*."

[78] BdF, 1,069,200,401 267 Guerre 1939—1945, Journal Résistance..., p. 4, "...such as that which happened to the wife of my friend, a Lorrainer by birth, who, upon leaving their apartment at the École des Mines, which was still occupied by the Germans, was suspected of being a spy, by a brainless idiot, and had to spend the day and night at the police station in the 5$^{th}$ arrondissement."

on the wall, indicating that mines had been buried underneath the sand.[79] The entry to the bank on Rue de Raziwill was blocked, but it meant that the *Banque*'s vehicle pool was effectively immobilised. An argument, concerning its removal, broke out with the military commander in the 1st arrondissement. The peace was kept with the offer of a requisitioned two-tonne truck, housed outside of the bank's defensive perimeter.

The return of the daily press was celebrated. On Wednesday morning, newspapers, including *Le Figaro* and *L'Aube*, began to appear on the streets. During the Occupation, many newspaper vendors had been driven from their jobs. However, by this point, the authoritarian regime was teetering on the verge of collapse. Even *L'Humanité*, which had been originally established by the socialist Jean Jaurès, before becoming the mouthpiece for the French Communist Party, reappeared with a poster at the *Arts et Métiers* underground station. Behind the Atlantic Wall, the diffusion of information had been a vital preoccupation for resistance groups. Now that they were able to print without hindrance, aspects of civil life that had been silenced could begin to be freely debated, once again. Metropolitan French politics was beginning to emerge from the fog of war.

The *Banque de France* received a delivery of a hundred kilograms of potatoes, ten kilograms of butter and eight kilograms of gruyere. This food served to feed the members of the *Banque*'s F.F.I. and supplied a buffet. Like the *Maquis* camps, resistance activity was reliant upon the organisation of supply lines. While no indication is given as to the source of the large quantities of products, it can only be presumed to have originated from the black market. Potatoes were in short supply for the entirety of the Occupation[80] and access to gruyere cheese, originally from Switzerland and the Jura, was also difficult. Considering the ingredients brought to the F.F.I. members, dishes such as mashed potato, or a type of gratin, could have been cooked. All that was missing was the champagne…until a gift of fifty bottles arrived the following morning, worth somewhere in the region of 40,000 francs.[81]

[79] BdF, 1,069,200,401 267 Guerre 1939–1945, Journal, *Incidents de la journée de 23 août 1944*, undated.

[80] TAYLOR, '*The Black Market…*', 1997, p. 155.

[81] BdF, 1069200401 267 Guerre 1939–1945, Journal, p. 3, "Thursday August 24 - 9:30 am, Gift from a nightclub, rue Montmartre: 50 bottles of champagnes, aperitif";

On the penultimate day of fighting in central Paris, the proliferation of barricades continued unabated. In the 10th *Arrondissement*, near to the *Marché Saint-Quentin*, all seemed to be calm, before a volley of rifle fire caused the cyclist to flee towards the town hall. Along their route, heading south from the *Gare de l'Est*, shop windows had been shattered by rifle shot and tank shells. Rue Lafayette, leading to *Gare de Nord*, was blockaded. This is shown, in Fig. 9.3, by the absence of reconnaissance in the northern Parisian areas. The transport hubs were clear targets for both the Germans and the F.F.I., and much of the combat was concentrated around these locations. By the end of the day, Parisian radio was free from German control, meaning that both branches of the press had been freed from censorship. The city's liberation continued with the retaking of the German post, in the *Banque*'s Ventadour office, at 15:00, with the help of neighbouring groups of F.F.I. By 21:00, the American scouts, who had begun to enter the city in the afternoon, had fought their way to the *Hôtel de Ville*.

The arrival of Leclerc's troops, at the *Portes de Paris*, on 25th August, gave the opportunity for equipment comparisons to be made, when the F.F.I. met the Allied troops, whose quartermasters had been helping to organise and supply them. In a process similar to those experienced by the British civilians upon meeting the U.S. troops for the first time, exchanges were swiftly made, with exotic offerings being given, like Chesterfield and Camel cigarettes. Due to the absence of rationing in the United States, G.I. rations were of a far higher quality than those available locally. Furthermore, they also included luxury items, such as premium cigarettes or chocolate, which served as excellent icebreakers when encountering the local populace. In this case, the F.F.I. from the *Banque de France* met the chauffeur of a high-ranking American colonel who had come to discuss monetary policy. They compared their equipment with that of the driver, Harry Morgan, including the helmet, which, as well as protecting the head of the wearer, could serve as an improvised latrine. Operational necessities of a soldier's life were not neglected either and the American rifle was judged very favourably against the weapons that the F.F.I. were carrying. While the report does not specify the model of the rifle, it mentions that the magazines held fifteen rounds, thus meaning that they were referring to the M1

CORDIER Daniel, *La victoire en pleurant: Alias Caracalla 1943–1946*, Paris, Éditions Gallimard, 2021, 310p., p. 295, "Champagne is 800 francs a bottle…".

carbine, which came with either fifteen- or thirty-round box magazines. The rifle's sights were commented upon, explaining that they offered greater precision than the F.F.I.'s own models. The rear sights of the M1917 and the M1 carbine were identical, and both were used in wartime France. The former was provided under Lend-Lease and the latter arrived with the G.I.'s. The manner in which the ammunition could be carried meant that each rifleman was carrying 105 rounds, in seven magazines, which offered a great deal of individual protection and afforded greater tactical independence, freed from the burden of bulkier and less-transportable rounds. The cartridges used by both weapons were 0.30 carbine, providing great stopping power against unarmoured targets. While their ammunition may have come from the same source, they would have taken vastly different routes into France. Those rounds brought by the American chauffeur, Morgan, would have travelled with the S.H.A.E.F. forces, which were disembarked in the wake of D-Day, in June 1944; those belonging to the F.F.I. would, in all likelihood, have constituted those that were found in the airdropped containers.

Paris awoke, on Saturday 26th August, liberated. The German facilities at the Concorde and Tuileries, the *Hôtel Majestic* and the *Quai d'Orsay* were the final areas of the city to fall. On that day, the sellers of trinkets and other patriotic symbols did a roaring trade. This marked the end of the cyclist's mission. However, the battles were far from finished. The *Caisse centrale* remained in Algiers and, while Paris may have been freed, the focus rapidly shifted towards forcing the Germans from the rest of metropolitan France.

# Conclusion

The funding for French resistance came, in large part, from the British, but also from Francophone and Francophile communities in neutral countries and those living in the rallied territories. From the earliest days of the conflict, Britain helped to incubate the Free French movement by providing military support and funding. The colonial contributions were largely seen in the provision of natural resources, as well as monetarily through the 'Subscription to Help the Resistance' which began in September 1943. This money was sent into France which greatly increased spending to their highest levels yet seen in the conflict.

The personal and professional networks that contributed to the development of funding for French resistance activities have been underlined. These matrices showed the transnational relationships existing between different financial interlocuters, who acted as vectors for the funds which drove resistance activity, including the formation of escape lines, sabotage groups or intelligence collection, within France. Acting as a conduit for Gaullist money, the role of the REX mission and Jean Moulin with the sending of nearly 351.5 million francs into the Non-Occupied Zone cannot be understated. Money that was despatched to the mission came in dollars and francs but, despite its lower nominal value, the U.S. currency was worth much more than its French counterpart. This underlines that the world's hegemonic currency was no longer the pound but the dollar.

The financing was heavily linked to the Gaullist external resistance, but it would not have been possible had it not been for the support and



D. Foulk, *The Price of Freedom*,
https://doi.org/10.1007/978-3-031-09066-0

infrastructure furnished by the American and the British governments. It also had a highly transnational inflection, which was offered by the Free French delegations, in neutral and allied countries, which helped to provide a form of irregular income. These delegations, notably those in South and Central America, assisted through their fundraising efforts, publications and educative role. Through the monetary support that the Bank of England and H.M. Treasury provided, the Free French were able to manage the economies of those colonies which rallied to de Gaulle. This relationship continued until mid-1943 and beyond, but it was during this initial period that the most substantial financial assistance came.

The Free French were a supported 'government-in-exile' in all but name, at least by Churchill's government. It was viewed as being in the British interest to support General de Gaulle's movement, especially after the rallying of the African French territories which neighboured their own. These relations risked becoming economically and monetarily fractious but, by integrating some of them into the 'Sterling Area', including Syria and Lebanon, this allowed the British to continue protecting vital interests, such as the Suez Canal and the eastern Mediterranean. These territories also represented a major boon for resourcing the Allied war effort, as the Free French controlled areas represented some of the world's most plentiful sources of nickel and ground nuts, to name but two. In part, British support was a recognition of the importance of these natural deposits and resources.

Furthermore, this cooperation occurred at far deeper strata than simply between de Gaulle, Churchill, Spears, Morton and Catroux. This is an aspect that has yet to be fully emphasised by either the anglophone or francophone historiography. The harmonious interactions between such actors as John Lithiby, André Diethelm, René Pleven, Pierre Denis, Allen Bartholomew, André Postel-Vinay or Jean Monnet, in spite of the challenging circumstances, proved that centralisation of policy decisions was viewed as necessitous. Ultimately, this was helped by the fact that their goals were similar; those being the economic stabilisation of the French colonial world and the continued military riposte against the Axis powers.

Despite the reticence of the U.S. government to diplomatically engage with the Free French, it was also recognised that, after 1943, French resistance was beneficial for the ongoing Allied war effort. This change of perspective was due to the increasing awareness that French colonial territories were ideally placed, strategically, to allow the counterattack against both Germany and Japan. The liberation of North Africa and the strategic importance of New Caledonia represented ideal launching pads for the forthcoming invasions of continental Europe and the Japanese-held islands. The growing importance of Lend-Lease and Reciprocal Lend-Lease, over 1941 and 1942, reflected the Roosevelt administration's acceptance of the premise that helping one's ally was more productive than hindering them.

Furthermore, much of this external funding came from private donors who wished to support General de Gaulle's movement. These donations were subsequently channelled towards resistance activity in France. Fund raising and economic management were important parts of external resistance efforts and, as has been seen, greatly occupied the thoughts of a significant number of supporters across the planet.

Jean Moulin's REX Mission was largely responsible for issuing the received funds to French internal resistance groups during the period from 1942 into 1943. Daniel Cordier played a key role as the mission's money handler. However, when Moulin was captured, his successors were not able to replicate his unifying exploits and the REX Mission broke apart. It is important to underline Moulin's role as a centralising figure, not just politically but monetarily. This became more visible through the difficulties experienced by his successors, Bouchinet-Serreulles and Bingen. Largely, this was due to the asynchronous nature of communications between the headquarters, in London and, eventually, Algiers, and those operating in France. With money lacking and links severed, decisions could not be taken as easily, which hampered the continued development of resistance. However, the ground had been prepared for future missions. Nonetheless, financing resistance action was a complex and thankless task, as it often incited many arguments and much ill-feeling for the participants.

Money was the cause of much rancour which occurred between the various hierarchical levels within the movements in France. Incandescent disputes have been covered, notably those concerning Pierre-Camille Rayon (*Archiduc*) or Henri Manhès (*Frédéric*), which have helped to explain the difficulties that some experienced when they felt that they had received too little or the harassment that others faced when confronted by those who wanted what they considered to be their fair share. This resentment was largely linked to the scarcity of the funds available.

It appears that the Section 'F' networks of S.O.E., which were controlled by the British armed forces, seem to have been better adapted to regularly receive money. The Section 'RF' groups, run in conjunction with the Gaullist B.C.R.A., used more people to receive funds and even their official history was highly critical of the inefficient functioning. This work has shown that Section 'RF' were paid far more than Section 'F', which was due to the fact that large portions of their money came from external sources and they were, therefore, not wholly dependent upon direct government funding by the British.

However, it is important to recognise that this was all occurring under war conditions so nothing will ever be optimal. Ideally, it appears that it is better to attempt to centralise the transfer of funds, but not to such a degree that operational security is compromised.

Money was clearly an important sinew of resistance activity. However, the money required to further French resistance activity has often been treated in a perfunctory manner in the historiography, often being relegating to little more than a one-page afterthought. However, without funds, underground activity would have been virtually impossible and those most intimately involved in resistance activity, whose testimony has been covered in this work, have all explained as much.

Independent of Allied forces, the most quantitatively successful method of money procuration by resistance forces appears to have been 'patriotic hold-ups'. The Neuvic train robbery, with its 2.2-billion-franc haul, was the largest single acquisition. However, this requisition was simply too great and too disruptive for the funds to be easily secreted into the local, rural economy. Moreover, for such actions to be successful, the military context within which they took place must be considered. The Neuvic robbery simply could not have taken place earlier in the conflict, as the conditions were not conducive for such an audacious action.

The same could be argued for the 'wartime withdrawals', which were robberies of *Banque de France* branches in local towns of note. Using extortion and, paradoxically, often with the support of those whom they were robbing, the local *maquis* sometimes 'shook down' multiple branches in the same day. The stolen money could support thousands of troops, covering their food, equipment, pay and limited levels of social security. Equally as important were those working directly for the *Banque de France* and who served in their non-homologated resistance group. The liberation of Paris has been recorded by one of the participants and this showed the final days of the occupation of the French capital through an economic prism. Their bicycle reconnaissance mission, conducted around the war-torn city, showed a vision of the liberation of the capital in August 1944.

Towards the end of November, the *Caisse centrale de la France d'Outre-mer* began relocating to Paris from Algiers. For the Gaullists, this organisation helped to ensure that the money supply in their rallied territories did not evaporate, as had very nearly been the case prior to the organisation's inception in December 1941. As it survives to this day, the *Agence Française de Développement* is one of the remaining vestiges of the Second World War and a living monument to the transnational resistance effort.[1]

French resistance funding was far more complex than could ever have been imagined, both monetarily and geographically, with links to countries far beyond those that may have ordinarily been envisaged from a reading of traditional military histories of the Second World War. The price of freedom had a heavy cost—one which was borne by a transnational Allied network and was reliant upon a global funding effort, driven by donations, fund-raising activities, illicit military action and the Bank of England's institutional support.

[1] AFD History, https://www.afd.fr/en/our-history, Consulted 19 August 2021.

# Chronology

### *1939*

- September 1939—Jean Monnet is sent to London to discuss the organisation of the economic war effort.
- 18 October 1939—Correspondence between the British prime minister, Neville Chamberlain, and the French president of the council of ministers, Edouard Daladier, concerning proposed economic collaboration between the two countries.
- 2 November 1939—Agreement creating the Anglo-French Coordinating Committee.
- 17 November 1939—The Anglo-French Economic Agreement is announced.
- 29 November 1939—Jean Monnet is appointed Chairman of the Anglo-French Coordinating Committee.
- 6 December 1939—First meeting of the Anglo-French Coordinating Committee.

### *1940*

- 10 May 1940—German invasion of France and the Low Countries begins.
- 18 June 1940—Charles de Gaulle's Call of 18th June.
- 22 June 1940—Armistice is signed between France and Germany.



D. Foulk, *The Price of Freedom*,
https://doi.org/10.1007/978-3-031-09066-0

- 1 July 1940—Captain André Dewavrin, *Passy*, is named head of the Free French 2nd and 3rd Bureau (Military Intelligence) in London.
- 18 July 1940—Free French radio programmes begin to be broadcast by the B.B.C.
- 7 August 1940—General Agreement between the Free French and the British government, whereby Britain recognises the Free French Forces.
- 9 August 1940—Memorandum of Agreement setting out the conditions of employment of Free French troops.
- 10 August 1940—Cameroon and French Equatorial Africa, with the exception of Gabon, rally to General de Gaulle.
- 27 October 1940—Creation of the Empire Defence Council by General de Gaulle in Brazzaville, French Equatorial Africa.
- November 1940—Captain Henri Frenay's Manifesto which announced the creation of the National Liberation Movement (Mouvement de Libération nationale). Creation of France-Freedom (France-Liberté), the future Franc-Tireur.
- 12 November 1940—Conquest of Gabon by the Free French.
- 25 November 1940—First issue of *Liberté* is published.
- 1 December 1940—Christian Pineau releases the first issue of *Libération-nord*.

### *1941*

- 14 January 1941—Beginning of the 'V' campaign, originally launched by the Belgian B.B.C. presenter, Victor de Laveleye, but which is adopted across occupied Europe.
- 11 March 1941—U.S. president, Franklin D. Roosevelt, signs the Lend-Lease Act into law.
- 15 March 1941—Operation Savanna, the first mission of the 2nd Bureau, is despatched to destroy aircraft near to Vannes, Brittany.
- 19 March 1941—Both the Financial and the Monetary Agreements are signed between the Free French and the British government.
- 6 May 1941—Infiltration of the first agent belonging to Section 'F' of the Special Operations Executive.
- 8 June 1941—Beginning of the Syria campaign. General Georges Catroux proclaims the independence of Syria and Lebanon.
- 22 June 1941—Beginning of Operation Barbarossa.

- July 1941—First issue of *Libération-sud* is published.
- 18 August 1941—Act of Concession of the Caisse centrale de la France libre.
- 29 August 1941—Statutes of the Caisse centrale de la France libre received by the Bank of England.
- 24 September 1941—De Gaulle establishes the French National Committee (Comité national français).
- 20 October 1941—Former prefect of Eure-et-Loir, Jean Moulin, arrives in London with a report on nascent resistance activity in southern France.
- 25 October 1941—First meeting between de Gaulle and Moulin.
- November—Liberté and Libération nationale fuse to form the movement Combat.
- 2 December 1941—Ordonnance N° 21 of 2nd December 1941 creates the Caisse centrale de la France libre.
- 7 December 1941—Entry of the United States into the war, following the Japanese attack on Pearl Harbor.
- 24 December 1941—Disagreement between the U.S. State Department and the Bank of England over the opening of an account for the Caisse centrale de la France libre at the Federal Reserve.

## *1942*

- 2 January 1942—Jean Moulin parachutes back into the southern zone of France.
- 14 January 1942—Premises rented to the Caisse centrale de la France libre on the 3rd floor of N° 1, Bank Buildings, Princes Street, London.
- February 1942—*L'Humanité* announces the creation of Francs-Tireurs et Partisans.
- 10 February 1942—Decree N° 137 on the emission of bank notes in the Free French African territories.
- 26 April 1942—American troops arrive to help defend New Caledonia.
- 28 April 1942—Christian Pineau returns to France, from London, bringing the political manifesto of General de Gaulle.
- 22 June 1942—Pierre Laval announces the system of *la Relève* and states that he hopes to see a German victory.

- 14 July 1942—The Free French change their name to the Fighting French.
- 4 September 1942—First Vichyite law on the requisition of workers.
- October 1942—Agreement in London between the Fighting French and the southern resistance movements to form a coordinating committee and a 'secret army', to be led by General Charles Delestraint.
- 11 November 1942—The Germans invade the French southern zone.
- 26 December 1942—General Henri Giraud is named as high commissioner, civil and military commander in North Africa.

## *1943*

- 26 January 1943—The three largest movements in the southern zone join forces to create the Unified Movements of the Resistance (Mouvements unis de la Résistance).
- 27 February 1943—Arrival in France of Colonel Passy and the beginning of the Mission Brumaire-Arquebuse, alongside Pierre Brossolette and Forest Yeo-Thomas.
- 27 May 1943—First meeting of the National Resistance Council (C.N.R.) in Paris.
- 30 May 1943—Arrival of General de Gaulle in Algiers.
- 3 June 1943—Creation of the French Committee of National Libération (C.F.L.N.).
- 21 June 1943—In Caluire, the arrest of Jean Moulin and other Resistance leaders.
- 17 September 1943—Ordonnance calling for the creation of a Provisional Consultative Assembly in Algiers.
- 30 October 1943—Closure of the London office of the Caisse centrale.
- 3 November 1943—Inaugural session of the Consultative Assembly in Algiers.
- 1 December 1943—Request lodged for the retention of a bank account with the Bank of England by the Caisse centrale.

### *1944*

- 4 January 1944—Departure from the offices at Princes Street, London, by the Caisse centrale.
- 1 February 1944—Creation of the French Forces of the Interior (F.F.I.).
- 2 February 1944—Ordonnance renaming the Caisse centrale de la France libre as the Caisse centrale de la France d'Outre-mer.
- 8 February 1944—Nomination of André Postel-Vinay as the director of the Caisse centrale de la France d'Outre-mer.
- 3 April 1944—New premises of the Caisse centrale de la France d'Outre-mer transferred to 12 Boulevard Laferrière, Algiers.
- 30 May 1944—General Pierre Koenig recognised by the Allies as commander of the F.F.I.
- 3 June 1944—The C.F.L.N. becomes the Provisional Government of the French Republic (G.P.R.F.).
- 6 June 1944—Allied landings in Normandy.
- 26 July 1944—Neuvic Train Robbery
- 18 August 1944—Beginning of the Parisian insurrection.
- 26 August 1944—The Liberation of Paris.
- 10 November 1944—New premises of the Caisse centrale in the Ministry of Economic Affairs, 110 rue de l'Université, Paris, 7th *arrondissement*.

### *1945*

- 8 May 1945—German capitulation.
- 15 May 1945—Notification of the closure of the office of the representative of the Caisse centrale, Allan G. Bartholomew.

# Appendix

## Social Network Analysis

This study has utilised data visualisation software, notably Gephi, which has allowed for social network analysis (S.N.A.) to be conducted on suitable archival files. These generally include correspondences between named or identifiable individuals. Other documents of interest include those which contain records of meetings, with minutes, notably those concerning governmental committees, in which those present are identified. The former demonstrates direct forms of interaction between an expeditor, or 'source', and recipients, or 'targets'. Meetings between three or more participants will record far higher numbers of interactions than letters, as each participant is counted as having met each one of the others. This highlights those who interacted most frequently within the organisations being studied and, therefore, helps to underline the role of intermediaries within the network.

The programme 'Gephi version 0.9.2.' has been used to create the maps. The software is open source, meaning that it is free to use and allows for modifications, like filters, and for different functions to be applied to the maps. Rather than creating matrices, as was the case for other social network analysis programmes like UCINET, Gephi relies on.csv (comma separated values) files, using a database from the names of the sender, the recipient and additional columns if weighting is to be applied to the map. Gephi also offers tools to manipulate the nodes, in



D. Foulk, *The Price of Freedom*,
https://doi.org/10.1007/978-3-031-09066-0

order to correct entries, and to adjust the space between nodes. 'Nodes' are the individual actors. The number of interactions can be shown either through the thickness of the connecting link, or 'edge', or on the node itself. Different communities, or 'cliques', can be represented by changing the coloration of the nodes. This software allows for the quantitative identification of relations between different actors in archival research.

Upon opening the software and a prepared.csv file, Gephi produces an import report which indicates how many nodes (actors) will appear in the network and how many edges (links) appear and whether these are directed or undirected relationships. Directed graphs show the direction of relations that have occurred between actors. Undirected graphs demonstrate those relations for which it makes little difference as to who talks with whom. Once produced, a graph will be displayed but with random positions attributed to the nodes. The graph can be manipulated using various settings, known as 'layouts'. The ranking value can be displayed by the use of different colours. Moreover, different analytical calculations can be performed, including the average path length, meaning the average number of nodes passed to get from one side of the network to another or the betweenness centrality. A particular node may have many direct ties, but if those do not link different parts of a network, the actor is of less importance to bridging two communities than a different actor, with fewer ties, but a greater number of links to other parts of the network. Those with a high rating of betweenness, centrality can exert influence over the network's handling of information. This can be displayed as the size of the node, meaning that those with a high betweenness centrality can appear larger on the map, or with a different colouration. In order to improve the map's readability, filters can be applied, including those related to the 'degree' or the number of interactions that occurred between different members of the network. If this characteristic is filtered, the graph will generally show fewer nodes. Once the map is finished, it can be exported as an image file.

# References

## Primary Sources


**Archives**

**French Archives**

*Archives départementales de la Haute Vienne, Limoges, France*

Adrien Tixier dossier

88 J 6

88 J 7

88 J 10

88 J 11

88 J 13 88 J 15

88 J 16 88 J 17

88 J 18

88 J 19

*Archives nationales d'Outre-mer, Aix-en-Provence, France*

1AFF-POL 873

1AFF-POL 879

1AFF-POL 2556

*Archives nationales, Pierrefitte, France*

382 AP 32

AG 3 (2) 276

AG 3 (2) 277

AG 3 (2) 278

AG 3 (1) 314

AG 3 (1)268





D. Foulk, *The Price of Freedom*,
https://doi.org/10.1007/978-3-031-09066-0

3 AG 1 301
3 AG 1 302
3 AG 1 303
3 AG 1 305
560 AP 25
*Banque de France, Paris, France*
1064198804
1069199410 1
1069199410 2
1069200401 267
1245198815 208
*Centre Jean Moulin, Bordeaux, France*
L'Affaire Grandclément ou la Résistance à Bordeaux de 1940–44 par Guy PENAUD
*Service des Archives économiques et financières, Savigny-le-Temple, France*
B 0062799
B 0062801
B 0062804
B 0062805
B 0062806
B 0062810
B 0062824
B 0062825
B 0062829
B 0062835
B 0062836
**U.K. Archives**
*Bank of England, London, U.K.*
C92 57
OV45 129
OV45 130
OV100 13
*Churchill Archives, Churchill College, University of Cambridge, U.K.*
CHAR 2/396, Image 11 and 12
CHAR 20/97A/35 Image 1 and 2
CHAR 20/97A/36, Images 3 to 14
CHAR 20/78/126, Image 1
CHAR 20/230/55, Image 1
CHAR 20/76/79, Image 1
CHAR 20/22A/94-95, Images 1 and 2
CHAR 20/47/122, Image 1
CHAR 20/128/39, Image 1

CHAR 20/193A/62-64, Image 1 to 3
CHAR 20/42A/25, Image 1
CHAR 20/85/68, Image 1
CHAR 20/85/90-91, Image 1 and 2
CHAR 23/13, Image 75 to 77
CHAR 20/106/10, Image 1
*Middle East Centre Archive, Saint Antony's College, University of Oxford, U.K.*
(N1) GB165-0269 Sir Edward Spears BOX 2 Files 5–7
(N2) GB165-0269 Sir Edward Spears BOX 2 Files 5–7
GB165-0269 Sir Edward Spears BOX 2 Files 1, 3, 4
*The National Archives, Kew, U.K.*
Air Ministry Papers
AIR/27/1068/1
AIR/27/1068/2
AIR/27/1068/3
AIR/27/1068/4
AIR/27/1068/5
AIR/27/1068/6
AIR/27/1068/7
AIR/27/1068/8
AIR/27/1068/9
AIR/27/1068/10
AIR/27/1068/11
AIR/27/1068/12
AIR/27/1068/13
AIR/27/1068/14
AIR/27/1068/15
AIR/27/1068/16
AIR/27/1068/17
AIR/27/1068/18
AIR/27/1068/19
AIR/27/1068/20
AIR/27/1068/21
AIR/27/1068/22
AIR/27/1068/23
AIR/27/1068/24
AIR/27/1068/25
AIR/27/1068/26
AIR/27/1068/27
AIR/27/1068/28
AIR/27/1068/29
AIR/27/1068/30

AIR/27/1068/31
AIR/27/1068/32
Cabinet Office Papers
CAB/21/1269
CAB/65/7/71
CAB/65/7/81
CAB/65/30/19
CAB/66/15/3
CAB/66/18/44
CAB/66/23/6
CAB/66/27/29
CAB/66/30/48
CAB/66/33/48
CAB/66/39/28
CAB/66/39/41
CAB/66/50/47
CAB/66/56/20
CAB/67/7/5
CAB/68/6/3
CAB/68/6/59
CAB/68/7/10
CAB/68/7/17
CAB/68/7/23
CAB/68/8/27
CAB/68/8/37
CAB/68/8/41
CAB/68/8/52
CAB/85/22/1
CAB/85/25
CAB/85/29
CAB/85/40
CAB/85/42
CAB/85/50
CAB/85/55
CAB/85/59
CAB/85/62
CAB/85/65
CAB/85/67
CAB/85/69
CAB/85/71
CAB/85/72
CAB/85/88

CAB 101/131
CAB/101/282
CAB/101/301
CAB/106/982
CAB/109/78
CAB/109/79
CAB/109/83
CAB/111/299
CAB/111/301
CAB/122/780
CAB/122/781
CAB/301/55
Colonial Office Papers
CO/968/29 10
Foreign Office Papers
FO/1055/4
FO/1055/7
FO/371/31990
FO/371/36046
FO/371/41912
FO/371 1944
FO/371 41925
FO/371 41925
FO/892/3
FO/892/60
FO/892/79
FO/892/101
FO/892/112
Records of Special Operations Executive
HS/7/121
HS/7/122
HS/7/124
HS7/135
HS/8/897/15
HS/8/897/16
HS/8/897/34
HS/8/897/36
HS/8/897/38
HS/8/897/106
HS/8/897/107
HS/8/899/4
HS/8/899/5

HS/8/899/6
HS/8/899/7
HS/9/12/2
HS/9/232/8
HS/9/1166/3
HS/9/415/6
HS/9/877/5
HS/9/1070/6
The Security Service Papers
KV6/24
The War Office Papers
WO/106/2903
WO/202/38
WO/202/63
WO/202/72
WO/229/14
WO/229/33/1
WO/229/33/2
WO/229/68/1
WO/229/68/2
WO/372/12/103333
**U.S. Archives**
*National Archives and Records Administration, College Park, United States*
RG 226 199 34
RG 226 199 35
RG 226 199 36
RG 226 199 38
RG 313 76 1
RG 313 76 5
RG 313 76 6
RG 313 76 9
RG 313 76 10
RG 313 76 11
RG 313 76 28
RG 331 314 7
*U.S. Office of the Historian, United States*
Foreign Relations of the United States Diplomatic Papers, 1940, General and Europe, Volume II
881.01/93
Foreign Relations of the United States Diplomatic Papers, 1940, General and Europe, Volume II—Interest of the United States in political and economic conditions in French North Africa

123 M 956/294
611.8131/50
611.8131/60
611.8131/61
611.8131/63
611.8131/64
611.8131/64a
611.8131/65
611.8131/72
611.8131/74
611.8131/78
611.8131/80
681.00/8
Foreign Relations of the United States Diplomatic Papers, 1940, General and Europe, Volume II—Assumption of control over French Equatorial Africa by the Free French; non-committal attitude of the United States
848L.00/28
740.00112 European War 1939/1772
740.00112 Navicert/207
740.0011 European War 1939/4176
740.0011 European War 1939/5258
740.0011 European War 1939/5291
740.0011 European War 1939/5299
740.0011 European War 1939/5334
740.0011 European War 1939/5352
740.0011 European War 1939/5420
740.0011 European War 1939/5258
740.0011 European War 1939/5299
740.0011 European War 1939/5960
740.0011 European War 1939/6208
740.0011 European War 1939/6348
740.0011 European War 1939/6612
740.0011 European War 1939/6712
740.0011 European War 1939/6704
740.0011 European War 1939/6878
Foreign Relations of the United States Diplomatic Papers, 1940, General and Europe, Volume II—Interest of the United States in political and economic conditions in French North Africa
881.00/1753
811.79680/3
851.01/164
740.0011 European War 1939/6697

740.0011 European War 1939/6724
740.0011 European War 1039/6752
862.20281/8
740.0011 European War 1939/7035
740.0011 European War 1939/7094
Foreign Relations of the United States Diplomatic Papers, 1941, Europe, Volume II—Protests by the French Government regarding lend-lease aid to Free French in Equatorial Africa and sending there of American military and naval observers
740.0011 European War 1939/11872
740.00118 European War 1939/532
740.00118 European War 1939/821
740.0011 European War 1939/17091
740.0011 European War 1939/17478
740.00118 European War 1939/866
740.00118 European War 1939/886
851.24/251
Relations of the United States with the Free French forces
711.51/198½
Foreign Relations of the United States Diplomatic Papers, 1939, General, Volume I, Appeals of President Roosevelt to the belligerents against aerial bombardment of civil populations
740.0011 European War 1939/27782
Foreign Relations of the United States Diplomatic Papers, 1944, the British Commonwealth and Europe, Volume III—Concern of the United States over civil administration of France immediately following liberation from the Germans; recognition of the French Provisional Government
740.0011 European War 1939/33516
851.515/210a
851.515/210b
851.515/211
Foreign Relations of the United States Diplomatic Papers, 1940, General and Europe, Volume II—Efforts by the United States to secure release by France of certain strategic materials held in Indochina
811.20 Defense (M)/471/22
811.20 Defense (M)/473/22
811.20 Defense (M)/474/22
811.20 Defense (M)/479/22a
811.20 Defense (M)/479/22a
811.20 Defense (M)/4713/22
811.20 Defense (M)/106a
811.20 Defense (M)/105

811.20 Defense (M)/150
811.20 Defense (M)/163
811.20 Defense (M)/230
811.20 Defense (M)/236
811.20 Defense (M)/230
Foreign Relations of the United States Diplomatic Papers, 1940, General and Europe, Volume II—Consideration of problem of giving food relief to France without aiding Germany
851.5018/45
840.48/4540
Foreign Relations of the United States Diplomatic Papers, 1942, Europe, Volume II
851A.01/1/1842
Foreign Relations of the United States Diplomatic Papers, 1941, Europe, Volume II
851A.01/58 851A.01/72
851A.74/5
Foreign Relations of the United States Diplomatic Papers, 1942, Europe, Volume II, Relations of the United States with the Free French forces
851.01/368 851.01/390
851.01/533
851.01/536
Foreign Relations, 1942, Volume II—Concern of the United States over the Seizure of St. Pierre-Miquelon Islands by Free French Forces
851A.01/28
Foreign Relations of the United States: Diplomatic Papers, 1942, Europe, Volume II
851.01/651
851.01/677
851.01/847
851R.24/7
Foreign Relations of the United States: Diplomatic Papers, 1943, Europe, Volume II
851.01/2216
851.01/6-1943
851.01/6-2443
851.01/2223
851.01/2830
851.01/2832
Foreign Relations of the United States: Diplomatic Papers, 1944, the British Commonwealth and Europe, Volume III
351.01/3336

851.01/3342
851.01/3881
851.01/3644
851.01/3788
851.01/3921
851.01/3938
851.01/3951
851.01/4066
851.24/370
851.48/104
851.48/109½
851.50/4-745
851.50/7–245
Foreign Relations of the United States: Diplomatic Papers, 1944, the British Commonwealth and Europe, Volume III, Special economic mission to French North Africa and Morocco
851R.50/9-844
Foreign Relations of the United States: Diplomatic Papers, 1943, Europe, Volume II, Concern of the United States over methods used by the Free French in recruiting French sailors in American ports
851.86/62
Oral History Interviews
Daniel Bouyjou-Cordier, 10th and 11th May 2017, Cannes, France.

## Primary Printed Sources

**Series**

Congressional Record: Proceedings and Debates of the 80th Congress, Second Session, Appendix Vol. 94—Part 11, May 11, 1948 to June 19, 1948, Pages A2881 to A4174, United States Government Printing Office, Washington, 1948

*Registres de nationalité ouverts par les Forces françaises libres à Londres*, Premier carnet (20000247/1), Acte n° 27, MAERSCHALCH, Suzanne Marie José, https://www.siv.archives-nationales.culture.gouv.fr/siv/rechercheconsultation/consultation/ir/consultationIR.action;jsessionid=64C6C403B36FA47B0A2825FBAFEF6E44?irId=FRAN_IR_023109&udId=RLc1a_27&details=true&gotoArchivesNums=false&auSeinIR=true

*USA Report on Lend-Lease Operations*, Reports 1–20, Washington United States Government Printing Office, 1941–1945

*USA Report on Lend-Lease Operations*, Reports 21–40, Washington, United States Government Printing Office, 1945–1958

**Authored Works**


AGLION Raoul, *The Fighting French*, New York, Henry Holt and Co., 1943, 315p.

AGLION Raoul, *Roosevelt and de Gaulle: Allies in Conflict, A Personal Memoir*, New York, The Free Press, 1988, 239p.

BLAIR John, ULMER Melville, NELSON Saul (Ed.), 'Wartime Prices', *Bulletin of the United States Bureau of Labor Statistics*, No. 749, 272p., https://fraser.stlouisfed.org/title/wartime-prices-4235

BLOCH Marc, *L'Étrange défaite*, Paris, Éditions Gallimard, 1990, 326p.

BUCKMASTER Maurice, *They Fought Alone*, London, Biteback Publishing, 1958 (Ed. 2014), 304p.

Committee on International Relations, University of California, *Africa, The Near East and The War—Lectures Delivered Under the Auspices of the Committee on International Relations on the Los Angeles Campus of the University of California—Spring 1942*, Berkeley and Los Angeles, University of California Press, 1943, 212p.

CORDIER Daniel, *Alias Caracalla*, Paris, Éditions Gallimard, 2011, 1152p.

CORDIER Daniel, *La victoire en pleurant: Alias Caracalla 1943–1946*, Paris, Éditions Gallimard, 2021, 310p.

CHURCHILL Winston, *The Second World War Vol. 1 'The Gathering Storm'*, New York, Houghton Miffin Company, 1948, 527p.

CHURCHILL Winston, *The Second World War Vol. 2 'Their Finest Hour'*, New York, Houghton Miffin Company, 1976, 556p.

CHURCHILL Winston, *The Second World War Vol. 3 'The Grand Alliance'*, New York, Houghton Miffin Company, 1977, 630p.

CHURCHILL Winston, *The Second World War Vol. 4 'The Hinge of Fate'*, New York, Houghton Miffin Company, 1978, 744p.

CHURCHILL Winston, *The Second World War Vol. 5 'Closing the Ring'*, New York, Houghton Miffin Company, 1951, 558p.

CHURCHILL Winston, *The Second World War Vol. 6 'Triumph and Tragedy'*, New York, Houghton Miffin Company, 1981, 584p.

CLOSON Francis Louis, *Le Temps des Passions: De Jean Moulin à la Libération 1943–1944*, Éditions du Félin, 1998 (Ed. 2021), 325p.

DE CURTON Émile, *Tahiti 40 - Récit du ralliement à la France libre des Établissements français d'Océanie*, Paris, Société des Océanistes, 1973, 176p.

DE GAULLE Charles, *Mémoires de guerre*, Paris, Plon, 1989, 1518p.

DE GAULLE Charles, *Lettres, notes et carnets, tome 3: 1940–41*, Paris, Plon, 2014, 459p.

DENIS Pierre, *Souvenirs de la France Libre*, Paris, Éditions Berger-Levrault, 1947, 242p.

DE ROUSSY DE SALES Raoul, *The Making of Yesterday*, New York, Reynal & Hitchcock, 1947, 310p.

FRASER W. Lionel, *All to the Good*, Kingswood, Heinemann, 1963, 275p.

FRENAY Henri, *La nuit finira: Mémoires de Résistance 1940–1945*, Paris, Éditions Robert Laffont, 1973, 607p.

GRAUMAN J., REMBERT E. W., *The French Iron and Steel Industry*, Washington DC, International Bank for Reconstruction and Development, 1949

HESLOP Richard, *Xavier: A British Secret Agent with the French Resistance*, London, Biteback Publishing, 1970 (Ed. 2014), 306p.

HOOVER Ethel, WILLIAMS Faith, 'Cost of Living in 1941', *Bulletin of the United States Bureau of Labor Statistics*, No. 710, 41p., https://fraser.stlouisfed.org/title/cost-living-1941-4209

HULL Cordell, BERDING Andrew H. T., *The Memoirs of Cordell Hull*, New York, Macmillan Co., 1948, 1804p.

McCAIRNS James Atterby, *Lysander Pilot: Secret Operations with 161 Squadron*, Tangmere, Tangmere Military Aviation Museum, 2016 (Ebook)

MONNET Jean, *Mémoires*, Paris, Fayard, 1976, 642p.

MOULIN Jean, *Premier Combat*, Paris, Les Éditions de Minuit, 1983, 169p.

MURPHY Robert, *Diplomat Among Warriors: The Unique World of a Foreign Service Expert*, Garden City, New York, Doubleday & Company, Inc., 1964, 470p.

PASSY Colonel, *Mémoires du chef des services secrets de la France Libre*, Paris, Éditions Odile Jacob, 2000, 801p.

PENAUD Guy, *L'affaire Grandclément ou La Résistance à Bordeaux de 1940 à la fin 1944*, Bordeaux, Centre Jean Moulin, Folder dating from 1989

PIKETTY Guillaume (Ed.), *Français en Résistance: Carnets de guerre, correspondances, journaux personnels*, Paris, Éditions Robert Laffont, 2009

PINEAU Christian, *La Simple vérité 1940–1945*, Paris, René Julliard, 1960, 632p.

POSTEL-VINAY André, *Un fou s'évade: Souvenirs de 1941–1942*, Paris, Éditions du Félin, 1997

POSTEL-VINAY André, PACQUEMENT François (Ed.), *La passion du développement - 32 ans de Caisse centrale: Mémoires d'André Postel-Vinay*, Paris, Agence Française du Développement, 2019, 314p.

RÉE Harry, RÉE Jonathan (Ed.), *A Schoolmaster's War: Harry Rée, British Agent in the French Resistance*, Padstow, Yale University Press, 2020, 211p.

Secrétariat d'Etat à l'Economie Nationale et aux Finances, *L'Action économique en France depuis l'armistice*, Macon, Protat Frères, 1941, 181p.

SOUSTELLE Jacques, *Envers et contre tout: De Londres à Alger (1940–1942)*, Paris, Robert Laffont, 1947, 470p.

SPEARS Edward, *Fulfilment of a Mission: The Spears Mission to Syria and Lebanon, 1941–1944*, London, Leo Cooper, 1977, 311p.

VERITY Hugh, *We Landed By Moonlight*, Manchester, Crecy Publishing, 1998 (2nd Edition), 256p.

**Digital Primary Sources: Magazines and Newspapers**
Journal Officiel de la France Libre
https://gallica.bnf.fr/ark:/12148/cb328020711/date
25/2/41
25/3/41
29/4/41
27/5/41
28/6/41
26/8/41
14/10/41
18/11/41
9/12/41
30/12/41
20/1/42
10/2/42
10/3/42
14/4/42
12/5/42
30/5/42
30/6/42
14/7/42
28/8/42
30/9/42
28/10/42
24/11/42
8/12/42
30/12/42
20/1/43
24/2/43
18/3/43
30/3/43
19/4/43
03/05/43
24/5/43
15/6/43
10/08/43
16/9/43
The Economist
https://www.gale.com/intl/c/the-economist-historical-archive
29/6/40
29/6/40
6/7/40

6/7/40
9/11/40
9/11/40
25/1/41
1/2/41
8/2/41
1/3/41
8/3/41
8/3/41
22/3/41
12/4/41
19/4/41
10/5/41
24/5/41
7/6/41
28/6/41
28/6/41
12/7/41
19/7/41
19/7/41
26/7/41
26/7/41
9/8/41
20/9/41
27/9/41
29/11/41
3/1/42
3/1/42
21/2/42
21/2/42
28/2/42
7/3/42
11/4/42
2/5/42
9/5/42
16/5/42
16/5/42
23/5/42
23/5/42
30/5/42
30/5/42
6/6/42

6/6/42
13/6/42
4/7/42
11/7/42
18/7/42
1/8/42
15/8/42
26/9/42
3/10/42
3/10/42
24/10/42
21/11/42
21/11/42
21/11/42
28/11/42
5/12/42
12/12/42
19/12/42
2/1/43
9/1/43
6/2/43
13/2/43
20/2/43
27/2/43
20/3/43
27/3/43
17/4/43
24/4/43
1/5/43
5/6/43
12/6/43
12/6/43
19/6/43
26/6/43
10/7/43
17/7/43
24/7/43
14/8/43
28/8/43
4/9/43
11/9/43
2/10/43

2/10/43
13/11/43
13/11/43
20/11/43
18/12/43
25/12/43
12/2/43
12/2/44
12/2/44
12/2/44
25/3/44
15/4/44
22/4/44
13/5/44
10/6/44
8/7/44
5/8/44
20/1/45
The Times
https://www.gale.com/intl/c/the-times-digital-archive
6/9/40
26/9/40
27/7/41
20/8/41
20/8/41
19/9/41
23/10/41
21/11/41
12/1/42

## Secondary Sources

**Books**

AGLAN Alya, *La France à l'envers: La guerre de Vichy 1940–1945*, Paris, Éditions Gallimard, 2020, 720p.

AGLAN Alya, *La Résistance sacrifiée: Histoire du mouvement «Libération-Nord»*, Paris, Éditions Flammarion, 1995, 323p.

AGLAN Alya (Ed.), FEIERTAG Olivier (Ed.), MAREC Yannick (Ed.), *Les Français et l'argent: Entre fantasmes et réalités*, Rennes, Presses Universitaires de Rennes, 2011, 352p.

AGLIETTA Michel, *Macroéconomie financière*, Paris, Éditions La Découverte, 2008, 255p.

AGLION Raoul, *Roosevelt and de Gaulle: Allies in Conflict, A Personal Memoir*, New York, The Free Press, 1988, 239p.

AHAMED Liaquat, *Lords of Finance: 1929, The Great Depression and the Bankers who Broke the World*, London, Cornerstone Digital, 2011, 588p.

ALBERTELLI Sébastien, *Atlas de la France Libre: De Gaulle et la France Libre, une aventure politique*, Paris, Éditions Autrements, 2010, 79p.

ALBERTELLI Sébastien, *Les services secrets de la France libre*, Paris, Chronos - Éditions Nouvelle Monde, 2017, 222p.

ALBERTELLI Sébastien, *Les services secrets du général De Gaulle, Le BCRA 1940–1944*, Paris, Perrin, 2009, 624p.

ALBERTELLI Sébastien, BLANC Julien, DOUZOU Laurent, *La lutte clandestine en France: Une histoire de la Résistance 1940–1944*, Paris, Éditions du Seuil, 2019, 442p. (Edition Ebook)

ALBORD Maurice, *L'Armée Française & les États du Levant 1936–1946*, Paris, CNRS Éditions, 2000, 336p.

ALEXANDER Martin (Ed.), PHILPOTT William (Ed.), *Anglo-French Defence Relations Between the Wars*, Basingstoke, Palgrave Macmillan, 2002, 256p.

ALMERAS Philippe, *De Gaulle à Londres*, Paris, Editions Dualpha, 2001, 232p.

AMYOT Éric, *Le Québec entre Pétain et de Gaulle: Vichy, la France libre et les Canadiens français, 1940–1945*, Montreal, Éditions Fides, 1999, 365p.

ANDREWS Ahmed, 'Sociological analysis of Jammat-i-Islami in the United Kingdom' in BAROT Rohit (Ed.) *Religion and Ethnicity: Minorities and Social Change in the Metropolis*, Kampen, Kok Pharos Pub. House, 1993, pp. 68–79

ANDREWS Ahmed, 'The Importance of Individual Networks: Network Analysis as a Means of Understanding the Significance of Social Barriers in Religious Conversion' in GÖRMAN Ulf (Ed.), *Towards a New Understanding of Conversion*, Lund, Skrifter Utgivna Av Teologiska Institutionen I Lund, 1999, pp. 38–48

ARISTOTLE, JOWETT Benjamin (Trad.), *Politics*, Cambridge, Clarendon Press, 1885, 485p.

ASHDOWN Paddy, *A Brilliant Little Operation: The Cockleshell Heroes and the Most Courageous Raid of WW2*, London, Aurum Press, 2013, 416p.

ASHDOWN Paddy, *The Cruel Victory: The French Resistance, D-Day and the Battle for the Vercours 1944*, Saint-Ives, William Collins, 2014, 472p.

ASSELAIN Jean-Charles, *Histoire économique de la France du XVIIIe siècle à nos jours, Tome I – De l'Ancien Régime à la Première Guerre mondiale*, Paris, Points Histoire, 2014, 221p.

ASSELAIN Jean-Charles, *Histoire économique de la France du XVIIIe siècle à nos jours, Tome II – Depuis 1918*, Paris, Points Histoire, 2014, 274p.

ATKIN Nicholas, *The Forgotten French: Exiles in the British Isles, 1940–44*, Glasgow, Manchester University Press, 2003, 304p.

AZÉMA Jean-Pierre (Ed.), *Jean Moulin face à l'Histoire*, Paris, Flammarion, 2000, 418p.

AZÉMA Jean-Pierre, *Jean Moulin: Le politique, le rebelle, le résistant*, Paris, Éditions Perrin, 2006, 597p.

BARBIER Colette, *Henri Hoppenot. Diplomate (25 octobre 1891–10 août 1977)*, Paris, Comité d'Histoire Économique et Financière en France, 1999, 630p.

BARR James, *A Line in the Sand: Britain, France and the Struggle for the Mastery of the Middle East*, London, Simon & Schuster UK, 2011, 350p.

BELLUSH Bernard, *He Walked Alone: A Biography of John Gilbert Winant*, The Hague, Mouton, 1968, 248p.

BELOT Robert, KARPMAN Gilbert, *L'affaire suisse: La Résistance a-t-elle trahi de Gaulle?*, Paris, Armand Colin, 2009, 432p.

BELTRAN Alain, GRISET Pascal, *L'économie française 1914–1945*, Paris, Armand Colin, 1994, 187p.

BENAMOU Georges-Marc, *Les rebelles de l'an 40*, Paris, Éditions Robert Laffont, 2010, 375p.

BERGÈS Louis (Ed.), JAMET Delphine (Ed.), LAUX Frédéric (Ed.), *La Seconde guerre mondiale en Gironde par les textes*, Toulouse, Archives départementales de la Gironde, 2006, 331p.

BEZBAKH Pierre, *Le Petit Larousse de l'histoire de France*, Paris, Larousse, 2003 (Ed. 2011), 1023p.

BINOT Jean-Marc, BOYER Bernard, *L'argent de la Résistance*, Paris, Larousse, 2010, 175p.

BINOT Jean-Marc, BOYER Bernard, *Nom de code: Brutus – Histoire d'un réseau de la France Libre*, Paris, Fayard, 2007, 481p.

BLAKE Robert (Ed.), LEWIS William R. (Ed.), *Churchill*, London, Oxford University Press, 1993, 581p.

BLANCPAIN Jean-Pierre, *Le Chili et la France*, Paris, Harmattan, 1999, 242p.

BONIN Hubert, 'The Political Influence of Bankers and Financiers in France in the Years, 1850–1960' in CASSIS Youssef (Ed.), *Finance and Financiers in European History 1880–1960*, Cambridge, Cambridge University Press, 1992, 464p.

BONIN Hubert, BOUNEAU Christophe, JOLY Hervé, *Les entreprises et l'outre-mer français pendant la Seconde Guerre mondiale*, Pessac, MSHA, 2010, 339p.

BOUGEARD Christian, *René Pleven: Un Français libre en politique*, Rennes, Presse universitaires de Rennes, 1995 (Ed. 2015), 473p.

BOURGES-MANOURY Maurice, *Les réseaux action de la France combattante 1940–1944*, Paris, Amicale des réseaux action de la France combattante, 1987, 293p.

BRADFORD James (Ed.), *International Encyclopedia of Military History*, London, Routledge, 2006, 1600p.

BRICKHILL Paul, *The Dam Busters*, London, Pan, 2009, 304p.

CARDONI Fabien (Ed.), CARRÉ de MALBERG Nathalie (Ed.), MARGAIRAZ Michel (Ed.), *Dictionnaire Historique des Inspecteurs des Finances 1801–2009*, Comité pour l'Histoire économique et financière de la France, https://books.openedition.org/igpde/3653l?lang=en

COBB Matthew, *Eleven Days in August: The Liberation of Paris in 1944*, London, Simon and Schuster, 2014, 544p.

COGNEAU Denis, DUPRAZ Yannick, MESPLÉ-SOMPS Sandrine, 'African States & Development in Historical Perspective: Colonial Public Finances in British and French West Africa', *Paris School of Economics Working Paper*, N° 2018-29, 2018, 37p.

COGNEAU Denis, DUPRAZ Yannick, MESPLÉ-SOMPS Sandrine, 'Fiscal Capacity and Dualism in Colonial States: The French Empire 1830–1962', *Paris School of Economics Working Paper*, N° 2018–27, 2019, 126p.

COINTET Michèle, *De Gaulle et Giraud; L'affrontement (1942–1944)*, Paris, Perrin, 2005, 549p.

COINTET Michèle, COINTET Jean-Paul, *La France à Londres 1940–1943*, Paris, Editions Complexe, 1990, 272p.

COLLECTIVE, Amicale des Réseaux Action de la France Combattante, *Les Réseaux Action de la France Combattante*, Fondation de la Résistance (édition électronique), 2008, 293p.

CONWAY Martin (Ed.), GOTOVITCH, José (Ed.), *Europe in Exile: European Exile Communities in Britain 1940–45*, United States, Berghahn Books, 2001, 281p.

CORDIER Daniel, *Jean Moulin: La République des catacombes (Tome I)*, Paris, Éditions Gallimard, 1999 (Ed. 2011), 976p.

CORDIER Daniel, *Jean Moulin: La République des catacombes (Tome II)*, Paris, Éditions Gallimard, 1999 (Ed. 2011), 898p.

CORNIL-FRERROT Sylvain (Ed.), OULMONT Philippe (Ed.), *Les Français Libres et le Monde*, Paris, Éditions Nouveau Monde, 2015, 431p.

COSTAGLIOLA Jacques, *La Guerre anglo-française*, Coulommiers, Dualpha Editions, 2005, 641p.

COURTEAUX Olivier, *Canada Between Vichy & Free France, 1940–1945*, Toronto, University of Toronto Press, 2013, 280p.

CRÉMIEUX-BRILHAC Jean-Louis, *De Gaulle, la République et la France Libre*, Paris, Tempus Perrin, 2014, 493p.

CRÉMIEUX-BRILHAC Jean-Louis, *La France Libre, Vol. 1: De l'appel du 18 juin à la libération*, Paris, Éditions Gallimard, 1998 (Ed. 2013), 816p.

CRÉMIEUX-BRILHAC Jean-Louis, *La France Libre, Vol. 2: De l'appel du 18 juin à la libération*, Paris, Éditions Gallimard, 1998 (Ed. 2013), 660p.

CRÉMIEUX-BRILHAC Jean-Louis, *Les Français de l'an 40, Tome II - ouvriers et soldats*, Paris, Éditions Gallimard, 1990, 672p.
CROMPTON Constance, LANE Richard, SIEMENS Ray, *Doing Digital Humanities: Practice, Training, Research*, Abingdon, Routledge, 2016, 408p.
DARWIN John, *The Empire Project: The Rise and Fall of the British World System 1830–1970*, Cambridge, Cambridge University Press, 2009, 811p.
DAVET Michel-Christian, *La Double Affaire de Syrie*, Paris, Fayard, 1967, 356p.
DE GAULLE Charles, *Vers l'Armée de métier*, Paris, Berger-Levrault, 1934, 211p.
DOBRY Michel, *Sociologie des crises politiques; la dynamique des mobilisations multisectorielles*, Paris, Presse de la Fondation nationale des sciences politiques, 320p.
DORMOIS Jean-Pierre, *The French Economy in the Twentieth Century*, Cambridge, CUP, 2004 (Ed. 2010), 156p.
DOUZOU Laurent, *La Désobeissance: Histoire du mouvement Libération-Sud*, Paris, Éditions Odile Jacob, 1995, 480p.
DU MOULIN DE LE LABARTHETE Jean, *Des marins dans la tourmente: témoignages*, Paris, Nouvelles Editions Latines, 1990, 158p.
EDGERTON David, *Britain's War Machine*, London, Penguin Press, 2012, 442p.
ESCHOLIER Raymond, *Maquis de Gascogne*, Genève, Éditions du milieu du monde, 1945, 354p.
ESPOSITO Marie-Claude, GUILLAUME André, *Londres: Histoire d'une place financière*, Paris, PUF, 1993, 320p.
FARGEAUDOUX Éric, *1944 Tombés du Ciel Missions alliées en Bazadais*, Toulenne, Sauternes Impression, 2014, 112p.
FENBY Jonathan, *The General Charles De Gaulle and the France He Saved*, Sydney, Simon and Schuster UK, 2010, 720p.
FERNÁNDEZ-DOMINGO Enrique, *Le Négoce Français au Chili – 1880–1929*, Rennes, Presses universitaires de Rennes, 2015, 379p.
FFORDE John, *The Bank of England and Public Policy, 1941–1958*, Cambridge, Cambridge University Press, 1992, 884p.
FLOUD Roderick, JOHNSON Paul, *The Cambridge Economic History of Modern Britain*, Cambridge, Cambridge University Press, 2004.
FONDATION CHARLES DE GAULLE, *De Gaulle Chef de Guerre, De l'Appel de Londres à la libération de Paris 1940–1944*, Paris, Plon, 2008, 633p.
FOOT Michael, *Des anglais dans la Résistance, le S.O.E. en France*, Paris, Tallandier, 2014, 816p.
GATES Eleanor, *End of the Affaire, the Collapse of the Anglo-French Alliance, 1939–1940*, Berkeley, University of California Press, 1992, 648p.
GILDEA Robert, *Fighters in the Shadows: A New History of the French Resistance*, London, Faber and Faber, 2015, 608p.

GILDEA Robert, *Marianne in Chains: Daily Life in the Heart of France During the German Occupation*, New York, Picador, 2004, 528p.

GILLOT Jean-Jacques, LAGRANGE Jacques, *Le partage des milliards de la Résistance*, Périgueux, Pilote 24 éditions, 2004, 315p.

GRANDCLÉMENT Daniel, *L'affaire Grandclément: Le résistant qui négociait avec les SS*, Saint-Amand-Montrond, Éditions Lucien Souny, 2007, 221p.

GRENARD Fabrice, *La France du marché noir (1940–1949)*, Barcelona, Éditions Payot & Rivages, 2008 (Ed. 2012), 431p.

GRENARD Fabrice, LE BOT Florent, PERRIN Cédric, *Histoire économique de Vichy*, Paris, Perrin, 2017, 500p.

GUNN Simon (Ed.), FAIRE Lucy (Ed.), *Research Methods for History*, Edinburgh, Edinburgh University Press, 2016, 278p.

HANCOCK William Keith, GOWING Margaret, *The British War Economy (HMSO Official History of WWII)*, London, Her Majesty's Stationery Office, 2012, 1310p.

HARRISON Mark, *The Economics of World War II: Six Great Powers in International Comparison*, Cambridge, Cambridge University Press, 1998, 331p.

HEILBRONER Robert, *The Worldly Philosophers: The Lives, Times and Ideas of the Great Economic Thinkers*, New York, Touchstone, 1999, 365p.

HENNESSY Elizabeth, *A Domestic History of the Bank of England 1930–1960*, Cambridge, Cambridge University Press, 1992, 449p.

HORN Alexander, *The Fall of Paris: The Siege and the Commune 1870–1871*, London, Penguin, 2007, 480p.

HORN Martin, *Britain, France & the Financing of the First World War*, Montreal, McGill-Queen's University Press, 2002, 249p.

*How to Be a Spy: The World War II SOE Training Manuel* (Introduction by RIGDEN Denis), Toronto, The Dundurn Group, 2004, 433p.

JACKSON Julian, *A Certain Idea of France: The Life of Charles de Gaulle*, London, Penguin, 2018, 906p.

JACKSON Julian, *La France sous l'occupation 1940–1944*, Paris, Flammarion, 2004, 847p.

JENNINGS Eric, *Free French Africa in World War II: The African Resistance*, United States of America, Cambridge University Press, 2015, 300p. (Ebook)

JENNINGS Eric, *La France libre fut africaine*, Paris, Perrin, 2014, 350p. (Ebook)

JONES Benjamin, *Eisenhower's Guerrillas: The Jedburghs, The Maquis & The Liberation of France*, Oxford, Oxford University Press, 2016, 384p.

KEDWARD Harry R., *A la recherché du Maquis*, Paris, L'édition du Cerf, Paris, 1999, 472p.

KEDWARD Harry R., *Occupied France: Collaboration and Resistance, 1940–44*, London, Blackwell Publishers, 1985, 108p.

KEEN Bernard, *The Agricultural Development of the Middle East*, London, H.M. Stationery Office, 1946, 164p.

KERSAUDY François, *De Gaulle et Churchill*, Paris, Perrin, 2003, 512p. (Ebook)

KERSAUDY François, *De Gaulle et Roosevelt. Le duel au sommet*, Paris, Perrin, 2004, 552p. (Ebook)

KERSCHBAUMER Florian (Ed.), VON KEYSERLINGK-REHBEIN Linda (Ed.), STARK Martin (Ed.), DÜRING Marten (Ed.), *The Power of Networks: Prospects of Historical Network Research*, Abingdon-on-Thames, Routledge, 2020, 302p.

KEYNES John Maynard, 'How to Pay for the War' in *Essays in Persuasion*, Cambridge, Macmillan Press Ltd. 1972, pp. 367–439, 451p.

LAWREY John, *The Cross of Lorrain in the South Pacific: Australia and the Free French Movement 1940–1942*, Canberra, The Journal of Pacific History, 1982, 152p.

LORMIER Dominique, *La résistance dans le Sud-Ouest*, Bordeaux, Éditions Sud-Ouest, 1989, 253p.

LORMIER Dominique, *Le Livre d'Or de la Résistance dans le Sud-Ouest*, Bordeaux, Éditions Sud-Ouest, 1991, 383p.

LOYER Emmanuelle, *Paris à New York: Intellectuels et artistes français en exil 1940–1947*, Paris, Éditions Grasset et Fasquelle, 2005, 497p.

MAGUIRE Gloria, *Anglo-American Policy Towards the Free French*, London, Macmillan Press, 1995, 210p.

MANAS Arnaud, *L'Or de Vichy*, Paris, Éditions Vendémiaire, 2016, 198p.

MANGOLD Peter, *Britain and the Defeated French: From Occupation to Liberation*, 1940–1944, London, Bloomsbury, 2010, 252p.

MARGAIRAZ Michel (Ed.), *Banques, Banque de France et Seconde Guerre mondiale*, Paris, Albin Michel, 2015, 208p.

MAUSS Marcel, *The Gift: The Form and Reason for Exchange in Archaic Societies*, London, Routledge, 1990, 200p.

MILL John Stewart, *On Liberty*, New York, Cosimo Classics, 2005, 185p.

MILWARD Alan, *War, Economy and Society, 1939–1945*, London, Allen Lane, 1977, 395p.

MOUTANGOU Fabrice Anicet, *Une entreprise coloniale et ses travailleurs: la Société du Haut-Ogooué et la main d'œuvre africaine (1893–1963)*, Sociologie, Université Toulouse le Mirail – Toulouse II, 2013, 513p.

MUNHOLLAND Kim, *Rock of Contention: Free French and Americans at War in New Caledonia*, 1940–1945, New York, Berghahn Books, 2005, 251p.

MURACCIOLE Jean-François, *Histoire de la France Libre*, Paris, Presse Universitaire de France, 2006, 126p.

MURACCIOLE Jean-François, *Les Français Libres, L'autre résistance*, Paris, Éditions Tallandier, 2009, 424p.

NANCY Michel (Ed.), PICARD Élisabeth (Ed.), *Les Arabes du Levant en Argentine*, Aix-en-Provence, Institut de recherches et d'études sur les mondes arabes et musulmans, 2014, 144p.

NNANG NDONG Léon Modeste, *L'effort de guerre de l'Afrique: Le Gabon dans la Deuxième Guerre mondiale (1939–1947)*, Paris, L'Harmattan, 2011, 286p.

OLLANDET Jérôme, *Brazzaville, capitale de la France libre: Histoire de la résistance française en Afrique 1940–1944*, Paris, La Savane, 1981 (Ed. L'Harmattan, 2013), 278p.

OLSON Lynne, *Citizens of London*, New York, Random House, 2010, 496p.

OUAHES Idir, *Syria and Lebanon Under the French Mandate: Cultural Imperialism and the Workings of Empire*, London, I.B. Tauris, 2018, 320p.

OULMONT Philippe, *Pierre Denis; Français libre et citoyen du monde*, Paris, Éditions Nouveau Monde, 2012, 480p.

PAILLAT Claude, *L'Échiquier d'Alger (I) Avantage à Vichy - Juin 1940–Novembre 1942*, Paris, Robert Laffont, 1966, 434p.

PAILLAT Claude, *L'Échiquier d'Alger (II) De Gaulle Joue et Gagne-Novembre 1942–Août 1944*, Paris, Robert Laffont, 1967, 415p.

PAXTON Robert, *Vichy France Old Guard and New Order 1940–1944*, New York, Columbia University Press, 2001, 478p.

PÉAN Pierre, *Vies et morts de Jean Moulin*, Paris, Fayard, 715p.

PHILLIPS Peter, *The Economics of Terrorism*, Abingdon, Routledge, 2016, 212p.

PIKETTY Guillaume, *Pierre Brossolette: Un héros de la Résistance*, Paris, Éditions Odile Jacob, 1998, 416p.

RAGACHE Gilles, *De Gaulle, L'or, le dollar et la France (1940–1970)*, Antony, Éditions Clefs pour l'Histoire de France, 2017, 206p.

RAGACHE Gilles, *Juin 1940*, Paris, Perrin, 2020, 334p.

REID Donald, *Whose Pharaohs? Archaeology, Museums and Egyptian National Identity from Napoleon to World War I*, Berkeley, University of California Press, 2003, 428p.

RIGDEN Denis (Introduction), *How to Be a Spy: The World War II SOE Training Manual*, Bury St. Edmunds, The Dundurn Group Toronto, 2001, 433p.

RIVALLAN Josette (Ed.), D'ALMEIDA-TOPOR Hélène (Ed.), *Eboué, soixante ans après*, Paris, Société Française d'Histoire d'Outre-mer, 2008, 432p.

ROLLAND Denis, *Vichy et la France Libre au Mexique: Guerre, cultures et propagandes pendant la Deuxième Guerre mondiale*, Paris, L'Harmattan, 1990, 443p.

RUBY Marcel, *Résistance civile et résistance militaire*, Lyon, Éditions L'Hermès, 1984, 156p.

SAUVY Alfred, *La vie économique des Français de 1939 à 1945*, Paris, Flammarion, 1978, 226p.

SAYERS Richard Sidney, *Financial Policy 1939–1945*, London, Her Majesty's Stationery Office & Longmans, Green and Co., 1956, 630p.
SCOTT John, *Social Network Analysis (3rd Edition)*, London, Sage, 2013, 201p.
Secrétariat d'Etat à l'Economie Nationale et aux Finances, *L'Action économique en France depuis l'armistice*, Macon, Protat Frères, 1941, 181p.
SÉDILLOT René, *Du franc Bonaparte au franc De Gaulle*, Paris, Calmann-Lévy, 1959, 237p.
SÉDILLOT René, *Histoire des Marchés Noirs*, Paris, Éditions Tallandier, 1985, 365p.
SEED Philip, *Introducing Network Analysis in Social Work*, London, Jessica Kingsley Ltd., 1991, 185p.
SHIPLEY-WHITE Dorothy, *Les origines de la discorde; de Gaulle, la France Libre et les Alliées*, Paris, Éditions de Trévise, 1967, 498p.
SOULEAU Philippe, *La ligne de démarcation en Gironde 1940–1944*, Périgueux, Éditions Fanlac, 1998, 362p.
SOULEAU Philippe, *La Région de Langon sous l'Occupation*, Breil-sur-Roya, Éditions du Cabri, 1991 (Ed. Fenixx Réédition Numérique, Ebook), 112p.
STRACHAN Hew, *Financing the First World War*, Oxford, Oxford University Press, 2004, 268p.
TAYLOR Alan J. P., *The Origins of the Second World War*, London, Hamish Hamilton, 1961, 357p. (Ed. Penguin, 2001, Ebook)
TERRISSE René, *Bordeaux 1940–1944*, Paris, Perrin, 1993, 343p.
THOMAS Martin, *The French Empire at War 1939–1945*, Manchester, Manchester University Press, 2000, 320p.
TODMAN Daniel, *Britain's War: Into Battle 1937–1941*, London, Penguin, 2016, 722p. (Ebook)
TODMAN Daniel, *Britain's War: A New World 1942–1947*, London, Penguin, 2020, 976p. (Ebook)
TOMBS Robert (Ed.), CHABAL Emile (Ed.), *Britain and France in Two World Wars*, London, Bloomsbury Academic, 2013, 232p.
TOOZE Adam, *The Wages of Destruction: The Making and Breaking of the Nazi Economy*, New York, Penguin, 2007, 832p.
TURPIN Frédéric, *André Diethelm 1896–1954; De Georges Mandel à Charles de Gaulle*, Paris, Les Indes Savantes, 2004, 276p.
VANDENBUSSCHE Robert (Ed.), *La Clandestinité en Belgique et en Zone Interdite (1940–1944)*, Lille, Publications de l'Institut de recherches historiques du Septentrion, 2009, 265p.
VIATTE Auguste, *D'un Monde à l'autre: Journal d'un intellectuel jurassien au Québec (1939–1949), V. 1 mars 1939–novembre 1942*, Paris, L'Harmattan, 2001, 516p.
VIGNERAS Marcel, *Rearming the French*, CreateSpace Independent Publishing Platform, 1957, ed. 2015, 466p.

VINCENT Isabel, *Hitler's Silent Partners: Swiss Banks, Nazi Gold, and the Pursuit of Justice*, New York, William Morrow, 1997, 351p.

VINEN Richard, *The Unfree French: Life Under the Occupation*, St. Ives, Penguin Books, 2006 (Ed. 2007), 477p.

WIEVIORKA Oliver, *Histoire de la Résistance*, Paris, Perrin, 2013, 588p.

WIEVIORKA Olivier, *Une Histoire de la Résistance en Europe Occidentale*, Paris, Perrin, 2017, 476p.

ZIELINSKI Rosella Cappella, *How States Pay for Wars*, Ithaca, Cornell University Press, 2016, 208p.

**Articles**

ADAMS R. J. Q., 'Hoare, Samuel John Gurney, Viscount Templewood', *Oxford Dictionary of National Biography*, 23 September 2004, p. 2, https://doi.org/10.1093/ref:odnb/33898, Consulted 24 May 2021

AGLAN Alya, 'Des syndicalistes dans la résistance', *Vingtième Siècle, Revue d'histoire*, N° 67, Juillet–septembre 2000, pp. 119–127

A.J.B., 'The Sterling Area', *Bulletin of International News*, Vol. 21, N° 24, November 1944, pp. 1000–1005

ALMEIDA Mónica, 'Los Sirio-Libaneses en el espacio social ecuatoriano: cohesión étnica y asimilación cultural', *Journal de la société des américainistes*, N° 83, 1997, pp. 201–227

AZEMA Jean-Pierre, 'Ce que la Résistance doit aux Anglais: Entretien avec Jean-Louis Crémieux-Brilhac' in *L'Histoire*, N° 381, November 2012

BARKER Nancy Nichols, 'The French Colony in Mexico, 1821–61: Generator of Intervention' in *French Historical Studies*, Vol. 9, N° 4, Autumn, 1976, pp. 596–618, Duke University Press

BELOT, Robert. 'Les comités de la France Libre en Amérique latine pendant la guerre: enjeu symbolique, politique et diplomatique' in VAÏSSE Maurice (Ed.), *De Gaulle et l'Amérique latine*, Rennes, Presses universitaires de Rennes, 2014, 280p.

BLANC Jérôme, 'Pouvoirs et monnaie durant la seconde guerre mondiale en France: la monnaie subordonnée au politique', International Conference on War, Monet and Finance, *Monetary and Financial Structures: The Impact of Political Unrests and Wars*, June 2008, Paris, Nanterre, 32p., https://halshs.archives-ouvertes.fr/halshs-00652826

BLOCH-LAINÉ François, 'Le Financement de la Résistance', *Revue d'histoire de la Deuxième Guerre mondiale*, 1ère année, N° 1, Novembre 1950, pp. 6–19

BOUGEARD Christian, 'La vie quotidienne des Bretons pendant la guerre: Quelques aspects' in *Annales de Bretagne et des pays de l'Ouest*, Vol. 92, N° 1, 1985, pp. 79–102, p. 97

BRAUDEL Fernand, 'Histoire et Sciences Sociaux: La longue durée' in *Reseaux*, Vol. 5, N° 27, Armand Colin, 1987, pp. 7–37

BRUNET Luc-André, 'Jean Monnet et l'organisation des économies alliées pour la guerre (1939–1940)' in BOSSUAT Gérard (Ed.), *Jean Monnet et l'économie*, Brussels, Euroclio, Peter Lang, 2018, 14p.

CARRELLÁN RUIZ Juan Luis, DE LA LLOSA Alvar, 'L'Appel de la Patrie: Les Réservistes et les Volontaires Français du Chili pendant la Première Guerre mondiale', *Guerres mondiales et conflits contemporains*, PUF, 2018/2, N° 270, pp. 7–23

CARROLL Francis M., 'United States Armed Forces in Northern Ireland During World War II', *New Hibernia Review / Iris Éireannach Nua*, Samhradh/Summer 2008, Vol. 12, N° 2, pp. 15–36

CHABORD Marie-Thérèse, 'Le Bureau Central de Renseignements et d'Action de la France libre (BCRA)' in *Guerres mondiales et conflits contemporains*, 2003/4, N° 212, pp. 105–111.

CHIN Rachel, 'Who Speaks for France? Vichy, Free France and the Battle over French Legitimacy: 1940–1942', *British Journal for Military History*, Vol. 6, N° 3 (2020), pp. 2–22

CITROEN H. A., 'European Emigration in the Inter-War Period' in *European Emigration Overseas Past and Future*, Publications of the Research Group for European Migration Problems, vol 2, Dordrecht, Springer, 1951, pp. 17–20

COATES Ken, MORRISON W. R., 'The American Rampant: Reflections on the Impact of United States Troops in Allied Countries During World War II', *Journal of World History*, Vol. 2, N° 2, Fall, 1991, pp. 201–221

COLSON Justin, 'Geocoding Historical Data Using QGIS', *The Programming Historian* 6, 2017, https://programminghistorian.org/en/lessons/geocoding-qgis

CORBINOS Lorenzo Agar, 'Árabes y Judíos en Chile: Apuntes Sobre La Inmigración y la Integración Social' in KLICH Ignacio (Ed.) *Árabes y judíos en América Latina. Historia, representaciones y desafíos*, Buenos Aires, Siglo XXI Editoria Iberoamericana, 2006, 21p.

COTTER Joseph, OSBORNE Michael A., 'Agronomía Afranceada: The French Contribution to Mexican Agronomy, 1880–1940' in *Science, Technology & Society*, Vol. 1, N° 1, 1996, Sage Publications, New Delhi, pp. 25–49

COUGHLAN Sean, 'The Scientists Who Escaped the Nazis', *BBC News*, 17 July 2013, https://www.bbc.com/news/business-23261289

CUCHE Denys, 'L'immigration libanaise au Pérou: Une immigration ignorée', *Journal de la société des américainistes*, N° 83, 1997, pp. 173–199

DAUGHTON J. P., 'When Argentina Was "French": Rethinking Cultural Politics and European Imperialism in Belle-Époque Buenos Aires' in *The Journal of Modern History*, 80, December 2008, pp. 831–864

DENIS Pierre, 'Les finances de la France Libre' in *Revue de la Deuxième Guerre mondiale*, PUF, N° 1, November 1950, pp. 20–27

DRAKE HALL Marian, 'The Belgian Congo as a Fats-and-Oils Source' in *Foreign Commerce Weekly*, Vol. 24, 24 August 1946, pp. 3–5

DREYFUS Michel, PENNETIER Claude, 'FOURGUES Julien', *Le Maitron*, 2009, https://maitron.fr/spip.php?article50708 , Consulted 2 November 2020

DUCARME Bernard, 'Le Financement de la Résistance Armée en Belgique: 1940–1944', *Courrier hebdomadaire du CRISP*, 1970/11, N° 476–477, pp. 1–62

DÜRING Marten, 'From Hermeneutics to Data to Networks: Data Extraction and Network Visualization of Historical Sources', *The Programming Historian* 4, 2015, https://programminghistorian.org/en/lessons/creating-network-diagrams-from-historical-sources

EICHENGREEN Barry, 'The British Economy Between the Wars', April 2002, https://eml.berkeley.edu/~eichengr/research/floudjohnsonchaptersep16-03.pdf

ENOCH Charles, GULDE Anne-Marie, 'Are Currency Boards a Cure for All Monetary Problems?', *Finance & Development*, Vol. 35, N° 4, December 1998, https://www.imf.org/external/pubs/ft/fandd/1998/12/enoch.htm

Federal Reserve Bank, New York, *Monthly Review of Credit and Business Conditions, Second Federal Reserve District, Monthly Review*, 1 March 1939

FETTER Bruce, 'Changing War Aims: Central Africa's Role, 1940–41, As Seen from Léopoldville' in *African Affairs*, Vol 87, N° 348, July 1988, pp. 377–392

FEUER Lewis, 'Cartel Control in New Caledonia' in *Far Eastern Survey*, Vol. 15, N° 12, 19 June 1946, pp. 184–187

GALLAIS-HAMONNO Georges, HOANG Thi Hong Van, OOSTERLINCK Kim, 'Price Formation on Clandestine Markets: The Case of the Paris Gold Market During World War II' in *Economic History Review*, Vol. 72, N° 3, 2019, pp. 1048–1072

GAUNSON A. B., 'Churchill, de Gaulle, Spears and the Levant Affaire, 1941' in *The Historical Journal*, Vol. 27, N° 3, September 1984, pp. 697–713

GRANOVETTER Mark, 'The Strength of Weak Ties' in *American Journal of Sociology*, Vol. 78, N° 6, May 1973, University of Chicago Press, pp. 1360–1380

HALL H. D., 'Arthur Blaikie Purvis (1890–1941)', *Oxford Dictionary of National Biography*, Published 23 September 2004, p. 1, https://www.oxforddnb.com/view/10.1093/ref:odnb/9780198614128.001.0001/odnb-9780198614128-e-35635;jsessionid=1D3D45901F777C6671A5F7ACF7F27DFC, Consulted 24 May 2021

HENNINGHAM Stephen, 'Some Australian Official Views of New Caledonia's Melanesians, 1941 to 1953', *Journal de la Société des Océanistes*, Vol. 141, 2015, pp. 323–336

HENNINGHAM Stephen, 'The French Administration, the Local Population and the American Presence in New Caledonia, 1943–1944' in *Journal de la Société des Océanistes*, 98, 1994, pp. 21–41

HOFFMAN Stanley, 'Collaborationism in France During World War II' in *The Journal of Modern History*, Vol. 40, N° 3, September 1968, pp. 375–395

HOWARD Michael, 'La Pensée Stratégique' in *Revue d'histoire de la Deuxième Guerre mondiale*, PUF, N° 90, April 1973, pp. 1–9

HOWLETT Peter, 'The War-Time Economy, 1939–1945', in FLOUD Roderick (Ed.), JOHNSON Paul (Ed.), *The Cambridge Economic History of Modern Britain*, Cambridge, Cambridge University Press, 2004, pp. 1–26

JEANNESSON Stanislas, 'Pourquoi la France a-t-elle occupé la Ruhr?' in *Vingtième Siècle, revue d'histoire*, Vol. 51, N° 1, 1996, pp. 56–67

KEDWARD H. Rod, 'Mapping the Resistance: An Essay on Roots and Routes', *Modern & Contemporary France*, Vol. 20, N° 4, 2012, pp. 491–503

KELLY Debra, 'Mapping Free French London: Places, Spaces, Traces' in *A History of the French in London: Liberty, Equality, Opportunity*, London, School of Advanced Study, University of London, Institute of Historical Research, 2013, pp. 299–341

KENT Hilary, 'Sir Ronald Hibbert Cross (1896–1968)', *Australian Dictionary of Biography*, https://adb.anu.edu.au/biography/cross-sir-ronald-hibbert-9870

KURIHARA Kenneth, 'Toward A New Theory of Monetary Sovereignty', *Journal of Political Economy*, Vol. 57, N°2, April 1949, pp. 162–170

LAMBAUR Barbara, 'Occupation – collaboration – répression: une affaire allemande', Delivered During *Vichy et l'occupation: Militaires, civils, justice, économie*, CEMMC, Université Bordeaux Montaigne, 7 April 2016

LAWREY John, 'A Catch on the Boundary: Australia and the Free French Movement in 1940' in *The Journal of Pacific History*, Vol. 10, N° 3, 1975, pp. 64–82

LE CROM Jean-Pierre, 'Syndicalisme et Résistance' in DOUZOU Laurent (Ed.), FRANK Robert (Ed.), PESCHANSKI Denis (Ed.), VEILLON Dominique (Ed.), *La Résistance et les Français: villes, centres etlogiques de décision*, Actes du colloque de Cachan– IHTP, 1995, pp. 395–413

LEIGHLEY Jan, 'Social Interaction and Contextual Influences on Political Participation' in *American Politics Research*, Vol. 18, N° 4, October 1990

LEMERCIER Claire, 'Analyse de réseaux et histoire' in *Revue d'histoire moderne et contemporaine*, Belin, 2005/2, N° 52-2, pp. 88–122

MARBEAU Michel, 'Un acteur des nouvelles relations multilatérales: le Service Français de la Société des Nations (1919–1940)' in *Matériaux pour l'histoire de notre temps*, Vol. 36, N° 1, 1994, pp. 11–20

M.B. & H.G.L., 'Syria & Lebanon: The States of the Levant Under French Mandate' in *Bulletin of International News*, Vol. 17, N°14, 13 July 1940, pp. 841–851

MEMOLI-AUBRY Crécence, 'Le Mbam dans la Seconde Guerre Mondiale: contribution d'une région administrative du Cameroun à l'effort de guerre français' in *Outre-mers*, Vol. 96, N° 362–363, 1st Quarter 2009, L'Atlantique Français, pp. 241–266

MICKELSEN Martin, 'Another Fashoda: The Anglo-Free French Conflict over the Levant, May-September 1941' in *Revue française d'histoire d'outre-mer*, Vol. 63, N° 230, 1st Quarter 1976, pp. 75–100

MIKESELL Raymond F., 'Sterling Area Currencies of the Middle East' in *Middle East Journal*, Vol. 2, N° 2, April 1948, pp. 160–174

MILLS Geoffrey, ROCKOFF Hugh, 'Complaisance with Price Controls in the United States and the United Kingdom During World War II' in *The Journal of Economic History*, Vol. 47, N° 1, March 1987, pp. 197–213

MOURÉ Kenneth, 'Spearhead Currency: Monetary Sovereignty and the Liberation of France' in *The International History Review*, Vol. 42, N° 2, 2020, pp. 278–297

MUNDELL Robert, 'Monetary Unions and the Problem of Sovereignty', *The Annals of the American Academy of Political and Social Science*, Vol. 579, Exchange Rate Regimes and Capital Flows (January 2002), pp. 123–152

MUNHOLLAND Kim, 'The Trials of the Free French in New Caledonia, 1940–1942', *French Historical Studies*, Vol. 14, N° 14, Autumn 1986, pp. 547–579

'Neutrality Act of 1939', *The American Journal of International Law*, Vol. 34, N° 1, Supplement: Official Documents (January 1940), pp. 47–74

NEWTON Ronald, 'The United States, the German-Argentines and the Myth of the Fourth Reich, 1943–47' in *The Hispanic American Historical Review*, Vol. 64, N° 1, February 1984, pp. 81–103

NYE Joseph, 'Soft Power', *Foreign Policy*, N° 80, Twentieth Anniversary (Autumn, 1990), Washingtonpost Newsweek Interactive, LLC, pp. 153–171

OBSTFELD Maurice, SHAMBAUGH Jay, TAYLOR Alan, 'Monetary Sovereignty, Exchange Rates and Capital Controls: The Trilemma in the Interwar Period', *IMF Staff Papers*, Vol. 51, IMF Fourth Annual Research Conference, 2004, pp. 75–108

OSTENDORP Peter, 'Nickel: Hidden in Plain Sight', Dartmouth Toxic Metals, National Institute of Environmental Health Sciences Superfund Research Program, Dartmouth College, Undated, https://sites.dartmouth.edu/toxmetal/more-metals/nickel-hidden-in-plain-sight/

OTERO Hernán, 'Emigración, movilización militar y cultura de guerra. Los franceses de la Argentina durante la Gran Guerra' in *Amnis*, 10 | 2011, https://journals.openedition.org/amnis/1137

PAXTON Robert, 'La collaboration d'état' in AZEMA J.P. (Ed.), BEDARIDA F. (Ed.), *La France des années noires, Vol. 1*, Paris, Seuil, 1993, pp. 334–361

POGGIOLI Morgan, 'La CGT et la répression antisyndicale (août 1939–décembre 1940): Entre légalisme et apprentissage de la clandestinité, *Vingtième Siècle. Revue d'histoire*, 2016/2, N° 130, pp. 149–162

POPE Arthur Upham, 'The Importance of Morale', *The Journal of Educational Sociology*, Vol. 15, N° 4, Civilian Morale, December 1941, pp. 195–205

RASKIN Richard, 'CASABLANCA and United States Foreign Policy', *Film History*, Vol. 4, N° 2, 1990, pp. 153–164

RICHARDSON J. Henry, 'Consumer Rationing in Great Britain' in *The Canadian Journal of Economics and Political Science*, Vol. 8, N° 1, February 1942, pp. 69–82

RICKETT Denis, 'Salter, (James) Arthur, Baron Salter', *Oxford Dictionary of National Biography*, 23 September 2004, p. 1, https://www.oxforddnb.com/view/10.1093/ref:odnb/9780198614128.001.0001/odnb-9780198614128-e-31651

RIPPY J. Fred, 'French Investments in Argentina and Brazil' in *Political Science Quarterly*, Vol. 64, N° 4, December 1949, pp. 560–578

ROE Teiva, 'Les Français d'Australie et la France libre (1940–1944)' in *Outre-mers*, Vol. 95, N° 360–361, 2nd semester 2008, *L'Afrique des Indiens*, pp. 209–222

ROLLAND Denis, 'Jacques Soustelle, De l'Ethnologie à la Politique' in *Guerres mondiales et conflits contemporains*, N° 180, October 1995, pp. 171–185

ROLLAND Denis, 'L'exil structure l'émigration (Mexique, Seconde Guerre mondiale)' in *Matériaux pour l'histoire de notre temps*, N° 67, Pour une histoire de l'Exil français et belge, 2002, pp. 66–77

SACQUETY Troy, 'Supplying the Resistance: OSS Logistics Support to Special Operations in Europe', *Veritas*, Vol. 3, N° 1, 2007, pp. 38–50

SAS Louis Furman, 'The Spirit of France in Argentina' in *The French Review*, Vol. 15, N° 6, May 1942, pp. 468–477

SCHLAIM Avi, 'Prelude to Downfall: The British Offer of Union to France, June 1940' in *Journal of Contemporary History*, Vol. 9, N° 3, July 1974, pp. 27–63

SCHOFIELD Hugh, 'A Farewell to France's War Broadcaster', *BBC News*, 9 April 2015, https://www.bbc.com/news/world-europe-32237764

SHEFFIELD Hazel, 'BMW Admits 'Profound Regret' for Using Nazi Slave Labour During the Second World War', *The Independent*, 8 March 2016, https://www.independent.co.uk/news/business/news/bmw-admits-profound-regret-for-the-enormous-suffering-it-caused-by-using-nazi-slave-labour-during-the-second-world-war-a6919081.html

SMITH Andrew W. M., 'Eclipse in the Dark Years: Pick-Up Flights, Routes of Resistance and the Free French', *European Review of History: Revue europćene d'histoire*, Vol. 25, N° 2, 2018, pp. 392–414

Statista, Population of Belgium from 1800 to 2020, https://www.statista.com/statistics/1008201/total-population-belgium-1816-2020/

Statista, Population of France from 1700 to 2020, https://www.statista.com/statistics/1016777/total-population-norway-1769-2020/

Statista, Population of the Netherlands from 1800 to 2020, https://www.statista.com/statistics/1016675/total-population-netherlands-1816-2020/

Statista, Population of Norway from 1769 to 2020, https://www.statista.com/statistics/1016777/total-population-norway-1769-2020/

SUDOL Stan, 'Nickel Closest Thing to a True 'War Metal'', *Republic of Mining*, 13 February 2009, https://republicofmining.com/2009/02/13/nickel-closest-thing-to-a-true-%E2%80%98war-metal%E2%80%99-by-stan-sudol/

SUNDERLAND David, 'Chapter 4—The Management of the Joint Colonial Fund and the Joint Miscellaneous Fund' in *Managing British Colonial and Post-Colonial Development: The Crown Agents, 1914–1974*, Woodbridge, Boydell & Brewer, 2007, 312p., pp. 97–114

TAGLIABUE John, 'Henri Ziegler, Aviation Figure, Is Dead at 91', *New York Times*, 28 July 1998

TAYLOR Lynne, 'The Black Market in Occupied Northern France, 1940–4' in *Contemporary European History*, Vol. 6, N° 2, July 1997, pp. 153–176

THOMAS Martin, 'Economic Conditions and the Limits to Mobilization in the French Empire, 1936–1939' in *The Historical Journal*, Vol. 48, N° 2, 2005, pp. 471–498

THOMAS Martin, 'Le Royaume-Uni et la France Libre' in *Relations Internationales*, Vol. 108, N°. Hiver, 2001, pp. 575–593

THOMAS Martin, 'Resource War, Civil War, Rights War: Factoring Empire into French North Africa's Second World War' in *War in History*, Vol. 18, N° 2, April 2011, pp. 225–248

WALEY David, 'The Treasury During World War II' in *Oxford Economic Papers*, Vol. 5, Supplement; Sir Hubert Henderson 1890–1952, 1953, pp. 47–54

WALL Irwin M., RAVIART Philippe-Etienne, 'Jean Monnet, les États-Unis et le plan français' in *Vingtième Siècle - Revue d'histoire*, N°. 30, April–June 1991, pp. 3–21

WARD Rowena, 'Female Japanese Citizens in New Caledonia: Pre-December 1941', *Pacific Dynamics—Journal of Interdisciplinary Research*, Vol. 2, N° 1, pp. 45–52

WARD Rowena, 'Repatriating the Japanese from New Caledonia, 1941–46', *The Journal of Pacific History*, Vol. 51, N° 4, pp. 392–408

WARD Rowena, 'The Internment and Repatriation of the Japanese-French Nationals Resident in New Caledonia, 1941–1946', *PORTAL Journal of*

*Multidisciplinary International Studies*, Vol. 14, N° 2, September 2017, pp. 55–67

WETHERELL Charles, 'Historical Social Network Analysis' in *International Review of Social History* 43, 1998, Supplement, pp. 125–144

WILMINGTON Martin, 'The Middle East Supply Center: A Reappraisal', *Middle East Journal*, Vol. 6, N° 2, Spring 1952, pp. 144–166

WRIGHT Gordon, 'Bullitt and the Fall of France', *World Politics*, Vol. 10, N° 1 (October 1957), pp. 63–90

YLÄ-ANTTILA Tuukka, 'Familiarity as a Tool of Populism: Political Appropriation of Shared Experiences and the Case of the Suvivirsi' in *Acta Sociologica*, Vol. 60, N° 4, pp. 342–357

ZAMIR Meir, 'De Gaulle and the Question of Syria and Lebanon During the Second World War: Part I' in *Middle Eastern Studies*, Taylor & Francis Ltd., Vol. 43, N° 5, September 2007, pp. 675–708

**Theses**

CAPDEPUY Arlette, *Félix Éboué, 1884–1944: mythe et réalités coloniales*, Doctoral Thesis, Université Michel de Montaigne – Bordeaux III, France, 2013, 509p.

COUTINHO Priscilla, *Lavoura Arcaica: Un Romain de la diaspora libanaise au Brésil*, Doctoral Thesis, Université Sorbonne Paris Cité, Universidade de São Paulo, France & Brazil, 2018, 250p.

COUTTS Matthew, *The Political Career of Sir Samuel Hoare During the National Government 1931–40*, Doctoral Thesis, University of Leicester, UK, 2010, 298p.

COX Nechama, *The Ministry of Economic Warfare and Britain's Conduct of Economic Warfare, 1939–1945*, Doctoral Thesis, King's College London, U.K. 2001, 366p.

MANAS Arnaud, 'L'Or de Vichy: L'État Français et la monnaie', Doctoral Thesis, Université Paris I – Sorbonne, France, 2013, 757p.

McLEARY Luke, *Rethinking Africa's GDP, 1796–1950*, Master's Thesis, Universitat de Barcelona School of Economics, Spain, 2018, 40p.

NZUME Anastasia Nlende, *British and French Administration of Peoples on the Southern Borderlands of Cameroon: The Case of the Anglo-French Inter-Cameroons Boundary, 1916–61*, Doctoral Thesis, School of African and Oriental Studies (S.O.A.S.), University of London, UK, 2004, 410p.

VAST Cécile, *Une histoire des Mouvements Unis de Résistance (de 1941 à l'après-guerre): Essai sur l'expérience de la Résistance et l'identité résistante*, Doctoral Thesis, Université de Franche-Comté, France, 2008, 399p.

VIVIER Thierry, *Guerre et Résistance en Touraine à l'ère des conflits de masse au cours de 1870 à 1945: une approche multiscalaire, de l'ego-histoire à l'histoire globale.*, Oral Viva for *Habilitation à diriger des recherches*, Université Bordeaux Montaigne, 5 September 2016

WILMINGTON Martin, *Economic Regionalism in the Middle East During World War II (The Middle East Supply Center)*, Doctoral Thesis, New York University, United States of America, 1960, 448p.

**Mediography**

'Alias «ARCHIDUC», Terroriste à la retraite', https://vimeo.com/67803592

'Avec ce "de Gaulle" là, vous ne prendrez rien M. Mrs...', Propaganda image, edited by the *Ligue Française Antibritannique*, 1940, BnF Gallica, https://gallica.bnf.fr/ark:/12148/btv1b9013935t/f1.item

ASHDOWN Paddy, WHATELEY Francis, *The Most Courageous Raid of WWII*, BBC Productions, 1 November 2011, BBC2, 59'04

'Billet de banque AMGOT Recto-Verso', Musée de la Résistance En Ligne, http://museedelaresistanceenligne.org/media.php?media=811&expo=&sens=recto

BRIDGE Joe (John Steer, 1886–1967), 'Cigares Diplomates' poster, Ateliers Joe Bridge, Paris, 1930, 120 x 159.4cm, https://auctions.posterauctions.com/lots/view/1-HG2MO/cigares-diplomates-1930

CORDIER Daniel (Author), TASMA Alain (Director), BENAMOU Georges-Marc (Producer), *Alias Caracalla*, Telefilm, Arté Fr., 93 minutes, 2013

CREMIEUX-BRILHAC Jean-Louis, L'ALLINEC Laurène, *Les anglais dans la résistance*, BFC Productions, France 5, 52 minutes, 2012

'La Maison Familiale de Jean Moulin À Saint-Andiol', http://museedelaresistancenligne.org/media6044-La-maison-familiale-de-Jean-Moulin-A

LEVISSE-TOUZÉ Christine, 'Faux Papiers de Jean Moulin', 25 October 1941, http://museedelaresistanceenligne.org/media3331-Faux-papiers-de-Jean-Moulin

*M. Malfait et M. Fertein: Témoignages sur le réseau de Résistance du capitaine Michel*, Office national de radiodiffusion télévision française Lille, Nord actualités télé, 27 November 1973, 2'22, https://www.ina.fr/video/RCC970923 2006

OVERY Richard, *Writing the History of the Second World War: Anything More to Say?*, Talk given at the inauguration of the Sir Michael Howard Centre, King's College London, 9 March 2015, https://www.youtube.com/watch?v=eub0JuAMSiI&ucbcb=1

PETAIN Philippe, *Discours radiophonique de Philippe Pétain: Le lancement de la collaboration avec l'Allemagne*, Fonds Vichy disques de la BDIC, 30 October 1940, 8'18, https://www.ina.fr/audio/PHD95079031

'Tracé de la Ligne de démarcation de la Zone Occupée', December 1941, Institut géographique national, Bibliothèque nationale de France, Gallica.bnf.fr, https://gallica.bnf.fr/ark:/12148/btv1b525070033/f1.highres

'Tracé de la Ligne de démarcation de la Zone Occupée', December 1941, Institut géographique national, Bibliothèque nationale de France, Gallica.bnf.fr, https://gallica.bnf.fr/ark:/12148/btv1b525070033/f2.item

WERTHER Maurice, '*Témoignage Aubrac*', Antenne 2 Midi, 5 February 1983

**Webography and Software**

AFD History, https://www.afd.fr/en/our-history

Agence Française de Développement, 'Our History', https://www.afd.fr/en/our-history

American Chemical Society, 'The Houdry Process for the Catalytic Conversion of Crude Petroleum to High-Octane Gasoline', 1996, https://www.acs.org/content/acs/en/education/whatischemistry/landmarks/houdry.html

Amicale de la 1e Division Française Libre, '1940: Gabon', https://web.archive.org/web/20161124075631/http://1dfl.fr/-1940-Gabon-.html

Association Nationale des Anciens Combattants de la Banque de France, https://web.archive.org/web/20181220173856/http://www.anac-fr.com/f_2gm.htm

'August Brusset', Les Français Libres, de juin 1940 à juillet 1943, http://www.francaislibres.net/liste/fiche.php?index=58514

BARRETT Margaret, '*BRENAC André (1902–1999)*', *The French-Australian Dictionary of Biography*, Sydney, March 2019, https://www.isfar.org.au/bio/brenac-andre-1902-1999/

BASTIAN Mathieu, RAMOS IBANEZ Eduardo, JACOMY Mathieu, BARTOSIAK Cezary, HEYMANN Sébastien, BILCKE Julian, McSWEENEY Patrick, PANISSON André, SUBTIL Jérémy, SUZUKI Helder, SKURLA Martin, PATRIARCA Antonio, *Gephi 0.9.1*, Gephi Contributors, 2008–2016, https://gephi.org/

'Biographie – Édouard Daladier', Assemblée nationale, https://www2.assemblee-nationale.fr/sycomore/bio/(num_dept)/2105

'Biography of Frederic René Coudert Jr.', History, Art & Archives: United States House of Representatives, https://history.house.gov/People/Detail/11462

Biographical information on Albert Guérin, Ordre de la Libération, https://www.ordredelaliberation.fr/fr/compagnons/albert-guerin

Biographical information on André Boulloche, Ordre de la Libération, https://www.ordredelaliberation.fr/fr/compagnons/andre-boulloche

Biographical information on André Schock, Ordre de la Libération, https://www.ordredelaliberation.fr/fr/compagnons/andre-schock

Biographical information on Émile Bollaert, Ordre de la Libération, https://www.ordredelaliberation.fr/fr/compagnons/emile-bollaert

Biographical information on Ft. Lt. Charles Peter Clark, Commonwealth War Graves Commission, https://www.cwgc.org/find-records/find-war-dead/casualty-details/1084454/clark,-charles-peter/#&gid=null&pid=1

Biographical information on Henri Frenay, Ordre de la Libération, https://www.ordredelaliberation.fr/fr/compagnons/henri-frenay

Biographical information on Henri Goiran Papers, https://dl.tufts.edu/concern/eads/dr26z763h

Biographical information on Henri Jaboulay, Ordre de la Libération, https://www.ordredelaliberation.fr/fr/compagnons/henri-jaboulay
Biographical information on Henri Manhès, Ordre de la Libération, https://www.ordredelaliberation.fr/fr/compagnons/henri-manhes
Biographical information on Jacques Bingen, Ordre de la Libération, https://www.ordredelaliberation.fr/fr/compagnons/jacques-bingen
Biographical information on Jean-François Clouët des Pesruches, Ordre de la Libération, https://www.ordredelaliberation.fr/fr/compagnons/jean-francois-clouet-des-pesruches
Biographical information on Jean Rosenthal, Ordre de la Libération, https://www.ordredelaliberation.fr/fr/compagnons/jean-rosenthal
Biographical information on Laure Diebold, Ordre de la Libération, https://www.ordredelaliberation.fr/fr/compagnons/laure-diebold
Biographical information on Maurice Bourgès-Manoury, Ordre de la Libération, https://www.ordredelaliberation.fr/fr/compagnons/maurice-bourges-maunoury
Biographical information on Michel Pichard, Ordre de la Libération, https://www.ordredelaliberation.fr/fr/compagnons/michel-pichard
Biographical information on Paul Rivière, Ordre de la Libération, https://www.ordredelaliberation.fr/fr/compagnons/paul-riviere
Biographical information on Pierre Louis Bourgoin, Ordre de la Libération, https://www.ordredelaliberation.fr/fr/compagnons/pierre-deshayes
Biographical information on Pierre Louis Bourgoin, Ordre de la Libération, https://www.ordredelaliberation.fr/fr/compagnons/pierre-louis-bourgoin
Biographical information on Pierre Wellhoff, Les Amis de la Fondation de la Résistance, https://www.memoresist.org/resistant/pierre-wellhoff/
Biographical information on Raymond Fassin, Les Amis de la Fondation de la Résistance, https://www.memoresist.org/resistant/raymond-fassin/
Biographical information on Serge Ravanel, Ordre de la Libération, https://www.ordredelaliberation.fr/fr/compagnons/serge-ravanel
Biographical information on Tony de Graaf, Les Amis de la Fondation de la Résistance, https://www.memoresist.org/resistant/antoine-de-graaff/
Biographical information on Valentin Abeille, Ordre de la Libération, https://www.ordredelaliberation.fr/fr/compagnons/valentin-abeille
Biographical information on Yves Bouthillier, National Economy and Finance Minister (1940–1942), https://www.economie.gouv.fr/saef/yves-bouthillier
BONNAUD Pierre, 'Notice Annonay (Ardèche) et sa région: les fusillés de l'été 1944', 16 March 2020, https://maitron.fr/spip.php?article222028
BORGATTI Steve, EVERETT Martin, FREEMAN Lin, *Ucinet for Windows: Software for Social Network Analysis*, Harvard, Analytic Technologies, 2002

BOURRÉE Fabrice, 'Plaque en Hommage à Henri Frager, dit «Paul»', Musée de la Résistance en Ligne, http://museedelaresistanceenligne.org/media5261-Plaque-en-hommage-A

BROWN Derek, 'Bartenders Are Liars, but It's Not Their Fault', *The Atlantic*, 10 August 2010, https://www.theatlantic.com/health/archive/2010/08/bartenders-are-liars-but-its-not-their-fault/61259/

CALDER John, *Obituary: Tony Mayer*, The Independent, 6 November 1997, https://www.independent.co.uk/news/obituaries/obituary-tony-mayer-129 2389.html

'Camille Rayon bâtisseur de port est décédé à l'âge de 101 ans', France 3, Provence Alpes Côte d'Azur, 18 September 2014, https://france3-regions.francetvinfo.fr/provence-alpes-cote-d-azur/alpes-maritimes/cannes/camille-rayon-batisseur-de-port-est-decede-l-age-de-101-ans-553258.html

CASSIN René, 'Rauzan (Pierre Denis), Fondation de la France Libre', https://www.france-libre.net/pierre-denis-rauzan/#2

CHILDS Martin, 'Obituary: Margot Duhalde, Chile's First Female Pilot Who Came to Europe to Help Allies Fight Axis Forces', *The Scotsman*, 22 March 2018, https://www.scotsman.com/news/obituary-margot-duhalde-chiles-first-female-pilot-who-came-europe-help-allies-fight-axis-forces-316718

'Couvre-feu pendant la Seconde Guerre mondiale', Mémoire Alpine, https://web.archive.org/web/20200807220144/http://www.memoire-alpine.com/couvre-feu-pendant-la-seconde-guerre-mondiale_pat325.php

DALLEY Jessica, 'What Would $50 In 1940 Rent a New Yorker Today?', *Curbed New York*, 21 July 2013, https://ny.curbed.com/2013/11/21/10172014/what-would-50-in-1940-rent-a-new-yorker-today

Discovery, National Archives, Kew Gardens, https://discovery.nationalarchives.gov.uk/, Consulted on multiple occasions between 2016 and 2021

'Disparition du Margot Duhalde, symbole des Forces françaises libres', Délégation à l'Information et à la communication de la Défense (DICoD), 14 February 2018, https://www.defense.gouv.fr/actualites/international/dispar ition-de-margot-duhalde-symbole-des-forces-francaises-libres

Dossiers GR16P du SHD, http://www.francaislibres.net/liste/gr16p.php?&pro=1&cot=95581, Consulted 12 September 2019

ECOCHARD Henri, 'Liste Ecochard, 40e version', http://www.francaislibres.net/liste/ecochardv40.php?&lie=35187

EDVINSSON Rodney, 'Historical Statistics: Portal for Historical Statistics', https://www.historicalstatistics.org/

'Entretien avec Joseph MONJARET', Magazine 39–45, N° 88, October 1993, http://www.memorialjeanmoulin.fr/articles.php?lng=fr&pg=495#mai nContent

'Étienne Hirsch alias Bernard', Les Français Libres, de juin 1940 à juillet 1943 http://www.francaislibres.net/liste/fiche.php?index=110311

'Étienne Hirsch', *L'Entreprise*, Société du nouvel économiste, N° 2, 15 April 1953, http://clio.ish-lyon.cnrs.fr/patrons/AC000008015/AC000008015Doc1214.pdf

Eurostat, 'Police, Court and Prison Personnel Statistics', July 2018, https://ec.europa.eu/eurostat/statistics-explained/index.php?title=Police,_court_and_prison_personnel_statistics

*Fondation Charles de Gaulle*, https://www.charles-de-gaulle.org/

'GEISMAR Jeanne épouse Marais', Les Français Libres, de juin 1940 à juillet 1943, http://www.francaislibres.net/liste/fiche.php?index=83278

'Georges Pinson (France) v. United Mexican States, 19 October 1928', https://legal.un.org/riaa/cases/vol_V/327-466.pdf

'History', Port Camille Rayon, https://www.portcamillerayon.net/en/history/

Institut national de l'audiovisuel, https://www.ina.fr/

'Juin 1944 - Un Vent de Liberté', http://stephane.delogu.pagesperso-orange.fr/libe2.html,

La Fondation de la France Libre, https://www.france-libre.net/

'La inmigración árabe a Chile (1885–1950)' Memoria Chilena – Biblioteca Nacional de Chile, http://www.memoriachilena.gob.cl/602/w3-article-3523.html#presentacion

'Le Comité de la France Libre du Mexique, par René Dubernaud', *Revue de la France Libre*, n° 126 - juin 1960, 12 November 2009, https://www.france-libre.net/comite-fl-mexique/

'Le Comité de la France Libre en Uruguay', «Note établie d'après les renseignements fournis» par M. E. Darnet, Extrait de la *Revue de la France Libre*, n° 126 - juin 1960, 13 November 2009, https://www.france-libre.net/comite-fl-uruguay/

Legifrance, 'Loi n° 45–15 du 2 décembre 1945 relative à la nationalisation de la Banque de France et des grandes banques et à l'organisation du crédit', https://www.legifrance.gouv.fr/loda/id/LEGITEXT000006072686/

'Les frères Dubernard seront honorés, aujourd'hui, à Meymac', *La Montagne*, 11 November 2014

'Lord Killearn, 84, Retired Diplomat; Ambassador to Egypt as Sir Miles Lampson Is Dead', *The New York Times*, 19 September 1964, https://www.nytimes.com/1964/09/19/archives/lord-killearn84-retired-diplomat-ambassador-to-egypt-as-sir-miles.html

'Louis Eugène Mangin', Les Français Libres, de juin 1940 à juillet 1943, http://www.francaislibres.net/liste/fiche.php?index=83142

'M. Louis Joxe est nommé secrétaire général du Comité de la libération', *L'Écho d'Alger*, 14 October 1943, https://www.retronews.fr/journal/l-echo-d-alger/14-octobre-1943/30/1295515/1

'MARAIS Henri Octave', Les Français Libres, de juin 1940 à juillet 1943, http://www.francaislibres.net/liste/fiche.php?index=83276

'Margot Duhalde, wartime ATA Pilot—Obituary' *The Telegraph*, 16 February 2018, https://www.telegraph.co.uk/obituaries/2018/02/16/margot-duhalde-wartime-ata-pilot-obituary/

MARTIN Emmie, 'Here's How Much Housing Prices Have Skyrocketed over the Last 50 Years in Every U.S. State', CNBC, 27 June 2017, https://www.cnbc.com/2017/06/27/how-much-housing-prices-have-increased-since-1940-in-every-state.html

Mass Observation, http://www.massobs.org.uk/

'Jacques Chaban-Delmas', Musée de la Résistance En Ligne, http://museedelaresistanceenligne.org/media3347-Jacques-Chaban-Delmas

'Joseph Monjaret', http://francoisemorvan.com/histoire/petites-chroniques-de-la-resistance/joseph-monjaret-herve/

Musée de la Résistance online, http://www.museedelaresistanceenligne.org/

National Archives (TNA) Currency Converter, http://www.nationalarchives.gov.uk/currency-converter/

O'CONNOR J., ROBERTSON E. F, 'Raphaël Salem', MacTutor, https://mathshistory.st-andrews.ac.uk/Biographies/Salem/

'Ordonnance du 3 juin 1944s substituant au nom du Comité français de la Libération nationale celui de Gouvernement provisoire de la République française', https://mjp.univ-perp.fr/france/co1944.htm#3/06/44

Ordre de la Libération, https://www.ordredelaliberation.fr/fr/

OULMONT Philippe, 'Français libre et citoyen du monde: Pierre Denis', 2 May 2015, https://www.memoresist.org/lecture/francais-libre-et-citoyen-du-monde-philippe-oulmont/

Pan Am Historical Foundation, 'The Mat @ LaGuardia', 2020, https://www.panam.org/war-years/374-marine-air-terminal-laguardia-2

'Philippe Etlin', Les Français Libres, de juin 1940 à juillet 1943, http://www.francaislibres.net/liste/fiche.php?index=67621

PIKETTY Thomas, 'Historical Gold Prices—1833 to Present', http://piketty.pse.ens.fr/files/capital21c/xls/RawDataFiles/GoldPrices17922012.pdf

'Plane Pulled Across Canadian Border in Houlton, 1940', Maine Memory Network, https://www.mainememory.net/artifact/103726

QGIS Development Team, QGIS Geographic Information System, Open-Source Geospatial Foundation Project, 2009, https://qgis.org/en/site/

'*René Mayer*', Service des Archives économiques et financières, https://www.economie.gouv.fr/saef/rene-mayer

SERRE Robert, 'Relève et S.T.O.', *Musée de la Résistance 1940–1945 En Ligne*, http://www.museedelaresistanceenligne.org/expo.php?expo=2&theme=6&stheme=24&sstheme=47#English

Site of the former Canadian Governor-General, Lord Bessborough, Canada, https://www.gg.ca/en/governor-general/former-governors-general/earl-bessborough

'Plaque Commémorative: PC du Sous-Secteur FFI Nord II', Musée de la Résistance En Ligne, http://museedelaresistanceenligne.org/media4851-Plaque-commA

The Fédération des Associations Françaises en Grande-Bretagne, http://fafgb.org/

The History of The Neutrality Acts, 1930s, https://history.state.gov/milestones/1921-1936/neutrality-acts

TOMBS Robert, '*St Paul's Convent Through the Eyes of a Pupil*', Saint Peter's Catholic Church, Bloxwich, https://www.stpetersbloxwich.org.uk/history-of-st-pauls-convent.html

TURKEL Stanley, 'Hotel History: Shepheard's Hotel in Cairo Known for Opulence, Famous Guests and the Military', 9 June 2019, https://eturbonews.com/254665/hotel-history-shepheards-hotel-in-cairo-known-for-opulence-famous-guests-and-the-military/

WILSON Theodore, 'Oral History Interview with Étienne Hirsch', 30 June 1970, https://www.trumanlibrary.gov/library/oral-histories/hirsche

YOUNG Richard, 'Charles de Gaulle's Time in Hertfordshire', *Hertfordshire Life*, 30 January 2017, https://www.greatbritishlife.co.uk/charles-de-gaulle-s-time-in-hertfordshire-7205042

ZINSOU Cameron, 'The Forgotten Story of Operation Anvil', *The New York Times*, 15 August 2019, https://www.nytimes.com/2019/08/15/opinion/the-forgotten-story-of-operation-anvil.html

# Index




D. Foulk, *The Price of Freedom*,
https://doi.org/10.1007/978-3-031-09066-0

The manufacturer's authorised representative in the EU is Springer Nature Customer Service Centre GmbH, Europaplatz 3, 69115 Heidelberg, Germany. If you have any concerns regarding our products, please contact ProductSafety@springernature.com

Printed and bound by CPI Group (UK) Ltd, Croydon, CR0 4YY
30/09/2026
02225492-0006